# THE WORLD ALMANAC® FOR KIDS 2000

**WORLD ALMANAC BOOKS**
A PRIMEDIA Company

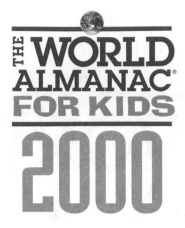

# THE WORLD ALMANAC FOR KIDS 2000

**EDITOR:**
Elaine Israel

**CURRICULUM CONSULTANT:**
Jean Craven
Director of Instructional Support
Albuquerque, NM, Public Schools

**CONTRIBUTORS:**
Michael Cusack, Rose Ann DeRupo, Monica M. Gallen, Bill Gutman,Charles Hirsch,
Judith S. Levey, Randi Metsch-Ampel, Allen Mogol, Brenda Pilson, Terry Simon
**Consultants:** Lee T. Shapiro, Ph.D. (Astronomy); Michelle Bender, M.D. (Health);
Anthony T. Padovano, S.T.D., Ph.D., and Abdulaziz Sachedina, Ph.D. (Religion)

**DESIGN:**
Bill SMITH STUDIO

**WORLD ALMANAC BOOKS**

| Vice President– Sales and Marketing: | Deputy Editor: | Marketing Manager: |
|---|---|---|
| James R. Keenley | William McGeveran, Jr. | Jacqueline J. Sloan |

**Editorial Staff:** Lori P. Wiesenfeld, Senior Editor;
Beth R. Ellis, Mark S. O'Malley, Associate Editors;
Elizabeth J. Lazzara, Desktop Publishing Associate

**PRIMEDIA REFERENCE INC.**
**Vice President and Editorial Director:** Robert Famighetti
**Director of Editorial Production:** Andrea J. Pitluk
**Director–Purchasing and Production:** Edward Thomas
**Director of Indexing Services:** Marjorie B. Bank
**Index Editor:** Walter Kronenberg
**Desktop Publishing Assistant:** Hana Shaki

**THE WORLD ALMANAC FOR KIDS 2000**
Copyright © 1999 by PRIMEDIA Reference Inc.
A PRIMEDIA Company

The World Almanac and The World Almanac for Kids are registered trademarks of
PRIMEDIA Reference Inc.

ISBN (softcover) 0-88687-840-3
ISBN (hardcover) 0-88687-841-1

Printed in the United States of America

The softcover and hardcover editions are distributed to the
trade in the United States by St. Martin's Press.

WORLD ALMANAC® BOOKS
An Imprint of PRIMEDIA Reference Inc.
One International Boulevard
Mahwah, New Jersey 07495-0017
E-Mail: Waforkids@aol.com

The addresses and content of Web sites referred to in this book
are subject to change. Although The World Almanac for Kids carefully
reviews these sites, we cannot take responsibility for their content.

# CONTENTS

*▲ Facto the Factosaurus, mascot of* The World Almanac for Kids.

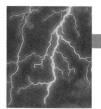

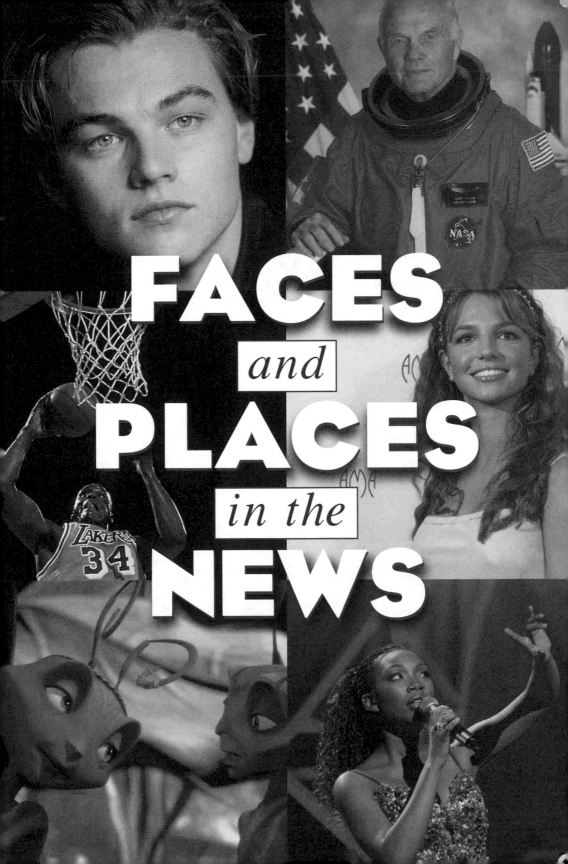

# FACES *and* PLACES *in the* NEWS

**Will SMITH**

His busy singing and acting careers left him just about enough time to accept a 1999 Grammy.

## Keri RUSSELL

A former Mouseketeer, Keri starred in the TV series *Felicity* (and won a Golden Globe Award for it).

## BRANDY

As Cinderella on TV, she went from rags to riches. Her real life is not too shabby either. Brandy is singing, producing, *and* acting!

# BIG NAMES

**Leonardo DiCAPRIO**

He went from *Titanic* to *The Beach*. . .
Where's Leo headed next?

## Adam SANDLER

Now a star of comedies like *The Waterboy*, Adam was the class clown at his New Hampshire high school.

## Sarah Michelle GELLAR

Sarah starred in the cult TV hit *Buffy the Vampire Slayer*, while also launching a career in movies.

# NEW LIVES

## Tara LIPINSKI

This Olympic champion skater recently turned professional and now performs in ice shows.

## John GLENN

He orbited Earth in 1962, became a senator, and at age 77 returned to space in a 1998 shuttle mission.

**Michael JORDAN**

Jordan retired in 1999. But not before he boosted the Chicago Bulls to their sixth NBA championship.

EPISODE I

### Episode I: THE PHANTOM MENACE

The newest Star Wars movie goes back to the childhood of Anakin Skywalker, who was to become Darth Vader.

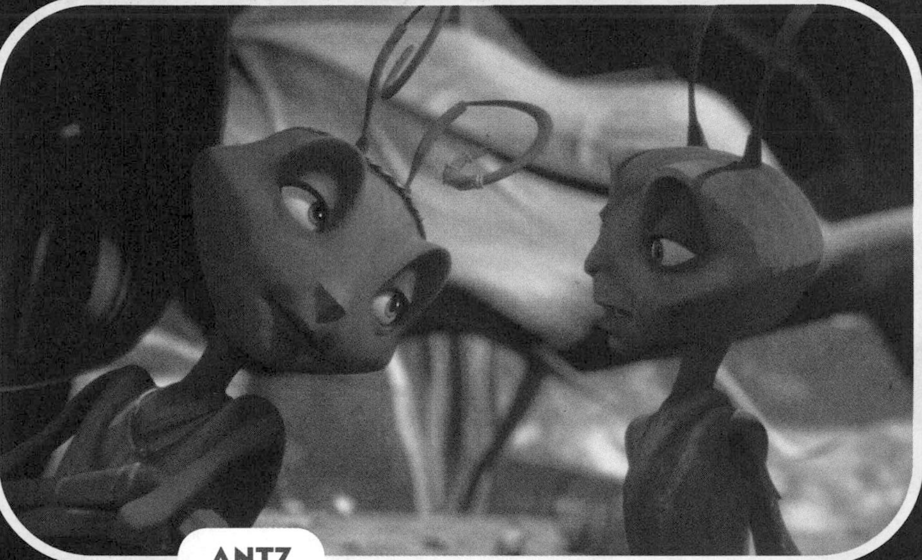

**ANTZ**

Two computer-animated films about creepy crawlies were recent hits. One was *Antz* (above); the other was *A Bug's Life*.

**Alicia SILVERSTONE**

Between starring in movies like *A Blast From the Past*, Alicia works for her animal rescue group.

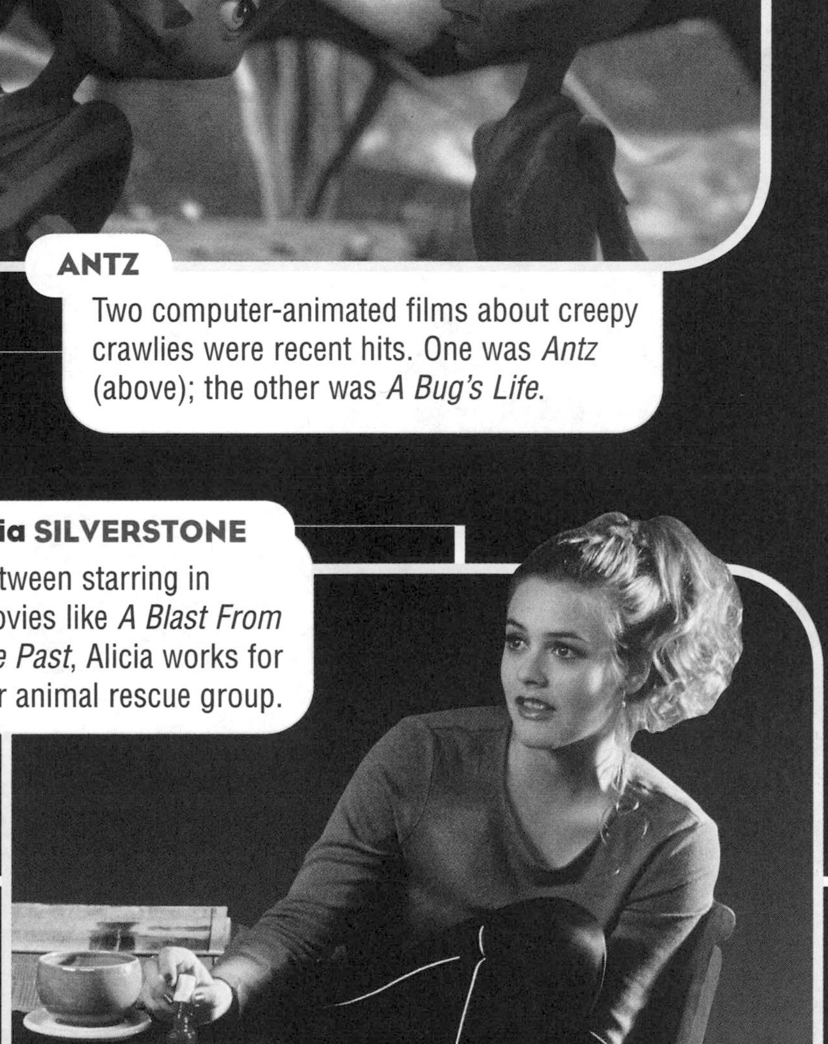

# THE MUSIC SCENE

## 'N SYNC
The five members of 'N Sync have millions of young fans.

## BACKSTREET BOYS
The five Backstreet Boys have taken the music world by storm.

**Britney SPEARS**

Britney had bragging rights to a No. 1 single and album at the same time. A top designer even signed her to model his new spring line.

19

**Mark McGWIRE and Sammy SOSA**

When McGwire hit homer number 62 in 1998, breaking the major league single-season record, Sosa—who was close behind—congratulated him.

## Shaquille O'NEAL

One of the NBA's biggest superstars, Shaq plays for the LA Lakers.

## Jeff GORDON

A three-time Winston Cup winner, Jeff roared off to a good start in 1999 when he won the NASCAR Daytona 500.

# SPORTS CHAMPS

**Martina HINGIS**

The popular Swiss star racked up her fifth grand slam victory when she won the 1999 Australian Open.

**Richard HAMILTON**

Hamilton led Connecticut to the 1999 NCAA title and was named MVP of the tournament.

**John ELWAY**

In January 1999, Elway led the Denver Broncos to their second Super Bowl victory in a row. Later, he announced his retirement.

# MAKING NEWS
## *Around* THE WORLD

### Prince WILLIAM and Prince HARRY

William will probably be king of England some day. He and his younger brother, Prince Harry, already reign—as teen idols.

### Bertrand PICCARD and Brian JONES

In 1999, Piccard (left) of Switzerland and Jones of Great Britain became the first people to fly around the world nonstop in a balloon.

# The All-New Millennium
## Turn of the Millennium

Unless you've spent the last year or so in another galaxy, you have most likely heard of the new millennium. It will be starting soon, if it hasn't started by the time you read this. What exactly is it? And why are we celebrating twice?

The calendar used by most people in the Western world counts years from the year we call A.D. 1. (A.D. is an abbreviation from Latin, meaning "in the year of the Lord.") This was once believed to be the first year after Jesus Christ was born. Historians now think he was born a few years before then, but the calendar still starts from the later year.

A millennium is a period of 1,000 years. The first millennium started with the year 1 and ended with the year 1000. So the second millennium really ends on December 31, 2000, and the new millennium does not officially begin until January 1, 2001. However, because 2000 is a round number—and because it comes before 2001—most people won't be waiting that long. Most of the world will celebrate the start of the new millennium at the stroke of midnight on December 31, 1999. It is a big event for many people!

On this page and on the next few pages, you can read about:
- the "Y2K problem"
- how people around the world will celebrate 2000
- anniversaries in 2000 and 2001
- past predictions—some silly ones, some that really came true
- making a time capsule
- 50 big events of the past 1,000 years

HAPPY NEW MILLENNIUM!

## The Millennium Bug

Will telephone systems crash? Will traffic lights get stuck? Will cash machines stop working? Questions like these were on many people's minds as the world approached the new millennium. The reason: the Y2K problem. Y2K stands for year 2000 (K is the symbol for thousand in Greek). The problem is that computer programs have used only the last two numbers of a year to represent that year. For example, 99 has been used for 1999. So 00 should mean 2000. However, 00 could also mean 1900. Many computer programs and systems have not been able to tell. They were being checked to make corrections in time for January 1, 2000. Since computers are used in almost every aspect of our lives, this has been a huge and costly project. By the time you read this, you might know how well it worked.

People around the world have planned huge parties and events to welcome the year 2000. Here are some of the celebrations that are expected to take place to mark the new millennium.

New York City will hold a 24-hour party that begins at 7 A.M. Eastern Standard Time on December 31, 1999, and continues until the new millennium has arrived in each of the world's 24 time zones. Celebrations from around the world will flash across giant TV screens in Times Square. At midnight, the New Year's Eve ball (a brand-new one) will be lowered from high above Times Square.

## Bells, Bells, Bells

All across Great Britain, thousands of bells will ring on New Year's Day. Beginning at noon, 30,000 or more bells in about 6,000 churches will ring for five minutes. These large bells weigh from 50 pounds to several tons. In London, a Ferris wheel 500 feet in diameter is expected to carry riders high above the city. Passengers on the Millennium Wheel will be able to enjoy breath-taking views for 30 miles in all directions.

Greenwich, England, is home to the prime meridian, an imaginary line going from the north pole to the south pole. The world measures time and distance from the prime meridian. Greenwich will ring in the year 2000 with fireworks, a river pageant, a concert, and the opening of a big new exhibition hall known as the Millennium Dome.

## Dawn of a New Era

Gisborne, New Zealand, says it will be "the first city to see the light of the new millennium." A 24-hour party is planned for the city's waterfront, with performers, fireworks, and a laser show. On New Year's Day, canoes from seven Pacific nations and tall ships from around the world will arrive in the Gisborne harbor to join the celebration.

In Fiji (a group of islands in the Pacific Ocean), people will celebrate with an ancient fire ceremony. At midnight, fires will glow on hilltops and a Chinese fireworks display will take place. Fijians will dedicate a time capsule, to be opened 1,000 years from now. It will be filled with photos, messages to the future, and items from the celebration. Islanders are also building a special millennium wall, using hollow bricks. Messages from people around the world will be sealed inside the bricks.

## Lights and Lasers

A spectacular light and laser show will highlight the celebration at the Pyramids in Giza, Egypt. Dancers, singers, and actors will perform in a celebration of artistic achievements of the past 2,000 years. Visitors will float lighted candles down the Nile River.

Beginning in Cairo, Egypt, a chain of drummers will relay a drum beat from drummer to drummer until the sound reaches a stadium in Durban, South Africa. At midnight, 4,000 drummers in the stadium will hear it and beat their drums to welcome the year 2000.

**WEB SITES** Find out more about these and other millennium celebrations at:

http://www.eventsworldwide.com

http://www.greenwich2000.com

# In 2000

## 50 Years Ago - 1950

- The Federal Bureau of Investigation (FBI) began its "Ten Most Wanted Fugitives" lists.
- The first "Peanuts" comic strip, by Charles Schulz, appeared in newspapers.
- The Diner's Club issued the first credit card.
- The Korean War began.
- The first successful kidney transplant was performed, in Chicago, Illinois.
- Walt Disney's *Cinderella* was shown in movie theaters for the first time.

## 100 Years Ago - 1900

- In Galveston, Texas, the worst hurricane in U.S. history left 6,000 people dead.
- Troops from the United States and other countries entered China to end the Boxer Rebellion, a movement that tried to drive foreigners out of the country.
- The first "zeppelin," a rigid gas-filled airship, was launched by Count Ferdinand von Zeppelin, a German inventor.
- The first U.S. national automobile show opened. At that time, there were only about 8,000 cars in the United States.
- *The Wonderful World of Oz*, by L. Frank Baum, was published.

# In 2001

## 50 Years Ago - 1951

- United Nations headquarters opened in New York City.
- The *I Love Lucy* show, which is still in reruns, was first broadcast on television.
- The 22nd amendment to the U.S. Constitution was ratified (approved). It says that no president can be elected to more than two terms in office.
- The first commercial computer went into service at the U.S. Census Bureau. It was known as UNIVAC.
- The New York Yankees' great centerfielder Joe DiMaggio retired from baseball.
- The National Basketball Association's first All-Star game was played.
- The first color TV program was broadcast by CBS. But color TVs remained rare for many years.

## 100 Years Ago - 1901

- President William McKinley was assassinated in Buffalo, New York. Vice President Theodore Roosevelt became president.
- New York reportedly became the first state to require license plates for cars. The plates cost $1 each.
- Memorial Day was observed for the first time in the United States.
- The first Nobel Prizes were awarded.
- Guglielmo Marconi sent and received the first transatlantic radio signals.

NY

1 bUK

# Predicting the Future

What does the new millennium have in store for us? Since ancient times, people have been making predictions about the future. What seems likely to one person can seem like nonsense to someone else. Of course, predictions that sound far-fetched sometimes come true, while many predictions that seem reasonable do not. Here are some predictions made in the past, which may or may not have come true.

**MOSTLY**

| | Correct | Incorrect |
|---|---|---|
| • In the middle of the 1500s, a French doctor named Nostradamus wrote poetry that seems to have predicted the French Revolution, the deaths of the French rulers, the rise and fall of Napoleon Bonaparte, World War I, and the Russian Revolution. | X | |
| • In 1796, respectable doctors spoke out against Dr. Edward Jenner's efforts to develop the smallpox vaccine. The doctors predicted it would cause people to grow cow-like features. | | X |
| • Alfred Velpeau, a well-known surgeon in the early 1800s, predicted that anesthesia could not work and that painless surgery is impossible. | | X |
| • In 1825, British journalists predicted that railroads would not work because they "would prevent cows grazing and hens laying. The poisoned air...would kill birds." | | X |
| • Leo Tolstoy, a Russian writer who lived from 1828 to 1910, predicted that a "great conflagration will start about 1912, set by the torch of the first arm in the countries of southeastern Europe." World War I actually started in 1914 when Archduke Francis Ferdinand was murdered in the Balkan region of Europe. | X | |
| • About seven days before Orville and Wilbur Wright successfully flew their plane for the first time, editors of *The New York Times* predicted that "airship experiments" were a waste of time. | | X |
| • In 1945, a science fiction writer, Arthur C. Clarke, predicted the invention of communication satellites, which were actually created in 1960. He also predicted that the first rocket to the moon would be launched around then. | X | |

## What Jules Verne Dreamed of

In the 1860s and '70s, in books like *20,000 Leagues Under the Sea*, *Around the World in Eighty Days*, and *From the Earth to the Moon*, Jules Verne foresaw the invention of submarines, airplanes, spaceships, electric lights, air conditioning, guided missiles, and many more discoveries and advances in technology. At the time, most of these ideas were not even close to becoming a reality. Yet Verne described them in such believable detail that later inventors and explorers gave him part of the credit for their own accomplishments. Richard Byrd said Jules Verne inspired him to make the first flight over the North Pole in 1926. Robert Goddard, who launched the first liquid fuel rocket, said he began to dream of rockets and space travel after reading one of Verne's books. Verne did not have a mysterious or magical ability to look into the future. He said that all of his predictions were based on careful research into ideas or projects that scientists were studying at the time.

Here are some predictions made by scientists and others about the late 20th century.

- By 1980, we will be able to put information on handwritten papers directly into a computer.
- By 1990, inexpensive anti-aging pills will be available.
- By 1990 there will be a World Wide Weather Watch, which will be able to calm hurricanes and change local weather.
- By 1995, complete vacation centers will be built underwater.

# Your Gift to the Future

We learn about the past in many ways. One of the most exciting is by digging up artifacts—objects buried long ago. For example, the Shetland Islands, off the northern coast of Scotland, are the site of a big dig. Workers there found an ancient garbage dump that may have been left by Norse invaders. It was filled with trash many centuries old. The pots, pans, and utensils, which may already have been old when they were tossed away, give clues to the way people lived at a certain time in that part of the world.

What could people in the future learn from your artifacts? You can make a time capsule for your own artifacts. A metal box will most likely last best. You can even buy inexpensive containers for this purpose, in a card store or other store.

Bury the capsule in your backyard or, better yet, ask your parents to suggest a safe place in your home. One day, when you are an adult, it will be interesting to open the container up. Or you could leave it for others to find.

What should your time capsule hold? The answer depends on what message you want to pass on about being a kid in the year 2000. Here are just a few of the items you could include. (Be sure to ask your parents for permission before burying anything!)

- audiocassettes and videos you like
- photographs of your family, pets and friends
- items of clothing, such as T-shirts
- a book you enjoyed
- comic books
- old school notebooks
- a menu from a restaurant
- a light bulb
- a baseball cap
- a ball point pen
- a football or tennis ball
- a newspaper or magazine, including TV listings
- a list of current cool words
- a personal letter from you telling about your life, with a date on top
- a printout from your favorite Web site

# Fifty Big Events

Many of these events changed the way we live, forever! Some of them are important dates in history or have to do with famous people or historic achievements. Others affect the way we live today.

| | |
|---|---|
| c.1000 | Norseman Leif Ericson lands in Newfoundland. He is probably the first European to reach the western hemisphere. |
| 1066 | William, Duke of Normandy, conquers England. |
| 1071 | A two-pronged fork for eating is introduced in Venice, Italy. |
| 1095 | Christians launch the Crusades, to capture Jerusalem from Muslims. |
| 1148 | Sugar is introduced to Europe. |
| 1211 | Genghis Khan invades China and starts to build the largest empire in history. |
| 1215 | English nobles accept the Magna Carta, which limited royal power and led the way to democracy. |
| 1230 | The Mali kingdom begins in North Africa. It became a center of learning and trade. |
| 1232 | The Chinese fire the first-known rockets powered by gunpowder. |
| 1250 | Arabic numerals and the decimal system are introduced to Europe. |
| 1290 | Eyeglasses are invented. |
| 1325 | The Aztecs establish the capital of their empire in Mexico. |
| 1348 | The Black Death (bubonic plague) strikes Europe. It killed up to half the population. |
| 1450s | Johann Gutenberg starts printing Bibles, opening up a new era in communications. |
| 1492 | Christopher Columbus lands in the New World. |
| 1510 | The first Africans are brought to the Americas as slaves. |
| 1517 | Martin Luther launches the Protestant Reformation. |
| 1521 | Hernando Cortés defeats the Aztecs, and Spain takes control of Mexico. |
| 1564 | William Shakespeare, considered the world's greatest playwright, is born. |
| 1607 | English colonists settle in Jamestown, Virginia. |
| 1769 | James Watt invents the steam engine. The Industrial Revolution begins. |
| 1776 | English colonies in America sign the Declaration of Independence. |
| 1789 | The French Revolution begins. |
| 1796 | Edward Jenner discovers a vaccine for smallpox, a milestone in preventing disease. |

| | |
|---|---|
| 1821 | Simón Bolívar wins independence for Venezuela. |
| 1850 | Levi Strauss makes the first pair of jeans. |
| 1854 | Commmodore Matthew Perry opens up trade between Japan and the Western world. |
| 1859 | Charles Darwin introduces the theory of evolution. |
| 1865 | The Civil War ends, and slavery is abolished in the United States. |
| 1869 | The Suez Canal opens, and a railroad across the United States is completed. |
| 1876 | Alexander Graham Bell makes the first telephone call. |
| 1884 | The first roller coaster opens at Coney Island, in Brooklyn, New York. |
| 1895 | The first motion picture (a silent film) is shown to the public. |
| 1903 | The Wright brothers make the first successful airplane flight. |
| 1905 | Albert Einstein publishes his first major works, changing our understanding of the universe. |
| 1908 | Henry Ford introduces the Model T car, opening a new era in transportation. |
| 1914 | World War I begins. |
| 1917 | The Russian Revolution takes place, creating the Soviet Union. |
| 1920 | U.S. women are granted the right to vote. |
| 1927 | TV is successfully demonstrated in the United States. |
| 1933 | Adolf Hitler assumes power in Germany. Under his rule, almost six million Jews died in the Holocaust. |
| 1941 | Japan attacks Pearl Harbor, and the United States enters World War II. |
| 1945 | The United States drops an atom bomb on Hiroshima, Japan. World War II ends. |
| 1946 | Jackie Robinson breaks "the color barrier" in baseball. |
| 1946 | The world's first all-electronic computer (ENIAC) is introduced, starting the computer age. |
| 1947 | After a nonviolent campaign led by Mohandas K. Gandhi, India wins independence from Great Britain. |
| 1949 | The People's Republic of China is established, under Communist rule. |
| 1953 | Scientists map the structure of DNA, the basis of heredity. |
| 1969 | Neil Armstrong becomes the first human to walk on the moon. |
| 1991 | The Soviet Union breaks up. |

Do you agree? It's your turn to make history by selecting your own top 50 events. It may help to look through sections of *The World Almanac for Kids*, especially the chapters on Inventions, Science, Sports, United States, and World History.

31

❷ **What do turkeys and bears have in common?**
*You can find the answer on page 33.*

# AMAZING ANIMAL FACTS

**F**acts about animals are often surprising. Here are a few.

**AN OCTOPUS** in danger can squirt a stream of ink at its attacker. After that, the octopus can change its shape and color to blend in with its surroundings.

**VAMPIRE BATS** of Central and South America drink the blood of cows, horses, chickens, pigs, birds, and other animals. They use their sharp, pointy teeth to pierce the skin of their sleeping victims. The bloodsucking alone doesn't kill the animals, but it sometimes gives them the deadly disease known as rabies. Fortunately, these vampire bats do not like the taste of human blood.

**THE NILE CROCODILE** can stay underwater for more than an hour waiting to surprise its prey. Its varied diet includes mammals, fish, reptiles, birds, insects, frogs, and even stones—which help the crocodile stay on the bottom of the river or water hole.

**AT NIGHT TIME, SEA OTTERS** tuck themselves into beds of kelp, a kind of large seaweed. They wrap long pieces of kelp around their bodies so that the current cannot carry them out to sea while they sleep floating on the water.

**DARWIN'S FROGS AND GAFF-TOPSAIL CATFISH** care for their young in their mouths! Darwin's frogs store their eggs in their vocal sacs until the eggs hatch into tadpoles. The tadpoles stay in Dad's mouth until they grow into tiny adults. Male gaff-topsail catfish also keep eggs in their mouths until they hatch. The baby fish swim in and out of Dad's mouth to allow him to eat. They live there until they get to be about three inches long.

**DID YOU KNOW?**

*Do you remember the whale from the movie* Free Willy? *His real name is Keiko. After he was captured in 1982, he lived a hard life in tanks and pools that were too small for him. In 1998, he was moved to a large pen in Iceland. Scientists there hope he can someday become healthy enough to return to real freedom in the Atlantic Ocean.*

**THE HORNED TOAD** is actually a lizard that has pointy scales on its head and sides. When it is attacked it tries to scare away the enemy by hissing, biting, and shooting blood from its eyes!

**SOME LIZARDS** can make their own tails fall off in order to avoid being caught by another animal. It's no big deal for a lizard. In a short time, a new tail will grow in place of the old one.

# CLASSIFYING ANIMALS

There are so many different types of animals that scientists had to find a way to organize them into groups. A Swedish scientist named Carolus Linnaeus (1707–1778) worked out a system for classifying both animals and plants. We still use it today.

## ANIMAL KINGDOM

The animal kingdom is separated into two large groups—animals with backbones, called **vertebrates,** and animals without backbones, called **invertebrates.**

These large groups are divided into smaller groups called **phyla**. And phyla are divided into even smaller groups called **classes**. The animals in each group are classified together when their bodies are similar in certain ways.

Below are examples of some of the animals in these groups.

| VERTEBRATES:<br>Animals With Backbones | INVERTEBRATES:<br>Animals Without Backbones |
|---|---|

**VERTEBRATES: Animals With Backbones**

**FISH:** Swordfish, tuna, salmon, trout, halibut

**AMPHIBIANS:** Frogs, toads, mud puppies

**REPTILES:** Turtles, alligators, crocodiles, lizards

**BIRDS:** Sparrows, owls, turkeys, hawks

**MAMMALS:** Kangaroos, opossums, dogs, cats, bears, seals, rats, squirrels, rabbits, chipmunks, porcupines, horses, pigs, cows, deer, bats, whales, dolphins, monkeys, apes, humans

**INVERTEBRATES: Animals Without Backbones**

**PROTOZOA** The simplest form of animals

**COELENTERATES** Jellyfish, hydra, sea anemones, coral

**MOLLUSKS** Clams, snails, squid, oysters

**ANNELIDS** Earthworms

**ARTHROPODS**
**Crustaceans:**
  Lobsters, crayfish
**Centipedes and Millipedes** 
**Arachnids:**
  Spiders, scorpions
**Insects:**
  Butterflies, grasshoppers, bees, termites, cockroaches

**ECHINODERMS** Starfish, sea urchins, sea cucumbers

# WHAT'S the DIFFERENCE

## BETWEEN...

### A CROCODILE AND AN ALLIGATOR?

**Crocodile**
Pointed snout
More fierce
Fourth tooth on each
side on the bottom sticks
out over the upper lip

**Alligator**
Broad, flat snout
Less fierce

### A LEOPARD, A JAGUAR, AND A CHEETAH?

**Leopard**
Lives in Africa and Asia

Spots are broken circles,
no dot in the center
Black markings on the
backs of the ears

**Jaguar**
Lives in Central and South
America
Spots are circles, with a
dot in the center
Belly is white

**Cheetah**
Lives in Africa and Arabian
Peninsula
Spots are solid circles

Black mark from the nose
to the eye

### AN AFRICAN ELEPHANT AND AN INDIAN ELEPHANT?

**African elephant**
Larger than the Indian elephant
Huge ears

Two lobes at the end of
the trunk
Both males and females
have long tusks
Usually lives in the wild

**Indian elephant**
Smaller than the African elephant
Small ears
One lobe at the end
of the trunk
Only the males (bulls)
have long tusks
More easily trained
to do work for humans

### A FROG AND A TOAD?

**Frog**
Slim
Lighter skin, often green
Long back legs for jumping
Smooth skin
Spends most of its
time in water

**Toad**
Stout
Darker skin
Shorter back legs
Warty skin
Spends most of its
time on land

### A MOUNTAIN LION, A PUMA, AND A COUGAR?

Nothing! These are all names for the same large cats, *Felis concolor*, whose original range extended through North and South America. In some areas these animals are also called **panthers**; the name panther is also used for a leopard with a black coat.

# The LARGEST and the FASTEST

## The Largest Animals

**WORLD'S LARGEST ANIMAL:** blue whale (110 feet long, 209 tons)
**LARGEST LAND ANIMAL:** African bush elephant (13 feet high, 8 tons)
**TALLEST ANIMAL:** giraffe (19 feet tall)
**LARGEST REPTILE:** saltwater crocodile (16 feet long, 1,150 pounds)
**LARGEST SNAKE: Heaviest:** anaconda (27 feet, 9 inches long, 500 pounds)
                  **Longest:** reticulated python (26–32 feet long)
**LONGEST FISH:** whale shark (41 ½ feet long)
**LARGEST BIRD:** ostrich (9 feet tall, 345 pounds)
**LARGEST INSECT:** stick insect (15 inches long)

## The Fastest Animals

**WORLD'S FASTEST ANIMAL:** swift, a bird (100–200 miles per hour)
**FASTEST MARINE ANIMAL:** blue whale (30 miles per hour)
**FASTEST LAND ANIMAL:** cheetah (70 miles per hour)
**FASTEST FISH:** sailfish (68 miles per hour)
**FASTEST BIRD:** swift (100–200 miles per hour)
**FASTEST INSECT:** dragonfly (36 miles per hour)

# How Fast Do Animals Run?

**D**id you know that some animals can run as fast as a car can move or that a snail would need more than 30 hours just to go one mile? If you look at this table, you will see how fast some common land animals can move.

**DID YOU KNOW?**

The blue whale may be the largest animal that ever lived. But it is no match for humans. Tens of thousands of blue whales were killed in the early 1900s. They are now protected, and there are about 5,000 of them in the world.

These fussy eaters feed mainly on tiny shrimp-like creatures called krill, which they find in their summer homes near the North and South Poles. They eat about four tons of food a day.

When winter sets in, the whales head for warmer water, and go on a diet. That is also the time when they mate.

### MILES PER HOUR

| Animal | Miles per hour |
|---|---|
| Cheetah | 70 |
| Lion | 50 |
| Cape hunting dog | 45 |
| Zebra | 40 |
| Rabbit | 35 |
| Grizzly bear | 30 |
| Cat (domestic) | 30 |
| Elephant | 25 |
| Squirrel | 12 |
| Pig (domestic) | 11 |
| Chicken | 9 |
| Snail | 0.03 |

# HABITATS: Where Animals Live

The area in nature where an animal lives is called its habitat. The table below lists some large habitats and some of the animals that live in them.

| HABITAT | SOME ANIMALS THAT LIVE THERE |
| --- | --- |
| Deserts (hot, dry regions) | camels, bobcats, coyotes, kangaroos, mice, gila monsters, scorpions, rattlesnakes |
| Tropical Forests (warm, humid climate) | orangutans, gibbons, leopards, tamandua anteaters, tapirs, iguanas, parrots, tarantulas |
| Grasslands (flat, open lands) | African elephants, kangaroos, Indian rhinoceroses, giraffes, zebras, prairie dogs, ostriches, tigers |
| Mountains (highlands) | yaks, snow leopards, vicunas, bighorn sheep, chinchillas, pikas, eagles, mountain goats |
| Polar Regions (cold climate) | polar bears, musk oxen, caribou, ermines, arctic foxes, walruses, penguins, Siberian huskies |
| Oceans (sea water) | whales, dolphins, seals, manatees, octopuses, stingrays, coral, starfish, lobsters, many kinds of fish |

# FOSSILS: Clues to Ancient Animals

A fossil is the remains of an animal or plant that lived long ago. Most fossils are formed from the hard parts of an animal's body, such as bones, shells, or teeth. Some are large, like dinosaur footprints. Some are so tiny that you need a microscope to see them. Most fossils are found in rocks formed from the mud or sand that collects at the bottom of oceans, rivers, and lakes. Fossils offer scientists clues to ancient animals.

### WHAT DO FOSSILS TELL US?

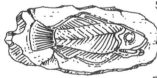

Scientists study fossils to help them understand plant and animal life in ancient periods of the world's history. The age and structure of the rocks in which fossils are found can help scientists tell how long ago certain kinds of animals or plants lived. For example, dinosaurs lived millions of years ago, but people have known about dinosaurs only since the first dinosaur fossils were uncovered, less than 200 years ago.

### WHERE ARE FOSSILS FOUND?

Fossils, including dinosaur fossils, are found on every continent on the Earth. In eastern and southern Africa, people have found fossils that are ancestors of early humans. Insects that lived millions of years ago are sometimes found preserved in amber. Amber is hardened tree sap. Fossils have also been found in ice and tar. In 1991 a frozen corpse of a man believed to have lived over 5,000 years ago was found in the Austrian Alps.

| | |
|---|---|
| Box turtle | 100 years |
| Asian elephant | 40 years |
| Grizzly bear | 25 years |
| Horse | 20 years |
| Gorilla | 20 years |
| Polar bear | 20 years |
| Rhinoceros (white) | 20 years |
| Black bear | 18 years |
| Lion | 15 years |
| Lobster | 15 years |
| Rhesus monkey | 15 years |
| Rhinoceros (black) | 15 years |
| Camel (Bactrian) | 12 years |
| Cat (domestic) | 12 years |
| Dog (domestic) | 12 years |
| Leopard | 12 years |
| Giraffe | 10 years |
| Pig | 10 years |
| Squirrel | 10 years |
| Red fox | 7 years |
| Kangaroo | 7 years |
| Chipmunk | 6 years |
| Rabbit | 5 years |
| Guinea pig | 4 years |
| Mouse | 3 years |
| Opossum | 1 year |

## How Long Do Animals Live?

Most animals do not live as long as human beings do. A monkey that is 14 years old is thought to be old. A person who is 14 is still considered young. The average life span of a human being today is 70 to 80 years. The average life spans of some animals are shown here. Only one of these animals lives longer than human beings.

## Bunnies, Kids, and Other ANIMAL BABIES

| ANIMAL | MALE | FEMALE | YOUNG |
|---|---|---|---|
| bear | boar | sow | cub |
| pig | boar | sow | piglet |
| horse | stallion | mare | foal, filly (female), colt (male) |
| lion | lion | lioness | cub |
| cattle, elephant, giraffe, whale | bull | cow | calf |
| deer | buck | doe | fawn |
| goat | buck, billy goat | doe, nanny goat | kid |
| rabbit | buck | doe | bunny, kit |
| duck | drake | duck | duckling |
| goose | gander | goose | gosling |
| sheep | ram | ewe | lamb |
| tiger | tiger | tigress | cub |

# ENDANGERED SPECIES

## A Few Endangered Species

**Mammals:** *Giant panda* in China; *Gray whale* in North Pacific Ocean

**Fish:** *Sockeye (red) salmon* in North Pacific from the United States to Russia

**Bird:** *Piping Plover* along East Coast and Great Lakes region of the United States

**Reptile:** *American crocodile* from the southeastern United States to South America

**W**hen an animal becomes less and less plentiful on one part of the Earth or in the entire world, the animal is said to be endangered or threatened. The U.S. Department of the Interior keeps track of endangered and threatened animals. Throughout the world today, 1,034 species of animals are endangered or threatened. Among them are:

| | |
|---|---|
| **Mammals:** 331 species | **Reptiles:** 114 species |
| **Birds:** 274 species | **Clams:** 64 species |
| **Fish:** 119 species | **Insects:** 41 species |

## How Do Animals Become Endangered?

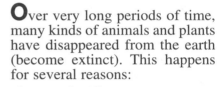

**O**ver very long periods of time, many kinds of animals and plants have disappeared from the earth (become extinct). This happens for several reasons:

**Changes in Climate.** Animals are threatened when the climate of their habitat (where they live) changes in a major way. For example, if an area becomes very hot and dry and a river dries up, the fish and other plant and animal life in the river will die.

**Habitat Destruction.** Sometimes animal habitats are destroyed when people need the land. Wetlands, for example, where many types of waterfowl, fish, and insects live, might be drained for new houses or a mall. The animals that lived there would either have to find a new home or else die out.

**Over-hunting.** Bison or buffalo once ranged over the entire Great Plains of the United States, but they were hunted almost to extinction in the 19th century. Since then, they have been protected by laws, and their numbers are increasing. Sometimes, when an animal population is too large, controlled hunting may reduce the number of animals enough so that the surviving animals can live comfortably with the food available to them.

# Do You Want a PET?

**P**ets can be lots of fun, but they may need a lot of care. This takes time, effort, and money. If you are thinking of getting a pet, these questions will help you choose the best kind for you and your family. Look for information on pets at a library, pet shelter, or veterinarian's office.

### QUESTIONS TO ASK BEFORE YOU GET A PET

Why do you want a pet? Do you want an animal to cuddle or keep you company? Do you want to teach a bird to talk? Or watch fish swim?

How much space do you need for the pet you want?

What kind of shelter should it live in?

Does the animal like to be held or left alone?

What kind of food is best for the animal? How often and how much food does it eat? How much does the food cost?

What kind of exercise should the pet get? How often?

What kind of grooming does the animal need?

Is there a veterinarian nearby to meet your pet's health needs? Will this care be expensive?

Are you or anyone in your family allergic to any animals?

### TRAVELING WITH YOUR PET

With careful planning, traveling with your pet can be safe and fun. Think about these tips before you leave home. Share them with the adults going with you.

Ask your veterinarian for advice on how to prepare for your trip. Make sure your pet is up to making the trip.

Make reservations to stay somewhere that allows pets. Let the place know what kind of pet you'll be bringing and ask about any special rules and fees.

Just as you need a seat belt to travel safely in a car, animals should be restrained by an animal seat belt, car seat, or animal carrier.

During long car rides, stop often so your pet can get water and exercise.

If you must leave your pet alone in a car, be quick, keep a window open a crack, and make sure the car does not get too hot or too cold.

## What Are Groups of Animals Called?

**T**he next time you describe a group of animals, try using one of the expressions below.

**ants:** *colony* of ants
**bees:** *swarm* of bees
**chicks:** *clutch* of chicks
**clams:** *bed* of clams
**ducks:** *brace* of ducks
**elks:** *gang* of elks
**fish:** *school* of fish
**geese:** *flock* or *gaggle*
**gorillas:** *band* of gorillas
**hares:** *down* of hares

**kangaroos:** *troop* of kangaroos
**leopards:** *leap* of leopards
**lions:** *pride* of lions
**monkeys:** *troop* of monkeys
**oxen:** *yoke* of oxen
**sheep:** *flock* of sheep
**swans:** *bevy* of swans
**whales:** *pod* of whales

# ANIMAL LIFE on Earth

This time line shows how animal life developed on Earth and when land plants developed. The earliest animals are at the top of the chart. The most recent are at the bottom of the chart.

| | YEARS AGO | | ANIMAL LIFE ON EARTH |
|---|---|---|---|
| PRECAMBRIAN | 4.5 billion | | Formation of the Earth. No signs of life. |
| | 2.5 billion | | First evidence of life in the form of bacteria and algae. All life is in water. |
| PALEOZOIC | 570–500 million | | Animals with shells (called trilobites) and some mollusks. Some fossils begin to form. |
| | 500–430 million | | Jawless fish appear, oldest known animals with backbones (vertebrates). |
| | 430–395 million | | Many coral reefs, jawed fishes, and scorpion-like animals. First land plants. |
| | 395–345 million | | Many fishes. Earliest known insect. Amphibians (animals living in water and on land) appear. |
| | 345–280 million | | Large insects appear. Amphibians increase in numbers. First trees appear. |
| | 280–225 million | | Reptiles and modern insects appear. Trilobites, many corals, and fishes become extinct. |
| MESOZOIC | 225–195 million | | Dinosaurs and turtles appear. Many reptiles and insects develop further. Mammals appear. |
| | 195–135 million | | Many giant dinosaurs. Reptiles increase in number. First birds and crablike animals appear. |
| | 135–65 million | | Dinosaurs develop further and then become extinct. Flowering plants begin to appear. |
| CENOZOIC | 65–2.5 million | | Modern-day land and sea animals begin to develop, including such mammals as rhinoceroses, whales, cats, dogs, apes, seals. |
| | 2.5 million–10,000 | | Earliest humans appear. Mastodon, mammoths, and other huge animals become extinct. |
| | 10,000–present | | Modern human beings and animals. |

# All About DINOSAURS

Dinosaurs lived during the Mesozoic era, from 225 to 65 million years ago. The Mesozoic era is divided into the three periods shown below.

## TRIASSIC PERIOD, from 225 to 195 million years ago

▶ **First dinosaurs** appeared during the **Triassic period.**
   Most early dinosaurs were small, rarely longer than 15 feet.
▶ **Early meat-eating dinosaurs** were called **Theropods.**
▶ **Earliest-known dinosaurs** were meat-eaters, found in Argentina: **Eoraptor** (the most primitive dinosaur, only about 40 inches long) and **Herrerasaurus.**
▶ **Early plant-eating dinosaurs** were called **Prosauropods. Plateosaurus** and **Anchisaurus** were two early plant-eating dinosaurs.

## JURASSIC PERIOD, from 195 to 135 million years ago

▶ Dinosaurs that lived during the **Jurassic period** were gigantic.
▶ Jurassic dinosaurs included the **Sauropods,** giant long-necked plant-eaters, the **largest land animals** ever. **Apatosaurus** and **Brachiosaurus** (70–80 feet) and **Diplodocus** (over 80 feet) were Sauropods.
▶ **Stegosaurus** (30 feet), a large plant-eater, had sharp, bony plates along its back.
▶ **Allosaurus** and **Megalosaurus,** two giant meat-eaters, fed on large plant-eating dinosaurs like the Apatosaurus and Stegosaurus. Megalosaurus grew to 30 feet in length; Allosaurus, 30-36 feet.

## CRETACEOUS PERIOD, from 135 to 65 million years ago

▶ New dinosaurs appeared during the **Cretaceous period,** but by the end of this period, all dinosaurs had died out.
▶ New plant-eaters: **Triceratops** and other horned dinosaurs, **Anatosaurus** and other duckbilled dinosaurs, **Ankylosaurus** and other armored dinosaurs.
▶ New meat-eater: **Tyrannosaurus Rex**, one of the largest and fiercest meat-eaters, growing to 20 feet high and 40 feet long.

**DID YOU KNOW?**

*Using footprints as clues, dinosaur experts can tell how fast a dinosaur traveled, whether it ate alone or in a pack, and whether it was a meat– or plant–eater. Plant eaters tended to wander in groups, while meat eaters ran quickly after their prey.*

*Scientists once thought Tyrannosaurus Rex was the biggest of all dinosaurs. But in 1993 and 1995, they found evidence of two dinosaurs—Giganotosaurus and Carcharodontosaurus— that were even bigger.*

## EGGS MAY HELP UNSCRAMBLE DINOSAUR MYSTERIES

In 1998, scientists working in Argentina found thousands of dinosaur egg fossils in a nesting ground 70 to 90 million years old. Some of the eggs contained fossilized bits of skin, bones, and teeth of baby titanosaurs, a kind of sauropod. Researchers believe a flood buried the eggs just before they hatched, helping to preserve these remains. They say the fossils show what baby dinosaur skin felt and looked like. They hope these fossils will help explain how dinosaurs evolved.

# Which U.S. ZOOS Have the Largest Numbers of Species?

## San Diego Zoo

2920 Zoo Drive
San Diego, California 92101
Phone: (619) 234-3153
Number of Species: 800
*Popular Exhibits:* Tiger
   River, Komodo dragons,
   koalas, Hippo Beach

## St. Louis Zoological Park

Forest Park
St. Louis, Missouri 63110
Phone: (314) 781-0900
Number of Species: 713
*Popular Exhibits:* Living World,
   Bear Pits, Jungle of the Apes

## Cincinnati Zoo

3400 Vine Street
Cincinnati, Ohio 45220
Phone: (800) 94-HIPPO
Number of Species: 712
*Popular Exhibits:* Gorilla World,
   white Bengal tigers, Jungle Trails

## Houston Zoological Gardens

Hermann Park
1513 North MacGregor
Houston, Texas 77030
Phone: (713) 284-1300
Number of Species: 700
*Popular Exhibits:* Wortham World of
   Primates, Mexican wolves, cheetahs

## Denver Zoo

City Park
Denver, Colorado 80205
Phone:  (303) 376-4800
Number of Species: 672
*Popular Exhibits:*
   Tropical Discovery,
   Northern Shores,
   Primate Panorama

## Columbus Zoo

9990 Riverside Drive
Powell, Ohio 43065-0400
Phone: (800) MONKEYS
Number of Species: 650
*Popular Exhibits:* Discovery
   Reef, Ohio Wetlands,
   Tidepool Touch Tank

## Toledo Zoological Gardens

2700 Broadway
Toledo, OH 43609
Phone: (419) 385-5721
Number of Species: 633
*Popular Exhibits:* Hippoquarium, Primate
   Forest, aviary

## Omaha's Henry Doorly Zoo

3701 South 10th Street
Omaha, Nebraska 68107
Phone: (402) 733-8401
Number of Species: 630
*Popular Exhibits:* Indoor rain forest,
   aquarium, cat complex

## Bronx Zoo/Wildlife Conservation Park

Fordham Road and Bronx River Pkwy.
Bronx, New York 10460
Phone: (718) 367-1010
Number of Species: 607
*Popular Exhibits:* Himalayan Highlands,
   Jungle World, endangered species

## Cleveland Metroparks Zoo

3900 Brookside Drive
Cleveland, Ohio 44109
Phone: (216) 661-6500
Number of Species: 599
*Popular Exhibits:*
   Rain Forest with 600
   animals and 7,000
   plants

# ANIMAL PUZZLE

## FIND THE HIDDEN ANIMAL WORDS

To find out which words are hidden in this word search puzzle, first fill in the blanks. All the answers can be found in the ANIMALS chapter.

1. An animal with a backbone is called a __ __ __ __ __ __ __ __ __ __.
2. A turtle is a __ __ __ __ __ __ __.
3. A type of __ __ __ __ __ __ __ __ is the largest land animal.
4. The whale shark is the longest __ __ __ __.
5. A type of __ __ __ __ __ is the world's largest animal.
6. A __ __ __ can run as fast as a grizzly bear.
7. A female pig is called a __ __ __.
8. __ __ __ __ __ __ __ are the remains of long-dead animals or plants.
9. A group of kangaroos is called a __ __ __ __ __.
10. Triceratops was a __ __ __ __ __ __ dinosaur that lived at least 65 million years ago.
11. A fawn is a young __ __ __ __.
12. The __ __ __ __ __ __ is one animal that lives in polar regions.
13. __ __ __ __ hunting dogs run almost as fast as lions.
14. A __ __ __ __ lives for about 15 years.
15. A young sheep is called a __ __ __ __.
16. More than one __ __ __ is called a colony.
17. The first evidence of life was found during the __ __ __ cambrian period.
18. A pig lives an average of __ __ __ years.
19. The __ __ __ __ __ panda is endangered in China.

The words you found above are hidden in the puzzle below. They run across, backward, diagonally, up, or down. Some of them are backward.

| V | E | R | T | E | B | R | A | T | E |
|---|---|---|---|---|---|---|---|---|---|
| D | E | E | R | M | I | N | E | A | R |
| E | E | P | A | C | W | O | S | C | P |
| N | E | T | F | H | B | M | A | L | O |
| R | G | I | A | N | T | N | A | I | O |
| O | S | L | I | S | S | O | F | O | R |
| H | E | E | L | E | P | H | A | N | T |

*Answers are on pages 317-320.*

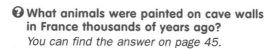

# ART

❓ **What animals were painted on cave walls in France thousands of years ago?**
*You can find the answer on page 45.*

## Painting: LANDSCAPE, PORTRAIT, and STILL LIFE

Art can be real or imaginary, funny or sad, beautiful or disturbing. Before photography was invented, most artists tried to show things as they saw them or as they imagined them to look. Throughout history, artists have painted pictures of nature (called landscapes); or pictures of people (called portraits); or pictures of flowers in vases, food, and other objects (known as still lifes). When artists paint people and things to look as they do in real life, their art is called realistic, or representational.

### LANDSCAPES

A drawing or painting of nature is called a **landscape**. A picture of the sea is called a **seascape**. A picture of city buildings is called a **cityscape**. Below are a few famous painters, when they lived, their nationality, and the name of one of their landscapes.

▲ *A landscape*

**El Greco** (1541-1614), Spanish painter: "View of Toledo" (cityscape)
**Jan Vermeer** (1632-1675), Dutch painter: "View of Delft" (cityscape)
**Katsushika Hokusai** (1760-1849), Japanese painter: "Views of Mount Fuji" (landscape)
**John Constable** (1776-1837), English painter: "The Cornfield" (landscape)
**Winslow Homer** (1836-1910), American painter: "Northeaster" (seascape)
**Georgia O'Keeffe** (1887-1986), American painter: "Grey Hills" (landscape)

### PORTRAITS

A painting of a person (or more than one person) is called a **portrait**. When a person paints a picture of himself or herself, it is called a **self-portrait**. Below is a list of some famous painters,

▲ *A portrait*

when they lived, their nationality, and the name of one of their portraits.

**Leonardo da Vinci** (1452-1519), Italian painter: "Mona Lisa"
**Rembrandt** (1606-1669), Dutch painter: "Self Portrait"
**John Singleton Copley** (1737-1815), American painter: "Paul Revere"
**Edouard Manet** (1832-1883), French painter: "The Fifer"
**Pierre Auguste Renoir** (1841-1919), French painter: "Madame Charpentier and Her Children"
**Mary Cassatt** (1844-1926), American painter: "The Bath"

## STILL LIFES

A picture of small objects—like flowers, bottles, books, food, and other things—is called a **still life**. Below are a few famous painters, when they lived, their nationality, and the name of one of their still-life paintings.

**Henri Fantin-Latour** (1836-1904), French painter: "Still Life With Flowers and Fruit"
**Paul Cézanne** (1839-1906), French painter: "Apples and Pears"
**William Michael Harnett** (1848-1892), American painter: "Still Life—Violin and Music"
**Vincent van Gogh** (1853-1890), Dutch painter: "Sunflowers"

▲ A still life

# Modern Art

**M**any artists still paint pictures that can be recognized as landscapes and portraits. But some artists today create pictures using shapes or colors or textures in interesting ways that do not look like anything in the real world. These paintings are called abstract, or nonrepresentational. Abstract art is also called modern art.

 **DID YOU KNOW?**

▶ Thousands of years ago, people painted pictures on the walls of caves.

▶ Many of these paintings—of bison, horses, deer, and other wild animals— can be found in caves in Altamira, Spain, and Lascaux, France.

▶ These caves were discovered by accident (Altamira in 1879 and Lascaux in 1940).

▶ Some of the cave art in France is believed to be as much as 30,000 years old.

## ABSTRACT PAINTINGS

Here are a few famous painters known for their abstract paintings, along with the years they lived, their nationality, and the name of one of their paintings. Sometimes an abstract painting has a name that sounds realistic—like Picasso's "Three Musicians"— even though the painting is abstract.

▲ An abstract painting

**Pablo Picasso** (1881-1973), Spanish painter: "Three Musicians"
**Joan Miró** (1893-1983), Spanish painter: "Composition"
**Helen Frankenthaler** (born 1928), American painter: "Blue Territory"
**Wassily Kandinsky** (1866-1944), Russian painter: "Impression No. 30"
**Piet Mondrian** (1872-1944), Dutch painter: "Composition"
**Jackson Pollock** (1912-1956), American painter: "Number 1"

▲ Cave painting

# MAKING ORIGAMI

## THE ART OF ORIGAMI

Origami is the art of folding paper into different shapes. The name comes from the Japanese words for *ori,* which means "to fold" and *gami,* which means "paper."

Origami is not just a Japanese art, though many great origami artists are Japanese. The Chinese, inventors of paper, used beautiful folded paper shapes to decorate temples and shrines. Many origami shapes are of animals, especially the crane. It is said that folding 1,000 cranes ensures that you will have a long and prosperous life.

With practice, you can create a roomful of lovely origami creations. All you need is patience and squares of thin paper. Some stores sell special origami paper that is colored on one side and plain on the other, but it's not necessary to have it.

## LEARNING MORE ABOUT ORIGAMI

You don't have to know special words to do origami, though it helps to know what the arrows and lines on diagrams stand for. Each of the books listed here gives complete instructions. The projects they include range from easy to complicated.

Visit your local library to look at some of the many books on origami. You can usually find them in the 700 section under 736.98.

### Paperback Books

▶ *Easy Origami,* by Dokuohtei Nakano (Puffin Books)
▶ *Easy Origami,* by John Montrall (Dover Publications)
▶ *Folding Paper Toys,* by Shari Lewis and Lillian Oppenheimer (Stein and Day)
▶ *The Magic of Origami,* by Alice Gray and Kunihiko Kasahara with cooperation of Lillian Oppenheimer and Origami Center of America (Japan Publications)
▶ *Origami in Action/Paper Toys that Fly, Flap, Gobble, and Inflate,* by Robert J. Lang (St. Martin's Griffin)
▶ *Origami Made Easy,* by Kunihiko Kasahara (Japan Publications)
▶ *Origami, Plain and Simple,* by Thomas Hull with models by Robert Neale (St. Martin's Griffin)
▶ *Origami Treasure Chest,* by Keiji Kitamura (Japan Publications Trading Company)
▶ *Paper Pandas and Jumping Frogs,* by Florence Temko (China Books)
▶ *The World of Origami,* by Isao Honda (Japan Publications Trading Company)

For more information about origami, send a self-stamped (two first-class stamps), self-addressed business-size envelope to Origami USA, 15 West 77th Street, New York, NY 10024-5192.

## AN ORIGAMI WHALE

As a first project in origami, try making this whale.

Use a square piece of medium-weight paper; an eight-inch square works nicely.

As you become more expert, you can create a whole group, or pod, of origami whales in different colors and kinds of paper. Whales made of wrapping-paper scraps make perfect decorations for gifts.

**1** Place the paper on a flat surface with one corner on top, in the shape of a diamond.

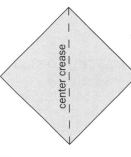

**2** Fold the point on the left over to meet the right point, then unfold it. You will have a crease in the center.

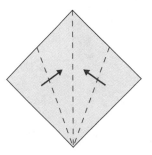

**3** Fold the lower left and lower right sides so they meet at the crease. Make your folds as sharp as possible.

**4** What you have should look like a kite. Now fold down the top point to make a small triangle.

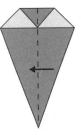

**5** Fold over the right side to meet the left side.

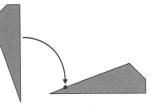

**6** Turn the shape so that the long side is facing you.

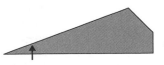

**7** Fold up the point at the end to make a tail.

**8** Draw a face on your whale.

# SCULPTURE

**S**culpture is a three-dimensional form made from clay, stone, metal, or other material. Many sculptures stand freely so that you can walk around them. Some are mobiles that hang from the ceiling. Sculptures can be large, like the Statue of Liberty, or small. Some sculpture is representational (looks like the person or animal it represents). Some modern sculpture is abstract and has no form that can be recognized.

## SOME FAMOUS SCULPTORS AND SCULPTURE

Below is a list of a few sculptors, when they lived, their nationality, and the name of one of their sculptures.

**Michelangelo Buonarroti** (1475-1564) Italian sculptor and painter: "Pietà" (representational)

**Edgar Degas** (1834-1917) French painter and sculptor: "Little Fourteen-Year-Old Dancer" (representational)

**Auguste Rodin** (1840-1917) French sculptor: "The Thinker" (representational)

**Henry Moore** (1898-1986) English sculptor: "Family Group" (abstract)

**Louise Nevelson** (1899-1988) American sculptor: "Royal Tide II" (abstract)

**Isamu Noguchi** (1904-1988) American sculptor, "Unidentified Object" (abstract)

▲ A sculpture

# Where to Look at Art

**T**here are art museums in many cities in the United States. Some of them are general art museums, where you can see art from many different countries and from many different time periods—sometimes from early Egyptian art to modern art. Many cities also have museums of American art, museums of modern art, and other special collections. For museums that focus on ethnic art, culture, and history, such as African or Asian culture, see the section called Ethnic Museums, on page 130. A few general art museums are listed below.

Art Institute of Chicago
Baltimore Museum of Art
Boston Museum of Fine Arts
Cleveland Museum of Art
Dallas Museum of Art
Denver Art Museum
Detroit Institute of Arts
Getty Center (Los Angeles, CA)
Houston Museum of Fine Arts
Kansas City Art Institute

Los Angeles County Museum of Art
Metropolitan Museum of Art (New York)
Minneapolis Institute of Arts
National Gallery of Art (Washington, D.C.)
North Carolina Museum of Art (Raleigh, NC)
Philadelphia Museum of Art
San Antonio Museum of Art
San Francisco Museum of Art

❓ **Where can you visit both Avi and Virginia Hamilton, two famous children's authors?**
*You can find the answer on page 50.*

# Book AWARDS, 1998–1999

**A**re you in the mood for unforgettable characters? For exciting stories? For an experience that will make you think about life in a fresh way? Then read one of the following award-winning books.

SNOWFLAKE BENTLEY

Jacqueline Briggs Martin   Illustrated by Mary Azarian

**Boston Globe-Horn Book Award**
—These are given every year.
   **1998 winners:**
      Fiction: *The Circuit: Stories From the Life of a Migrant Child*, by Francisco Jimenez
      Nonfiction: *Leon's Story*, by Leon Walter Tillage
      Picture Book: *And if the Moon Could Talk*,
         by Kate Banks, illustrated by Georg Hallensleben

**Caldecott Medal**—This is the highest honor a picture book can receive.
   **1999 winner:** *Snowflake Bentley*, illustrated by Mary Azarian

**Coretta Scott King Awards**—These are given to artists and authors whose works promote the cause of peace and world brotherhood.
   **1998 winners:**
      Author Award: *Heaven*, by Angela Johnson
      Illustrator Award: *i see the rhythm*, illustrated by Michele Wood

**Newbery Medal**—This is an award for writing. It is the highest honor for a children's book that is not a picture book.
   **1999 winner:** *Holes*, by Louis Sachar

**Poetry Awards**—The **Lee Bennett Hopkins/International Reading Association Award** is presented every three years to a poet who has had up to two books published.
   **Current winner:** Kristine O'Connell George for *The Great Frog Race and Other Poems* and *Old Elm Speaks*.
The **Lee Bennett Hopkins Poetry Award** is given annually to a distinguished poetry book.
   **1999 winner:** *The Other Side: Shorter Poems*, by Angela Johnson.

**Hans Christian Andersen Awards**—These are given every two years.
   **1998 winners:**
      Author Award: *Bridge to Terabithia*, by Katherine Peterson
      Illustrator Award: Tommi Ungerer

# BEST NEW BOOKS of the Year

(Some of those chosen in 1999 by the American Library Association)

*Alien for Rent,* by Betsy Duffey

*Animals Eat the Weirdest Things,* by Diane Swanson

*Apple Island; or the Truth About Teachers,* by Douglas Evans

*The Barefoot Book of Trickster Tales,* by Richard Walker

*By Truck to the North,* by Alan Turnbull

*Collecting Baseball Cards,* by Tomas S. Owens

*Forty Acres and Maybe a Mule,* by Harriett Gillem Robinet

*Frozen Summer,* by Mary Jane Auch

*Living on Mars: Mission to the Red Planet,* by Michael D. Cole

*Maniac Monkeys on Magnolia Street,* by Angela Johnson

*McGwire and Sosa: A Season to Remember,* by James Preller

*Powwow, A Good Day to Dance,* by Jacqueline D. Greene

*A Street Through Time,* by Anne Millard, illustrated by Steve Noon

*Strudle Stories,* by Joanne Rocklin

*Wise Words of Paul Tiulana: An Inupait Alaskan's Life,* by Vivian Senungetuk

## MEET VIRGINIA HAMILTON AND AVI

**Virginia Hamilton** was born in 1936 on a small farm in Ohio and raised by a family of storytellers. Her childhood was filled with tales of her African-American heritage.

With her award-winning books *The People Could Fly: American Black Folktales* and *Her Stories: African American Folktales, Fairy Tales and True Tales*, Virginia has rescued dusty manuscripts from old library shelves and brought them back to life.

To learn more about her many other highly praised books and fascinating personality, check out her Web site at

**WEB SITE**
*http://www.virginiahamilton.com*

Did you know that she loves frog jokes? If you send her one, she would probably enjoy it!

**Avi** was born in 1937 and grew up in Brooklyn, New York. He has written everything from historical novels to science fiction, mysteries, comedies, and animal tales. He has won many awards.

As a child Avi's teachers criticized him for spelling words wrong. He later learned that this was caused by a learning disability. Avi likes to show kids the many spelling mistakes that still must be corrected before his manuscripts are published. Luckily, this never stops him from writing.

If you liked his book *Poppy,* try its sequel *Poppy and Rye,* or *Amanda Joins the Circus.* You can also check out Avi's Web site at

**WEB SITE** *http://www.avi-writer.com*

## Ten ALL-TIME BEST-SELLING Paperbacks

*Charlotte's Web,* by E. B. White, illustrated by Garth Williams

*The Outsiders,* by S. E. Hinton

*Tales of a Fourth Grade Nothing,* by Judy Blume

*Shane,* by Jack Schaefer

*Are You There, God? It's Me, Margaret,* by Judy Blume

*Where the Red Fern Grows,* by Wilson Rawls

*A Wrinkle in Time,* by Madeleine L'Engle

*Island of the Blue Dolphins,* by Scott O'Dell

*Little House on the Prairie,* by Laura Ingalls Wilder

*Little House in the Big Woods,* by Laura Ingalls Wilder

# BOOKS You May ENJOY

The books listed on this page and the next one have been praised by many people. For more on children's books, go to:

**WEB SITE** http://www.lacs.ucalgary.cal~dkbrown/index.html

### Fiction

Fiction books are stories that come out of the writer's imagination. They are not true. Some fiction books are set in a world of fantasy. Others seem incredibly real.

*Center Court Sting*, by Matt Christopher
When Daren McCall's basketball team plays badly, Daren blames everyone but himself. His teammates decide to teach him a lesson.

*The Friends*, by Kazumi Yumoto
Fascinated with death after Yamashita's grandmother passes away, three friends follow an old man they think is about to die. They end up learning much more about living than dying.

*From the Mixed-Up Files of Mrs. Basil E. Frankweiler*, E. L. Konigsburg
When Claudia and her brother Jamie run away from home, they hide in the Metropolitan Museum of Art and try to solve a mystery.

*The Giver*, by Lois Lowry
Twelve-year-old Jonas lives in a world with no pain, fear, or war. But life is not nearly as perfect as it seems.

*The Moorchild*, by Eloise McGraw
A moving story about a half-fairy, half-human being who has to leave her place of birth and go to live with humans who are afraid of her.

*Mrs. Frisby and the Rats of NIMH*, by Robert C. O'Brien
When Mrs. Frisby, the mother of a family of field mice, sees her home threatened by the farmer's plow, she seeks help from a group of intelligent rats who escaped from a laboratory.

*The Quicksand Pony*, by Alison Lester
Set along the rugged coastline of Australia, this is a story about a young boy who lives alone in the wilderness until he meets Biddy and her family.

*Thank You, Jackie Robinson*, by Barbara Cohen
Sam and Davy come from different races, religions, and generations. But their interest in baseball brings them together, and they find they have more in common than they ever imagined.

*The Thief*, by Megan Whalen Turner
A young thief searches for a gemstone so that he can be freed from prison forever. Set in a long-ago land of fantasy, this adventure story has a surprise ending.

*Walk Two Moons*, by Sharon Creech
During a long car ride with her strange grandparents, Sal Hiddle tells stories that help her accept the truth about her mother's disappearance.

*Wringer*, by Jerry Spinelli
A suspenseful tale about a 10-year-old boy who must choose between doing something he thinks is wrong and disappointing and possibly losing his friends.

*Yolanda's Genius*, by Carol Fenner
Yolanda is determined to prove to her family that her brother—who is having trouble learning to read—is really a musical genius.

## Poetry

Poems use language in creative and imaginative ways, sometimes in rhyme.

*The Beauty of the Beast: Poems From the Animal Kingdom*
selected by Jack Prelutsky, illustrated by Mielo So
An illustrated multicultural collection of poems about animals, insects, and birds.

*Classic Poetry: An Illustrated Collection*, edited by Michael Rosen
There are short biographies and portraits of the poets with each of these poems.

*At the Crack of the Bat: Baseball Poems*, by Lillian Morrison
Lots of illustrated poems for baseball lovers.

## Nonfiction

The books below prove that fact can be just as interesting as fiction.

*Cowboy With a Camera, Erwin E. Smith: Cowboy Photographer*, by Don Worcester
Photographs taken by a real cowboy in the American West around 1900.

*Laura's Album: A Remembrance Scrapbook of Laura Ingalls Wilder*
by William Anderson
This collection of letters and mementos gives a glimpse into Wilder's life.

*House*, by Albert Lorenz
From a serf's cabin to the Mir space station, this detailed and lively book will show you the different kinds of places people have lived.

*Orphan Train Rider: One Boy's True Story*, by Andrea Warren
One of the 200 orphans who rode the Orphan Train to the Midwest in search of a new family tells his exciting story.

*Pearl Harbor Child: A Child's View of Pearl Harbor—From Attack to Peace*,
by Dorinda Nicholson
The first book to describe the Japanese attack on Pearl Harbor from the viewpoint of a child who lived there. Family photos and official documents help tell the story.

*Pharmacy in the Forest: How Medicines Are Found in the Natural World*,
by Fred Powledge
This book warns us to protect our forests before we miss the chance to discover the powerful cures they hold.

*Shannon Lucid,* by Carmen Bredeson
An entertaining biography of the brave and charming astronaut who spent 188 days aboard the Mir space station.

*Story Painter: The Life of Jacob Lawrence*, by John Duggleby
A fast-moving illustrated biography of the famous African-American artist whose paintings make the past come alive.

*Winning Ways: A Photohistory of Women in Sports*, by Sue Macy
About women's struggle to be taken seriously as athletes.

## Reference Books

**WHERE THE ANSWERS ARE**
Many reference materials are stored on CD-ROMs and are also available on the Internet.

**Almanac:** A one-volume book of facts and statistics.

**Atlas:** A collection of maps.

**Dictionary:** A book of words in alphabetical order. A dictionary gives the meanings and spelling of words and shows how they are pronounced.

**Encyclopedia:** A place to go for information on almost any subject in the world.

# Make Your Own Book

**M**ake a scrapbook for yourself or to give as a gift.

## YOU NEED

▶ sheets of three-hole loose-leaf paper
▶ two feet or more of yarn
▶ two sheets of heavy colored paper
▶ three-hole punch (if possible)
▶ stamps, stickers, glitter, picture scraps, fabric

## WHAT TO DO

1 Make a paper sandwich with the loose-leaf sheets in between the heavy paper.
2 Make holes in the cover papers that exactly line up with the loose-leaf paper. (If you can use a three-hole punch, that would be best.)
3 Run the yarn through the holes. Make tight bows or knots so the book is securely fastened.
4 Decorate the cover.

What can you do with your book? Here are some ideas. You'll probably come up with many more.

class photo album to give to your teacher at the end of the school year

your personal diary

family scrapbook, including your photos, artwork, jokes, menus of places you like to eat, poems

sports scrapbook with photos and info about favorite teams

Web scrapbook with downloads from the Net

celebrity scrapbook

scrapbook about places you've been or would like to visit

holiday-theme book to give to someone you care about

reviews of books you've read, movies you've seen, music you've heard—anything you want to remember or share with friends and classmates

puzzles you've created

## MORE IDEAS

_____

_____

_____

# BUILDINGS, BRIDGES, AND TUNNELS

**❓ In what country would you find the world's tallest building?**
*You can find the answer below.*

## TALLEST BUILDINGS in the World

Here are some of the world's tallest buildings.

1. **Petronas Towers 1 & 2,** Kuala Lumpur, Malaysia (completed 1996)
   Height: each building 88 stories, 1,483 feet
2. **Sears Tower,** Chicago, Illinois (completed 1974)
   Height: 110 stories, 1,454 feet
3. **Jin Mao Building,** Shanghai, China (completed 1997)
   Height: 88 stories, 1,379 feet
4. **World Trade Center 1 & 2,** New York City (completed 1972, 1973)
   Height: each building 110 stories, over 1,360 feet
5. **Empire State Building,** New York City (completed 1931)
   Height: 102 stories, 1,250 feet
6. **Central Plaza,** Hong Kong, China (completed 1992)
   Height: 78 stories, 1,227 feet
7. **Bank of China Tower,** Hong Kong (completed 1989)
   Height: 70 stories, 1,209 feet
8. **The Centre,** Hong Kong, China (completed 1998)
   Height: 73 stories, 1,149 feet
9. **T & C Tower,** Kaohsiung, Taiwan (completed 1997)
   Height: 85 stories, 1,140 feet
10. **Amoco Building,** Chicago, Illinois (completed 1973)
    Height: 80 stories, 1,136 feet

## The 7 WONDERS of the Ancient World

These were considered the most remarkable structures of the time. Only the pyramids survive today.

**Pyramids of Egypt**
At Giza, Egypt, built as royal tombs from 3000 to 1800 B.C. The largest is the Great Pyramid of Khufu (or Cheops).

**Hanging Gardens of Babylon**
Terraced gardens built by King Nebuchadnezzar II around 600 B.C. for his wife.

**Temple of Artemis**
At Ephesus (now part of Turkey), built mostly of marble around 550 B.C. in honor of a Greek goddess, Artemis.

# LONGEST TUNNELS in the World

A **tunnel** is a long underground passageway, dug through rock or earth or built underwater. Vehicular tunnels (on land and under water) are for automobiles, trucks, and the like. Railroad tunnels are for trains and subway traffic. Water tunnels are for water mains, drainage, sewage, mining, and storage. Here are the longest tunnels of each type:

| TYPE OF TUNNEL | NAME | LOCATION | LENGTH |
|---|---|---|---|
| Land Vehicular | St. Gotthard | Switzerland | 10.1 miles |
| Underwater Vehicular | Brooklyn-Battery | New York, USA | 1.7 miles |
| Railroad | Seikan | Japan | 33.5 miles |
| Water | Delaware Aqueduct | New York, USA | 85.0 miles |

# LONGEST BRIDGES in the World

*Main Span*

**T**he **span** of a bridge is the distance between its supports. The bridges below, as measured by main spans, are the world's longest suspension bridges (those that hang from cables). The longest suspension bridge in the U.S. is the Verrazano-Narrows Bridge in New York (4,260 feet).

| NAME OF BRIDGE | LOCATION | MAIN SPAN |
|---|---|---|
| Akashi Kaikyo | Japan | 6,570 feet |
| Storebaelt | Denmark | 5,328 feet |
| Humber | England | 4,626 feet |

**Colossus of Rhodes**

In the harbor on the island of Rhodes (Greece). A bronze statue of the sun god Helios, built about 280 B.C.

**Statue of Zeus**

At Olympia, Greece. The statue, made about 462 B.C. by the sculptor Phidias from ivory and gold, showed the king of the gods.

**Mausoleum of Halicarnassus**

(Now part of Turkey), built about 353 B.C. in honor of King Mausolus, a ruler of ancient Caria.

**Lighthouse of Alexandria, Egypt**

Built about 270 B.C. during the reign of King Ptolemy II. It may have been around 500 feet tall.

# CALENDARS AND TIME

❓ **If your birthstone is a diamond, what month were you born in?**
*You can find the answer below.*

# CALENDARS

Calendars divide time into days, weeks, months, and years. Calendar divisions are based on movements of Earth and on the sun and the moon. A day is the average time it takes for one rotation of Earth on its axis. A year is the average time it takes for one revolution of Earth around the sun. Early calendars were based on the movements of the moon across the sky. The ancient Egyptians were the first to develop a calendar based on the movements of Earth in relation to the sun.

## ROMAN CALENDARS:
### The Julian and Gregorian Calendars
At first the ancient Romans had a calendar with a year of 304 days, but it was not a solar calendar and became confusing. In 45 B.C., the emperor Julius Caesar decided to use a calendar based on movements of the sun. This calendar, called the **Julian calendar**, fixed the normal year at 365 days and added one day every fourth year (leap year). It also established the months of the year and the days of the week.

The Julian calendar was used until A.D. 1582, when it was revised by Pope Gregory XIII, because it was 11 minutes and 14 seconds longer than the solar year. The new calendar, called the **Gregorian calendar**, is the one used today in most of the world.

## OTHER CALENDARS:
### Jewish and Islamic Calendars
Other calendars are also used. The Jewish calendar, which starts in the year 3761 B.C., is the official calendar of the State of Israel. The year 2000 is equivalent to the year 5760–5761 on the Jewish calendar, which starts at Rosh Hashanah. The Islamic calendar starts counting years in A.D. 622. The year 2000 is equivalent to 1420–1421 on the Islamic calendar, which begins at Muharram (New Year).

| BIRTHSTONES | |
| --- | --- |
| MONTH | BIRTHSTONE |
| January | Garnet |
| February | Amethyst |
| March | Aquamarine |
| April | Diamond |
| May | Emerald |
| June | Pearl |
| July | Ruby |
| August | Peridot |
| September | Sapphire |
| October | Opal |
| November | Topaz |
| December | Turquoise |

**DID YOU KNOW?** Stonehenge, the ancient stone monument in Salisbury, England, is between 3,000 and 5,000 years old. Most scientists think it was used to predict the positions of the sun and moon—a kind of huge calendar.

# What Are TIME ZONES?

The length of a day is 24 hours—the time it takes Earth to complete one rotation on its axis. The system we use to tell time is called standard time. In standard time, Earth is divided into 24 time zones. They each run north to south, from the North Pole to the South Pole.

To figure out the time in a particular zone, count the number of zones east or west of the prime meridian, or 0 degrees, which runs through Greenwich, England. When it is midnight, or 0 hour, in Greenwich, it is five hours earlier in New York, because New York is five zones away.

Pacific Standard Time

Mountain Standard Time

Central Standard Time

Eastern Standard Time

Alaska Standard Time

Hawaii-Aleutian Standard Time

## WHEN IT IS 12 NOON IN NEW YORK, IT IS

| 12 noon | 11 A.M. | 11 A.M. | 10 A.M. | 9 A.M. | 8 A.M. | 7 A.M. |
|---------|---------|---------|---------|--------|--------|--------|
| Atlanta, Georgia | St. Louis, Missouri | Dallas, Texas | Denver, Colorado | Los Angeles, California | Juneau, Alaska | Honolulu, Hawaii |

## HOW LONG DID IT TAKE?

**1492** — Christopher Columbus's first trip across the Atlantic Ocean, from Spain to San Salvador, took 70 days.

**1650s** — It took 50 days to sail across the ocean from London, England, to Boston, Massachusetts.

**1829** — The first Atlantic Ocean crossing by a ship powered in part by steam (*Savannah*, sailing from Savannah, Georgia, to Liverpool, England) took 29 days.

**1903** — The first flight in a heavier-than-air craft was made by Orville Wright at Kitty Hawk, North Carolina, and lasted for 12 seconds.

**1927** — Charles Lindbergh flew from New York to Paris in 33 hours, 29 minutes, 30 seconds. It was the first nonstop flight made across the Atlantic Ocean by one person.

**1961** — The flight of the first U.S. satellite carrying an astronaut (Alan Shepard, Jr.) lasted 15 minutes.

**1976** — Passengers can fly by supersonic plane, the Concorde, between London and New York in only $3\frac{1}{2}$ hours.

# COMPUTERS

❓ If you are inputting a URL, what are you hoping to reach?
*You can find the answer on page 64.*

# WHAT Do COMPUTERS Do?

At first, computers were used to add, subtract, multiply, and divide big numbers. Today they are used to do much more. A pizza shop owner can use a computer to keep track of what pizzas people buy every day and what toppings need to be ordered. This information is organized and saved in a database. A student can use a computer to get information from the Internet (see page 64), play games, or do homework.

### COMPUTERS HELP PEOPLE COMMUNICATE.
Computers can be used to write letters or stories or reports for school.

Computers help create newspapers, magazines, and books.

People use computers to send electronic mail (e-mail), sometimes across the continent or to other countries.

People who cannot speak can type in messages that the computer translates into speech. People who cannot type can speak into a computer that translates their speech into text.

### COMPUTERS HELP PEOPLE CREATE.
People use computers to create artwork and music or to design buildings.

Computers are used to create special effects for movies and television.

### COMPUTERS HELP PEOPLE LEARN.
Programs on computers help teach school subjects.

Computer programs can keep track of students' progress.

Pilots and astronauts use computer flight simulators.

### COMPUTERS KEEP INFORMATION ORGANIZED.
Many companies and organizations keep a database with information. The FBI has a database that police departments can use to find information about criminals or stolen goods from all around the United States.

### COMPUTERS HELP PREDICT THE FUTURE.
Companies use computer programs to help them make decisions.

Computer programs use data from satellites to help forecast weather.

### COMPUTERS ARE USED TO MANUFACTURE PRODUCTS.
Engineers use special software to create detailed drawings of an object and then test it to see how to make it stronger or cheaper.

Computers can control machinery used to make the new product.

### COMPUTERS AREN'T JUST FOUND ON DESKS.
Computers are used in automatic teller machines at the bank and with the price scanner at the supermarket checkout.

Cars, VCRs, and digital watches all have built-in computers.

# COMPUTER TALK

**artificial intelligence or AI**
The ability of computers and robots to imitate human intelligence by learning and making decisions.

**bit**
The smallest unit of data.

**boot**
To turn on a computer.

**browser**
A program to help get around the Internet.

**bug or glitch**
An error in a program or in the computer.

**byte**
An amount of data equal to 8 bits.

**database**
A large collection of information organized so that it can be retrieved and used in different ways.

**desktop publishing**
The use of computers for combining text and pictures to design and produce magazines, newspapers, and books.

**download**
To transfer information from a host computer to a personal computer, often through a modem.

**e-mail or electronic mail**
Messages sent from one computer to another over a network.

**gig or gigabyte (GB)**
An amount of information equal to 1,000 (or 1,024) megabytes.

**hard copy**
Computer output printed on paper or similar material.

**Internet**
A worldwide system of linked computer networks.

**K**
This means "thousands" in Greek. It is used to represent bytes of data or memory.

**laptop or notebook**
A portable personal computer that can run on batteries.

**megabyte (MB)**
An amount of information equal to 1 million (or 1,048,516) bytes.

**multimedia**
Software that includes pictures, video, and sound. In multimedia software, you can see pictures move and hear music and other sounds.

**network**
A group of computers linked together so that they can share information.

**password**
A secret code that keeps people who do not know it from using a computer or software.

**program**
Instructions for a computer to follow.

**RAM or random access memory**
The memory your computer uses to open programs and store your work until you save it to the hard drive or a disk. The information in RAM disappears when the computer is turned off.

**ROM or read only memory**
ROM contains permanent instructions for the computer and cannot be changed. The information in ROM remains after the computer is turned off.

**scanner**
A device that can transfer words and pictures from a printed page into the computer.

**upload**
To send information from a personal computer to a host computer.

**virtual reality**
Three-dimensional images on a screen that are viewed using special equipment (like gloves and goggles). The user feels as if he or she is part of the image and can interact with everything around.

**virus**
A program that damages other programs and data. It gets into a computer through telephone lines or shared disks.

**Web site**
A place on the Internet's World Wide Web where text and pictures are stored. The contents are sent to computers when the correct World Wide Web address (which begins with http://) is entered.

# HOW COMPUTERS WORK

**C**omputers perform tasks by using programs called **software**. These programs tell the computer what to do when the user enters certain information or commands. This is called **input**.

The computer then processes the information and gives the user the results (**output**). The computer can also save, or **store**, the information so that it can be used again and again.

The machines that make up a computer system are kinds of **hardware**. The largest and most powerful computers are called **mainframes**. Scientists use them to perform calculations that would take years to do by hand. The computers most people are familiar with are personal computers (**PCs**). These can be used at a desk (**desktops**), carried around (**laptops**), even held in your hand (**palm computers**).

## SOFTWARE

▶ **Kinds of Software**

To write a story (or letter or school report) you use a type of software called a word-processing program. This program can be selected by using the **keyboard** or a **mouse**.

Other common types of software include programs for doing mathematics, keeping records, playing games, and creating pictures.

▶ **Entering Data**

In a word processing program, you can input your words by typing on the **keyboard**. The backspace and delete keys are like electronic erasers. You can also press special keys (called **function keys**) or click on certain symbols (**icons**), to center or underline words, move words and sentences around, check your spelling, print out a page, and do other tasks. When you input a command, the word-processing program tells the computer what to do.

## HARDWARE

▶ **Inside the Computer**

The instructions from the program you use are carried out inside the computer by the **central processing unit**, or **CPU**. The CPU is the computer's brain.

▶ **Getting the Results**

The **monitor** and **printer** are the most commonly used output devices in a computer system. When you type a story, the words appear on a **monitor**, which is similar to a television screen. Your story can then be printed on paper by using a **printer**.

If you print out a story, you can mail it to a friend. But if you and your friend both have **modems**, the story can be sent from your computer directly to your friend's computer. A **modem** allows information from a computer to travel over telephone lines.

# A COMPUTER SYSTEM

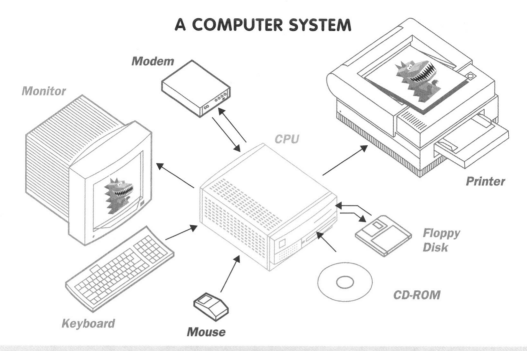

Modem

Monitor

CPU

Printer

Floppy Disk

CD-ROM

Keyboard

Mouse

# STORAGE

### Keeping Data to Use It Later

A computer also stores information that you may want to use later. Suppose you want to stop working and eat lunch. You can save your work and go back to it later.

### Floppy Disk

Information can be saved on a "floppy" disk that goes into a slot in the computer called a disk drive. If you use a disk to save your story, you can use the disk on another computer and your story will be there to work on. Disks today are usually stiff. Older computers used larger disks that were light and easy to bend, so people began calling them floppy disks.

### Zip Disk

Zip disks hold much more information than a floppy disk. They are used in special zip drives.

### Hard Disk

Most computers have a hard drive. The hard drive contains a hard disk that is not removed. It holds much more information than zip or floppy disks. It stores your software and information you have entered into the computer.

## CD-ROMS

Many computers have a CD-ROM drive. This allows you to play special disks called CD-ROMs, similar to music CDs. A CD-ROM can hold a huge amount of information, including pictures and sound. Almanacs, games, encyclopedias, and many other types of information and entertainment are on CD-ROMs.

### DVDs

Digital Versatile Disks look like CD-ROMs, but hold about eight times more information on a single side. DVDs are currently used to store movies, encyclopedias, and other products with lots of data.

# The BINARY SYSTEM

A computer can do many impressive things, but one thing it cannot do is understand English. For a computer to do its work, every piece of information given to it must be translated into binary code. You are probably used to using 10 digits, 0 through 9, when you do arithmetic. When the computer uses the **binary code**, it uses only two digits, 0 and 1. Think of it as sending messages to the computer by switching a light on and off.

Each 0 or 1 digit is called a **bit**, and most computers use a sequence of 8 bits (called a **byte**) for each piece of data. Almost all computers use the same code, called ASCII (pronounced "askey"), to stand for letters of the alphabet, number digits, punctuation, and other special characters that control the computer's operation. Below is a list of ASCII bytes for the alphabet.

| | | | | | |
|---|---|---|---|---|---|
| A | 01000001 | J | 01001010 | S | 01010011 |
| B | 01000010 | K | 01001011 | T | 01010100 |
| C | 01000011 | L | 01001100 | U | 01010101 |
| D | 01000100 | M | 01001101 | V | 01010110 |
| E | 01000101 | N | 01001110 | W | 01010111 |
| F | 01000110 | O | 01001111 | X | 01011000 |
| G | 01000111 | P | 01010000 | Y | 01011001 |
| H | 01001000 | Q | 01010001 | Z | 01011010 |
| I | 01001001 | R | 01010010 | | |

Many of the words in "computer talk" can be turned into English words. Try to turn the binary code into English in each of the sentences below. Put a mark after every eight numbers, so you won't lose your place. Then find the letter that each group of eight numbers stands for, and fill in the blanks. (Answers are on pages 317–320.)

Computer language is translated into this code: ___ ___ ___ ___ ___ ___ .
01000010010010010100111001000001010100100101011001

Very few people have been to this place. It's called the ___ ___ ___ ___ .
01001101010010111010011110100111101001110

Another one is coming soon. It's the ___ ___ ___ ___ ___ ___ ___ ___ ___ .
01001101010010010100110001001100010001010100111001001110
01001001010101010101001101

# What Is a Programming Language?

If you decoded the words above, you saw how slow it is to work with binary code. The first computer programs were written in binary code. Today, programs use languages both humans and computers can understand. They are translated by the computer into binary code.

On the screen at right you can see a very simple program in a language called BASIC. It tells the computer to print the sum of 1 + 2, or 3. Some other programming languages you might hear about are FORTRAN, COBOL, Pascal, Java, and C++.

```
LET A=1
LET B=2
LET C=A+B
PRINT C
```

# SUPER SOFTWARE

You can learn and have a lot of fun with software programs. Here are a few popular ones.

**Carmen San Diego Word Detective,** Broderbund. PC, Mac. Carmen has invented a Babble-On Machine in hopes of turning words into gibberish. Help foil her plans.

**Make a Masterpiece,** IBM. PC, Mac. Experiment with different art materials and ways of creating art.

**Thinkin' Things Sky Island Mysteries,** Edmark. PC, Mac. Use your creativity to unravel mysteries and solve puzzles.

**Somebody Catch My Homework,** Discis. PC, Mac. Join in the fun with 20 poems by David Harrison that are funny and fun to read. There's also an interview with the poet.

**Chicka Chicka Boom Boom,** Davidson. PC, Mac. Everyone will be singing with you. You can also record your own songs and "play" instruments.

 **DID YOU KNOW?**

*In ancient times people did computing with numbers using an abacus, which is made up of rods and beads. A modern version of the abacus is still used today in Japan. A person who is skilled with an abacus can add more than 15 numbers in one minute.*

*Charles Babbage (1791–1871), an English mathematician, is the "father" of the computer. He was the first person to figure out how a machine could perform calculations and store the results.*

*A compact disk can store 72 minutes of cartoon or video, 2 hours of music, or 19 hours of speech.*

# COMPUTER MUSEUMS

Some museums have sections where you can learn about computers and use them to do many fascinating things. A few museums are devoted entirely to the computer. Here are three:

**AMERICAN COMPUTER MUSEUM**
234 East Babcock Street
Bozeman, MT 59715
**Phone:** (406) 587-7545
**WEB SITE** *http://www.compustory.com*
**E-MAIL** americancomputermuseum @computer.org

**THE COMPUTER MUSEUM, INC.**
300 Congress Street
Boston, MA 02210
**Phone:** (617) 426-2800
**WEB SITE** *http://www.net.org*

**TECH MUSEUM OF INNOVATION**
145 West San Carlos Street
San Jose, CA 95113
**Phone:** (408) 279-7150
**WEB SITE** *http://www.thetech.org*
**E-MAIL** info@thetech.org

# << The INTERNET >>

## What is the Internet?

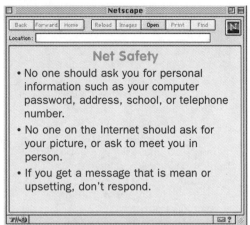

### Net Safety

• No one should ask you for personal information such as your computer password, address, school, or telephone number.

• No one on the Internet should ask for your picture, or ask to meet you in person.

• If you get a message that is mean or upsetting, don't respond.

The Internet ("Net") is a way of connecting computers from around the world so people can share information. You can play games on the Net, send electronic mail (e-mail), shop, and find information. The World Wide Web (www) is a part of the Internet that lets you see information using pictures, colors, and sounds. Most people just call it the Web. Information on the Web lives on a Web site. To get to the Web site you want, you need to use the right Universal Resource Locator (URL), or address. If you know the address, just find the place for it on the screen and type it in carefully.

If you don't know the address, hit Search. You may have to pick a search engine. When you have the search engine you want, type in words that tell exactly what or whom you're searching for. The result will be a list giving you a choice of sites and descriptions of them. You can choose the site that seems most likely to have the information you want. Some sites have links—names of other sites on the same subject that you can click on.

 **DID YOU KNOW?**

*If you want to use the Internet to write to* The World Almanac for Kids, *the e-mail address is:* **Waforkids@aol.com** *Look for information from* The World Almanac for Kids *at* **www.eplay.com**

## Can you depend on information from the Internet?

Watch out when you use information from the Internet. Because people can put whatever they want on it, you cannot always be sure the information is correct. Keep in mind where the information is coming from. Try to use more than one source.

## SMILEYS
Smileys are typed letters and symbols that look like faces when you turn them sideways. They are used to express feelings or tell other things about yourself in messages you send.

| | | | | | |
|---|---|---|---|---|---|
| :-) | Smile | :-O | Shout | :-& | Tongue-tied |
| :-( | Sad | ;-) | Wink | :-() | Can't stop talking |
| :-D | Laugh | :-* | Kiss | [:-) | I wear headphones |
| :'( | Cry | {*} | Hug and kiss | :-# | I wear braces |

# INTERNET TREASURE HUNT

## WHAT TO DO

❶ Go to each of the Web sites listed below.

❷ There, find the answers to the questions shown under the addresses.

❸ Write the answers in the boxes, one letter in each box.

❹ Take the letters in the numbered boxes and arrange them according to their numbers.

❺ When you write the letters in the spaces at the bottom of the page, you'll find a secret message.

**WEB SITE** ➤ *http://www.whitehouse.gov/WH/kids/html/home.html*

**What is the name of the pet cat that lives in the White House?**

— — — — —
   2  1

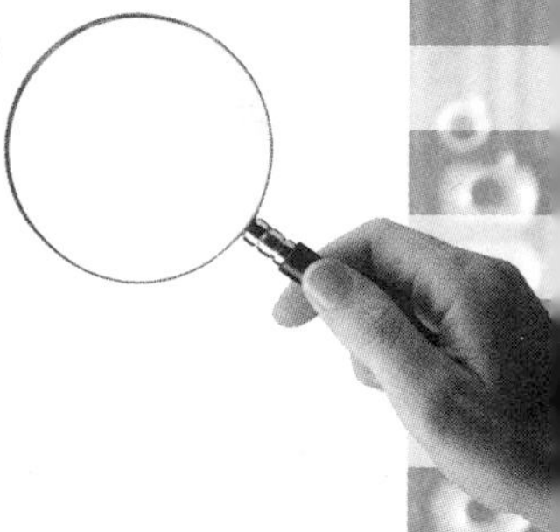

**What was the name of the pony that lived at the White House? (It belonged to Caroline Kennedy.)**

— — — — — — — —
3

**On what avenue is the White House?**

— — — — — — — — — — — — —
4

— — — — —
       5

**WEB SITE** ➤ *http://www.amnh.org/explore/elephants*

**What was the first elephant called?**

— — — — — — — — — —
      6     7   8

**WEB SITE** ➤ *http://www.exploratorium.edu/frogs/mainstory/index.html*

**What was the earliest kind of frog, actually a four-legged fish, called?**

— — — — — — — — — — —
         9          10

**WEB SITE** ➤ *http://spaceplace.jpl.nasa.gov/friends.htm*

**What kind of code did the Voyager spacecraft use to send back photos of the planets?**

— — — — — — — —
   11         12

**What will the Deep Space 2 mission drop onto Mars?**

— — — — —
 13   14

**What is the name of a moon close to Jupiter?**

— —
 15

**What number system do humans use?**

— — — — — —
      16

## EXTRA! EXTRA!

Do you have your own favorite Web sites?

Make up your own version of this game and challenge your friends and family.

— — — — — — — — —    — — —    — — — — !
1  2  3  4  5  6  7  8  9    10 11 12    13 14 15 16

*Answers are on pages 317-320.*

❓ **What is the connection between long-dead plants and how we heat our homes?**
*You can find the answer on page 67.*

# ENERGY Keeps Us Moving

**Y**ou can't touch or smell or taste energy, but you can observe what energy can do. You can feel that sunlight warms objects, and you can see that electricity lights up a light bulb, even if you can't see the heat or the electricity.

**WHAT IS ENERGY?** Things that you see and touch every day use some form of energy to work: your body, a bike, a basketball, a car. Energy enables things to move. Scientists define **energy** as the ability to do work.

**WHY DO WE NEED ENERGY TO DO WORK?** Scientists define **work** as a force moving an object. Scientifically speaking, throwing a ball is work, but studying for a test isn't! When you throw a ball, you use energy from the food you eat to do work on the ball. The engine in a car uses energy from gasoline to make the car move.

## Are There Different Kinds of Energy?

**Potential**

When we rest or sleep we still have the ability to move. We do not lose our energy. We simply store it for another time. Stored energy is called **potential energy**. When we get up and begin to move around, we are using stored energy.

**Kinetic**

As we move around and walk, our stored (potential) energy changes into **kinetic energy**, which is the energy of moving things. A parked car has potential energy. A moving car has kinetic energy. A sled stopped at the top of the hill has potential energy. As the sled goes down the hill, its potential energy changes to kinetic energy.

**HOW IS ENERGY CREATED?** Energy cannot be created or destroyed, but it can be changed or converted into different forms. **Heat**, **light**, and **electricity** are forms of energy. Other forms of energy are **sound**, **chemical energy**, **mechanical energy**, and **nuclear energy**.

**WHERE DOES ENERGY COME FROM?** All of the forms of energy we use come from the energy stored in **natural resources**. Sunlight, water, wind, petroleum, coal, and natural gas are natural resources. From these resources, we get heat and electricity.

# The SUN and Its ENERGY

Most of our energy comes from the Sun. The Sun is a big ball of glowing gases, made up mostly of hydrogen. Inside the Sun, hydrogen atoms join together (through a process called nuclear fusion) and become helium. During the fusion process, large amounts of energy are released. This energy works its way to the Sun's surface and then radiates out into space in the form of waves. These waves give us heat and light. The energy from the Sun is stored in our food, which provides fuel for our bodies.

## THE SUN STORES ITS ENERGY IN FOSSIL FUELS

The Sun also provides the energy stored in fossil fuels. Coal, petroleum, and natural gas are **fossil fuels**. Fossil fuels come from the remains of ancient plants and animals over millions and millions of years. This is what happened:

1. Hundreds of millions of years ago, before people lived on Earth, trees and other plants absorbed energy from the Sun, just as they do today.

2. Animals ate plants and smaller animals.

3. After the plants and animals died, they slowly became buried deeper and deeper underground.

4. After millions of years, they turned into coal and petroleum.

Although the buried prehistoric plants and animals changed form over time, they still contained stored energy.

When we burn fossil fuels today, the stored energy from the Sun is released in the form of heat. The heat is used to warm our homes and other buildings and produce electricity for our lights and appliances.

## From the Sun to You

Plants absorb energy from the Sun (solar energy) and convert absorbed energy to chemical energy for storage.

Animals eat plants and gain the stored chemical energy.

People eat plants and meat.

Food provides the body with energy to work and play.

# How Does ENERGY GET to YOU?

## ENERGY FROM FOSSIL FUELS

Most of our energy comes from fossil fuels. Your home may be heated with oil or natural gas. You may have a kitchen stove that uses natural gas. Cars need gasoline to run. Here is how a power plant uses fossil fuel to make electricity.

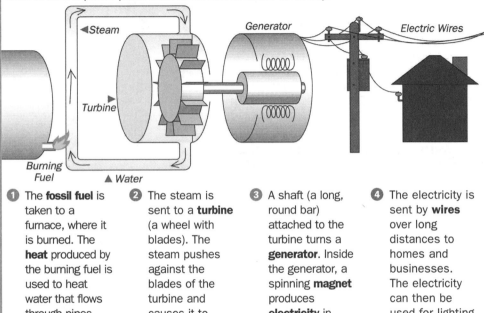

1. The **fossil fuel** is taken to a furnace, where it is burned. The **heat** produced by the burning fuel is used to heat water that flows through pipes. When the water boils, it becomes **steam**.

2. The steam is sent to a **turbine** (a wheel with blades). The steam pushes against the blades of the turbine and causes it to spin.

3. A shaft (a long, round bar) attached to the turbine turns a **generator**. Inside the generator, a spinning **magnet** produces **electricity** in coils nearby.

4. The electricity is sent by **wires** over long distances to homes and businesses. The electricity can then be used for lighting and for running appliances or machines.

## NUCLEAR ENERGY

In **nuclear reactors**, uranium atoms are split into smaller atoms to produce heat. The heat is then used to produce electricity, just as the heat from burning coal is used.

## ENERGY FROM WATER

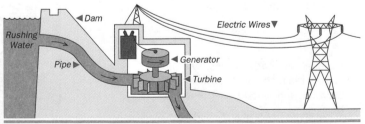

For centuries, people have been getting energy from rushing water. In a **hydroelectric plant**, water from rivers or dams is used to drive machinery like a turbine. The turbine is connected to a generator, which produces electricity.

# Who Produces and Uses the MOST ENERGY?

The United States produces and uses more energy than any other country in the world. Below you can see which countries produced the most energy in 1996 and which countries used the most. A unit that is often used to measure energy is the British Thermal Unit, abbreviated Btu. A 60-watt light bulb uses about 205 Btus of energy in the form of electricity every hour. In these charts, the amounts of energy are written in quadrillions of Btus. One quadrillion is the same as 1,000,000,000,000,000.

## Countries That Produce the Most Energy
### (in quadrillion Btus)

|  |  |
| --- | --- |
| United States | 72.32 |
| Russia | 39.68 |
| China | 37.41 |
| Saudi Arabia | 20.39 |
| Canada | 17.29 |
| Great Britain | 11.49 |
| Iran | 9.60 |
| India | 9.33 |
| Norway | 9.28 |
| Venezuela | 8.84 |

## Countries That Use the Most Energy
### (in quadrillion Btus)

|  |  |
| --- | --- |
| United States | 93.87 |
| China | 37.04 |
| Russia | 25.98 |
| Japan | 21.37 |
| Germany | 14.44 |
| Canada | 12.20 |
| India | 11.55 |
| Great Britain | 10.05 |
| France | 9.87 |
| Italy | 7.63 |

**DID YOU KNOW?**
Do you know which countries produce the most fossil fuels?

The country that produces the most crude oil is Saudi Arabia. The country that produces the most natural gas is Russia. The country that produces the most coal is China.

**DID YOU KNOW?**
The United States uses more energy than it produces. To meet its energy needs, the United States must import large amounts of fossil fuels from other countries. The United States gets its crude oil mainly from Venezuela, Mexico, Saudi Arabia, Canada, and Nigeria. It also imports natural gas from Canada.

**DID YOU KNOW?**
Alaska used more energy per person than any other state in the United States in 1996. The 10 other states that used the greatest amount of energy per person were Louisiana, Wyoming, Texas, North Dakota, Alabama, Kentucky, Indiana, Montana, West Virginia, and Maine.

# Will We Have Enough ENERGY?

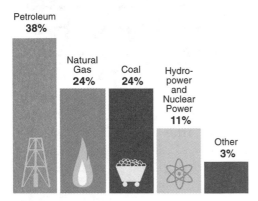

Petroleum
**38%**

Natural
Gas
**24%**

Coal
**24%**

Hydro-
power
and
Nuclear
Power
**11%**

Other
**3%**

## WHERE DOES OUR ENERGY COME FROM?

In 1997, most of the energy used in the United States came from fossil fuels (about 38% from petroleum, 24% from natural gas, and 24% from coal). The rest came mostly from hydropower (water power) and nuclear energy. Fossil fuels are **nonrenewable** sources of energy. That means the amount of fossil fuel available for use is limited and that all this fuel might get used up after many years.

## LOOKING FOR RENEWABLE RESOURCES

Scientists are trying to find more sources of energy that will reduce pollution and save some of the fossil fuels. People are using several types of **renewable resources**. Some of these forms of energy exist in an unlimited supply.

▶ **Solar power.** Solar power uses energy from sunlight. Solar panels can collect the sun's rays for heating. Solar cells can convert light energy directly into electricity.

▶ **Water from the ocean.** Ocean waves and tides can be used to drive generators to produce electricity.

▶ **The wind.** Windmills can be used to drive machinery. Today, some people are using wind turbines to generate electricity.

▶ **Biomass energy.** Biomass includes wood from trees and other plants, animal wastes, and garbage. When these are burned or allowed to decay, they produce natural gas. Biomass energy is widely available and used in some parts of the world, although it is limited.

▶ **Geothermal energy.** Geothermal energy is energy that comes from the hot, molten rock inside Earth. In certain parts of the world, such as Iceland and New Zealand, people use this kind of energy for electricity and to heat buildings.

## SAVING ENERGY FOR TOMORROW

▶ Many businesses are trying to find ways to reuse heat from steam turbine generators.

▶ Recycling reduces the energy that would be used for making new products.

▶ Riding buses and trains, car pooling, and driving fuel-efficient cars reduces the use of fossil fuels.

▶ Using less heat, less hot water, and less air-conditioning also helps save energy.

❓ **What may be causing global warming?**
*You can find the answer on page 77.*

# What Is the ENVIRONMENT?

**E**verything that surrounds us is part of the environment. Not just living things like plants and animals, but also the air we breathe, the sunlight that provides warmth and energy, the water that we use in our homes, schools, and businesses, and even rocks.

## People and the Environment

People have existed for many thousands of years. For a long time people thought the Earth was so huge that it would always absorb any kind of pollution. And they thought that Earth's natural resources would never be used up.

Even prehistoric life affected the environment. People killed animals for food and built fires to cook food and keep themselves warm. They cut down trees for fuel, and their fires released gases into the air. In prehistoric times, though, there were so few people that their activities had little impact on the environment.

In modern times, the world's population has been growing very fast. In 1850 there were around a billion people in the world. In 1950 there were around 2.5 billion, and by 1998 there were more than 5.9 billion. Because there are so many people on the planet Earth, the things we do can affect the environment dramatically.

## Sharing the Earth

People share the planet with trees, flowers, insects, fish, whales, dogs, and many other plants and animals. Each species (type) of animal or plant has its place on Earth, and each one is dependent on the others. Plants give off oxygen that animals need to breathe. Animals pollinate plants and spread their seeds. Animals eat plants and are in turn eaten by larger animals. When plants and animals die, they become part of the soil in which new plants, in their turn, take root and grow.

## Watching Over the Earth

Many people are becoming more aware that some of the things humans do could seriously damage the planet and the animals and plants on it. Sometimes this damage can be reversed or slowed down. But it is often permanent. On the following pages you'll learn about the damage, and about what can be done to clean up and protect our planet.

**WEB SITE** You can learn more about the environment at:
http://www.nwf.org/nwf/kids/index.html

# What Is BIODIVERSITY?

Our planet, Earth, is shared by more than five million species of living things. Human beings of all colors, races, and nationalities make up just one species, *Homo sapiens*. All of the species together form the variety of life we call "biodiversity" (*bio* means "life" and *diversity* means "variety").

## How Many Species Are There?
### This list is just a sampling of how diverse Earth is.

BEETLES: 290,000 species
Fascinating Fact ▼
There are more kinds of
beetles than any other
animal on Earth.

FLOWERING PLANTS: 250,000 species
Fascinating Fact ▶ The 750,000
species of insects and the 250,000
species of flowering
plants depend on one
another. The insects
need the plants for
food, the plants need
the insects for pollination.

EDIBLE PLANTS: 30,000 species
Fascinating Fact ▶ Although 30,000
are edible, 90% of the world's food
comes from only 20 species.

ANTS: 20,000 species
Fascinating Fact ▶ If you were to
weigh all the insects on Earth, ants
would make up almost half of the total.

BIRDS: 9,040 species
Fascinating Fact ▼
More than 1,000 of these
species are in danger of
becoming extinct.

BATS: 1,000 species
Fascinating Fact ▼
There are more species
of bats than of any other
mammal.

PET DOGS: 1 species
Fascinating Fact ▼
Even though they can look
very different, all dogs
belong to the same species.

HUMAN BEINGS: 1 species
Fascinating Fact ▼
This one species holds
the fate of all the other
species in its hands. People
can affect the environment more
than any other form of living thing.

**Some Threats to Biodiversity** Plants and animals are harmed by air, water, and land pollution, and their habitats are often destroyed by deforestation. For example, in recent years, large areas of rain forests have been cleared for wood, farmland, and cattle ranches, and people have become concerned that rain forests may be disappearing. Another threat is overharvesting, or the use of too many animals for food or other products. For example, the number of whales has been steadily declining, and some species of whales could eventually be wiped out entirely.

**Protecting Biodiversity** Efforts to reduce pollutants in air, water, and soil, to preserve rain forests, and to limit deforestation and overharvesting help to preserve biodiversity. A few species that were once endangered now will probably survive.

**DID YOU KNOW?** *Bats should be valued by humans rather than feared. These winged mammals are often killed because of superstition. Except in rare cases, bats do not attack people. Some species help Earth's ecosystem by eating insects and by pollinating plants.*

# Environment GLOSSARY

**climate** The average weather in a region of the world.

**compost heap** A pile of food scraps and yard waste that is gradually broken down by worms and tiny insects. The result looks like plain dirt. It can be used to enrich the soil.

**conservation** The planned and wise use of water, forests, and other natural resources so they will not be damaged or wasted.

**deforestation** The cutting down of most of the trees from forested land, usually so that the land can be used for something besides a forest.

**ecosystem** A community of living things and the place where they live, such as a forest or pond.

**environment** All living and non-living things in an area at a given time. The environment affects the growth of living things.

**extinction** The disappearance of a type (species) of plant or animal from Earth. Some species become extinct because of natural forces, but many others are becoming endangered or threatened with extinction because of the activities of people.

**fossil fuel** Anything that comes from once-living matter deep in the earth, such as oil, gas, and coal.

**global warming** An increase in Earth's temperature due to a buildup of certain gases in the atmosphere.

**greenhouse effect** Warming of Earth caused by certain gases (called **greenhouse gases**) that form a blanket in the atmosphere high over Earth. Small amounts of these gases keep Earth warm so we can live here, but the larger amounts produced by factories, cars, and burning trees may hold in too much heat and cause global warming.

**groundwater** Water in the ground that flows in the spaces between soil particles and rocks. Groundwater supplies water for wells and springs.

**habitat** The natural home of an animal or a plant.

**pollution** Contamination of air, water, or soil by materials that can injure health, the quality of life, or the working of ecosystems.

**recycling** Using something more than once, either just the way it is, or treated and made into something else.

**reforestation** Planting new trees where other trees have been cut down.

**soil erosion** The washing away or blowing away of topsoil. Trees and other plants hold the soil in place and help reduce the force of the wind. Soil erosion happens when trees and plants are cut down.

# RECYCLING Garbage

Look around. Everything you see will probably be replaced or thrown away someday. Skates, clothes, the toaster, the refrigerator, furniture—they may break or wear out, or you may get tired of them and want new ones sooner or later. Where will they go when they are thrown out? What kinds of waste will they create, and how will it affect the environment?

## What Happens to Things We Throw Away?

### LANDFILLS

Most of our trash goes to places called landfills. A **landfill** (or dump) is a low area of land that is filled with garbage. Most modern landfills are lined with a layer of plastic or clay to try to keep dangerous liquids from seeping out.

### The Problem with Landfills

There is so much trash that we are quickly running out of room for it. In less than 10 years, all the landfills in more than half of the states of the United States will be full. Some of the household trash in landfills is hazardous. It includes batteries, paint, motor oil, and antifreeze. These things can poison land, air, and water.

### INCINERATORS

Another way to get rid of trash is to burn it. Trash is burned in a device like a furnace called an **incinerator**. Because incinerators can get rid of almost all of the bulk of the trash, some communities would rather use incinerators than landfills.

### The Problem with Incinerators

Leftover ash and smoke from burning trash may contain harmful chemicals, called **pollutants**. They can harm plants, animals, and people.

 **DID YOU KNOW?** *The average American produces more than four pounds of trash every day, and only one pound of that is recycled or made into compost.*

## Look at What Is Now in U.S. Landfills

Metal **8%**

Plastic **24%**

Food and Yard Waste **11%**

Rubber and Leather **6%**

Other Trash **21%**

Paper **30%**

# REUSE, RECYCLE, REDUCE

You can help reduce waste by reusing containers, batteries, and paper. You can also recycle newspaper, glass, and plastics to provide materials for making other products.

At right are some of the things you can do.

## What is made from RECYCLED MATERIALS?

▶ From **RECYCLED PAPER** we get newspapers, cereal boxes, wrapping paper, cardboard containers, and insulation.

▶ From **RECYCLED PLASTIC** we get soda bottles, tables, benches, bicycle racks, cameras, backpacks, carpeting, shoes, and clothes.

▶ From **RECYCLED STEEL** we get steel cans, cars, bicycles, nails, and refrigerators.

▶ From **RECYCLED GLASS** we get glass jars and tiles.

▶ From **RECYCLED RUBBER** we get bulletin boards, floor tiles, playground equipment, and speed bumps.

| | TO RECYCLE | TO REDUCE WASTE |
|---|---|---|
| Paper | Recycle newspapers, magazines, comic books, catalogs, cardboard, and junk mail. | Use both sides of the paper. Use cloth towels instead of paper towels. |
| Plastic | Return soda bottles to the store. | Wash food containers and store leftovers in them. Reuse plastic bags. |
| Glass | Recycle glass bottles and jars. | Keep glass bottles and jars to store other things. |
| Clothes | Cut unwearable clothing into rags to use instead of paper towels. | Give clothes to younger relatives or friends. Donate clothes to thrift shops. |
| Metal | Recycle aluminum cans and foil trays. Return wire hangers to the dry cleaner. | Keep leftovers in storage containers instead of wrapping them in foil. Use glass or stainless steel pans instead of disposable pans. |
| Food/Yard Waste | Make a compost heap using food scraps, leaves, grass clippings, and the like. | |
| Batteries | Find out about your town's rules for recycling or disposing of batteries. | Use rechargeable batteries for toys and games, radios, tape players, and flashlights. |

# The AIR We Breathe

All human beings and animals need air to survive. Without air we would die. Plants also need air to live. Plants use sunlight and the carbon dioxide in air to make food, and then give off oxygen.

We all breathe the air that surrounds Earth. The air is made up mainly of gases: around 78% nitrogen, 21% oxygen, and 1% carbon dioxide, other gases, and water vapor. Human beings breathe more than six quarts of air every minute. Because air is so basic to life, it is very important to keep the air clean by reducing or preventing air pollution. Today, air pollution causes problems worldwide, such as **acid rain, global warming,** and the **breakdown of the ozone layer**.

Nitrogen 78%

Oxygen 21%

Carbon Dioxide, Other Gases, Water Vapor 1%

**What Is Air Pollution and Where Does It Come From?** **Air pollution** is dirtying the air with chemicals or other materials that can injure health, the enjoyment of life, or the working of ecosystems. The major sources of air pollution are cars, trucks and buses, waste incinerators, factories, and some electric power plants, especially those that burn fossil fuels.

**What Is Acid Rain and Where Does It Come From?** **Acid rain** is a kind of air pollution. It is caused by chemicals that are released into the air and cause rain, snow, and fog to be more acidic than usual. The main sources of these chemicals are fumes from cars' exhaust pipes, and power plants that burn coal. When these chemicals mix with moisture and other particles in the air, they create sulfuric acid and nitric acid. The wind often carries these acids many miles before they fall to the ground in rain, snow, and fog, or even as dry particles.

**Why Worry About Air Pollution and Acid Rain?** Air pollution and acid rain can harm people, animals, and plants. Air pollution can cause our eyes to sting and can make some people sick. It can also damage crops and trees.

Air pollution (especially acid rain) is also harmful to water in lakes, often killing plants and fish that live there. Hundreds of lakes in the northeastern United States and 14,000 lakes in Canada are so acidic that fish can no longer live there. Acid rain has affected trees in U.S. national parks. In the Appalachian Mountains, for example, it has harmed spruce trees growing in the Shenandoah and Great Smoky Mountain National Parks. And it can turn buildings and statues black and damage them by eating away at metal, stone, and paint. Monuments and statues that have survived hundreds of years are suddenly disintegrating.

*A factory on Lake Superior in northern Michigan*

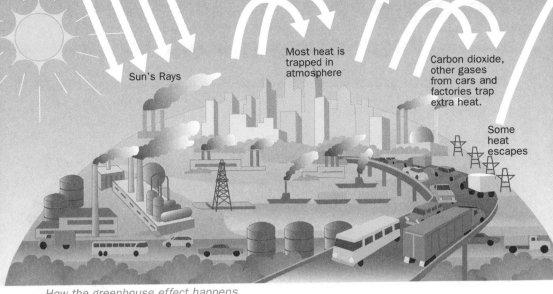

Sun's Rays

Most heat is trapped in atmosphere

Carbon dioxide, other gases from cars and factories trap extra heat.

Some heat escapes

*How the greenhouse effect happens*

# Global Warming and the Greenhouse Effect

Many scientists believe that gases in the air are causing Earth's climate to gradually become warmer. This is called **global warming**. If the climate becomes so warm that a great deal of ice near the north and south poles melts and more water goes into the oceans, many areas along the coasts may be flooded.

In Earth's atmosphere there are tiny amounts of gases called **greenhouse gases**. These gases let the rays of the sun pass through to the planet, but they hold in the heat that comes up from the sun-warmed Earth—in much the same way as the glass of a greenhouse holds in the warmth of the sun.

As cities increased in size and population, factories and businesses have also grown. People have needed more and more electricity, cars, and other things that must be manufactured. As industries in the world have increased, more greenhouse gases have been added to the atmosphere. These gases increase the thickness of the greenhouse "glass," causing too much heat to be trapped. This is called **the greenhouse effect**.

# Good and Bad Ozone

**Good Ozone.** A layer in the atmosphere high above Earth, called the **ozone layer**, protects us from the harsh rays of the sun. When refrigerators, air conditioners, and similar items are thrown away, gases from them (called chlorofluorocarbons or CFCs) rise into the air and destroy some of the ozone in this layer.

**Bad Ozone.** There is also ozone near the ground that forms when sunlight hits air pollutants from cars and smokestacks, causing smog. This ozone near the ground can be harmful.

# What Are We Doing to Reduce Air Pollution?

Many countries, including the United States, are trying to reduce air pollution. Today's cars can go farther on a gallon of gasoline than cars of 20 or 30 years ago. In the United States, cars must have a special device to remove harmful chemicals from their smoke before it comes out of the tailpipe. Many power plants and factories have devices on their smokestacks to catch harmful chemicals before they can enter the air. Many people try not to use more electricity than they really need, so that less coal will have to be burned to produce electricity. And in some places, power companies use windmills or other equipment that does not pollute the air.

# PROTECTING Our WATER

Every living thing needs water to live. Many animals also depend on water as a home. People not only drink water, but also use it to cook, clean, cool machinery in factories, produce power, and irrigate farmland.

## Where Does WATER Come From?

Although about two thirds of the Earth's surface is water, we are able to use only a tiny fraction of it. Seawater makes up 97% of Earth's water, and 2% is frozen in glaciers and ice around the north and south poles. **Freshwater** makes up only 1% of our water, and only part of that is close enough to Earth's surface for us to use.

The water we can use comes from lakes, rivers, reservoirs, and groundwater. **Groundwater** is melted snow or rain that seeps deep below the surface of the Earth and collects in pools called aquifers.

Overall, the world has enough freshwater, but sometimes it is not available exactly where it is needed. Extreme water shortages, or **droughts,** can occur when an area gets too little rain or has very hot weather over a long period of time, causing water supplies to dry up. To protect against this, we must keep our water sources clean and use our water supplies wisely through conservation.

## How Much Water Do We Use?

**Average American's daily cooking, washing, flushing, and lawn care**: 183 gallons

**One load of wash in a washing machine:** 50 gallons

**10-minute shower or a bath:** 25–50 gallons

**One load of dishes in a dishwasher:** 12–20 gallons

**One person's daily drinking and eating:** 2 ½ quarts

### How Water is Used at Home

Bathroom 74%

Laundry and cleaning 21%

Kitchen 5%

## What Is Threatening Our Water?

Water is said to be polluted when it is not fit for its intended uses, such as drinking, swimming, watering crops, or serving as a habitat. Polluted water can cause disease and kill fish and other animals. Some major water pollutants include sewage, chemicals from factories, fertilizers and weed killers, and leaking landfills. Water pollution is being reduced in some areas. Some lakes are being cleaned up. Companies continue to look for better ways to get rid of wastes, and many farmers are trying new ways to grow crops without using polluting fertilizers or chemicals.

# The Importance of Forests

Trees and forests are very important to the environment. In addition to holding water, trees hold the soil in place. Trees use carbon dioxide and give off oxygen, which animals and plants need for survival. And they provide homes and food for millions of types of animals.

**Why Do We Cut Down Trees?** People cut down trees for many reasons. When the population grows, people cut down trees to clear space to build houses, schools, factories, and other buildings. People may clear land to plant crops and graze livestock. Sometimes all the trees in an area are cut and sold for lumber and paper.

**What Happens When Trees Are Cut Down?** Cutting down trees—usually to use the land for something besides a forest—is called **deforestation**. Although people often have good reasons for cutting down trees, deforestation can have serious effects. If animal habitats are destroyed, many species will become extinct. Because of deforestation, thousands of species in the Amazon rain forest in South America are being lost before scientists can even learn about them. (For more about rain forests, see page 194.)

Cutting down trees can also affect the climate. After rain falls on a forest, mist starts rising and new rain clouds are created. When forests are cut down, this cycle is disrupted, and the area eventually grows drier, causing a change in the local climate.

If huge areas of trees are cut down, the carbon dioxide they would have used builds up in the atmosphere and contributes to the greenhouse effect. And without trees to hold the soil and absorb water, rain washes topsoil away into rivers and reservoirs, a process called **soil erosion**. Farming on the poorer soil that is left can be very hard.

**What Are We Doing to Save Forests?** Many European countries are planting trees faster than they are cutting them down. Also, trees are being planted to restock woodland areas and to create forests in some countries where timber is scarce. In addition, communities and individuals are helping to save forests by recycling paper.

**DID YOU KNOW?**

▶ *Because changes in climate affect how much a tree grows each year, scientists can tell what the climate was like in years past (in some cases 4,000 years!) by examining a tree's annual rings.*

▶ *Some trees, such as the northern red oak and the junipers, resist pollution better than others.*

▶ *Each year, the average American uses enough wood and wood products to add up to one tree 100 feet tall.*

▶ *By the mid-1990s, more paper in the United States was being recycled than was sent to landfills.*

# ENVIRONMENT PUZZLE

## A Double Puzzle Is Twice the Fun

The words in this puzzle are from pages 71 to 79. To find out what they are, first fill in the missing words in the sentences below. Then locate them in the puzzle. The words in the puzzle go up, down, backward, and forward. Some letters are used more than once. All but four letters are used.

All the words are in the Word Box. But it's more challenging to find them on your own.

1. Incinerators are used to burn _____.
2. Most of the Earth is covered in _____.
3. _____ help keep the air clean and soil in place.
4. A pile of food scraps, leaves, and grass clippings is a _____ heap.
5. One way to reduce garbage is by _____.
6. _____ aren't scary; they're helpful mammals.
7. _____ fuels come from once-living matter deep in the Earth.
8. _____, natural gas, and coal are types of fossil fuels.
9. A landfill is a kind of _____.
10. The _____ layer protects us from the sun's harsh rays.
11. Gasoline is one kind of _____.
12. Scientists are afraid ice caps will melt because of _____ warming.
13. Trees also keep _____ in place.

| R | E | C | Y | C | L | I | N | G |
|---|---|---|---|---|---|---|---|---|
| L | I | O | X | T | R | E | E | S |
| D | U | M | P | O | Z | O | N | E |
| X | J | P | W | A | T | E | R | E |
| G | L | O | B | A | L | I | O | S |
| F | O | S | S | I | L | E | U | F |
| B | A | T | S | H | S | A | R | T |

### WORD BOX

| | | | |
|---|---|---|---|
| BATS | OZONE | TRASH | GLOBAL |
| COMPOST | FUEL | SOIL | OIL |
| DUMP | RECYCLING | WATER | TREES |
| FOSSIL | | | |

*Answers are on pages 317–320.*

❓ **Where can you find the world's highest mountain?**
*You can find the answer on page 84.*

# LOOKING at Our WORLD

**D**id you ever travel on a spaceship? Whether you know it or not, you're traveling right now on the spaceship called Planet Earth. Earth is always speeding through space and around the sun.

A **globe** is a small model of Earth. Like Earth, a globe is shaped like a ball or sphere. Earth isn't exactly a sphere because it gets flat at the top and bottom and bulges a little in the middle, but a globe gives us the best idea of what Earth looks like.

Because Earth is round, most flat maps that are centered on the equator do not show the shapes of the land masses exactly right. The shapes at the top and bottom usually look too big. For example, the island of Greenland, which is next to North America, may look bigger than Australia, though it is really much smaller.

## Half of a Globe

North Pole

North America

40 degrees north latitude

20 degrees north latitude

Equator

Africa

South America

20 degrees south latitude

40 degrees south latitude

South Pole

## Which Hemisphere Do You Live In?

Draw an imaginary line around the middle of Earth. This is called the equator.

The equator splits Earth into two halves called **hemispheres**. The part that's north of the equator is called the **northern hemisphere**. The part that's south of the equator is called the **southern hemisphere**.

You can also divide Earth into the **western hemisphere** and the **eastern hemisphere**.

## Latitude and Longitude

Imaginary lines that run east and west around Earth, parallel to the equator, are called **parallels**. They tell you the **latitude** of a place, or how far it is from the equator. The equator is at 0 degrees latitude. As you go farther north or south, the latitude increases. The North Pole is at 90 degrees **north latitude**. The South Pole is at 90 degrees **south latitude**.

Imaginary lines that run north and south around the globe, from one pole to the other, are called **meridians**. They tell you the degree of **longitude**, or how far east or west a place is from an imaginary line called the **Greenwich meridian** or **prime meridian** (0 degrees). That line runs through the city of Greenwich in England.

# Reading a Map

There are many different kinds of maps. Physical maps mainly show features that are part of nature, such as mountains, rivers, oceans, and deserts. Political maps show features such as states and countries and the boundaries between them.

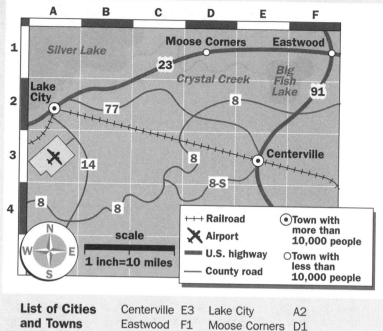

| List of Cities and Towns | Centerville E3 | Lake City | A2 |
| | Eastwood F1 | Moose Corners | D1 |

# CONTINENTS and OCEANS of the World

Almost two-thirds of Earth's surface is made up of water. The rest is land. Oceans are the largest areas of water. Continents are the biggest pieces of land. The Earth has seven continents and four oceans. Many islands in the Pacific Ocean are not counted as part of any of the continents. See pages 161-172 for maps of the continents.

## The Seven Continents

| | North America | South America | Europe |
|---|---|---|---|
| Area | 21,393,762 square miles | 17,522,371 square miles | 22,823,957 square miles |
| Population | 470,255,849 | 338,391,974 | 727,544,458 |
| Highest Point | Mount McKinley (Alaska), 20,320 feet | Mount Aconcagua (Argentina), 22,834 feet | Mount Elbrus (Russia), 18,510 feet |
| Lowest Point | Death Valley (California), 282 feet below sea level | Valdes Peninsula (Argentina), 131 feet below sea level | Caspian Sea (Russia, Azerbaijan; eastern Europe and western Asia), 92 feet below sea level |

## DISTANCE

Of course the distances on a map are much shorter than the distances in the real world. The **scale** shows you how to estimate the real distance. In the map at left, every inch on paper stands for a real distance of 10 miles.

## PICTURES

Maps usually have little pictures or symbols. The map key tells what they mean. At the bottom of this map, you can see the symbols for towns, roads, railroad tracks, and airports. Can you tell which are the two biggest cities on the map? Can you find the airport? How would you get from the airport to Centerville by car?

## DIRECTION

Maps usually have a compass rose that shows you which way is north. On most maps, north is toward the top. On this map, north is straight up. When north is straight up, south is down, east is to the right, and west is to the left.

## FINDING PLACES

To help you find places on a map, many maps have a list of places in alphabetical order, giving you a letter and number for each city or town. In the map to the left, you can find the first city on the list, Centerville (E3), by drawing a straight line down from the letter E on top, and another line going across from the number 3 on the side. Centerville should be near the place where these two lines meet.

# The Four Oceans

| The facts about the oceans include their size and average depth. |
| --- |
| **Pacific Ocean:** 64,186,300 square miles; 12,925 feet deep |
| **Atlantic Ocean:** 33,420,000 square miles; 11,730 feet deep |
| **Indian Ocean:** 28,350,500 square miles; 12,598 feet deep |
| **Arctic Ocean:** 5,105,700 square miles; 3,407 feet deep |

| Asia | Africa | Australia* | Antarctica |
| --- | --- | --- | --- |
| 31,027,230 square miles | 29,805,048 square miles | 3,300,000 square miles | 5,400,000 square miles |
| 3,592,816,983 | 759,954,511 | 30,000,000 | Zero |
| Mount Everest (Nepal, Tibet), 29,028 feet | Mount Kilimanjaro (Tanzania), 19,340 feet | Mount Kosciusko (New South Wales), 7,310 feet | Vinson Massif, 16,864 feet |
| Dead Sea (Israel, Jordan), 1,312 feet below sea level | Lake Assal (Djibouti), 512 feet below sea level | Lake Eyre (South Australia), 52 feet below sea level | Bentley Subglacial Trench, 8,327 feet below sea level |
| | | *(includes Australia, New Zealand, and many islands) | |

# Tallest, Longest, Highest, Deepest

**Longest River:** Nile, in Egypt and Sudan (4,160 miles)
**Highest Waterfall:** Angel Falls, in Venezuela (3,212 feet)
**Tallest Mountain:** Mount Everest, in Tibet and Nepal (29,028 feet)
**Deepest Lake:** Lake Baykal, in Asia (5,315 feet)
**Biggest Lake:** Caspian Sea, in Europe and Asia (143,244 square miles)
**Biggest Desert:** The Sahara, in Africa (3,500,000 square miles)
**Biggest Island:** Greenland, in the Atlantic Ocean (840,000 square miles)

# Some Important REGIONS of the World

**❶ BALKANS**
The Balkan region, in southeastern Europe, consists of Yugoslavia, Slovenia, Croatia, Bosnia and Herzegovina, Macedonia, and Albania. Bulgaria, southeastern Romania, northern Greece, and the portion of Turkey in Europe are also part of the Balkans. All the Balkan states were once part of the Ottoman Empire.

**❷ CARIBBEAN** This region is in the Caribbean Sea, an arm of the Atlantic Ocean between the United States and South America. The Caribbean has thousands of islands. The largest groups are the Greater Antilles and the Lesser Antilles. Among countries in the Greater Antilles are Cuba, Haiti, Dominican Republic, Jamaica, and the U.S. commonwealth of Puerto Rico. The Lesser Antilles include Dominica, Barbados, Grenada, and Trinidad and Tobago.

**❸ CENTRAL AMERICA** Central America is the region between Mexico and South America. It consists of Belize, Guatemala, Honduras, El Salvador, Nicaragua, Costa Rica, and Panama.

**❹ EASTERN EUROPE** Countries of Eastern Europe include Poland, the Czech Republic, Slovakia, Hungary, Romania, and Bulgaria. Three other Eastern European countries (Estonia, Latvia, and Lithuania) form a region known as the Baltic States.

**❺ MIDDLE EAST** One of the most famous regions in the news is the Middle East. It includes Egypt and Libya (in northeast Africa), Israel, Jordan, Lebanon, Syria, and Iraq, and countries of the Arabian Peninsula: Saudi Arabia, Kuwait, Bahrain, Qatar, United Arab Emirates, Oman, and Yemen (all in southwest Asia). The term "Middle East" sometimes also includes the other Islamic countries of North Africa: Morocco, Algeria, and Tunisia.

**❻ SOUTHEAST ASIA** The region of Southeast Asia lies east of India and south of China. It consists of 10 independent countries: Myanmar (Burma), Thailand, Vietnam, Laos, Cambodia, Malaysia, Singapore, the Philippines, Indonesia, and Brunei.

# Some FAMOUS European and American EXPLORERS

## THE AMERICAS

**around 1000** — **Leif Ericson,** from Iceland, explored "Vinland," which may have been the coasts of northeast Canada and New England.

**1492 to 1504** — **Christopher Columbus,** from Italy, sailed four times to America and started colonies there.

**1513** — **Juan Ponce de León,** from Spain, explored and named Florida.

**1513** — **Vasco Núñez de Balboa,** from Spain, explored Panama and reached the Pacific Ocean.

**1519-36** — **Hernando Cortés,** from Spain, conquered Mexico, traveling as far west as Baja California.

**1527-42** — **Alvar Núñez Cabeza de Vaca,** from Spain, explored the southwestern United States, Brazil, and Paraguay.

**1532-35** — **Francisco Pizarro,** from Spain, explored the west coast of South America and conquered Peru.

**1534-36** — **Jacques Cartier,** from France, sailed up the St. Lawrence River to the site of present-day Montreal.

**1539-42** — **Hernando de Soto,** from Spain, explored the southeastern United States and the lower Mississippi Valley.

**1603-13** — **Samuel de Champlain,** from France, traced the course of the St. Lawrence River and explored the northeastern United States.

**1609-10** — **Henry Hudson,** from England, explored the Hudson River, Hudson Bay, and Hudson Strait.

**1682** — **Robert Cavelier, sieur de La Salle,** from France, traced the Mississippi River to its mouth in the Gulf of Mexico.

**1804-6** — **Meriwether Lewis** and **William Clark,** from the United States, traveled from St. Louis along the Missouri and Columbia rivers to the Pacific Ocean and back.

## ASIA AND THE PACIFIC

**1271-95** — **Marco Polo,** from Venice, Italy, traveled through Central Asia, India, China, and Indonesia.

**1519-21** — **Ferdinand Magellan,** from Portugal, sailed around the tip of South America and across the Pacific Ocean to the Philippines, where he died. His expedition continued around the world.

**1768-78** — **James Cook,** from England, charted the world's major bodies of water and explored Hawaii and Antarctica.

## AFRICA

**1488** — **Bartolomeu Dias,** from Portugal, explored the Cape of Good Hope in southern Africa.

**1497-98** — **Vasco da Gama,** from Portugal, sailed farther than Dias, around the Cape of Good Hope to East Africa and India.

**1849-59** — **David Livingstone,** from Scotland, explored Southern Africa, including the Zambezi River and Victoria Falls.

# EARTHQUAKES

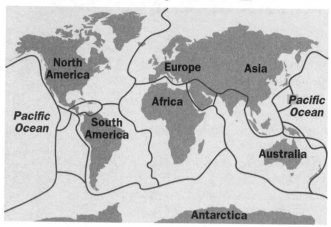

Earthquakes may be so weak that they are hardly felt, or they may be strong enough to do tremendous damage. There are thousands of earthquakes each year, but most of them are too small to be noticed. About 1 in 5 can be felt, and about 1 in 500 causes damage.

### What Causes Earthquakes?

The Earth's outer layer, its **crust,** is divided into huge pieces called **plates** (see map). These plates, made of rock, are constantly moving—away from each other, toward each other, or past each other. A crack in Earth's crust between two plates is called a **fault.** Many earthquakes occur along faults where two plates collide as they move toward each other or grind together as they move past each other. Earthquakes along the **San Andreas Fault** in California are caused by the grinding of two plates.

## Measuring Earthquakes

The Richter Scale goes from 0 to more than 8. These numbers are used to describe the strength of an earthquake. Each number on the Richter scale is 10 times greater than the one before it. An earthquake measuring 6 on the Richter scale is 10 times stronger than an earthquake measuring 5 and 100 times stronger than one measuring 4. Earthquakes that are below 4 on the Richter scale are considered minor. Those of 4 or above are considered major.

The strength of an earthquake, its *magnitude*, is registered on an instrument called a *seismograph* and is given a number on a scale called the *Richter scale.*

| Magnitude | Effects |
| --- | --- |
| 0-2 | Earthquake is recorded by instruments but is not felt by people. |
| 2-3 | Earthquake is felt slightly by a few people. |
| 3-4 | People feel tremors. Hanging objects like ceiling lights swing. |
| 4-5 | Earthquake causes some damage; walls crack; dishes and windows may break. |
| 5-6 | Furniture moves; earthquake seriously damages weak buildings. |
| 6-7 | Furniture may overturn; strong buildings are damaged; walls and buildings may collapse. |
| 7-8 | Many buildings are destroyed; underground pipes break; wide cracks appear in the ground. |
| Above 8 | Total devastation, including buildings and bridges; ground wavy. |

# Major Earthquakes of the 20th Century

The earthquakes listed below are among the largest and most destructive recorded in the 1900s. The list begins with recent earthquakes.

| YEAR | LOCATION | MAGNITUDE | DEATHS |
|------|----------|-----------|--------|
| 1999 | Colombia (western) | 6.0 | 930 |
| 1998 | Afghanistan (northeastern) | 6.9 | 4,700+ |
| 1998 | Bolivia (central) | 6.5 | 105 |
| 1998 | Afghanistan (northeastern) | 6.1 | 2,323 |
| 1997 | Iran (northern) | 7.5 | 1,560 |
| 1995 | Sakhalin Island (Russia) | 7.5 | 1,989 |
| 1995 | Japan (Kobe) | 6.9 | 5,502 |
| 1994 | United States (Los Angeles area) | 6.8 | 61 |
| 1993 | India (southern) | 6.3 | 9,748 |
| 1990 | Iran (western) | 7.7 | 40,000+ |
| 1989 | United States (San Francisco Bay area) | 7.1 | 62 |
| 1985 | Mexico (Michoacan) | 8.1 | 9,500 |
| 1976 | China (Tangshan) | 8.0 | 255,000 |
| 1976 | Guatemala | 7.5 | 23,000 |
| 1970 | Peru (northern) | 7.8 | 66,000 |
| 1960 | Chile (southern) | 9.5 | 5,000 |
| 1939 | Chile (Chillan) | 8.3 | 28,000 |
| 1934 | India (Bihar-Nepal) | 8.4 | 10,700 |
| 1927 | China (Nan-Shan) | 8.3 | 200,000 |
| 1923 | Japan (Yokohama) | 8.3 | 143,000 |
| 1920 | China (Gansu) | 8.6 | 200,000 |
| 1906 | Chile (Valparaiso) | 8.6 | 20,000 |
| 1906 | United States (San Francisco) | 8.3 | 503 |

**DID YOU KNOW?**

*Between December 16, 1811, and February 7, 1812, earthquakes near New Madrid, in Missouri, caused enormous damage in the midwestern United States.*

*The earthquakes (estimated at about 8.7 on the Richter scale) were so powerful that they caused the Mississippi River to change its course.*

*San Francisco earthquake, 1989*

ash and gas

crater

lava

magma

# VOLCANOES

A volcano is a mountain or hill with an opening on top known as a crater. Every once in a while, hot melted rock (magma), gases, ash, and other material from inside the earth may blast out, or erupt, through the opening. The magma is called lava when it reaches the air. This red-hot lava may have a temperature of more than 2,000 degrees Fahrenheit. The hill or mountain is made of lava and other materials that come out of the opening, and then cool off and harden.

Some islands are really the tops of undersea volcanoes. The Hawaiian islands developed when volcanoes erupted under the Pacific Ocean.

## Why Do Volcanoes Erupt?

More than 500 volcanoes have erupted over the centuries. Some have erupted many times. Volcanic eruptions come from pools of magma and other materials a few miles underground. The magma comes from rock far below. After the rock melts and mixes with gases, it rises up through cracks and weak spots in the mountain.

## SOME FAMOUS VOLCANIC ERUPTIONS

| Year | Volcano (Place) | Deaths (approximate) |
|---|---|---|
| 79 | Mount Vesuvius (Italy) | 16,000 |
| 1586 | Kelut (Indonesia) | 10,000 |
| 1792 | Mount Unzen (Japan) | 14,500 |
| 1815 | Tambora (Indonesia) | 10,000 |
| 1883 | Krakatau or Krakatoa (Indonesia) | 36,000 |
| 1902 | Mount Pelée (Martinique) | 28,000 |
| 1980 | Mount St. Helens (U.S.) | 57 |
| 1982 | El Chichon (Mexico) | 1,880 |
| 1985 | Nevado del Ruiz (Colombia) | 23,000 |
| 1986 | Lake Nyos (Cameroon) | 1,700 |
| 1991 | Mt. Pinatubo (Philippines) | 800 |

## WHERE IS THE RING OF FIRE?

Volcanoes are found on the bottom of the ocean and on every continent. Many of the active volcanoes are found on land along the edges of the Pacific Ocean. These volcanoes are often called the **Ring of Fire.**

The Ring of Fire marks the boundary between the plates under the Pacific Ocean and the plates under the continents around the Pacific Ocean (North America, South America, Asia). The plates of Earth are explained on page 86.

# HELP TOBY GET HOME

Toby ran out the open gate of his front yard to find an adventure. Instead, he found he was lost. Use the map key and compass rose to help Toby find his way home.

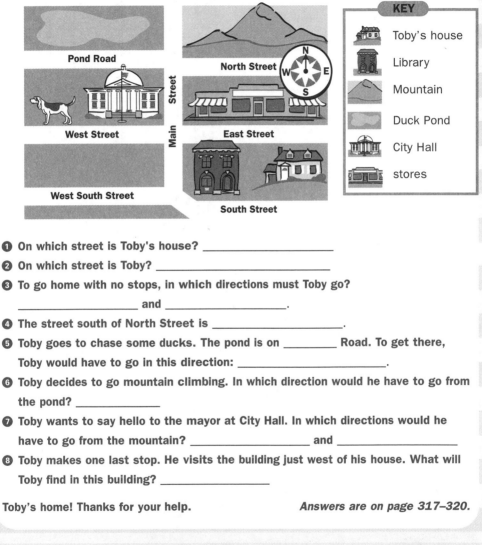

**KEY**

🏠 Toby's house
🏛 Library
⛰ Mountain
🌊 Duck Pond
🏛 City Hall
🏢 stores

❶ On which street is Toby's house? _____

❷ On which street is Toby? _____

❸ To go home with no stops, in which directions must Toby go?
_____ and _____.

❹ The street south of North Street is _____.

❺ Toby goes to chase some ducks. The pond is on _____ Road. To get there,
Toby would have to go in this direction: _____.

❻ Toby decides to go mountain climbing. In which direction would he have to go from
the pond? _____

❼ Toby wants to say hello to the mayor at City Hall. In which directions would he
have to go from the mountain? _____ and _____

❽ Toby makes one last stop. He visits the building just west of his house. What will
Toby find in this building? _____

Toby's home! Thanks for your help.          *Answers are on page 317–320.*

**DID YOU KNOW?**  *Canada's Northwest Territories broke in
two as of April 1, 1999. The eastern part, a large area of
Arctic wilderness that is one-fifth the size of Canada, became
Canada's newest territory. It is known as Nunavut, which
means "Our Land." Four out of five people in Nunavut are
members of the Inuit native group.*

# GEOGRAPHY PUZZLES

## MOUNTAIN Climbing

Find the names of some famous mountains by filling in the missing vowels below. (Hint: Volcanoes are mountains too!) Then, fit the names across the box so the climb up still spells "MOUNTAIN." Mountains are listed on pages 82–83 and 88.

P __ N __ T __ B __

K R __ K __ T __ __

MC K __ N L __ Y

ST. H __ L __ N S

__ C __ N C __ G __ __

V __ S __ V __ __ S

K __ S C __ __ S K __

__ N Z __ N

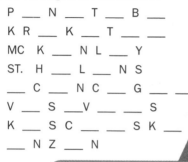

## MATCH the SIGHT with the SITE

1. Angel Falls
2. Death Valley
3. The Nile River
4. Dead Sea
5. Mount Everest

a. Egypt and Sudan
b. Venezuela
c. Tibet and Nepal
d. Israel and Jordan
e. California

*Learn more about these sights on pages 82–84.*

## RIVERS and MORE RIVERS

Change the spaces between the letters below to discover the rivers sailed by each of these explorers. For help, see page 85.

**EXPLORERS:**

Henry Hudson: _____

Meriwether Lewis and William Clark:

_____ & _____

David Livingstone: _____

Robert Cavalier, sieur de la Salle: _____

Samuel de Champlain: _____

**RIVERS:**

ZAM BE    ZIMIS

SIS SIP    PICOL

UMBI    AH

UDS    ONST    LAW    REN

CEMIS    SOUR    I

*Answers to puzzles are on page 317–320.*

# HEALTH

**❷ Who has more bones—a baby or an adult?**
*You can find the answer on page 93.*

# INSIDE YOUR BODY

**DID YOU KNOW?**

▶ Your body is made up of billions of tiny living units called **cells.** Different kinds of cells have different tasks to do in the body.

▶ Cells that do similar work form **tissue,** like nerve tissue or bone tissue.

▶ Tissues that work together form **organs,** like the heart, lungs, and kidneys.

▶ The **skin** is the body's largest organ. It protects the internal organs from infection, injury, and harmful sunlight. It also helps control body temperature.

▶ Organs work together as **systems,** and each system has a separate job to do.

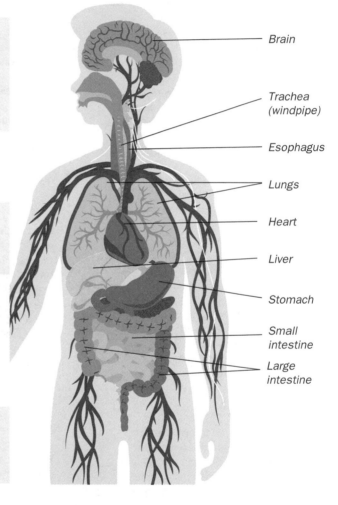

Brain

Trachea (windpipe)

Esophagus

Lungs

Heart

Liver

Stomach

Small intestine

Large intestine

**Y**our body is made up of many different parts that work together every minute of every day and night. Your body is more amazing than any machine or computer. Machines don't eat, run, have feelings, read and learn, or do other things that you do. Even though everyone's body looks different outside, people have the same parts inside.

# What the Body's Systems Do

Each system of the body has its own job. Some of the systems also work together in teams to keep you healthy and strong.

## CIRCULATORY SYSTEM

In the circulatory system, the **heart** pumps **blood**, which then travels through tubes, called **arteries**, to all parts of the body. The blood carries the oxygen and food that the body needs to stay alive. **Veins** carry the blood back to the heart.

## DIGESTIVE SYSTEM

The digestive system moves food through parts of the body called the **esophagus**, **stomach**, and **intestines**. As the food passes through, some of it is broken down into tiny particles called nutrients, which the body needs. Nutrients enter the bloodstream, which carries them to all parts of the body. The digestive system then changes the remaining food into waste that is eliminated from the body.

## ENDOCRINE SYSTEM

The endocrine system includes **glands** that are needed for some body functions. There are two kinds of glands. Exocrine glands produce liquids such as sweat and saliva. Endocrine glands produce chemicals called **hormones**. Hormones control body functions, such as growth.

## MUSCULAR SYSTEM

**Muscles** are made up of elastic fibers that help the body move. We use large muscles to walk and run, and small muscles to smile. Muscles also help protect organs.

## SKELETAL SYSTEM

The skeletal system is made up of the **bones** that hold your body upright. Some bones protect organs, such as the ribs that cover the lungs.

## NERVOUS SYSTEM

The nervous system enables us to think, feel, move, hear, and see. It includes the **brain**, the **spinal cord**, and **nerves** in all parts of the body. Nerves in the spinal cord carry signals back and forth between the brain and the rest of the body. The brain tells us what to do and how to respond. The brain has three major parts. The **cerebrum** controls our thinking, speech, and vision. The **cerebellum** is responsible for physical coordination. The **brain stem** controls the body's respiratory, circulatory, and digestive systems.

## RESPIRATORY SYSTEM

The respiratory system allows us to breathe. Air comes into the body through the nose and mouth. It goes through the windpipe (or trachea) to two tubes (called bronchi), which carry air to the **lungs**. Oxygen from the air is taken in by tiny blood vessels in the lungs. The blood then carries oxygen to the cells of the body.

## REPRODUCTIVE SYSTEM

Through the reproductive system, adult human beings are able to create new human beings. Reproduction begins when a sperm cell from a man fertilizes an egg cell from a woman.

## URINARY SYSTEM

This system, which includes the **kidneys**, cleans waste from the blood and regulates the amount of water in the body.

## Surprising Facts About the Body

**A newborn baby has more bones than an adult**. A baby's body has 350 bones, but an adult's body has 206 bones. That's because bones grow together to make fewer, larger bones as the baby grows up.

**The largest bone in your body is your thigh bone** (or femur). The smallest bone in your body is the stirrup (or stapes), a tiny bone in your middle ear.

**Children have 20 first teeth.** Adults have 32 teeth.

**The human body has more than 650 muscles**.

**The heart weighs less than one pound**. It beats about 100,000 times a day, and it pumps 2,000 gallons of blood in a day.

**An adult's large intestine is about 5 feet long**. The small intestine, which is much narrower than the large one, is about 25 feet long.

**Red blood cells live for about 120 days**. Then they are replaced by new ones. The bone cells in your body live for 25 to 30 years. Your brain cells live for a lifetime.

**About 70% of the average-sized adult body is made up of water.**

**It takes around 17 muscles to smile and around 43 to frown**.

# Stay Healthy with EXERCISE

Daily exercise is important for your good health, fitness, and appearance. Exercise makes you feel good. It helps you think better. And, believe it or not, it helps you sleep better and feel less tired and more relaxed. Once you start exercising regularly, you will feel stronger and keep improving at physical activities.

**What Happens When You Exercise?** When you exercise, you breathe more deeply and get more oxygen into your lungs with each breath. Your heart pumps more oxygen-filled blood to all parts of your body with each beat. Your muscles and joints feel more flexible. Exercise also helps you to stay at a healthy weight.

**What About People Who Don't Exercise?** People who don't exercise may have less strength and energy. They may not sleep well and may feel tired. And they may gain more weight than would be healthy.

**What Kind of Exercise Is Good?**
Almost all kinds of activity that move the body around are good. Bicycling, dancing, skating, swimming, running, roller-blading, and playing soccer are a few ways to exercise and have fun at the same time.

## WE ARE WHAT WE EAT

Have you ever noticed the labels on the packages of food you and your family buy? The labels provide information people need to make healthy choices about the foods they eat. Below are some terms you may see on labels.

### NUTRIENTS ARE NEEDED

**Nutrients** are the parts of food that the body can use. The body needs nutrients for growth, for energy, and to repair itself when something goes wrong. Carbohydrates, fats, proteins, vitamins, minerals, and water are different kinds of nutrients that are found in food. **Carbohydrates** and **fats** provide energy. **Proteins** help with growth and help to maintain and repair the body. **Vitamins** help the body to use food, help eyesight and skin, and help fight off infections. **Minerals** help build bones and teeth and work with the chemicals in the body. **Water** helps with growth and repair of the body. It also works with the blood and chemicals, and helps the body get rid of wastes.

### CALORIES COUNT

A **calorie** is a measure of how much energy we get from food. The government recommends the number of calories that should be taken in for different age groups. The number of calories recommended for children ages 7 to 10 is 2,400 a day. For ages 11 to 14, the government recommends 2,400 calories a day for girls and 2,800 for boys.

To maintain a **healthy weight**, it is important to balance the calories in the food you eat with the calories used by the body every day. Every activity uses up some calories. The more active you are, the more calories your body burns. If you eat more calories than your body uses, you will gain weight.

## A LITTLE FAT GOES A LONG WAY

**SOME LOWER-FAT FOODS:**
chicken or turkey hot dog
broiled chicken breast
tuna fish canned in water
pretzels
low-fat or nonfat frozen yogurt
plain popcorn (with no butter)
skim milk or 1% or 2% milk

**SOME FATTY FOODS:**
beef or pork hot dog
fried hamburger
tuna fish canned in oil
potato chips
ice cream
buttered popcorn
whole milk

**A little bit of fat** is important for your body. It keeps your body warm. It gives the muscles energy. It helps keep the skin soft and healthy. But the body needs only a small amount of fat to do all these things—just one tablespoon of fat each day is enough.

**Cholesterol.** Eating too much fat can make some people's bodies produce too much **cholesterol** (ko-LESS-ter-all). This waxy substance can build up over the years on the inside of arteries. Too much cholesterol keeps blood from flowing freely through the arteries and can cause serious health problems such as heart attacks.

**To eat less fat,** try eating lower-fat foods instead of fatty foods.

# Which FOODS Are the RIGHT FOODS?

To stay healthy, it is important to eat the right foods and to exercise. To help people choose the right foods for good health and fitness, the U.S. government developed the food pyramid shown below. The food pyramid shows the groups of foods that should be eaten every day.

## FOOD PYRAMID: A Guide to Daily Food Choices

**Fats, Oils, and Sweets**
*Use sparingly*

**Milk, Yogurt, and Cheese Group**
*2 to 3 servings*
1 serving = 1 cup of milk or yogurt; or 1½ to 2 ounces of cheese

**Meat, Poultry, Fish, Dry Beans, Eggs, and Nuts Group**
*2 to 3 servings*
1 serving = 2 to 3 ounces of cooked lean meat, fish, or poultry; ½ cup of cooked dry beans; 2 eggs; or 4 to 6 tablespoons of peanut butter

**Vegetable Group**
*3 to 5 servings*
1 serving = 1 cup of raw, leafy green vegetables; ½ cup of other vegetables (cooked or chopped raw); or ¾ cup vegetable juice

**Fruit Group**
*2 to 4 servings*
1 serving = 1 medium apple, banana, or orange; ½ cup of cooked, chopped, or canned fruit; or ¾ cup of fruit juice

**Bread, Cereal, Rice, and Pasta Group**
*6 to 11 servings*
1 serving = 1 slice of bread; 1 ounce of ready-to-eat cereal; or ½ cup of cooked cereal, rice, or pasta

The foods at the bottom (the widest part) of the pyramid are the ones you need to eat in the largest amounts. At the top are the foods to be eaten in the smallest amounts. The number of servings a person should eat depends on the person's age and body size. Younger, smaller people may eat fewer servings. Older, larger people may eat more.

# The TRUTH About COLDS

**C**olds are the most common illnesses we get. Schoolchildren often catch colds from one another—usually about five to eight colds a year. Here are some mistakes, and some facts, about colds.

**Fiction:** In low temperatures, you can catch a cold by going outside without a coat.

**Fact:** It's smart to dress warmly when it's cold out. But colds are caused by viruses, and not cold weather. Washing your hands is a good way to avoid catching many viruses.

**Fiction:** Some vitamins and medicines cure colds.

**Fact:** While some vitamins and medicines may make you feel better for a while, there is no cure for the cold. It usually lasts about one or two weeks.

**Fiction:** You can cure a cold by staying home.

**Fact:** There is no cure for the cold. Enough sleep, drinking juices, and eating well will help you feel better.

## Take Care of Your Teeth

**I**f you want to chew food properly and speak clearly, it is important to keep your teeth healthy. These tips will help you do that.

Brush your teeth at least twice a day—*after every meal if you can.*

*Floss. Use dental floss regularly to clean between your teeth.*

Eat healthful foods. *Eating too many sweets and sodas causes cavities.*

*Visit your dentist for a checkup and cleaning every six months.*

**What Causes Cavities in Your Teeth?** Cavities are caused by tiny pieces of food left on or between the teeth after eating. These pieces of food combine with the natural bacteria in your mouth to form an acid. The acid slowly eats away the tooth's enamel and causes tooth decay, or cavities.

## Which Doctor Does What?

A **dentist** is a doctor who takes general care of your teeth.

An **orthodontist** is a doctor who straightens teeth.

A **pediatrician** is a doctor who takes care of children.

An **orthopedist** is a doctor who fixes broken bones.

A **dermatologist** is a doctor who treats skin problems and diseases.

A **cardiologist** is a doctor who treats people who have heart problems.

A **psychiatrist** is a doctor who helps people with emotional problems.

# ALLERGIES: WHEEZES and SNEEZES

**A**h-choo! That's your umpteenth sneeze today. Your nose is running. Your eyes itch. Your sinuses are clogged. Your head aches. You feel completely yucky. Do you have a cold? Or, like 50 million other Americans, do you have an allergy? In general, people with allergies don't develop a fever, and people with colds don't feel itchy. But only a doctor can tell you for sure what your symptoms mean.

## What is an allergy?

A person with an allergy is super sensitive to stuff that is normally harmless. What is some of this "stuff"? It could be animal dander, traces of hair, feathers, or skin shed by pets. It could be mold spores, dust in the air, or pollen from plants. It could be something you touch (such as poison ivy, which affects many people). It could be something you ate. Just because a person is allergic to one kind of irritant doesn't mean he or she is allergic to the others. Different kinds of allergies have different names, causes, and symptoms.

## What is hay fever?

This is one of the most common allergies that affects sinuses. It is a reaction to pollen, from trees, grass, and weeds, which is in the air at certain times of the year. The pollen may come from the grass in your backyard. Or, as one allergy doctor (an allergist) discovered, it could even come on air currents from places hundreds of miles away.

## What is asthma?

It is an allergy in the lungs that can cause difficulty in breathing. Pollen and dust mites, as well as tobacco smoke, cold air, and certain foods can trigger an asthma attack.

## What are hives?

Hives are big itchy blotches, bumps, or red spots. They come from an allergy that occurs in the skin and is often caused by a reaction to certain foods.

## How can you protect yourself against allergies?

You should see a doctor to find out more about your allergy and what to do about it. You can also do some things to help yourself. If you're sensitive to pollen and molds, go out when they're at their lowest levels. Grass pollen, for example, is strongest between 6 and 10 A.M. Pollens are high on windy days, so those are good times to stay indoors. The middle of the day is the best time to avoid pollen from weeds.

People who have allergies to dust mites and molds must sometimes avoid using wall-to-wall carpeting in their homes because it holds in these things. Drugstore shelves are filled with medicines to fight allergies or slow down their symptoms. Always ask a doctor about medication before you buy it or take it.

## DOCTOR PUZZLE

**U**sing the letters in the word "dermatologist," see how many words you can make that have at least three letters. Plurals don't count.

*Answers are on pages 317–320.*

## Understanding AIDS

**What Is AIDS?** AIDS is a disease that is caused by a virus called HIV. AIDS attacks the body's immune system. The immune system is important because it helps the body fight off infections and diseases.

**How Do Kids Get AIDS?** A mother with AIDS may give it to her baby before the baby is born. Sometimes children (and adults, too) get AIDS from blood transfusions. But this happens less often, because blood banks now test all donations of blood for the AIDS virus.

**How Do Adults Get AIDS?** Adults get AIDS in two main ways: Having sex with a person who has AIDS, or sharing a needle used for drugs with a person who has AIDS.

**How Kids and Adults *Don't* Get AIDS.** People *don't* get AIDS from everyday contact with infected people at school, at home, or other places. People *don't* get AIDS from clothes, telephones, or toilet seats, or from food prepared by someone with AIDS. Children *don't* get AIDS from sitting near AIDS victims or from shaking hands with them.

**Is There a Cure for AIDS?** There is no cure for AIDS. But researchers are working to develop a vaccine to prevent AIDS or a drug to cure it. And new treatments are beginning to increase the lifespan of many AIDS victims.

# Say NO
# to Drugs, Alcohol, and Cigarettes

Drugs, alcohol, and cigarettes can do serious damage to people's bodies and minds. Most kids keep away from them. But some kids have a tough time saying "no" when they are offered harmful substances. Here are some ways to say "no." They're suggested by DARE, a U.S. government program. Add your own ideas to this list.

Say **"No thanks."** (Say it again and again if you have to.)

**Give reasons.** ("I don't like cigarettes" or "I'm going to soccer practice" or "I have asthma.")

**Change the subject** or offer a better suggestion.

**Walk away.** (Don't argue, don't discuss it. Just leave.)

**Avoid the situation.** (If you are asked to a party where kids will be drinking, smoking, or using drugs, make plans to do something else instead.)

**Find strength in numbers.** (Do things with friends who don't use harmful substances.)

# Stay SAFE, PREVENT ACCIDENTS

**B**eing careful and using common sense are the best ways to avoid accidents. No one can prevent every accident. But some—especially those in the home, where most accidents happen—can be prevented. Here are some safety tips.

▶ **In the Kitchen.** Check with an adult about whether you can use a knife. Handle sharp knives carefully. Always cut away from your body and put the knife down in a safe place. To avoid fire, keep paper or cloth (like napkins or towels) away from the stove. Keep sharp objects and matches out of the reach of babies and little children.

▶ **In the Bathroom.** Use a rubber mat or other non-slip surface to keep you from slipping in the tub. Keep soap in a soap dish. Keep electrical appliances, such as radios and hair dryers, away from water.

▶ **In Every Room.** Everyone in your home should know all the exits in case of fire. If an accident happens, call an adult to help. Never let strangers into your home. Don't give your name or address to strangers over the phone. Don't let anyone know if you are home alone.

▶ **On Bikes and Skates.** Wear a helmet. When skating, wear wrist, elbow, and knee guards. Be alert. Look for traffic and watch for bikes, skaters, and people walking. Learn the safety laws for cars. They apply to others on the road, too.

▶ **In Cars.** Always wear a seat belt. Don't distract the driver; don't jump around.

▶ **On the Street.** Watch for traffic. Look both ways. Cross only at corners. Stay on the curb until the light turns green and the "Walk" sign is on. Don't fool around near traffic.

## Be Ready for Any Emergency

**Tape a list of emergency numbers** near the phone or on the refrigerator. Numbers to include are:

▶ your parents' or guardians' telephone numbers at work

▶ the telephone number of a relative or other adult who lives nearby

▶ the numbers of your family doctor, a nearby hospital, the fire department, and the police department

*Emergency phone numbers can often be found inside the front cover of your local telephone book.*

**Remember 911.**
The number 911 is a special phone number for emergencies only. When a person who needs help right away calls 911, the operator asks the caller for his or her name and address and what the emergency is. Then the operator quickly sends the police, an ambulance, and, if needed, the fire department. Dial 0 (Operator) if your town doesn't have 911, and ask the operator for help.

❓ If you visited Japan on May 5, what holiday would you join in celebrating?
*You can find the answer below.*

# Legal or Public HOLIDAYS

There are no legal holidays for the whole United States. The U.S. government decides which days are holidays for its workers and for Washington, D.C. Each state picks its own holidays, but most states celebrate those listed here. On legal holidays, most banks and schools are closed, and so are many offices. Since 1971, Washington's Birthday (or Presidents' Day), Memorial Day, Columbus Day, and Veterans Day have been celebrated on a Monday so that many people can have a three-day weekend.

 **New Year's Day** Countries the world over celebrate the new year, although not always on January 1. The Chinese New Year falls between January 21 and February 19. In ancient Egypt, the New Year began around mid-June, when the Nile river overflowed and watered the crops.

**Martin Luther King, Jr., Day** Observed on the third Monday in January, this holiday marks the birth (January 15, 1929) of the African-American civil rights leader Martin Luther King, Jr.

**Washington's Birthday or Presidents' Day** On the third Monday in February, Americans often celebrate the births of both George Washington (born February 22, 1732) and Abraham Lincoln (born February 12, 1809).

 **Memorial Day or Decoration Day** Memorial Day, observed on the last Monday in May, is set aside to remember all those who died in United States wars.

## HOLIDAYS Around the WORLD

| | |
|---|---|
| Children's Day | In Japan, May 5 is set aside to honor children. |
| Canada Day | Canada's national holiday, July 1, commemorates the union of Canadian provinces under one government in 1867. |
| Chinese New Year | China's biggest holiday falls between January 21 and February 19 every year. Celebrations include lively parades, fireworks, and traditional family meals. |
| Independence Day | Mexico celebrates September 16 as its national holiday. |
| Boxing Day | December 26 is a holiday in Australia, Canada, Great Britain, and New Zealand. On this day, at one time, Christmas gifts were given in boxes to servants, tradespeople, and the poor. |

**Fourth of July or Independence Day** July 4 is the anniversary of the day in 1776 when the American colonies declared their independence from England. Kids and grownups celebrate with bands and parades, picnics, barbecues, and fireworks.

**Labor Day** Labor Day, the first Monday in September, honors the workers of America. It was first celebrated in 1882.

**Columbus Day** Celebrated on the second Monday in October, Columbus Day is the anniversary of October 12, 1492, the day when Christopher Columbus was traditionally thought to have arrived in America.

**Election Day** Election Day, the first Tuesday after the first Monday in November, is a legal holiday in some states.

**Veterans Day** Veterans Day, November 11, honors the veterans of United States wars. First called Armistice Day, it marked the armistice (agreement) that ended World War I. This was signed on the 11th hour (11 a.m.) of the 11th day of the 11th month of 1918.

**Thanksgiving** Celebrated on the fourth Thursday in November, Thanksgiving Day was first observed by the Pilgrims in 1621 as a harvest festival and a day for thanks and feasting.

**Christmas** Christmas is both a religious holiday and a legal holiday. (See p. 211.)

## SOME OTHER SPECIAL HOLIDAYS

 **Valentine's Day** February 14 is a day for sending cards or gifts to people you love.

**Arbor Day** We plant trees on Arbor Day to remind us of how they protect the environment. Each state observes the day at different times in the spring, depending on the state's climate.

**Mother's Day and Father's Day** Mothers are honored on the second Sunday in May. Fathers are honored on the third Sunday in June.

 **Halloween** In ancient Britain, Druids lit fires and wore grotesque costumes on October 31 to scare off evil spirits. Today, "trick or treating" children collect candy and other sweets. Some also collect money for UNICEF, the United Nations Children's Fund.

**Kwanzaa** This seven-day African-American festival begins December 26. It celebrates seven virtues including responsibility and cooperation. Kwanzaa means "first fruits" in Swahili, an African language.

## HOLIDAYS in 2000

**New Year's Day**
*January 1*
*Saturday*

**Martin Luther King, Jr., Day**
*January 17*
*Monday*

**Washington's Birthday**
*February 21*
*Monday*

**Memorial Day**
*May 29*
*Monday*

**Independence Day**
*July 4*
*Tuesday*

**Labor Day**
*September 4*
*Monday*

**Columbus Day**
*October 9*
*Monday*

**Election Day**
*November 7*
*Tuesday*

**Veterans Day**
*November 11*
*Saturday*

**Thanksgiving**
*November 23*
*Thursday*

**Christmas**
*December 25*
*Monday*

# INVENTIONS

❓**Who invented the dishwasher?**
*You can find the answer on page 103.*

# INVENTIONS Change Our Lives

**S**ome of the world's most important inventions were developed before history was written. These include tools and the wheel, pottery, and the ability to make and control fire. More recent inventions help us to travel faster, communicate better, and live longer.

## INVENTIONS TAKE US FROM ONE PLACE TO ANOTHER

Faster ways to travel have opened more of the world to more people.

| Year | Invention | Inventor | Country |
|------|-----------|----------|---------|
| 1785 | parachute | Jean Pierre Blanchard | France |
| 1807 | steamboat | Robert Fulton | U.S. |
| 1829 | steam locomotive | George Stephenson | England |
| 1852 | safety elevator | Elisha G. Otis | U.S. |
| 1885 | bicycle | James Starley | England |
| 1885 | motorcycle | Gottlieb Daimler | Germany |
| 1891 | escalator | Jesse W. Reno | U.S. |
| 1892 | automobile (gasoline) | Charles E. Duryea & J. Frank Duryea | U.S. |
| 1894 | submarine | Simon Lake | U.S. |
| 1895 | diesel engine | Rudolf Diesel | Germany |
| 1903 | propeller airplane | Orville & Wilbur Wright | U.S. |
| 1939 | helicopter | Igor Sikorsky | U.S. |
| 1939 | turbojet airplane | Hans von Ohain | Germany |
| 1969 | supersonic passenger airplane (Concorde) | Aérospatiale & British Aircraft Corp. | France & England |

## INVENTIONS HELP US LIVE HEALTHIER AND LONGER LIVES

CAT scanners and X rays find illnesses. Drugs help fight them.

| Year | Invention | Inventor | Country |
|------|-----------|----------|---------|
| 1780 | bifocal lenses for glasses | Benjamin Franklin | U.S. |
| 1819 | stethoscope | René T.M.H. Laënnec | France |
| 1842 | anesthesia (ether) | Crawford W. Long | U.S. |
| 1895 | X ray | Wilhelm Roentgen | Germany |
| 1922 | insulin | Sir Frederick G. Banting | Canada |
| 1929 | penicillin | Alexander Fleming | Scotland |
| 1954 | antibiotic for fungal diseases | Rachel F. Brown & Elizabeth L. Hazen | U.S. |
| 1955 | polio vaccine | Jonas E. Salk | U.S. |
| 1973 | CAT scanner | Godfrey N. Hounsfield | England |

## INVENTIONS HELP US COMMUNICATE WITH ONE ANOTHER

The pen, pencil, fax, phone, and computer are all tools for exchanging information.

| Year | Invention | Inventor | Country |
|------|-----------|----------|---------|
| A.D. 105 | paper | Ts'ai Lun | China |
| 1447 | movable type | Johann Gutenberg | Germany |
| 1795 | modern pencil | Nicolas Jacques Conté | France |
| 1837 | telegraph | Samuel F.B. Morse | U.S. |
| 1845 | rotary printing press | Richard M. Hoe | U.S. |
| 1867 | typewriter | Christopher L. Sholes, Carlos Glidden, & Samuel W. Soulé | U.S. |
| 1876 | telephone | Alexander G. Bell | U.S. |
| 1888 | ballpoint pen | John Loud | U.S. |
| 1913 | modern radio receiver | Reginald A. Fessenden | U.S. |
| 1937 | xerography copies | Chester Carlson | U.S. |
| 1942 | electronic computer | John V. Atanasoff & Clifford Berry | U.S. |
| 1944 | auto sequence computer | Howard H. Aiken | U.S. |
| 1947 | transistor | William Shockley, Walter H. Brattain, & John Bardeen | U.S. |
| 1955 | fiber optics | Narinder S. Kapany | England |
| 1965 | word processor | IBM | U.S. |
| 1979 | cellular telephone | Ericsson Company | Sweden |

## INVENTIONS MAKE OUR LIVES EASIER

Modern inventions shorten the time it takes to do ordinary tasks.

| Year | Invention | Inventor | Country |
|------|-----------|----------|---------|
| 1800 | electric battery | Alessandro Volta | Italy |
| 1827 | matches | John Walker | England |
| 1831 | lawn mower | Edwin Budding & John Ferrabee | England |
| 1834 | refrigeration | Jacob Perkins | England |
| 1846 | sewing machine | Elias Howe | U.S. |
| 1851 | cylinder (door) lock | Linus Yale | U.S. |
| 1879 | first practical electric light bulb | Thomas A. Edison | U.S. |
| 1886 | dishwasher | Josephine Cochran | U.S. |
| 1891 | zipper | Whitcomb L. Judson | U.S. |
| 1901 | washing machine | Langmuir Fisher | U.S. |
| 1903 | windshield wipers | Mary Anderson | U.S. |
| 1907 | vacuum cleaner | J. Murray Spangler | U.S. |
| 1911 | air conditioning | Willis H. Carrier | U.S. |
| 1924 | frozen packaged food | Clarence Birdseye | U.S. |
| 1947 | microwave oven | Percy L. Spencer | U.S. |
| 1948 | Velcro | Georges de Mestral | Switzerland |
| 1969 | cash machine (ATM) | Don Wetzel | U.S. |
| 1971 | food processor | Pierre Verdon | France |

## CALIFORNIA BOY MAKES DELICIOUS DISCOVERY

When Frank Epperson was a boy in California, he liked to drink a fizzy mixture of soda powder and water. One cold night, Frank left his drink outside and it froze. In 1923, when Frank had his own business, he invented Epsicles—frozen desserts based on that mixture. You've probably had one. Today they're called Popsicles.

## INVENTIONS ENTERTAIN US

| Year | Invention | Inventor | Country |
|------|-----------|----------|---------|
| 1709 | piano | Bartolomeo Cristofori | Italy |
| 1877 | phonograph | Thomas A. Edison | U.S. |
| 1877 | microphone | Emile Berliner | U.S. |
| 1888 | portable camera | George Eastman | U.S. |
| 1893 | moving picture viewer | Thomas A. Edison | U.S. |
| 1894 | motion picture projector | Charles F. Jenkins | U.S. |
| 1899 | tape recorder | Valdemar Poulsen | Denmark |
| 1923 | television* | Vladimir K. Zworykin* | U.S. |
| 1951 | flexible kite | Gertrude Rogallo & Francis Rogallo | U.S. |
| 1963 | audiocassette | Phillips Corporation | Netherlands |
| 1969 | videotape cassette | Sony | Japan |
| 1972 | compact disc (CD) | RCA | U.S. |
| 1972 | video game (Pong) | Noland Buschnel | U.S. |
| 1979 | Walkman | Sony | Japan |

*Others who helped invent television include Philo T. Farnsworth (1926) and John Baird (1928).

## INVENTIONS HELP US EXPAND OUR UNIVERSE

| Year | Invention | Inventor | Country |
|------|-----------|----------|---------|
| 1250 | magnifying glass | Roger Bacon | England |
| 1590 | 2-lens microscope | Zacharias Janssen | Netherlands |
| 1608 | telescope | Hans Lippershey | Netherlands |
| 1714 | mercury thermometer | Gabriel D. Fahrenheit | Germany |
| 1926 | rocket engine | Robert H. Goddard | U.S. |
| 1930 | cyclotron (atom smasher) | Ernest O. Lawrence | U.S. |
| 1943 | Aqua Lung | Jacques-Yves Cousteau & Emile Gagnan | France |
| 1953 | bathyscaphe | August Piccard | France |
| 1977 | space shuttle | NASA | U.S. |

 **DID YOU KNOW?**

*Philo T. Farnsworth, an inventor of an early TV system, was 13 years old when he developed his idea. Today, kids are coming up with great ideas, too. For example, Richie Stachowski was in elementary school when he invented a water toy that allows swimmers to talk to each other underwater.*

### NATIONAL INVENTORS HALL OF FAME

To learn more about inventions and the people who created them, or to make your own invention, visit

Inventure Place
National Inventors Hall of Fame
221 S. Broadway St., Akron, Ohio 44308
Phone: (330) 762-4463.
E-mail: info@invent.org

**WEB SITE** *http://www.invent.org/book*

❓ What language is spoken by the most people in the world?
*You can find the answer on page 110.*

# SHORT and SHORTER

## ABBREVIATIONS and ACRONYMS

**An abbreviation** is a short form of a word or phrase used in order to save time or space. Here are some abbreviations:

Ave.   Avenue
oz.    ounce
pp.    pages
St.    Street
TV     television

**An acronym** is a kind of abbreviation. It is a word you can pronounce, formed from the first letters, or other parts, of a group of words. For example, NASA is an acronym for National Aeronautics and Space Administration.

Every day, the CIA (an abbreviation for the Central Intelligence Agency) sends the president of the United States a PICKLE — an acronym for the President's Intelligence Check List.

**The Long, Not the Short, of It.** One of the longest acronyms in English is **SWIFT ANSWER**. It stands for Special Word Indexed Full Text Alpha Numeric Storage With Easy Retrieval.

**TITLES** We often use abbreviations before or after people's names. For example, a doctor might be called Dr. I. M. Well or I. M. Well, M.D. (M.D. stands for medical doctor.)

## Technical Talk
**Special fields have their own abbreviations.**

**Computers.** To use your personal computer **(PC)**, you start, or boot up, the system. The computer works by using a central processing unit **(CPU)** that reads and writes using random access memory **(RAM)**. But a computer is only as good as what you write into it—garbage in, garbage out **(GIGO)**.

**Internet.** Abbreviations are a part of the everyday language of the Internet and electronic mail **(e-mail)**. **E.g.** (for example), **FWIW** (for what it's worth), **URL** stands for Uniform Resource Locator, which is the official name for Internet address. There's much more, but **TAFN** (that's all for now). See page 64 for more about the Internet.

**Sports.** All ranking college teams play in the **NCAA** (National Collegiate Athletic Association). Professional football, basketball, and hockey teams all belong to national leagues **(NFL, NBA**, and the **NHL)**. Baseball has two leagues, the National League **(NL)** and the American League **(AL)**. The abbreviations NL and AL are used chiefly in giving baseball **stats** (statistics).

# Words That SOUND ALIKE or Almost Alike

When words sound similar, sometimes their spellings and meanings are confusing. Words that sound alike are called **homophones**.

### CAPITAL or CAPITOL

A **capital** is the city where a country or state government is located. The **capitol** is the building where a legislative body meets.

### DIE or DYE

To **die** means to stop living. To **dye** means to change the color of an object.

### HAIR or HARE

**Hair** is what grows on the top of your head if you are not bald. A **hare** is a kind of rabbit.

### ITS or IT'S

**Its** is the possessive form of "it" (the bird flapped its wings). **It's** is a contraction of "it is."

### LOAN or LONE

A **loan** is something that you lend or someone borrows. **Lone** is an adjective that means single or alone.

### PRINCIPAL or PRINCIPLE

A **principal** is the person in charge of a school. **Principal** also means first in importance. A **principle** is a basic belief that a person strongly holds.

### ROLL or ROLE

A bun or muffin is a **roll**. A **role** is a part or character in a play.

### STEAL or STEEL

**Steal** means to take what does not belong to you. **Steel** is a very strong metal.

### THEIR, THEY'RE, or THERE

**Their** is the possessive form of "they." **They're** is a contraction of "they are." **There** means at or in that place. (They're going to put their packages there on the table.)

### VAIN, VANE, VEIN

To be **vain** means to be stuck-up or conceited. A **vane** shows what way the wind is blowing. But a **vein** is one of many tubes that carries blood to the heart.

**New Words**

The English language is always changing. New words become part of the vocabulary, while other words become outdated. Many new words come from the field of electronics and computers, from the media, even from slang.

**buffalo wing** • a deep-fried chicken wing coated with a spicy sauce and usually served with a blue cheese dressing; invented in Buffalo, New York.
(*We ate three plates of buffalo wings during the Super Bowl game.*)

**chat room** • a place or discussion room on the Internet where people can send messages for everybody to read.
(*There are dozens of chat rooms on the Internet, for everyone from Abyssinian cat breeders to zookeepers.*)

**comfort food** • food that people are used to having and that makes them feel good.
(*Mashed potatoes, meat loaf, and chocolate cake are my favorite comfort foods.*)

**family leave** • time off from a job, so that you can take care of a sick person or do other things you need to do for your family.
(*My mother took family leave when Grandpa came home from the hospital.*)

**trash talk** • nasty or boastful talk or teasing between people trying to make each other feel bad.
(*Did you hear that trash talk between Jane and Jill about each other's clothes?*)

# In Other Words: IDIOMS

Idioms are groups of words (phrases) or sentences that cannot be understood just by knowing the meaning of each of the words. They may often be slang. Idioms are confusing to people learning a new language. Here are some common idioms, with their meanings.

## ANIMAL LIFE

**dog-eat-dog:** fierce competition

**to open a can of worms:** to open up a lot of new problems

**to horse around:** to have fun; play around

**cold fish:** someone who is unfriendly or does not show feelings

**snake in the grass:** a liar, cheat, or sneaky person

**to cry wolf:** to alarm others or whine about something when there is no real danger

## BODY LANGUAGE

**arm in arm:** doing something with another person with arms connected; in agreement

**talking head:** a TV personality shown mostly from the shoulders up, just talking, not doing anything

**cap in hand:** in a humble or respectful manner

**to flip your wig:** to go crazy or get excited without warning

## FUN AND GAMES

**to play games:** to fool someone or keep the truth from someone

**to be on the ball:** to be alert or quick to catch on or understand

**to be off base:** to be wrong

**to strike someone funny:** to seem funny to someone

**the game is up:** a lie or other secret act has been discovered

**to go bananas:** to act silly or crazy

# WORD PUZZLE

Use the clues to figure out the idiom.

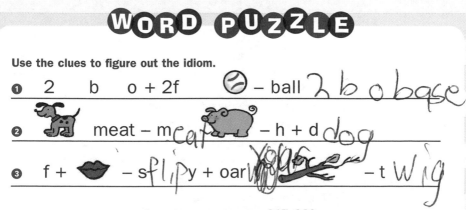

❶ 2    b    o + 2f    〇 – ball

❷ 🐶    meat – m    🐷 – h + d

❸ f + 👄 – s    y + oar        – t

*Answers are on pages 317–320.*

# Where Do ENGLISH WORDS Come From?

Words from many other languages have become part of the English language. Here are some words and where they come from.

**from French:** antique, beret, boulevard, camouflage, carousel, casserole, corsage, deluxe, fatigue, intrigue, menu, omelette, reservoir, souvenir, surgeon

**from German:** delicatessen, frankfurter, hamburger, kindergarten, knapsack, pretzel, snorkel, yodel

**from Hindi:** bungalow, lacquer, shampoo

**from Italian:** broccoli, macaroni, pasta, pizza, prima donna

**from Japanese:** haiku, karate, kimono, sushi, tofu

**from Spanish:** alligator, bonanza, cafeteria, canyon, chocolate, guitar, hammock, mosquito, mustang, rodeo, patio, plaza, pronto, stampede, tomato, tornado

# In OTHER WORDS

Some words we use come from place names. Others are based on people's names.

**Boycott:** In Ireland, people refused to use the services of Charles C. Boycott, a greedy land agent.

**Diesel:** The first diesel engine was built by Rudolph Diesel.

**Gardenia:** This flower was named after Alexander Garden, a botanist.

**Jersey:** This fine cloth was originally made on Jersey, one of the Channel Islands off the western coast of England.

**Limousine:** This luxury car is named after the Limousin region of France.

**Maverick:** This is someone who goes his or her own way. It may have come from Samuel A. Maverick, a rancher who wouldn't brand his calves.

**Panic:** Some ancient Greeks believed that this feeling was caused by the Greek god Pan.

**Sandwich:** It was invented by John Montagu, the Earl of Sandwich.

# JUMBO SHRIMP and Other OXYMORONS

Something jumbo is very large. A shrimp is very small. So what's a jumbo shrimp? It's an oxymoron, a pair of words that seem to contradict each other, or just look plain silly together. Many oxymorons have become part of our language. Here are a few. Can you think of others?

| Oxymoron | What It May Mean |
|---|---|
| bittersweet | The story was both sad and happy. |
| definite maybe | The answer may be yes . . . or no. |
| old news | It made headlines a while ago. |
| open secret | It's supposed to be a secret, but everyone knows it. |
| same difference | It's six of one, half a dozen of the other. |
| taped live | It happened hours ago, but it was taped as it happened. |
| working vacation | She's at the beach, but she's taken her laptop along. |

# Writing a LETTER

**D**id you know there are different kinds of letters?

Candace Kane
PO Box 44
Small Town, TN 37400

January 15, 2000

Customer Service
Gloppeys Chocolates, Inc.
183 Honey Place
Sweetland, OR 97075

To whom it may concern:

Gloppeys Chocolates are my absolute favorite. This week I bought three packages. In one package five pieces were missing chocolate centers. Then I looked at the other two packages. They were OK. However, one package had 13 pieces and the other had only 11 pieces. I have two suggestions:

1. Please make sure each piece has a chocolate center.
2. Put exactly the same amount of Gloppeys in each package.

Sincerely yours,

*Candace*

Candace Kane

## Writing a Business Letter

**A** letter to an official person—say, to your mayor or the head of a company—is a formal letter, and it should include your name and address, the date, the address of the person you're writing to, and an ending such as "Sincerely yours" or "Yours truly."

Hi Owen,

Greetings from Puppetville! Today we visited the Museum of Dummies. Tomorrow we're going to the Marionette Parade. This really is a vacation with strings attached.

Your friend,

Charlie

Owen Jones
15 Pleasant St.
Oak Bluff, NY 10000

---

| Ride Home | | | |
|---|---|---|---|
| Send | Compose | Send Later | Delete |

To: mypal@fun.com
From: me@allwork.net
Subject: Fireworks
Sent: Mon, 3 July 2000 10:33:58

Let's go to the fireworks festival at Big Bang Park. Picnic first. We're leaving at noon. Let me know ASAP.

## Writing to a Friend

A letter to a relative or friend is informal, and you can write it any way you like. The same is true of a friendly postcard or e-mail.

# Languages of the WORLD

**W**ould you have guessed that Mandarin, the principal language of China, is the world's most spoken language? You may find more surprises in the chart below, which lists languages spoken in 1998 by at least 50,000,000 native speakers (those for whom the language is their first language, or mother tongue) and some of the places where they are spoken.

| LANGUAGE | WHERE SPOKEN | NATIVE SPEAKERS |
|---|---|---|
| Mandarin | China, Taiwan | 874,000,000 |
| Hindi | India | 366,000,000 |
| Spanish | Spain, Latin America | 358,000,000 |
| English | U.S., Canada, Britain | 341,000,000 |
| Bengali | India, Bangladesh | 207,000,000 |
| Arabic | Arabian Peninsula | 206,000,000 |
| Portuguese | Portugal, Brazil | 176,000,000 |
| Russian | Russia | 167,000,000 |
| Japanese | Japan | 125,000,000 |
| German | Germany | 100,000,000 |
| French | France, Canada, Haiti | 77,000,000 |
| Malay-Indonesian | Indonesia | 60,000,000 |

Hello!
(English)

Konnichi wa!
(Japanese)

¡Hola!
(Spanish)

# Which LANGUAGES Are SPOKEN in the UNITED STATES?

| Language used at home | Speakers over 5 years old |
|---|---|
| ❶ Spanish | 17,339,000 |
| ❷ French | 1,702,000 |
| ❸ German | 1,547,000 |
| ❹ Italian | 1,309,000 |
| ❺ Chinese | 1,249,000 |
| ❻ Tagalog | 843,000 |
| ❼ Polish | 723,000 |
| ❽ Korean | 626,000 |
| ❾ Vietnamese | 507,000 |
| ❿ Portuguese | 430,000 |
| ⓫ Japanese | 428,000 |
| ⓬ Greek | 388,000 |
| ⓭ Arabic | 355,000 |
| ⓮ Hindi, Urdu,& related languages | 331,000 |
| ⓯ Russian | 242,000 |
| ⓰ Yiddish | 213,000 |
| ⓱ Thai | 206,000 |
| ⓲ Persian | 202,000 |

**S**ince the beginning of American history, immigrants have come to the United States from all over the world and brought their native languages with them. The table at left is a list of the most frequently spoken languages in the United States, not counting English.

# PICTURE WORD PUZZLE

Can you figure out the picture word puzzles on this page?

1  wear
   long

2  What ↗ must ↘

3  pig pig pig

4  league

5  somewhere

6

7  standing
   mis

8  read

9  stand

10  board

11  the rosie

12  e
    l
    t
    t
    a
    b

Try drawing this phrase:

Stand in line

Can you make up other picture word puzzles using pictures and words of your own?

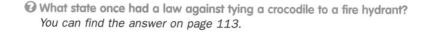

# LAW

❓ What state once had a law against tying a crocodile to a fire hydrant?
*You can find the answer on page 113.*

# Why Do We Need LAWS?

**D**id you ever wonder what your day would be like if there weren't any rules to follow? What if you could go to school any time you wanted? And what if there were no traffic lights or stop signs?

Life would be difficult and confusing without rules. We all need them.

The rules that a government makes are called laws. The government has the power to punish people who break laws. But U.S. laws assume that people are innocent until proven guilty in the courts.

**Laws are made to:**

Protect people from getting hurt

Help people do their jobs properly

Help people to be treated fairly

Help people know how to act in public

Protect animals, the environment, and property

## What Happens When You Break the Law?

**Kids** When children under 18 years old are accused of breaking the law, they are arrested by the police and usually must appear in **juvenile court**. This court has no jury. A judge decides whether or not there is strong enough evidence that the child has broken the law. If there is enough evidence, the judge decides how the child should be punished or helped. Sometimes the judge lets the child go home, but still under the watch of authorities. This is called **probation**. In other cases, a judge may decide that a child cannot be helped by juvenile court and should be tried as an adult in criminal court. This usually happens when a child who has broken the law several times in the past is accused of a very serious crime.

**Adults** When an adult breaks the law, the offense may be minor or it may be serious. An adult who gets a parking ticket, a minor crime, may have to pay a fine or may decide to go to court to argue against the ticket.

An adult who is accused of a serious crime would be arrested and have to appear in court. A trial might result if the evidence against the person seems strong enough. At the trial, a government lawyer, called a **prosecutor**, would present the case against the accused person (called the **defendant**). A person who is **acquitted**, or found "not guilty," is free to go home. If the defendant is **convicted**, or found "guilty," he or she will get a punishment, or a **sentence**, such as having to go to prison for a specific length of time. For very serious crimes, 38 U.S. states allow defendants who are convicted to be sentenced to death.

## LAWS FROM WAY BACK WHEN

Laws change over the years. Here are some laws in different states that people were supposed to follow a long time ago. You can see why these laws are no longer on the books.

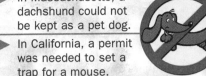

- ▶ In Massachusetts, a dachshund could not be kept as a pet dog.
- ▶ In California, a permit was needed to set a trap for a mouse.
- ▶ In Louisiana, it was illegal to lead a bear around with a rope.
- ▶ In Michigan, it was illegal to hitch a crocodile to a fire hydrant.
- ▶ In Waterville, Maine, it was illegal to blow your nose in public.

## THE RIGHTS AND RESPONSIBILITIES OF ADULTS AND CHILDREN

The Constitution is the basis of all laws in the United States. Specific rights are listed in the Bill of Rights, the first 10 amendments of the Constitution. Among other rights, the Bill of Rights grants Americans freedom of religion and freedom of speech, and the right of anyone who is arrested to have a lawyer and a fair trial.

The United States is a democracy; its citizens are free to disagree with one another and with their government. This is not true in many other countries of the world and is a great privilege. But with it comes the responsibility of being a good citizen. Adults' responsibilities include voting in elections and obeying laws, even those they disagree with. Children's responsibilities include going to school and obeying laws.

## WHEN CHILDREN DON'T HAVE RIGHTS: CHILD LABOR

Like many children around the world, you probably have chores to do. You must go to school, just as adults go to jobs. And you have to do homework. This is all within the law and not an abuse of children's rights.

But in some parts of the world, many children do not attend school. Instead, millions of children work in factories and fields. They may do backbreaking, often dangerous, work from early morning to late at night. UNICEF, the United Nations Children's Fund, estimates that 250 million children around the world work. This is a big problem in Asia, Africa, and Latin America. Even in the United States, from $2\frac{1}{2}$ to $3\frac{1}{2}$ million children work. These are usually the children of migrant workers, people who move from place to place depending on the season, picking fruits and vegetables.

The families of many child laborers could not survive without the money children bring home. This poverty is a big obstacle to stopping child labor.

*Child worker in Peru*

## MONEY AND BUSINESS

❓ **What new money will be printed in the year 2000?**
*You can find the answer on page 116.*

# HISTORY of MONEY

**Why Did People Start Using Money?** People first started using money in order to trade. A farmer who had cattle might want to have salt to preserve meat or cloth to make clothing. For this farmer, a cow became a "medium of exchange"—a way of getting things that the farmer did not make or grow. Cattle became a form of money. Whatever people agreed to use for trade became the earliest kinds of money.

**What Objects Have Been Used as Money Throughout History?** You may be surprised by some of the items that people have used every day as money. What does the form of money tell you about a society and its people?

▶ knives, rice, and spades in China around 3000 B.C.
▶ cattle and clay tablets in Babylonia around 2500 B.C.
▶ wampum (beads) and beaver fur by American Indians of the northeast around A.D. 1500
▶ tobacco by early American colonists around 1650
▶ whales' teeth by the Pacific peoples on the island of Fiji, until the early 1900s

### The First Paper Money

By the time of the Middle Ages in Europe (about A.D. 800-1100), gold had become a popular medium for trade. But gold was heavy and difficult to carry, and European cities and the roads of Europe at that time were dangerous places to carry large amounts of gold. So merchants and goldsmiths began issuing notes promising to pay gold to the person carrying the note. These "promissory notes" were the beginning of paper money in Europe. Paper money was probably also invented in China, where the explorer Marco Polo saw it in the 1280s.

### Why Did Governments Get Interested in Issuing Money?

The first government to make coins that looked alike and use them as money is thought to be the Greek city-state of Lydia in the 7th century B.C. These Lydian coins were actually bean-shaped lumps made from a mixture of gold and silver.

The first government in Europe to issue paper money that looked alike was France in the early 18th century. Governments were interested in issuing money because the money itself had value. If a government could gain control over the manufacture of money, it could increase its own wealth—often simply by making more money.

Today, money throughout the world is issued only by governments. In the United States, the Department of the Treasury and the U.S. Mint make all the paper money and coins we use. Nowadays, we also use checks and credit cards to pay for things we buy. These are not thought of as real money but more as "promises to pay."

# MONEY TALK:
## An Economics Glossary

### ATM or automated teller machine

An electronic machine in a public place where customers of a bank can withdraw cash from their accounts or make deposits by using a special plastic card.

### bank

A business establishment in which people and businesses keep money in savings accounts or checking accounts.

### bond

A certificate issued by a government or a business to a person or business from whom it has borrowed money. A bond promises to pay back the borrowed money with interest.

### CD or certificate of deposit

A kind of bank savings account that earns a fixed rate of interest over a specific period of time.

### cost of living

The average cost of the basic needs of life, including food, clothing, housing, medical care, and other services.

### debt

Something that is owed.

### depression

A period of severe economic decline. In a depression, many people are unemployed, many businesses fail, and people buy less. The last depression in the United States came in the 1930s.

### FDIC or Federal Deposit Insurance Corporation

A government agency created in 1933 to protect deposits when a bank fails. The FDIC guarantees to insure deposits up to $100,000 if they are in a bank that is a member of the FDIC.

### GDP or Gross Domestic Product

The total value of all goods made and services performed within a particular country during a period of time, usually one year.

### goods and services

**Goods** refer to real items such as cars, TVs, VCRs, wristwatches, and clothes. **Services** refer to work done for other people. Firefighters, nurses, waiters, actors, and lawyers all perform services.

### inflation

An increase in the level of prices.

### interest

The amount of money a borrower pays to borrow money. A bank pays interest on a savings account.

### money

Paper and coins issued by the government and used in exchange for all goods and services.

### recession

A period of economic decline. During a recession, more people become unemployed, some businesses fail, and people buy less than usual.

### stock

A share in a corporation. A corporation sells shares to individuals or other companies to raise money. The shares may increase or decrease in value. When the company makes a profit, it pays the stockholder a "dividend," or a part of the money.

◄ Stock certificate

115

# Making Money: THE U.S. MINT

**What Is the U.S. Mint?** The U.S. Mint is responsible for making all U.S. coins. It also safeguards the Treasury Department's stored gold and silver at Fort Knox, KY. The U.S. Mint was founded in 1792 and today is a part of the U.S. Treasury Department. The U.S. Mint's headquarters are in Washington, D.C. Local branches that produce coins are located in Philadelphia, PA; Denver, CO; San Francisco, CA; and West Point, NY.

Another division of the Treasury Department—the Bureau of Engraving and Printing, also in Washington, D.C—designs, engraves, and prints all U.S. paper money.

**What Kinds of Coins Does the Mint Make?** The U.S. Mint makes all the pennies, nickels, dimes, quarters, half dollars, and dollar coins that Americans use each day. These coins are made of a mixture of metals. For example, dimes, quarters, half dollars, and dollar coins look like silver but are a mixture of copper, nickel, and silver.

**Where Can I Get Information About the Mint?** Write to the United States Mint, Customer Service Center, 10003 Derekwood Lane, Lanham, MD 20706. Telephone: (202) 283-COIN. The Mint also offers free public tours at some of its facilities.

**Whose Portraits Are on Our Money?** On the front of all U.S. paper money are portraits of presidents and other famous Americans. Presidents also appear on the most commonly used coins. Starting in 1999, five new quarters will be coined every year for 10 years. Each one will feature the design of a different state on the back, with George Washington on the front. The quarters are being introduced in the same order as states entered the Union, starting with Delaware.

| Denomination | | Portrait |
|---|---|---|
| 1¢ | | Abraham Lincoln, 16th U.S. President |
| 5¢ | | Thomas Jefferson, 3rd U.S. President |
| 10¢ | | Franklin Delano Roosevelt, 32nd U.S. President |
| 25¢ |  | George Washington, 1st U.S. President |
| $1 | | George Washington, 1st U.S. President |
| $2 | | Thomas Jefferson, 3rd U.S. President |
| $5 | | Abraham Lincoln, 16th U.S. President |
| $10 | | Alexander Hamilton, 1st U.S. Treasury Secretary |
| $20 | | Andrew Jackson, 7th U.S. President |
| $50 | | Ulysses S. Grant, 18th U.S. President |
| $100 | | Benjamin Franklin, colonial inventor and U.S. patriot |

**WEB SITE** Read more about money at http://www.ustreas.gov/kids

**Paper Money.** In 1996 the U.S. Treasury printed a new $100 bill with many features to help prevent counterfeiting. A new $50 bill was printed in 1997, and a new $20 bill was issued in 1998. In 2000, new $10 and $5 bills will be issued.

# How Much MONEY Is in CIRCULATION?

As of March 31, 1998, the total amount of money in circulation in the United States came to $474,978,795,491 (nearly 475 billion dollars). About 24 billion dollars was in coins, the rest in paper money. The chart below shows the number of bills of each kind in circulation.

| Kind (Denomination) | Number of Bills in Circulation | Value of Money in Circulation |
|---|---|---|
| $1 bills | 6,428,507,478 | $6,428,507,478 |
| $2 bills | 567,147,372 | $1,134,294,744 |
| $5 bills | 1,489,249,459 | $7,446,247,295 |
| $10 bills | 1,328,332,102 | $13,283,321,020 |
| $20 bills | 4,135,807,748 | $82,716,154,960 |
| $50 bills | 933,741,275 | $46,687,063,750 |
| $100 bills | 2,926,001,233 | $292,600,123,300 |

# What Are EXCHANGE RATES?

When one country exports goods to another, the payment from the country buying the goods must be changed into the currency of the country selling them. An exchange rate is the price of one currency in terms of another. For example, 1 U.S. dollar could buy about $5\frac{5}{8}$ French francs in 1999. Exchange rates change as a nation's economy becomes stronger or weaker.

The chart below compares the exchange rates in 1970 and 1999 between the U.S. dollar and the currency of five of the country's biggest trading partners. The more foreign money the dollar can buy, the better the exchange rate for Americans.

| $1 Bought | | |
|---|---|---|
| COUNTRY | IN 1970 | IN 1999 |
| France | 6 francs | $5\frac{5}{8}$ francs |
| Germany | $3\frac{3}{5}$ marks | $1\frac{2}{3}$ marks |
| Great Britain | $\frac{2}{5}$ pound | $\frac{3}{5}$ pound |
| Italy | 600 lire | 1,700 lire |
| Japan | 350 yen | 114 yen |

$5 — United States   570 Yen — Japan

**DID YOU KNOW?** In January 1999, 11 European countries, including France, Germany, and Italy, began using the euro, a new currency, for some purposes. On July 1, 2002, the 11 countries will change over completely to the euro. The franc, mark, and lira will no longer be "real" money.

# Why BUDGETS Are Helpful

A budget is a plan that estimates how much money a person, a business, or a government will receive during a particular period of time, how much money will be spent and what it will be spent on, and how much money will be left over (if any).

## A Family Budget

Does your family have a budget? Do you know what your family spends money on? Do you know where your family's income comes from? The chart below shows some sources of income and typical yearly expenses for a family's budget.

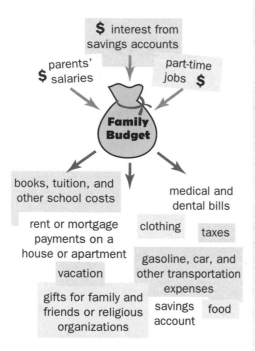

$ interest from savings accounts

parents' $ salaries

part-time jobs $

Family Budget

books, tuition, and other school costs

medical and dental bills

rent or mortgage payments on a house or apartment

clothing

taxes

vacation

gasoline, car, and other transportation expenses

gifts for family and friends or religious organizations

savings account

food

## A Balanced Budget

A budget is **balanced** when the amount of money you receive equals the amount of money you spend. A budget is **unbalanced** when the amount of money you spend is greater than the amount of money you have.

## MAKING YOUR OWN BUDGET

Imagine that you are given a weekly allowance of $10. With this money you must pay for things like snacks and magazines and also try to save up for special things you may want. A budget will help you plan how to do this. Here are examples of items you might want to put in your budget:

### Possible Purchases and Cost
Snacks: $.75 each
Video movie rental: $3.00
Magazine: $2.00

### Savings:
For gifts: $.50–$3.00
For something special for yourself (like a basketball, a compact disk, a computer game, or concert tickets): $1.00 or more.

On the lines below, list the items you want along with their price. You may also add any other items that interest you—and their prices. And don't forget to include any money you want to save.

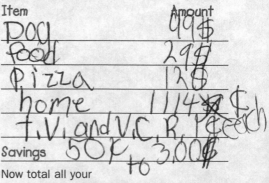

| Item | Amount |
|---|---|
| Dog Food | 99$ |
| | 299 |
| Pizza | 12$ |
| home | 1114$ each |
| T.V. and V.C.R. | each |
| Savings | 50¢ to 3.00$ |

Now total all your purchases and savings: _____

**Is your budget balanced?** Is the amount you plan to spend and save equal to the amount of your "income" ($10)?

# The U.S. BUDGET

**W**here does the U.S. government's income come from? And what are the government's biggest expenses?

## WHERE DOES THE U.S. GOVERNMENT GET MONEY?

Here is how the U.S. government got its money in the 1998 budget year.

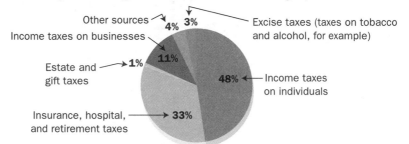

Other sources — 4%  3% — Excise taxes (taxes on tobacco and alcohol, for example)

Income taxes on businesses —

Estate and gift taxes — 1%  11%

48% — Income taxes on individuals

Insurance, hospital, and retirement taxes — 33%

## WHERE DOES THE U.S. GOVERNMENT SPEND MONEY?

Here is how the U.S. government spent its money in the 1998 budget year.

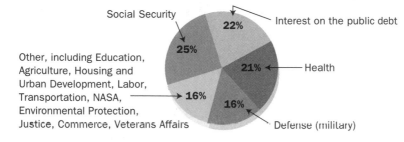

Social Security  22% — Interest on the public debt

25%

Other, including Education, Agriculture, Housing and Urban Development, Labor, Transportation, NASA, Environmental Protection, Justice, Commerce, Veterans Affairs — 16%

21% — Health

16% — Defense (military)

## THE UNITED STATES HAS BALANCED ITS BUDGET

The U.S. government has been trying to balance its budget for a long time. Every year from 1969 to 1997 the government spent more money than it took in through taxes. The difference between the higher amount spent and the amount taken in each year is called the **budget deficit**. Most economists say that paying interest on a large debt hurts the economy. Cutting the debt may mean raising taxes or cutting programs that many citizens depend on. But the budget deficit has been going down since 1993. And in 1998, for the first time since 1969, the U.S. took in more money than it spent. The United States had a budget **surplus**.

| YEAR | $ TAKEN IN | $ SPENT | DEFICIT |
|---|---|---|---|
| 1992 | $1.092 trillion | $1.382 trillion | $–290 billion |
| 1993 | $1.153 trillion | $1.408 trillion | $–255 billion |
| 1994 | $1.257 trillion | $1.460 trillion | $–203 billion |
| 1995 | $1.350 trillion | $1.514 trillion | $–164 billion |
| 1996 | $1.453 trillion | $1.560 trillion | $–107 billion |
| 1997 | $1.579 trillion | $1.602 trillion | $–23 billion |
| 1998 | $1.721 trillion | $1.651 trillion | $70 billion (surplus) |

MONEY AND BUSINESS

# What Do AMERICANS BUY?

The chart below shows how Americans spent their money in 1997.

| CATEGORY | AMOUNT SPENT |
|---|---|
| Medical and dental care | $957,300,000,000 |
| Food and tobacco | $832,300,000,000 |
| Housing | $829,800,000,000 |
| Transportation expenses (such as cars, gasoline, and train, bus, and plane tickets) | $636,400,000,000 |
| Household expenses (such as telephone, furniture, electricity, kitchen supplies) | $620,700,000,000 |
| Recreation (such as books, magazines, toys, videos, sports events, amusement parks) | $462,900,000,000 |
| Personal business expenses (such as bank charges, lawyers) | $459,100,000,000 |
| Clothing and jewelry | $353,300,000,000 |
| Religious and charitable contributions | $157,600,000,000 |
| School tuition and other educational expenses | $129,400,000,000 |
| Personal care (such as haircuts, health clubs) | $79,400,000,000 |

# Leading BUSINESSES in the United States

The following list shows the leading American business in many different categories and the money each company took in during 1998.

**Airplanes**
Boeing, $5,154,000,000

**Banks**
BankAmerica, $50,777,000,000

**Beverages**
Pepsi-Co, $22,348,000,000

**Cars and Other Motor Vehicles**
General Motors, $161,315,000,000

**Chemicals**
E. I. du Pont de Nemours, $39,130,000,000

**Clothing**
Nike, $9,553,000,000

**Computers and Office Equipment**
IBM, $81,667,000,000

**Electronics and Electrical Equipment**
General Electric, $100,694,000,000

**Entertainment**
Walt Disney, $22,976,000,000

**Food and Drug Stores**
Kroger, $28,203,000,000

**Industrial and Farm Equipment**
Caterpillar, $20,977,000,000

**Medicines and Drugs**
Merck, $26,898,000,000

**Petroleum Refining**
Exxon, $100,697,000,000

**Retail Stores**
Wal-Mart Stores, $139,208,000,000

**Rubber and Plastic Products**
Goodyear Tire & Rubber, $12,648,700,000

**Soaps and Cosmetics**
Procter & Gamble, $37,154,000,000

**Telecommunications**
AT&T, $53,588,000,000

**Toys, Sporting Goods**
Mattel, $4,782,000,000

# What Jobs Do Americans Have?

How are Americans employed? Each year the U.S. Department of Labor publishes information on employment in the United States. The following chart shows the number of men and women who worked full-time in different kinds of jobs during 1998. The column with weekly earnings shows the mid-range of earnings in 1997. This means that many people in each kind of job earned more than this amount and many earned less.

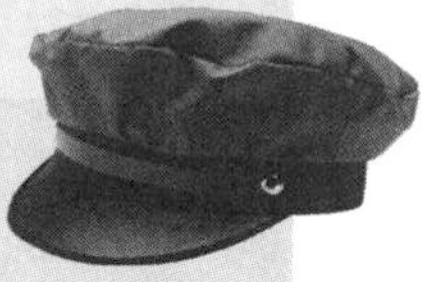

| Jobs | Number of Workers | Weekly Earnings |
|------|-------------------|-----------------|
| **Managers and professionals** (for example, business executives and supervisors, doctors, lawyers, teachers, nurses) | | |
| Men | 19,867,000 | $875 |
| Women | 19,070,000 | $632 |
| **Sales people, technicians, administrative workers** (including clerical workers) | | |
| Men | 13,792,000 | $588 |
| Women | 24,728,000 | $403 |
| **People who repair things, precision workers, crafts people** | | |
| Men | 13,208,000 | $569 |
| Women | 1,203,000 | $382 |
| **Machine operators and laborers, assemblers** | | |
| Men | 13,769,000 | $436 |
| Women | 4,487,000 | $313 |
| **Service jobs** (for example, police and firefighters, waiters, cooks, hairdressers) | | |
| Men | 7,222,000 | $372 |
| Women | 10,614,000 | $282 |
| **Farming, forestry, and fishing** | | |
| Men | 2,835,000 | $302 |
| Women | 668,000 | $257 |

## Occupations That Are Growing

Below is a list of some of the fastest-growing occupations in the United States:

**Computer science field:** computer programmers and scientists, systems analysts, desktop publishing specialists

**Health and medical field:** home health aides, medical assistants and secretaries, physical and occupational therapy assistants, technicians

**Teaching:** teachers' aides, high school teachers, and special education teachers

**Human services:** social workers, child care workers, gardeners and groundskeepers

**Paralegals**

# What the U.S. Buys and Sells

When companies or countries buy and sell their products or services to other companies or countries, we call this trade. Exports are goods that one country *sells* to another country. Imports are goods that one country *buys* from another country. The United States trades with many other countries. It exports and imports goods.

## EXPORTS ◀ 🗺 VALUE

| | |
|---|---|
| Electrical machinery | $65.4 billion |
| Motor vehicles | $53.4 billion |
| Farm products | $50.6 billion |
| Airplanes and parts | $50.3 billion |
| Computers and office machinery | $40.7 billion |

## IMPORTS ▶ 🗺 VALUE

| | |
|---|---|
| Motor vehicles | $121.3 billion |
| Electrical machinery | $79.4 billion |
| Computers and office machinery | $76.8 billion |
| Clothing | $53.7 billion |
| Crude oil | $37.5 billion |

**What Does the United States Sell to Other Countries?** The chart above shows some of the major products that the United States exported in 1998. In 1998, the total value of all U.S. exports was $683.0 billion.

**What Does the United States Buy From Other Countries?** The chart above shows some of the major products that the United States imported in 1998. Note that the United States exports *and* imports motor vehicles. In 1998, the total value of all U.S. imports was $913.8 billion.

**Who Are America's Leading Trading Partners?** In 1998, the countries with which the United States traded most were: Canada, Japan, Mexico, China, Germany, and Great Britain.

**Why Do Americans Buy Foreign-made Products?** Americans buy products from abroad that they do not make for themselves or that are less expensive or better-made than products made in the United States. For example, the United States imports most of its clothing partly because foreign-made products are less costly.

**What Happens If a Country Imports More Than It Exports?** When the United States sells to other countries (or exports), other countries pay the United States for the goods. When the United States buys from other countries (or imports), it makes payments to them. It is best for a country to export more than it imports, or to export and import an equal amount. When a country imports more than it exports, it has what is called a **trade deficit**. The United States imports more than it exports and has a trade deficit. That means it is spending more money abroad for foreign-made products than it is getting from selling American-made products overseas.

❓Can you name all three "Star Wars" films of the 1970s and 1980s?
*You can find the answer on page 124.*

Mulan

Doctor Dolittle

## 20 MOVIE HITS of 1998

Titanic (PG-13)
  Armageddon (PG-13)
The Waterboy (PG-13)
  Doctor Dolittle (PG-13)
Godzilla (PG-13)
  A Bug's Life (G)
The Truman Show (PG)
  Mulan (G)
The Mask of Zorro (PG-13)
  Antz (PG)
The Rugrats Movie (G)
  The Wedding Singer (PG-13)
Lost in Space (PG-13)
  The Parent Trap (PG)
Ever After (PG)
  You've Got Mail (PG)
The Prince of Egypt (PG)
  Mouse Hunt (PG)
Madeline (PG)
  Spice World (PG)

## 20 Popular KIDS' VIDEOS of 1998

Hercules
  Sleeping Beauty
The Little Mermaid: The Special Edition
  Anastasia
The Hunchback of Notre Dame
  The Jungle Book: 30th Anniversary
Peter Pan:
45th Anniversary Limited Edition
  Pooh's Grand Adventure
Elmopalooza!
  Creature Comforts
Bambi
  Swan Princess: Escape From
  Castle Mountain
Batman & Mr. Freeze: Subzero
  Cat's Don't Dance
The Lion King
  Pocahontas II:
  Journey to a New World
Melody Time
  Beauty and the Beast:
  The Enchanted Christmas
The Black Cauldron
  Belle's Magical World

# Some Popular MOVIES

*Snow White and the Seven Dwarfs* **(1937)** This Disney classic was the first full-length animated movie ever released. Since the late 1980s, Disney's new animated movies, such as *Beauty and the Beast, Aladdin, The Lion King,* and *Pocahontas,* have been popular with adults almost as much as with kids.

*The Sound of Music* **(1965)** Winner of five Academy Awards, including Best Picture, this musical tells the story of Maria Von Trapp, who becomes the governess to seven children and falls in love with their father. (G)

*Star Wars* **(1977)** Luke Skywalker, Princess Leia, and others battle Darth Vader and the forces of evil in a thriller set in outer space. The sequels *The Empire Strikes Back* (1980) and *The Return of the Jedi* (1983) were also huge hits. In 1999 a new Star Wars film came out, *Episode I: The Phantom Menace* (PG).

*E.T.: The Extra-Terrestrial* **(1982)** A heart-warming tale about a boy and a space alien whose deep relationship helps them both to grow. (G)

*Home Alone* **(1990)** An eight-year-old kid outwits the bad guys all by himself. (PG)

*Jurassic Park* **(1993)** A thriller about dinosaurs created in a lab from DNA found in fossils and put on a Caribbean island as the attraction in a park. (PG-13)

*Babe* **(1995)** This movie about an orphan pig who teaches himself how to be a sheepdog was nominated for seven Academy Awards, and won for Best Visual Effects. (G)

*Toy Story* **(1995)** The first full-length movie made entirely with computer animation, *Toy Story* stars the voices of Tom Hanks as Woody, a sheriff action figure, and Tim Allen as Buzz Lightyear, a space-traveling action figure. Both toys belong to six-year-old Andy, and compete to be Andy's favorite toy, leading to a wild and crazy adventure. (G)

# *The Wizard of Oz*

## STILL MAGICAL AFTER 60 YEARS

*The Wizard of Oz*, made in 1939, is so well-known that if you said "Follow the yellow brick road," almost everybody would think of this movie.

Based on a book by L. Frank Baum, it is the story of Dorothy, a Kansas farm girl. She is picked up by a tornado and dropped into a magical land with a talking scarecrow, a tin woodsman, a cowardly lion, and good and bad witches.

The movie was nominated for six Academy Awards, including Best Picture. It won two awards, for Best Original Score and Best Song ("Over the Rainbow"). That song was almost cut out of the movie because some people thought it slowed down the action. Judy Garland, who played Dorothy, won a special award for her acting.

*The Wizard of Oz*

# TELEVISION RATINGS

In 1997 the television industry came up with ratings to help parents choose programs that are OK for kids to watch.

The ratings may be followed by a letter such as (V) for violence or (L) for bad language.

| | |
|---|---|
| **TV-Y** | For all children—including those age 6 or younger. |
| **TV-Y7** | For children over age 6, especially those who can tell the difference between what is real and what is make-believe. |
| **TV-G** | General audience—suitable for all ages. Program has little or no violence. |
| **TV-PG** | Parental guidance suggested. Program may contain violence or bad language. |
| **TV-14** | Parents strongly warned. Program contains very violent or adult material. |
| **TV-M** | For adults—program may not be suitable for children under 17. |

## Popular TV SHOWS in 1998-1999

*(Source: Nielsen Media Research)*

**AGES 6-11**

1. Sabrina, the Teenage Witch
2. Boy Meets World
   Brother's Keeper (tied)
4. Two of a Kind
5. Wonderful World of Disney
6. The Simpsons
7. Family Guy
8. Pokemon
   The PJs (tied)
10. Futurama
    Power Rangers: Lost Galaxy (tied)

**AGES 12-17**

1. Family Guy
2. Sabrina, the Teenage Witch
   The Simpsons (tied)
4. Boy Meets World
5. Brother's Keeper
6. That 70's Show
7. Dawson's Creek
8. 7th Heaven
9. Two of a Kind
10. Friends
    Futurama (tied)

 **DID YOU KNOW?** *"Sabrina the Teenage Witch," starring Melissa Joan Hart, isn't the first TV series to feature Sabrina and her friends and family. An animated series with the same name was shown on Saturday mornings in the '70s.*

*Melissa Joan Hart*

## Popular VIDEO GAMES in 1998

| | | |
|---|---|---|
| Goldeneye 007–*Nintendo 64* | Tekken 3–*Playstation* | 6 in 1 Game Pack–*Genesis* |
| Gran Turismo Racing–*Playstation* | Super Mario Kart–*Super Nintendo* | Toy Story–*Genesis* |
| Banjo-Kazooie–*Nintendo 64* | Super Mario All-Stars–*Super Nintendo* | Lion King–*Super Nintendo* |
| | Resident Evil 2–*Playstation* | |

# Birthdays of Celebrities

**H**ere are the birthdays of your favorite stars, along with famous sports heroes, writers, and public figures.

## JANUARY

| | |
|---|---|
| Mel Gibson | Jan. 3, 1956 |
| Rowan Atkinson | Jan. 6, 1955 |
| A.J. McLean | Jan. 9, 1978 |
| Jim Carrey | Jan. 17, 1962 |
| Beverley Mitchell | Jan. 22, 1981 |
| Tiffani-Amber Thiessen | Jan. 23, 1974 |
| Wayne Gretzky | Jan. 26, 1961 |
| Nick Carter | Jan. 28, 1980 |
| Joey Fatone | Jan. 28, 1977 |
| Elijah Wood | Jan. 28, 1981 |
| Andrew Keegan | Jan. 29, 1979 |
| Oprah Winfrey | Jan. 29, 1954 |
| Justin Timberlake | Jan. 31, 1981 |

## FEBRUARY

| | |
|---|---|
| Natalie Imbruglia | Feb. 4, 1975 |
| Garth Brooks | Feb. 7, 1962 |
| David Gallagher | Feb. 9, 1985 |
| Jennifer Aniston | Feb. 11, 1969 |
| Brandy | Feb. 11, 1979 |
| Sheryl Crow | Feb. 11, 1963 |
| Judy Blume | Feb. 12, 1938 |
| Matt Groening | Feb. 15, 1954 |
| LeVar Burton | Feb. 16, 1957 |
| Michael Jordan | Feb. 17, 1963 |
| Brian Littrell | Feb. 20, 1975 |
| Jennifer Love Hewitt | Feb. 21, 1979 |
| Drew Barrymore | Feb. 22, 1975 |
| Chelsea Clinton | Feb. 27, 1980 |

## MARCH

| | |
|---|---|
| Jake Lloyd | March 5, 1989 |
| Shaquille O'Neal | March 6, 1972 |
| James Van Der Beek | March 8, 1977 |
| Billy Crystal | March 14, 1947 |
| Taylor Hanson | March 14, 1983 |
| Rosie O'Donnell | March 21, 1962 |
| Keri Russell | March 23, 1976 |
| Mariah Carey | March 27, 1970 |
| Celine Dion | March 30, 1968 |
| Al Gore | March 31, 1948 |
| Ewan McGregor | March 31, 1971 |

## APRIL

| | |
|---|---|
| Eddie Murphy | April 3, 1961 |
| Rick Schroder | April 3, 1970 |
| Maya Angelou | April 4, 1928 |
| Beverly Cleary | April 12, 1916 |
| Claire Danes | April 12, 1979 |
| Sarah Michelle Gellar | April 14, 1977 |
| Melissa Joan Hart | April 18, 1976 |
| Jerry Seinfeld | April 29, 1955 |

## MAY

| | |
|---|---|
| Jewel | May 3, 1974 |
| Lance Bass | May 4, 1979 |
| George Clooney | May 6, 1961 |
| George Lucas | May 14, 1944 |
| Madeleine Albright | May 15, 1937 |
| Cher | May 20, 1946 |
| Ricky Williams | May 21, 1977 |
| Drew Carey | May 23, 1961 |
| Lauryn Hill | May 25, 1975 |
| Mike Myers | May 25, 1963 |
| Sally Ride | May 26, 1951 |
| Clint Eastwood | May 31, 1930 |

## JUNE

| | |
|---|---|
| Alanis Morissette | June 1, 1974 |
| Scott Wolf | June 4, 1968 |
| Liam Neeson | June 7, 1952 |
| Natalie Portman | June 9, 1981 |
| Tara Lipinski | June 10, 1982 |
| Tim Allen | June 13, 1953 |
| Ashley Olsen | June 13, 1986 |
| Mary-Kate Olsen | June 13, 1986 |
| Courteney Cox | June 15, 1964 |
| Prince William | June 21, 1982 |
| John Elway | June 28, 1960 |

## JULY

| | |
|---|---|
| Tom Cruise | July 3, 1962 |
| Michelle Kwan | July 7, 1980 |
| Tom Hanks | July 9, 1956 |
| Fred Savage | July 9, 1976 |
| Bill Cosby | July 12, 1937 |
| Harrison Ford | July 13, 1942 |
| Matthew Fox | July 14, 1966 |
| Barry Sanders | July 16, 1968 |
| Robin Williams | July 21, 1952 |
| Jennifer Lopez | July 24, 1970 |
| Matt LeBlanc | July 25, 1967 |
| Brad Renfro | July 25, 1982 |
| Sandra Bullock | July 26, 1964 |
| Lisa Kudrow | July 30, 1963 |
| Arnold Schwarzenegger | July 30, 1947 |

## AUGUST

| | |
|---|---|
| Jeff Gordon | August 4, 1971 |
| David Duchovny | August 7, 1960 |
| Joshua "JC" Chasez | August 8, 1976 |
| Gillian Anderson | August 9, 1968 |
| Whitney Houston | August 9, 1963 |
| Ann Martin | August 12, 1955 |
| Pete Sampras | August 12, 1971 |
| Magic Johnson | August 14, 1959 |
| Ben Affleck | August 15, 1972 |
| Bill Clinton | August 19, 1946 |
| Matthew Perry | August 19, 1969 |
| Howie Dorough | August 22, 1973 |
| Kobe Bryant | August 23, 1978 |
| Shania Twain | August 28, 1965 |
| Michael Jackson | August 29, 1958 |
| Cameron Diaz | August 30, 1972 |

## SEPTEMBER

| | |
|---|---|
| Gloria Estefan | Sept. 1, 1957 |
| Devon Sawa | Sept. 7, 1978 |
| Jonathan Taylor Thomas | Sept. 8, 1981 |
| Adam Sandler | Sept. 9, 1966 |
| Prince Harry | Sept. 15, 1984 |
| Bill Murray | Sept. 21, 1950 |
| Bruce Springsteen | Sept. 23, 1949 |
| Will Smith | Sept. 25, 1968 |
| Se Ri Pak | Sept. 28, 1977 |
| Gwyneth Paltrow | Sept. 28, 1973 |
| Martina Hingis | Sept. 30, 1980 |

## OCTOBER

| | |
|---|---|
| Mark McGwire | Oct. 1, 1963 |
| Neve Campbell | Oct. 3, 1973 |
| Kevin Richardson | Oct. 3, 1972 |
| Alicia Silverstone | Oct. 4, 1976 |
| Grant Hill | Oct. 5, 1972 |
| Kate Winslet | Oct. 5, 1975 |
| Matt Damon | Oct. 8, 1970 |
| R. L. Stine | Oct. 8, 1943 |
| Brett Favre | Oct. 10, 1969 |
| Luke Perry | Oct. 11, 1966 |
| Chris Kirkpatrick | Oct. 17, 1971 |
| Zachary Hanson | Oct. 22, 1985 |
| Monica | Oct. 24, 1980 |
| Hillary Rodham Clinton | Oct. 26, 1947 |
| Terrell Davis | Oct. 28, 1972 |
| Bill Gates | Oct. 28, 1955 |

## NOVEMBER

| | |
|---|---|
| Sinbad | Nov. 10, 1956 |
| Leonardo DiCaprio | Nov. 11, 1974 |
| Calista Flockhart | Nov. 11, 1964 |
| Ryan Gosling | Nov. 12, 1980 |
| David Schwimmer | Nov. 12, 1966 |
| Sammy Sosa | Nov. 12, 1968 |
| Whoopi Goldberg | Nov. 13 1949 |
| Isaac Hanson | Nov. 17, 1980 |
| Ken Griffey, Jr. | Nov. 21, 1969 |

## DECEMBER

| | |
|---|---|
| Britney Spears | Dec. 2, 1981 |
| Brendan Fraser | Dec. 3, 1967 |
| Brad Pitt | Dec. 18, 1964 |
| Steven Spielberg | Dec. 18, 1947 |
| Samuel L. Jackson | Dec. 21, 1948 |
| Tiger Woods | Dec. 30, 1975 |

## PEOPLE to KNOW

Hundreds of young actors and actresses appear in TV shows and movies. But some really stand out. Here are two of today's most popular stars.

# BRANDY

*Brandy*

Born on February 11, 1979, Brandy Norwood has had more success in 20 years than most performers have in a lifetime. This singer and actress decided to become a musician when she was only four years old. Brandy's first single came out when she was 11, and by the time she was 15, she had one of the top 10 songs in the country.

Her 1994 hit single, "I Wanna Be Down," led to a hit album ("Brandy") in 1995. Brandy then went to work on her second smash album, "Never Say Never," which came out in 1998. She not only performed on this one, but produced it, too!

On TV, Brandy first appeared in *Thea,* then was chosen to star in *Moesha.* In 1997 she played the lead in the TV musical *Cinderella,* co-starring Whitney Houston.

In 1998, Brandy made her first movie, *I Still Know What You Did Last Summer*, playing Jennifer Love Hewitt's best friend. Confident about herself, Brandy told an interviewer, "This is my first movie, but you're gonna think I've done 20."

Brandy has big plans for more albums, more TV, and more movies. Expect to see a lot more of her. Though she's a big hit already, her career is just beginning!

# ADAM SANDLER

Adam Sandler's first comedy album was called *They're All Gonna Laugh at You!* The title got it right. Listeners did laugh... and laugh... and laugh.

Born in Brooklyn, New York, on September 9, 1966, Sandler grew up in New Hampshire. When he was 17 years old, he tried stand-up comedy for the first time at a comedy club in Boston. He continued performing while a student at New York University. He graduated from there in 1991.

While still in college, Sandler was "discovered" by comedian Dennis Miller. Miller helped him get a job on TV's *Saturday Night Live* as a writer and, once in a while, as a performer. Sandler became a regular on that show.

Who *is* Adam Sandler? Is he a comedian? He's done comedy albums. Is he an actor? He appeared in the movies *Coneheads* and *Airheads*. Is he a writer? He co-wrote and starred in *Billy Madison*. *Happy Gilmore*, which he also wrote with a partner, came next.

In 1998, his comedy *The Wedding Singer,* co-starring Drew Barrymore, was a big hit. Then came *The Waterboy,* an even bigger hit. It brought in more than $39 million in its opening weekend alone. So Sandler is a huge money maker, too.

If his winning streak continues, audiences will be laughing at Adam Sandler for a long, long time. And who knows what talents will show up next.

*Adam Sandler*

128

# MUSEUMS

❷ Where can you find a museum all about Elvis Presley?
*You can find the answer on page 130.*

## Visiting the Past and the Future

If you like to learn new things and have fun at the same time, museums are the places to go. Some museums, such as children's museums, have exhibits on many subjects, and some have exhibits from which you can learn a lot about one subject. In another kind of museum, you can walk in a village and watch people from an earlier century work and go about their daily lives. This type of museum is called a historic restoration.

The ancient Greeks were the first people to have public museums open to everyone. The oldest museum in the United States in continuous existence is the Charleston Museum, founded in South Carolina in 1773. The United States now has more than 7,700 museums. A few children's museums, ethnic museums, museums of entertainment, and historic restorations are listed here.

Many libraries have a *Directory of Museums in the United States*, and some museums have home pages on the Internet.

## Children's Museums

**Children's Museum,** Boston, Massachusetts. Has a full-size Japanese house, a Latino market, plus displays on Native Americans.
**WEB SITE** *http://www.bostonkids.org*

**Children's Museum of Indianapolis,** Indianapolis, Indiana. Has natural science exhibits, including a walk-through limestone cave; computer center; and an old-fashioned railway depot with a 19th-century locomotive.
**WEB SITE** *http://www.childrensmuseum.org*

**Children's Museum of Manhattan,** New York, New York. Hands-on displays of interest to kids on natural history, science, and art.
**WEB SITE** *http://www.cmom.org*

**Children's Museum,** Portland, Oregon. Hands-on displays allow kids 10 and under to shop for dinner, prepare a feast, or create with clay.

**Los Angeles Children's Museum,** Los Angeles, California. Exhibits on health and city life; has a TV studio.
**WEB SITE** *http://www.lacm.org*

# Museums of Entertainment

**Country Music Hall of Fame and Museum,** Nashville, Tennessee
Celebrates country music's history and stars.

**Graceland,** Memphis, Tennessee
The 14-acre estate of the King of Rock 'n' Roll, Elvis Presley.

**Museum of Television and Radio,** New York, New York
Contains 15,000 radio and 35,000 TV tapes from the 1920s
to the present.

## Ethnic Museums

Here are some museums that show the culture and history of groups of people who share traditions and customs.

**Arthur M. Sackler Gallery** and the **Freer Gallery of Art,** Washington, D.C.
Displays art from China, Japan, India, and other Asian countries.

**California African-American Museum,** Los Angeles, California
Displays art, books, and photographs on African-American culture.

**Heard Museum,** Phoenix, Arizona
Displays art by Native Americans and artists from Africa, Asia, Oceania, and the Upper Amazon.

**University of Texas Institute of Texan Cultures,** San Antonio, Texas
Shows material from 24 ethnic groups.

**Jewish Museum,** New York, New York
Has exhibits covering 40 centuries of Jewish history and culture.

**Museum of African-American History,** Detroit, Michigan
Features a large model of a slave ship, inventions by African-Americans, music by black composers, and the space suit worn by the first U.S. black female astronaut.

**National Museum of the American Indian,** New York, New York
Has displays on the ways of life and the history of Native Americans.

**DID YOU KNOW?**

You can find out about many of the pioneers who helped to develop the American West at the National Cowboy Hall of Fame and Western Heritage Center. It's at 1700 NE 63rd Street in Oklahoma City, Oklahoma.

**WEB SITE** http://www.cowboyhalloffame.org

**The Women's Museum,**
Dallas, Texas

One of the newest museums in the United States is expected to open in the fall of 1999 in Dallas, Texas. It celebrates the accomplishments of American women—as professionals and as leaders. One highlight of The Women's Museum is an electronic quilt. It is not made out of fabric, but out of video monitors. This super-modern museum is located inside an old and historic building. Built in 1909, it was used as an opera house at night and used for cattle auctions during the day. The building has been completely modernized on the inside.

# Museums of Natural History

**M**useums of natural history contain exhibits of things found in nature. These include animals, rocks, and fossils. Natural history museums allow you close-up looks at life-size models of coal mines, dinosaurs, desert and prairie life, or even whales.

**Academy of Natural Sciences of Philadelphia**, Philadelphia, Pennsylvania
**American Museum of Natural History**, New York, New York
**Carnegie Museum of Natural History**, Pittsburgh, Pennsylvania
**Denver Museum of Natural History**, Denver, Colorado
**Field Museum of Natural History**, Chicago, Illinois
**Museum of Comparative Zoology**, Cambridge, Massachusetts
**Museum of the Rockies**, Bozeman, Montana
**National Museum of Natural History**, Smithsonian Institution, Washington, D.C.
**New Mexico Museum of Natural History and Science**, Albuquerque, New Mexico
**University of Nebraska State Museum**, Lincoln, Nebraska

## Historic Restorations

**T**hese houses or parts of cities or towns have been restored to look the way they did many years ago.

**Colonial Williamsburg,**
Williamsburg, Virginia —
a restored 18th-century capital
(see photo below).

**Henry Ford Museum and Greenfield Village,**
Dearborn, Michigan — more than 80 historic buildings.

**Mystic Seaport,**
Mystic, Connecticut — re-creation of a New England whaling village, including ships and a museum.

**Old Sturbridge Village,**
Sturbridge, Massachusetts —
re-creation of a New England
farming community of the 1830s.

**Plimoth Plantation, Inc.,**
Plymouth, Massachusetts —
re-creation of the Pilgrims' first
settlement in the New World.

**St. Augustine Historic District,**
St. Augustine, Florida — includes the Oldest House (Gonzalez-Alvarez House), from the 1500s.

❓ **Which ballet are you most likely to see staged in December?**
*You can find the answer on page 136.*

# MUSIC and MUSIC MAKERS

## POP MUSIC

Pop music (short for popular music) puts more emphasis on melody (tune) than does rock and has a softer beat.
**Famous pop singers:** Frank Sinatra, Barbra Streisand, Whitney Houston, Madonna, Michael Jackson, Mariah Carey, Boyz II Men, Brandy, Celine Dion.

## RAP MUSIC

Rap is music in which words are spoken or chanted at a fast pace and are backed by music that emphasizes strong rhythm rather than melody. It was created by African-Americans in inner cities. Rap lyrics show strong feelings and may be about anger and violence. **Famous rappers:** Coolio, LL Cool J, TLC, The Fugees.

## JAZZ

Jazz has its roots in the work songs, spirituals, and folk music of African-Americans. It began in the South in the early 1900s. **Famous jazz artists:** Louis Armstrong, Fats Waller, Jelly Roll Morton, Duke Ellington, Benny Goodman, Billie Holiday, Sarah Vaughan, Ella Fitzgerald, Dizzy Gillespie, Charlie Parker, Miles Davis, Thelonious Monk, Wynton Marsalis.

## ROCK (also known as Rock 'n' Roll)

Rock music, which started in the 1950s, is based on black rhythm and blues and country music. It often uses electronic instruments and equipment. Folk rock, punk, heavy metal, and alternative music are types of rock music. **Famous rock musicians:** Elvis Presley, Bob Dylan, the Beatles, Janis Joplin, The Rolling Stones, Joni Mitchell, Bruce Springsteen, Aerosmith, R.E.M., Pearl Jam, Alanis Morissette, Jewel.

## BLUES

The music called "the blues" developed from work songs and religious folk songs (spirituals) sung by African-Americans. It was introduced early in the 1900s by African-American musicians. Blues songs are usually sad. (A type of jazz is also called "the blues.")
**Famous blues performers:** Ma Rainey, Bessie Smith, Billie Holiday, Buddy Guy, B. B. King, Muddy Waters.

# TOP ALBUMS of 1998

1. *Titanic*/Soundtrack, Various Artists
2. *Let's Talk About Love*, Celine Dion
3. *Backstreet Boys*, Backstreet Boys
4. *Come On Over*, Shania Twain
5. *'N Sync*, 'N Sync

*Celine Dion*

## COUNTRY MUSIC

American country music is based on Southern mountain music. Blues, jazz, and other musical styles have also influenced it. Country music became popular through the *Grand Ole Opry* radio show in Nashville, Tennessee, during the 1920s. **Famous country artists:** Johnny Cash, Dolly Parton, Willie Nelson, Garth Brooks, Vince Gill, Reba McEntire, Shania Twain.

## CLASSICAL MUSIC

Often more complex than other types of music, classical music is based on European musical traditions that go back several hundred years. Common forms of classical music include the symphony, chamber music, opera, and ballet music. **Famous early classical composers:** Johann Sebastian Bach, Ludwig van Beethoven, Johannes Brahms, Franz Joseph Haydn, Wolfgang Amadeus Mozart, Franz Schubert, Peter Ilyich Tchaikovsky. **Famous modern classical composers:** Aaron Copland, Virgil Thomson, Charles Ives, Igor Stravinsky.

## OPERA

An opera is a play whose words are sung to music. The music is played by an orchestra. The words of an opera are called the libretto, and a long song sung by one character (like a speech in a play) is called an aria. **Famous operas:** *Madama Butterfly* (Giacomo Puccini); *Aida* (Giuseppe Verdi); *Porgy and Bess* (George Gershwin).

## Rock and Roll HALL of FAME

The Rock and Roll Hall of Fame and Museum, located in Cleveland, Ohio, honors rock-and-roll musicians with exhibits and multi-media presentations. Musicians cannot be included until 25 years after their first record. Billy Joel, Paul McCartney, and Bruce Springsteen were among the performers to be added in 1999.

## CHAMBER MUSIC

**Chamber music** is written for a small group of musicians, often only three (a trio) or four (a quartet), to play together. In chamber music, each instrument plays a separate part. A **string quartet** (music written for two violins, viola, and cello) is an example of chamber music. Other instruments, such as a piano, are sometimes part of a chamber group.

## MUSICAL NOTATION

These are some of the symbols composers use when they write music.

| | |
|---|---|
| treble clef | 𝄞 |
| bass clef | 𝄢 |
| sharp | ♯ |
| flat | ♭ |
| natural | ♮ |
| whole note | o |
| half note | ♩ |
| quarter note | ♩ |
| eighth note | ♪ |
| sixteenth note | ♬ |
| whole rest | ▬ |
| half rest | ▬ |

## VOICE

There are six common types of voices, three for men and three for women. Women's voices usually range from *soprano* (highest) to *mezzo-soprano* (middle) to *alto* (lowest). Men's voices range from *tenor* (highest) to *baritone* (middle) to *bass* (lowest).

## SYMPHONY

A symphony is music written for an orchestra. The parts of a symphony are called movements.

# INSTRUMENTS of the ORCHESTRA

The instruments of an orchestra are divided into four groups, or sections: string, woodwind, brass, and percussion. In an orchestra with 100 musicians, usually more than 60 play string instruments. The rest play woodwinds, brasses, or percussion instruments.

## PERCUSSION INSTRUMENTS

Percussion instruments make sounds when they are struck. The most common percussion instrument is the drum, which comes in many forms. Other percussion instruments include cymbals, triangles, gongs, bells, and xylophone. Keyboard instruments, like the piano, are sometimes thought of as percussion instruments.

## BRASSES

Brass instruments are hollow inside. They make sounds when air is blown into a mouthpiece shaped like a cup or a funnel. The trumpet, French horn, trombone, and tuba are brasses.

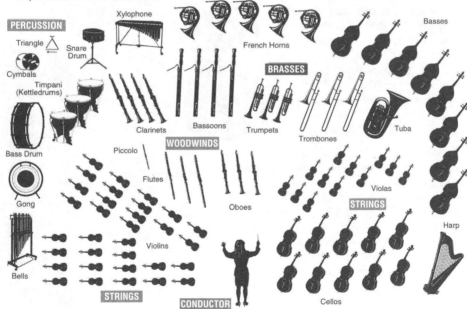

## WOODWINDS

Woodwind instruments are long and round and hollow inside. They make sounds when air is blown into them through a mouth hole or a reed. The clarinet, flute, oboe, bassoon, and piccolo are woodwinds.

## STRINGS

Stringed instruments make sounds when the strings are either stroked with a bow or plucked with the fingers. The violin, viola, cello, bass, and harp are stringed instruments used in an orchestra. The guitar, banjo, balalaika, mandolin, koto, and dulcimer are other examples of stringed instruments.

# AMERICAN MUSICAL THEATER

American musicals are plays known for their lively music and songs, comedy routines, dancing, colorful costumes, and elaborate stage sets. Tony (Antoinette Perry) Awards are given every year to outstanding Broadway plays. (Broadway is the theater district of New York City, which includes the street named Broadway and several surrounding blocks.) Some famous Broadway musicals are listed below. The date after the name of the play is the year it opened on Broadway.

**Annie** (1977), by Charles Strouse and Martin Charnin. Tony Award 1977.

**Annie Get Your Gun** (1946), by Irving Berlin.

**Anything Goes** (1930), by Cole Porter.

**Beauty and the Beast** (1994), by Alan Menken, Howard Ashman, and Tim Rice.

**Bring in 'da Noise, Bring in 'da Funk** (1996), by George C. Wolfe, Savion Glover, Daryl Waters, Zane Mark, and Ann Duquesnay.

**Carousel** (1945), by Richard Rodgers and Oscar Hammerstein II.

**Cats** (1982), by Andrew Lloyd Webber. Tony Award 1983.

**A Chorus Line** (1975), by Marvin Hamlisch and Edward Kleban. Tony Award 1976.

**Evita** (1979), by Andrew Lloyd Webber and Tim Rice. Tony Award 1980.

**Fiddler on the Roof** (1964), by Jerry Bock and Sheldon Harnick. Tony Award 1965.

**Grease** (1972), by Jim Jacobs and Warren Casey.

**Hello, Dolly!** (1964), by Jerry Herman. Tony Award 1964.

**The King and I** (1952), by Richard Rodgers and Oscar Hammerstein II. Tony Award 1952.

**Kiss Me Kate** (1948), by Cole Porter. Tony Award 1949.

**The Lion King** (1997), by Elton John, Tim Rice, Mark Mancina, Roger Allers, and Irene Meechi. Tony Award 1998

**The Music Man** (1957), by Meredith Willson. Tony Award 1958.

**My Fair Lady** (1956), by Alan Jay Lerner and Frederick Loewe. Tony Award 1957.

**Oklahoma!** (1943), by Richard Rodgers and Oscar Hammerstein II.

**The Pajama Game** (1954), by Richard Adler and Jerry Ross. Tony Award 1955.

**Rent** (1996), by Jonathan Larson. Tony Award 1996.

**Show Boat** (1927), by Jerome Kern and Oscar Hammerstein II.

**The Sound of Music** (1959), by Richard Rodgers and Oscar Hammerstein II. Tony Award 1960.

**South Pacific** (1949), by Richard Rodgers and Oscar Hammerstein II. Tony Award 1950.

**West Side Story** (1957), by Leonard Bernstein and Stephen Sondheim.

# MUSIC PUZZLE

Strings, woodwinds, brasses, and percussion Instruments combine to form an orchestra. In each of the following lists, which instrument doesn't belong because it's not in the same group as the others?

If you need to, look back on page 134 for help.

1. **Woodwinds:** clarinet, oboe, tuba, flute

2. **Strings:** cello, violin, harp, bass drum

3. **Percussion:** cymbals, triangle, xylophone, bassoon

4. **Brasses:** trombone, trumpet, French horn, violin

*Answers are on pages 317–320.*

# DANCE

In dance, the body performs patterns of movement, usually to music or rhythm. Dance may be a form of art, or part of a religious ceremony. Or it may be done just for fun. Ballet, modern dance, folk dance, and social dance are all important kinds of dance.

## BALLET

Ballet is a kind of dance that is based on formal steps. Ballet movements are often graceful and flowing. Ballets are almost always danced to music. They are performed for an audience and often tell a story. In the 15th century, ballet was part of the elaborate entertainment that was performed for the rulers of Europe. In the 1600s, professional dance companies existed, but without women. Women's parts were danced by men wearing masks. In the 1700s dancers wore bulky costumes and shoes with high heels. Women danced in hoopskirts—and so did men! In the 1800s ballet steps and costumes began to look the way they do now. Many of the most popular ballets today date back to the middle or late 1800s.

### NOTED BALLET DANCERS
Anna Pavlova (1885–1931)
Vaslav Nijinsky (1890–1950)
Margot Fonteyn (1919–1991)
Arthur Mitchell (born 1934)
Rudolph Nureyev (1938–1993)
Mikhail Baryshnikov (born 1948)

## SOME FAMOUS BALLETS

**Swan Lake.** First danced in St. Petersburg, Russia, in 1895. Perhaps the most popular ballet ever, *Swan Lake* is the story of a prince and his love for a maiden who was turned into a swan by an evil magician.

**The Nutcracker.** When this ballet was first performed in St. Petersburg, Russia, in 1892, it was a colossal flop. It has since become so popular that it is danced in many places every year at holiday time in December.

**The Sleeping Beauty.** Based on the fairy tale *The Sleeping Beauty*. The ballet was first danced in St. Petersburg in 1890.

**Jewels.** This ballet by the American choreographer George Balanchine was first performed in New York City in 1967. In *Jewels*, the dancers do not dance to a story. They explore patterns and movement of the human body.

**The River.** This 1970 ballet by Alvin Ailey is danced to music by the famous jazz musician Duke Ellington. It has been described as a ballet of imaginative movement and a celebration of life.

### NOTED CHOREOGRAPHERS
Marius Petipa (1818–1910)
Michel Fokine (1880–1942)
George Balanchine (1904–1983)
Agnes de Mille (1908–1993)
Jerome Robbins (1918–1998)
Kenneth MacMillan (1929-1992)

## SOCIAL DANCE

Social dance is the name for dances done just for fun by ordinary people. Social dancing has been around since at least the Middle Ages, when it was popular at fairs and festivals. In the 1400s social dance was part of fancy court pageants. It developed into dainty dances like the minuet and the waltz during the 1700s. New dances in the 20th century include the Charleston, lindy, twist, and tango, as well as disco dancing, break dancing, line dancing, and dances such as the macarena and electric slide.

## MODERN DANCE

Modern dance differs from classical ballet in many ways. It is often less concerned with graceful, flowing movement and with stories. Modern dance steps are often not performed in traditional ballet. Dancers may put their bodies into awkward, angular positions and turn their backs on the audience. Many modern dances are based on ancient art, such as Greek sculpture, or on dance styles found in Africa and Asia.

Here are some noted modern choreographers. (Many of them are also dancers.)

Alvin Ailey (1931–1989)               Martha Graham (1894–1991)
Trisha Brown (born 1936)              Mark Morris (born 1956)
Merce Cunningham (born 1919)         Paul Taylor (born 1930)
Isadora Duncan (1878–1927)           Twyla Tharp (born 1941)

## FOLK DANCE

Folk dance is the term for a dance that is passed on from generation to generation and that is part of the culture or way of life of people from a particular country or ethnic group. Virginia reel (American), czardas (Hungarian), jig, and the Israeli hora are some folk dances.

### THE LION KING BECOMES BROADWAY'S MANE EVENT

Anyone who has seen *The Lion King* movie might wonder how in the world it could be turned into a Broadway show. The main characters are lions and other jungle animals. Some scenes involve hundreds—if not thousands—of wild animals running across miles of fields. How could it all fit on a stage?

It was up to director Julie Taymor to make it work. How did she do it? She and her production team created masks and puppets for the characters. Even though the actors themselves can often be seen, the audience gets lost in the make-believe and in the music.

The Broadway musical keeps "Circle of Life," "Hakuna Matata," and other songs from the movie, and also adds some new songs. The result is a show that's very different from the movie, but one that audiences still love—the best seats are sold out way in advance!

# NATIONS

❷ If you had 1,700 lire in Italy, how many dollars would it be worth?
*You can find the answer on page 147.*

# NATIONS of the WORLD

There are 192 nations in the world. In this section, the information for each country goes across two pages. The left page gives the **name** and **capital** of each nation, its **location**, and its **area**. On the right page, the population column tells how many people lived in each country in 1998. The **language** column gives official languages or other commonly spoken languages. The currency column shows the name of each nation's money and how much one United States dollar was worth there at the start of 1999. This column also shows which countries now use the euro. Eleven members of the European Union started using this common currency in 1999. One euro was worth about $1.17 in early 1999. The euro is meant to make traveling and trading easier.

| COUNTRY | CAPITAL | LOCATION OF COUNTRY | AREA |
|---------|---------|---------------------|------|
| Afghanistan | Kabul | Southern Asia, between Iran and Pakistan | 250,000 sq. mi. (647,500 sq. km.) |
| Albania | Tiranë | Eastern Europe, between Greece and Yugoslavia | 11,100 sq. mi. (28,750 sq. km.) |
| Algeria | Algiers | North Africa on the Mediterranean Sea, between Libya and Morocco | 919,600 sq. mi. (2,381,740 sq. km.) |
| Andorra | Andorra la Vella | Europe, in the mountains between France and Spain | 170 sq. mi. (450 sq. km.) |
| Angola | Luanda | Southern Africa on the Atlantic Ocean, north of Namibia | 481,400 sq. mi. (1,246,700 sq. km.) |
| Antigua and Barbuda | St. John's | Islands on eastern edge of the Caribbean Sea | 170 sq. mi. (440 sq. km.) |
| Argentina | Buenos Aires | Fills up most of the southern part of South America | 1,068,300 sq. mi. (2,766,890 sq. km.) |
| Armenia | Yerevan | Western Asia, north of Turkey and Iran | 11,500 sq. mi. (29,800 sq. km.) |
| Australia | Canberra | Continent south of Asia, between Indian and Pacific Oceans | 2,967,900 sq. mi. (7,686,850 sq. km.) |
| Austria | Vienna | Central Europe, north of Italy | 32,378 sq. mi. (83,858 sq. km.) |
| Azerbaijan | Baku | Western Asia, north of Iran | 33,400 sq. mi. (86,600 sq. km.) |

| POPULATION | CURRENCY | LANGUAGE | COUNTRY |
|---|---|---|---|
| 24,792,375 | Afghani<br>$1 = 4,750 afghanis | Afghan Persian (Dari), Pashtu | **Afghanistan** |
| 3,330,754 | Lek<br>$1 = 140 leks | Albanian | **Albania** |
| 30,480,973 | Dinar<br>$1 = 60 dinars | Arabic, French | Algeria |
| 64,716 | French franc or Spanish peseta | Catalan, French | **Andorra** |
| 10,864,512 | New kwanza<br>$1 = 257,000 new kwanzas | Portuguese | **Angola** |
| 64,006 | East Caribbean dollar<br>$1 = 2$\frac{2}{3}$ EC dollars | English | **Antigua and Barbuda** |
| 36,265,463 | Peso<br>$1 = 1 peso | Spanish | Argentina |
| 3,421,775 | Dram<br>$1 = 500 drams | Armenian | **Armenia** |
| 18,613,087 | Australian dollar<br>$1 = 1$\frac{5}{8}$ Australian dollars | English | **Australia** |
| 8,133,611 | Schilling, also euro<br>$1 = 12 schillings | German | **Austria** |
| 785,576 | Manat<br>$1 = 4,000 manats | Azeri | Azerbaijan |

| COUNTRY | CAPITAL | LOCATION OF COUNTRY | AREA |
|---|---|---|---|
| The Bahamas | Nassau | Islands in the Atlantic Ocean, east of Florida | 5,400 sq. mi. (13,940 sq. km.) |
| Bahrain | Manama | In the Persian Gulf, near the coast of Qatar | 240 sq. mi. (620 sq. km.) |
| Bangladesh | Dhaka | Southern Asia, nearly surrounded by India | 55,600 sq. mi. (144,000 sq. km.) |
| Barbados | Bridgetown | Island in the Atlantic Ocean, north of Trinidad | 170 sq. mi. (430 sq. km.) |
| Belarus | Minsk | Eastern Europe, east of Poland | 80,200 sq. mi. (207,600 sq. km.) |
| Belgium | Brussels | Western Europe, on the North Sea, south of the Netherlands | 11,800 sq. mi. (30,510 sq. km.) |
| Belize | Belmopan | Central America, next to Mexico | 8,900 sq. mi. (22,960 sq. km.) |
| Benin | Porto-Novo | West Africa, on the Gulf of Guinea, west of Nigeria | 43,500 sq. mi. (112,620 sq. km.) |
| Bhutan | Thimphu | Asia, in the Himalaya Mountains, between China and India | 18,100 sq. mi. (47,000 sq. km.) |
| Bolivia | La Paz | South America, in the Andes Mountains, next to Brazil | 424,200 sq. mi. (1,098,580 sq. km.) |
| Bosnia and Herzegovina | Sarajevo | Southern Europe, on the Balkan Peninsula, west of Yugoslavia | 19,781 sq. mi. (51,233 sq. km.) |
| Botswana | Gaborone | Southern Africa, between South Africa and Zambia | 231,800 sq. mi. (600,370 sq. km.) |
| Brazil | Brasília | Occupies most of the eastern part of South America | 3,286,478 sq. mi. (8,511,965 sq. km.) |
| Brunei | Bandar Seri Begawan | On the island of Borneo, northwest of Australia in the Pacific Ocean | 2,200 sq. mi. (5,770 sq. km.) |
| Bulgaria | Sofia | Eastern Europe, on the Balkan Peninsula, bordering the Black Sea | 42,800 sq. mi. (110,910 sq. km.) |
| Burkina Faso | Ouagadougou | West Africa, between Mali and Ghana | 105,900 sq. mi. (274,200 sq. km.) |
| Burundi | Bujumbura | Central Africa, northwest of Tanzania | 10,700 sq. mi. (27,830 sq. km.) |
| Cambodia | Phnom Penh | Southeast Asia, between Vietnam and Thailand | 69,900 sq. mi. (181,040 sq. km.) |
| Cameroon | Yaoundé | Central Africa, between Nigeria and Central African Republic | 183,600 sq. mi. (475,440 sq. km.) |
| Canada | Ottawa | Occupies the northern part of North America, north of the United States | 3,851,800 sq. mi. (9,976,140 sq. km.) |
| Cape Verde | Praia | Islands off the western tip of Africa | 1,600 sq. mi. (4,030 sq. km.) |

| POPULATION | CURRENCY | LANGUAGE | COUNTRY |
|---|---|---|---|
| 279,833 | Bahamas dollar<br>Same value as U.S. dollar | English | **The Bahamas** |
| 616,342 | Dinar<br>$1 = $\frac{2}{5}$ dinars | Arabic | **Bahrain** |
| 127,567,002 | Taka<br>$1 = $48$\frac{1}{2}$ takas | Bangla | Bangladesh |
| 259,025 | Barbados dollar<br>$1 = 2 Barbados dollars | English | **Barbados** |
| 10,409,050 | Ruble<br>$1 = 58,500 rubles | Belarussian | **Belarus** |
| 10,174,922 | Franc, also euro<br>$1 = 35 francs | Flemish (Dutch),<br>French | **Belgium** |
| 230,160 | Belize dollar<br>$1 = 2 Belize dollars | English | Belize |
| 6,100,799 | CFA franc<br>$1 = 560 CFA francs | French | **Benin** |
| 1,408,307 | Ngultrum<br>$1 = 40 ngultrums | Dzongkha | **Bhutan** |
| 7,826,352 | Boliviano<br>$1 = 5$\frac{2}{3}$ Bolivianos | Spanish,<br>Quechua, Aymara | **Bolivia** |
| 3,365,727 | New dinar<br>$1 = 10$\frac{1}{2}$ new dinars | Serbo-Croatian | Bosnia and<br>Herzegovina |
| 1,448,454 | Pula<br>$1 = 4$\frac{1}{2}$ pula | English | **Botswana** |
| 169,806,557 | Real<br>$1 = 1$\frac{1}{5}$ real | Portuguese | **Brazil** |
| 315,292 | Brunei dollar<br>$1 = 1$\frac{2}{3}$ Brunei dollars | Malay | **Brunei** |
| 8,240,426 | Lev<br>$1 = 1,700 leva | Bulgarian | Bulgaria |
| 11,266,393 | CFA franc<br>$1 = 560 CFA francs | French | **Burkina Faso** |
| 5,537,387 | Franc<br>$1 = 500 francs | Kirundi,<br>French | **Burundi** |
| 11,339,562 | Riel<br>$1 = 4,000 riels | Khmer | **Cambodia** |
| 15,029,433 | CFA franc<br>$1 = 560 CFA francs | English,<br>French | Cameroon |
| 30,675,398 | Canadian dollar<br>$1 = 1$\frac{1}{2}$ Canadian dollars | English,<br>French | **Canada** |
| 399,857 | Escudo<br>$1 = 95 escudos | Portuguese | **Cape Verde** |

| COUNTRY | CAPITAL | LOCATION OF COUNTRY | AREA |
|---|---|---|---|
| Central African Republic | Bangui | Central Africa, south of Chad | 240,500 sq. mi. (622,980 sq. km.) |
| Chad | N'Djamena | North Africa, south of Libya | 496,000 sq. mi. (1,284,000 sq. km.) |
| Chile | Santiago | Along the western coast of South America | 292,300 sq. mi. (756,950 sq. km.) |
| China | Beijing | Occupies most of the mainland of eastern Asia | 3,705,400 sq. mi. (9,596,960 sq. km.) |
| Colombia | Bogotá | Northwestern South America, southeast of Panama | 439,700 sq. mi. (1,138,910 sq. km.) |
| Comoros | Moroni | Islands between Madagascar and the east coast of Africa | 800 sq. mi. (2,170 sq. km.) |
| Congo, Democratic Republic of the (formerly Zaire) | Kinshasa | Central Africa, north of Angola and Zambia | 905,600 sq. mi. (2,345,410 sq. km.) |
| Congo, Republic of the | Brazzaville | Central Africa, east of Gabon | 132,000 sq. mi. (342,000 sq. km.) |
| Costa Rica | San José | Central America, south of Nicaragua | 19,700 sq. mi (51,100 sq. km.) |
| Côte d'Ivoire (Ivory Coast) | Yamoussoukro | West Africa, on the Gulf of Guinea, west of Ghana | 124,500 sq. mi. (322,460 sq. km.) |
| Croatia | Zagreb | Southern Europe, south of Hungary | 21,829 sq. mi. (56,538 sq. km.) |
| Cuba | Havana | In the Caribbean Sea, south of Florida | 42,800 sq. mi. (110,860 sq. km.) |
| Cyprus | Nicosia | Island in the Mediterranean Sea, off the coast of Turkey | 3,600 sq. mi. (9,250 sq. km.) |
| Czech Republic | Prague | Central Europe, south of Poland, east of Germany | 30,387 sq. mi. (78,703 sq. km.) |
| Denmark | Copenhagen | Northern Europe, between the Baltic Sea and North Sea | 16,639 sq. mi. (43,094 sq. km.) |
| Djibouti | Djibouti | North Africa, on the Gulf of Aden, across from Saudi Arabia | 8,500 sq. mi. (22,000 sq. km.) |
| Dominica | Roseau | Island in the Caribbean Sea | 300 sq. mi. (750 sq. km.) |
| Dominican Republic | Santo Domingo | On an island, along with Haiti, in the Caribbean Sea | 18,800 sq. mi. (48,730 sq. km.) |
| Ecuador | Quito | South America, on the equator, bordering the Pacific Ocean | 109,500 sq. mi. (283,560 sq. km.) |
| Egypt | Cairo | Northeastern Africa, on the Red Sea and Mediterranean Sea | 386,700 sq. mi. (1,001,450 sq. km.) |

| POPULATION | CURRENCY | LANGUAGE | COUNTRY |
|---|---|---|---|
| 3,375,771 | CFA franc<br>$1 = 560 CFA francs | French,<br>Sangho | **Central African**<br>**Republic** |
| 7,359,512 | CFA franc<br>$1 = 560 CFA francs | French,<br>Arabic | **Chad** |
| 14,787,481 | Peso<br>$1 = 470 pesos | Spanish | Chile |
| 1,236,914,658 | Renminbi (yuan)<br>$1 = $8\frac{1}{4}$ renminbis | Mandarin | **China** |
| 38,580,949 | Peso<br>$1 = 1,550 pesos | Spanish | **Colombia** |
| 545,528 | Franc<br>$1 = 420 francs | Arabic,<br>French,<br>Comorian | **Comoros** |
| 49,000,511 | New zaire<br>$1 = 217,500 new zaires | French | Congo, Democratic<br>Republic of the<br>*(formerly Zaire)* |
| 2,658,123 | CFA franc<br>$1 = 560 CFA francs | French | **Congo,**<br>**Republic of the** |
| 3,604,642 | Colon<br>$1 = 270 colones | Spanish | **Costa Rica** |
| 15,446,231 | CFA franc<br>$1 = 560 CFA francs | French | **Côte d'Ivoire**<br>**(Ivory Coast)** |
| 4,671,584 | Kuna<br>$1 = $6\frac{1}{4}$ kunas | Croatian | Croatia |
| 11,050,729 | Peso<br>$1 = 23 pesos | Spanish | **Cuba** |
| 748,982 | Pound<br>$1 = $\frac{1}{2}$ pound | Greek,<br>Turkish | **Cyprus** |
| 10,286,470 | Koruna<br>$1 = 30 koruny | Czech | **Czech**<br>**Republic** |
| 5,333,617 | Krone<br>$1 = $6\frac{2}{5}$ kroner | Danish | Denmark |
| 440,727 | Franc<br>$1 = 180 francs | French,<br>Arabic | **Djibouti** |
| 65,777 | East Caribbean dollar<br>$1 = $2\frac{2}{3}$ EC dollars | English | **Dominica** |
| 7,998,766 | Peso<br>$1 = 16 pesos | Spanish | **Dominican**<br>**Republic** |
| 12,336,572 | Sucre<br>$1 = 6,800 sucres | Spanish | Ecuador |
| 66,050,004 | Pound<br>$1 = $3\frac{2}{5}$ pounds | Arabic | **Egypt** |

| COUNTRY | CAPITAL | LOCATION OF COUNTRY | AREA |
|---|---|---|---|
| El Salvador | San Salvador | Central America, southwest of Honduras | 8,100 sq. mi. (21,040 sq. km.) |
| Equatorial Guinea | Malabo | West Africa, on the Gulf of Guinea, off the west coast of Cameroon | 10,800 sq. mi. (28,050 sq. km.) |
| Eritrea | Asmara | Northeast Africa, north of Ethiopia | 46,800 sq. mi. (121,320 sq. km.) |
| Estonia | Tallinn | Northern Europe, on the Baltic Sea, north of Latvia | 17,462 sq. mi. (45,226 sq. km.) |
| Ethiopia | Addis Ababa | East Africa, east of Sudan | 435,185 sq. mi. (1,127,127 sq. km.) |
| Fiji | Suva | Islands in the South Pacific Ocean, east of Australia | 7,100 sq. mi. (18,270 sq. km.) |
| Finland | Helsinki | Northern Europe, between Sweden and Russia | 130,100 sq. mi. (337,030 sq. km.) |
| France | Paris | Western Europe, between Germany and Spain | 211,200 sq. mi. (547,030 sq. km.) |
| Gabon | Libreville | Central Africa, on the Atlantic coast, south of Cameroon | 103,300 sq. mi. (267,670 sq. km.) |
| The Gambia | Banjul | West Africa, on the Atlantic Ocean, surrounded by Senegal | 4,400 sq. mi. (11,300 sq. km.) |
| Georgia | Tbilisi | Western Asia, south of Russia, on the Black Sea | 26,900 sq. mi. (69,700 sq. km.) |
| Germany | Berlin | Central Europe, northeast of France | 137,800 sq. mi. (356,910 sq. km.) |
| Ghana | Accra | West Africa, on the southern coast | 92,100 sq. mi. (238,540 sq. km.) |
| Great Britain (United Kingdom) | London | Off the northwest coast of Europe | 94,500 sq. mi. (244,820 sq. km.) |
| Greece | Athens | Southern Europe, in the southern part of the Balkan Peninsula | 50,900 sq. mi. (131,940 sq. km.) |
| Grenada | Saint George's | Island on the eastern edge of the Caribbean Sea | 130 sq. mi. (340 sq. km.) |
| Guatemala | Guatemala City | Central America, southeast of Mexico | 42,000 sq. mi. (108,890 sq. km.) |
| Guinea | Conakry | West Africa, on the Atlantic Ocean, north of Sierra Leone | 94,900 sq. mi. (245,860 sq. km.) |
| Guinea-Bissau | Bissau | West Africa, on the Atlantic Ocean, south of Senegal | 13,900 sq. mi. (36,120 sq. km.) |
| Guyana | Georgetown | South America, on the northern coast, east of Venezuela | 83,000 sq. mi. (214,970 sq. km.) |
| Haiti | Port-au-Prince | On an island, along with Dominican Republic, in the Caribbean Sea | 10,700 sq. mi. (27,750 sq. km.) |

| POPULATION | CURRENCY | LANGUAGE | COUNTRY |
|---|---|---|---|
| 5,752,067 | Colon<br>$1 = 8\frac{3}{4}$ colones | Spanish | El Salvador |
| 454,001 | CFA franc<br>$1 = 560$ CFA francs | Spanish | Equatorial Guinea |
| 3,842,436 | Ethiopian birr<br>$1 = 7$ Ethiopian birr | Tigrinya | Eritrea |
| 1,421,335 | Kroon<br>$1 = 13$ kroons | Estonian | Estonia |
| 58,390,351 | Birr<br>$1 = 7$ birr | Amharic | Ethiopia |
| 802,611 | Fiji dollar<br>$1 = 2$ Fiji dollars | English | Fiji |
| 5,149,242 | Markka, also euro<br>$1 = 5$ markkaa | Finnish, Swedish | Finland |
| 58,804,944 | Franc, also euro<br>$1 = 5\frac{5}{8}$ francs | French | France |
| 1,207,844 | CFA franc<br>$1 = 560$ CFA francs | French | Gabon |
| 1,291,858 | Dalasi<br>$1 = 11$ dalasi | English | The Gambia |
| 5,108,527 | Lavi<br>$1 = 1\frac{1}{3}$ lavis | Georgian | Georgia |
| 82,079,454 | Mark, also euro<br>$1 = 1\frac{2}{3}$ marks | German | Germany |
| 18,497,206 | Cedi<br>$1 = 2,350$ cedis | English | Ghana |
| 58,970,119 | Pound<br>$1 = \frac{3}{5}$ pound | English | Great Britain (United Kingdom) |
| 10,662,138 | Drachma<br>$1 = 280$ drachmas | Greek | Greece |
| 96,217 | East Caribbean dollar<br>$1 = 2\frac{2}{3}$ EC dollars | English | Grenada |
| 12,007,580 | Quetzal<br>$1 = 6\frac{3}{4}$ quetzals | Spanish | Guatemala |
| 7,477,110 | Franc<br>$1 = 1,300$ francs | French | Guinea |
| 1,206,311 | CFA franc<br>$1 = 560$ CFA francs | Portuguese | Guinea-Bissau |
| 707,954 | Guyana dollar<br>$1 = 150$ Guyana dollars | English | Guyana |
| 6,780,501 | Gourde<br>$1 = 16\frac{1}{2}$ gourdes | Haitian Creole, French | Haiti |

| COUNTRY | CAPITAL | LOCATION OF COUNTRY | AREA |
|---|---|---|---|
| Honduras | Tegucigalpa | Central America, between Guatemala and Nicaragua | 43,300 sq. mi. (112,090 sq. km.) |
| Hungary | Budapest | Central Europe, north of Yugoslavia | 35,900 sq. mi. (93,030 sq. km.) |
| Iceland | Reykjavik | Island off the coast of Europe, in the North Atlantic Ocean, near Greenland | 40,000 sq. mi. (103,000 sq. km.) |
| India | New Delhi | Southern Asia, on a large peninsula on the Indian Ocean | 1,269,300 sq. mi. (3,287,590 sq. km.) |
| Indonesia | Jakarta | Islands south of Southeast Asia, along the equator | 741,100 sq. mi. (1,919,440 sq. km.) |
| Iran | Tehran | Southern Asia, between Iraq and Pakistan | 636,000 sq. mi. (1,648,000 sq. km.) |
| Iraq | Baghdad | In the Middle East, between Syria and Iran | 168,754 sq. mi. (437,072 sq. km.) |
| Ireland | Dublin | Off the coast of Europe, in the Atlantic Ocean, west of Great Britain | 27,100 sq. mi. (70,280 sq. km.) |
| Israel | Jerusalem | In the Middle East, between Jordan and the Mediterranean Sea | 8,000 sq. mi. (20,770 sq. km.) |
| Italy | Rome | Southern Europe, jutting out into the Mediterranean Sea | 116,300 sq. mi. (301,230 sq. km.) |
| Jamaica | Kingston | Island in the Caribbean Sea, south of Cuba | 4,200 sq. mi. (10,990 sq. km.) |
| Japan | Tokyo | Four big islands and many small ones, off the east coast of Asia | 145,882 sq. mi. (377,835 sq. km.) |
| Jordan | Amman | In the Middle East, south of Syria, east of Israel | 34,445 sq. mi. (89,213 sq. km.) |
| Kazakhstan | Astana | Central Asia, south of Russia | 1,049,200 sq. mi. (2,717,300 sq. km.) |
| Kenya | Nairobi | East Africa, on the Indian Ocean, south of Ethiopia | 225,000 sq. mi. (582,650 sq. km.) |
| Kiribati | Tarawa | Islands in the middle of the Pacific Ocean, near the equator | 277 sq. mi. (717 sq. km.) |
| Korea, North | Pyongyang | Eastern Asia, in the northern part of the Korean Peninsula; China is to the north | 46,500 sq. mi. (120,540 sq. km.) |
| Korea, South | Seoul | Eastern Asia, south of North Korea, on the Korean Peninsula | 38,000 sq. mi. (98,480 sq. km.) |
| Kuwait | Kuwait City | In the Middle East, on the northern end of the Persian Gulf | 6,900 sq. mi. (17,820 sq. km.) |
| Kyrgyzstan | Bishkek | Western Asia, between Kazakhstan and Tajikistan | 76,600 sq. mi. (198,500 sq. km.) |

| POPULATION | CURRENCY | LANGUAGE | COUNTRY |
|---:|---|---|---|
| 5,861,955 | Lempira<br>$1 = 14$ lempiras | Spanish | **Honduras** |
| 10,208,127 | Forint<br>$1 = 215$ forints | Hungarian<br>(Magyar) | **Hungary** |
| 271,033 | Krona<br>$1 = 70$ kronor | Icelandic | Iceland |
| 984,003,683 | Rupee<br>$1 = 40$ rupees | Hindi,<br>English | **India** |
| 212,941,810 | Rupiah<br>$1 = 8,000$ rupiah | Bahasa<br>Indonesian | **Indonesia** |
| 68,959,931 | Rial<br>$1 = 3,000$ rials | Persian<br>(Farsi) | **Iran** |
| 21,722,287 | Dinar<br>$1 = \frac{1}{3}$ dinar | Arabic | Iraq |
| 3,619,480 | Pound, also euro<br>$1 = \frac{2}{3}$ pound | English,<br>Gaelic | **Ireland** |
| 5,643,966 | New shekel<br>$1 = 4\frac{1}{5}$ new shekels | Hebrew,<br>Arabic | **Israel** |
| 56,782,748 | Lira, also euro<br>$1 = 1,700$ lire | Italian | **Italy** |
| 2,634,678 | Jamaican dollar<br>$1 = 37$ Jamaican dollars | English | Jamaica |
| 125,931,533 | Yen<br>$1 = 114$ yen | Japanese | **Japan** |
| 4,434,978 | Dinar<br>$1 = \frac{2}{3}$ dinar | Arabic | **Jordan** |
| 16,846,808 | Tenge<br>$1 = 80$ tenges | Kazakh | **Kazakhstan** |
| 28,337,071 | Shilling<br>$1 = 60$ shillings | Swahili,<br>English | Kenya |
| 83,976 | Australian dollar<br>$1 = 1\frac{5}{8}$ Australian dollars | English | **Kiribati** |
| 21,234,387 | Won<br>$1 = 2\frac{1}{5}$ won | Korean | **Korea, North** |
| 46,416,796 | Won<br>$1 = 1,200$ won | Korean | **Korea, South** |
| 1,913,285 | Dinar<br>$1 = \frac{1}{3}$ dinar | Arabic | Kuwait |
| 4,522,281 | Som<br>$1 = 20$ soms | Kyrgyz,<br>Russian | **Kyrgyzstan** |

| COUNTRY | CAPITAL | LOCATION OF COUNTRY | AREA |
|---------|---------|---------------------|------|
| Laos | Vientiane | Southeast Asia, between Vietnam and Thailand | 91,400 sq. mi. (236,800 sq. km.) |
| Latvia | Riga | On the Baltic Sea, between Lithuania and Estonia | 24,700 sq. mi. (64,100 sq. km.) |
| Lebanon | Beirut | In the Middle East, between the Mediterranean Sea and Syria | 4,000 sq. mi. (10,400 sq. km.) |
| Lesotho | Maseru | Southern Africa, surrounded by the nation of South Africa | 11,700 sq. mi. (30,350 sq. km.) |
| Liberia | Monrovia | Western Africa, on the Atlantic Ocean, southeast of Sierra Leone | 43,000 sq. mi. (111,370 sq. km.) |
| Libya | Tripoli | North Africa, on the Mediterranean Sea, to the west of Egypt | 679,400 sq. mi. (1,759,540 sq. km.) |
| Liechtenstein | Vaduz | Southern Europe, in the Alps between Austria and Switzerland | 60 sq. mi. (160 sq. km.) |
| Lithuania | Vilnius | Northern Europe, on the Baltic Sea, north of Poland | 25,200 sq. mi. (65,200 sq. km.) |
| Luxembourg | Luxembourg | Western Europe, between France and Germany | 998 sq. mi. (2,586 sq. km.) |
| Macedonia | Skopje | Southern Europe, north of Greece | 9,781 sq. mi. (25,333 sq. km.) |
| Madagascar | Antananarivo | Island in the Indian Ocean, off the east coast of Africa | 226,700 sq. mi. (587,040 sq. km.) |
| Malawi | Lilongwe | Southern Africa, south of Tanzania and east of Zambia | 45,700 sq. mi. (118,480 sq. km.) |
| Malaysia | Kuala Lumpur | Southeast Asia, on the island of Borneo | 127,300 sq. mi. (329,750 sq. km.) |
| Maldives | Male | Islands in the Indian Ocean, south of India | 100 sq. mi. (300 sq. km.) |
| Mali | Bamako | West Africa, between Algeria and Mauritania | 479,000 sq. mi. (1,240,000 sq. km.) |
| Malta | Valletta | Island in the Mediterranean Sea, south of Italy | 120 sq. mi. (320 sq. km.) |
| Marshall Islands | Majuro | Chain of small islands in the middle of the Pacific Ocean | 70 sq. mi. (181 sq. km.) |
| Mauritania | Nouakchott | West Africa, on the Atlantic Ocean, north of Senegal | 398,000 sq. mi. (1,030,700 sq. km.) |
| Mauritius | Port Louis | Islands in the Indian Ocean, east of Madagascar | 700 sq. mi. (1,860 sq. km.) |
| Mexico | Mexico City | North America, south of the United States | 761,600 sq. mi. (1,972,550 sq. km.) |
| Micronesia | Palikir | Islands in the western Pacific Ocean | 271 sq. mi. (702 sq. km.) |

| POPULATION | CURRENCY | LANGUAGE | COUNTRY |
|---:|---|---|---|
| 5,260,842 | Kip<br>$1 = 4,200 kip | Lao | **Laos** |
| 2,385,396 | Lat<br>$1 = $\frac{3}{5}$ lat | Latvian | **Latvia** |
| 3,505,794 | Pound<br>$1 = 1,500 pounds | Arabic,<br>French | Lebanon |
| 2,089,829 | Maloti<br>$1 = 5$\frac{5}{6}$ maloti | English,<br>Sesotho | **Lesotho** |
| 2,771,901 | Liberian dollar<br>Same as U.S. dollar | English | **Liberia** |
| 5,690,727 | Dinar<br>$1 = $\frac{1}{2}$ dinar | Arabic | **Libya** |
| 31,717 | Swiss franc<br>$1 = 1$\frac{2}{5}$ Swiss francs | German | Liechtenstein |
| 3,600,158 | Litas<br>$1 = 4 litas | Lithuanian | **Lithuania** |
| 425,017 | Franc, also euro<br>$1 = 35 francs | French,<br>German | **Luxembourg** |
| 2,009,387 | Denar<br>$1 = 52 denar | Macedonian | **Macedonia** |
| 14,462,509 | Franc<br>$1 = 5,200 francs | Malagasy,<br>French | Madagascar |
| 9,840,474 | Kwacha<br>$1 =45 kwacha | English,<br>Chichewa | **Malawi** |
| 20,932,901 | Ringgit<br>$1 = 4 ringgits | Malay | **Malaysia** |
| 290,211 | Rufiyaa<br>$1 = 12 rufiyaas | Divehi | **Maldives** |
| 10,108,569 | CFA franc<br>$1 = 560 CFA francs | French | Mali |
| 379,563 | Maltese lira<br>$1 = 2$\frac{2}{3}$ Maltese lira | Maltese,<br>English | **Malta** |
| 63,031 | U.S. dollar | English | **Marshall<br>Islands** |
| 2,511,473 | Ouguiya<br>$1 = 200 ouguiya | Wolof,<br>Arabic | **Mauritania** |
| 1,168,256 | Mauritian rupee<br>$1 = 25 Mauritian rupees | English | Mauritius |
| 98,552,776 | New peso<br>$1 = 10 new pesos | Spanish | **Mexico** |
| 129,658 | U.S. dollar | English | **Micronesia** |

| COUNTRY | CAPITAL | LOCATION OF COUNTRY | AREA |
|---|---|---|---|
| Moldova | Chisinau | Eastern Europe, between Ukraine and Romania | 13,000 sq. mi. (33,700 sq. km.) |
| Monaco | Monaco | Europe, on the Mediterranean Sea, surrounded by France | 3/4 of a sq. mi. (2 sq. km.) |
| Mongolia | Ulaanbaatar | Central Asia between Russia and China | 604,000 sq. mi. (1,565,000 sq. km.) |
| Morocco | Rabat | Northwest Africa, on the Atlantic Ocean and Mediterranean Sea | 172,400 sq. mi. (446,550 sq. km.) |
| Mozambique | Maputo | Southeastern Africa, on the Indian Ocean | 309,500 sq. mi. (801,590 sq. km.) |
| Myanmar (formerly Burma) | Yangon (Rangoon) | Southern Asia, to the east of India and Bangladesh | 262,000 sq. mi. (678,500 sq. km.) |
| Namibia | Windhoek | Southwestern Africa, on the Atlantic Ocean, west of Botswana | 318,695 sq. mi. (825,418 sq. km.) |
| Nauru | Yaren | Island in the western Pacific Ocean, just below the equator | 8 sq. mi. (21 sq. km.) |
| Nepal | Kathmandu | Asia, in the Himalaya Mountains, between China and India | 54,400 sq. mi. (140,800 sq. km.) |
| Netherlands | Amsterdam | Northern Europe, on the North Sea, to the west of Germany | 16,033 sq. mi. (41,526 sq. km.) |
| New Zealand | Wellington | Islands in the Pacific Ocean east of Australia | 103,700 sq. mi. (268,680 sq. km.) |
| Nicaragua | Managua | Central America, between Honduras and Costa Rica | 49,998 sq. mi. (129,494 sq. km.) |
| Niger | Niamey | North Africa, south of Algeria and Libya | 489,000 sq. mi. (1,267,000 sq. km.) |
| Nigeria | Abuja | West Africa, on the southern coast between Benin and Cameroon | 356,700 sq. mi. (923,770 sq. km.) |
| Norway | Oslo | Northern Europe, on the Scandinavian Peninsula, west of Sweden | 125,200 sq. mi. (324,220 sq. km.) |
| Oman | Muscat | On the Arabian Peninsula, southeast of Saudi Arabia | 82,000 sq. mi. (212,460 sq. km.) |
| Pakistan | Islamabad | South Asia, between Iran and India | 310,400 sq. mi. (803,940 sq. km.) |
| Palau | Koror | Islands in North Pacific Ocean, southeast of Philippines | 177 sq. mi. (458 sq. km.) |
| Panama | Panama City | Central America, between Costa Rica and Colombia | 30,200 sq. mi. (78,200 sq. km.) |
| Papua New Guinea | Port Moresby | Part of the island of New Guinea, north of Australia | 178,700 sq. mi. (462,840 sq. km.) |

| POPULATION | CURRENCY | LANGUAGE | COUNTRY |
|---:|---|---|---|
| 4,457,729 | Leu<br>$1 = 5 lei | Moldovan | **Moldova** |
| 32,035 | French franc<br>$1 = 5$\frac{5}{8}$ francs | French | **Monaco** |
| 2,578,530 | Tugrik<br>$1 = 800 tugriks | Khalkha<br>Mongolian | Mongolia |
| 29,114,497 | Dirham<br>$1 = 9 dirhams | Arabic | **Morocco** |
| 18,641,469 | Metical<br>$1 = 11,500 meticals | Portuguese | **Mozambique** |
| 47,305,319 | Kyat<br>$1 = 6$\frac{1}{8}$ kyats | Burmese | **Myanmar**<br>(*formerly* **Burma**) |
| 1,622,328 | Rand<br>$1 = 6 rand | Afrikaans,<br>English | Namibia |
| 10,501 | Australian dollar<br>$1 = 1$\frac{5}{8}$ Australian dollars | Nauruan | **Nauru** |
| 23,698,421 | Rupee<br>$1 = 68 rupees | Nepali | **Nepal** |
| 15,731,112 | Guilder, also euro<br>$1 = 1$\frac{7}{8}$ guilders | Dutch | **Netherlands** |
| 3,625,388 | New Zealand dollar<br>$1 = 1$\frac{5}{6}$ NZ dollars | English,<br>Maori | New Zealand |
| 4,583,379 | Gold cordoba<br>$1 = 11 gold cordobas | Spanish | **Nicaragua** |
| 9,671,848 | CFA franc<br>$1 = 560 CFA francs | French | **Niger** |
| 110,532,242 | Naira<br>$1 = 90 nairas | English | **Nigeria** |
| 4,419,955 | Krone<br>$1 = 7$\frac{5}{8}$ kroner | Norwegian | Norway |
| 2,363,591 | Rial Omani<br>$1 = $\frac{2}{8}$ rial Omani | Arabic | **Oman** |
| 135,135,195 | Rupee<br>$1 = 50 rupees | Urdu,<br>English | **Pakistan** |
| 18,110 | U.S. dollar | English,<br>Palauan | **Palau** |
| 2,735,943 | Balboa<br>Same value as U.S. dollar | Spanish | Panama |
| 4,599,785 | Kina<br>$1 = 2 kinas | English | **Papua<br>New Guinea** |

| COUNTRY | CAPITAL | LOCATION OF COUNTRY | AREA |
|---|---|---|---|
| Paraguay | Asunción | South America, between Argentina and Brazil | 157,000 sq. mi. (406,750 sq. km.) |
| Peru | Lima | South America, along the Pacific coast, north of Chile | 496,200 sq. mi. (1,285,220 sq. km.) |
| Philippines | Manila | Islands in the Pacific Ocean, off the coast of Southeast Asia | 116,000 sq. mi. (300,000 sq. km.) |
| Poland | Warsaw | Central Europe, on the Baltic Sea, east of Germany | 120,700 sq. mi. (312,683 sq. km.) |
| Portugal | Lisbon | Southern Europe, on the Iberian Peninsula, west of Spain | 35,672 sq. mi. (92,391 sq. km.) |
| Qatar | Doha | Arabian Peninsula, on the Persian Gulf | 4,416 sq. mi. (11,437 sq. km.) |
| Romania | Bucharest | Southern Europe, on the Black Sea, north of Bulgaria | 91,700 sq. mi. (237,500 sq. km.) |
| Russia | Moscow | Stretches from Eastern Europe across northern Asia to the Pacific Ocean | 6,592,800 sq. mi. (17,075,200 sq. km.) |
| Rwanda | Kigali | Central Africa, northwest of Tanzania | 10,200 sq. mi. (26,340 sq. km.) |
| Saint Kitts and Nevis | Basseterre | Islands in the Caribbean Sea, near Puerto Rico | 104 sq. mi. (269 sq. km.) |
| Saint Lucia | Castries | Island on eastern edge of the Caribbean Sea | 240 sq. mi. (620 sq. km.) |
| Saint Vincent and the Grenadines | Kingstown | Islands on eastern edge of the Caribbean Sea, north of Grenada | 130 sq. mi. (340 sq. km.) |
| Samoa (formerly Western Samoa) | Apia | Islands in the South Pacific Ocean | 1,100 sq. mi. (2,860 sq. km.) |
| San Marino | San Marino | Southern Europe, surrounded by Italy | 20 sq. mi. (60 sq. km.) |
| São Tomé and Príncipe | São Tomé | In the Gulf of Guinea, off the coast of West Africa | 400 sq. mi. (960 sq. km.) |
| Saudi Arabia | Riyadh | Western Asia, occupying most of the Arabian Peninsula | 756,983 sq. mi. (1,960,582 sq. km.) |
| Senegal | Dakar | West Africa, on the Atlantic Ocean, south of Mauritania | 75,700 sq. mi. (196,190 sq. km.) |
| Seychelles | Victoria | Islands off the coast of Africa, in the Indian Ocean, north of Madagascar | 176 sq. mi. (455 sq. km.) |
| Sierra Leone | Freetown | West Africa, on the Atlantic Ocean, south of Guinea | 27,700 sq. mi. (71,740 sq. km.) |

| POPULATION | CURRENCY | LANGUAGE | COUNTRY |
|---:|---|---|---|
| 5,291,020 | Guarani<br>$1 = 2,800 guarani | Spanish | **Paraguay** |
| 26,111,110 | New sol<br>$1 = 3$\frac{1}{8}$ new soles | Spanish,<br>Quechua | **Peru** |
| 77,725,862 | Peso<br>$1 = 39 pesos | Pilipino,<br>English | Philippines |
| 38,606,922 | Zloty<br>$1 = 3$\frac{1}{2}$ zlotys | Polish | **Poland** |
| 9,927,556 | Escudo, also euro<br>$1 = 170 escudos | Portuguese | **Portugal** |
| 697,126 | Riyal<br>$1 = 3$\frac{2}{3}$ riyals | Arabic | **Qatar** |
| 22,395,848 | Leu<br>$1 = 11,000 lei | Romanian | Romania |
| 146,861,022 | Ruble<br>$1 = 9 rubles | Russian | **Russia** |
| 7,956,172 | Franc<br>$1 = 320 francs | French,<br>Kinyarwanda | **Rwanda** |
| 42,291 | East Caribbean dollar<br>$1 = 2$\frac{2}{3}$ EC dollars | English | **Saint Kitts<br>and Nevis** |
| 152,335 | East Caribbean dollar<br>$1 = 2$\frac{2}{3}$ EC dollars | English | Saint Lucia |
| 119,818 | East Caribbean dollar<br>$1 = 2$\frac{2}{3}$ EC dollars | English | **Saint Vincent<br>and the<br>Grenadines** |
| 224,713 | Tala<br>$1 = 3 tala | English,<br>Samoan | **Samoa (formerly<br>Western Samoa)** |
| 24,894 | Italian lira<br>$1 = 1,700 lire | Italian | **San Marino** |
| 150,123 | Dobra<br>$1 = 2,400 dobras | Portuguese | São Tomé<br>and Príncipe |
| 20,785,955 | Riyal<br>$1 = 3$\frac{3}{4}$ riyals | Arabic | **Saudi Arabia** |
| 9,723,149 | CFA franc<br>$1 = 560 CFA francs | French | **Senegal** |
| 78,641 | Rupee<br>$1 = 5$\frac{1}{2}$ rupees | English,<br>French | **Seychelles** |
| 5,080,004 | Leone<br>$1 = 1,450 leones | English | Sierra Leone |

| COUNTRY | CAPITAL | LOCATION OF COUNTRY | AREA |
|---|---|---|---|
| Singapore | Singapore | Mostly on one island, off the tip of Southeast Asia | 250 sq. mi. (648 sq. km.) |
| Slovakia | Bratislava | Eastern Europe, between Poland and Hungary | 18,859 sq. mi. (48,845 sq. km.) |
| Slovenia | Ljubljana | Eastern Europe, between Austria and Croatia | 7,821 sq. mi. (20,256 sq. km.) |
| Solomon Islands | Honiara | Western Pacific Ocean | 11,000 sq. mi. (28,450 sq. km.) |
| Somalia | Mogadishu | East Africa, east of Ethiopia | 246,200 sq. mi. (637,660 sq. km.) |
| South Africa | Pretoria (executive) Cape Town (legislative) | At the southern tip of Africa | 471,009 sq. mi. (1,219,912 sq. km.) |
| Spain | Madrid | Europe, south of France, on the Iberian Peninsula | 194,880 sq. mi. (504,750 sq. km.) |
| Sri Lanka | Colombo | Island in the Indian Ocean, southeast of India | 25,300 sq. mi. (65,610 sq. km.) |
| Sudan | Khartoum | North Africa, south of Egypt, on the Red Sea | 967,500 sq. mi. (2,505,810 sq. km.) |
| Suriname | Paramaribo | South America, on the northern shore, east of Guyana | 63,000 sq. mi. (163,270 sq. km.) |
| Swaziland | Mbabane | Southern Africa, almost surrounded by South Africa | 6,700 sq. mi. (17,360 sq. km.) |
| Sweden | Stockholm | Northern Europe, on the Scandinavian Peninsula, east of Norway | 173,732 sq. mi. (449,964 sq. km.) |
| Switzerland | Bern | Central Europe, in the Alps, north of Italy | 15,900 sq. mi. (41,290 sq. km.) |
| Syria | Damascus | In the Middle East, north of Jordan and Iraq | 71,500 sq. mi. (185,180 sq. km.) |
| Taiwan | Taipei | Island off southeast coast of China | 13,900 sq. mi. (35,980 sq. km.) |
| Tajikistan | Dushanbe | Asia, west of China, south of Kyrgyzstan | 55,300 sq. mi. (143,100 sq. km.) |
| Tanzania | Dar-es-Salaam | East Africa, on the Indian Ocean, south of Kenya | 364,900 sq. mi. (945,090 sq. km.) |
| Thailand | Bangkok | Southeast Asia, west of Laos | 198,500 sq. mi. (514,000 sq. km.) |
| Togo | Lomé | West Africa, between Ghana and Benin | 21,900 sq. mi. (56,790 sq. km.) |
| Tonga | Nuku'alofa | Islands in the South Pacific Ocean | 289 sq. mi. (748 sq. km.) |

| POPULATION | CURRENCY | LANGUAGE | COUNTRY |
|---:|---|---|---|
| 3,490,356 | Singapore dollar<br>$1 = 1$\frac{5}{8}$ Singapore dollars | Chinese, Malay,<br>Tamil, English | **Singapore** |
| 5,392,982 | Koruna<br>$1 = 37 koruny | Slovak | **Slovakia** |
| 1,971,739 | Tolar<br>$1 = 160 tolars | Slovenian | Slovenia |
| 441,039 | Solomon Islands dollar<br>$1 = 4$\frac{7}{8}$ Solomon dollars | English | **Solomon Islands** |
| 6,841,695 | Shilling<br>$1 = 2,600 shillings | Somali | **Somalia** |
| 42,834,520 | Rand<br>$1 = 5$\frac{7}{8}$ rand | Afrikaans, English,<br>Ndebele, Sotho | **South Africa** |
| 39,133,996 | Peseta, also euro<br>$1 = 140 pesetas | Castilian<br>Spanish | Spain |
| 18,933,558 | Rupee<br>$1 = 68 rupees | Sinhala,<br>Tamil | **Sri Lanka** |
| 33,550,552 | Pound<br>$1 = 1,200 pounds | Arabic | **Sudan** |
| 427,980 | Guilder<br>$1 = 400 guilders | Dutch | **Suriname** |
| 966,462 | Lilangeni<br>$1 = 5$\frac{7}{8}$ emalangeni | English,<br>siSwati | Swaziland |
| 8,886,738 | Krona<br>$1 = 8$\frac{1}{8}$ kronur | Swedish | **Sweden** |
| 7,260,357 | Franc<br>$1 = 1$\frac{2}{5}$ francs | German,<br>French, Italian | **Switzerland** |
| 16,673,282 | Pound<br>$1 = 46 pounds | Arabic | **Syria** |
| 21,908,135 | New Taiwan dollar<br>$1 = 32 new Taiwan dollars | Mandarin<br>Chinese | Taiwan |
| 6,020,095 | Tajik ruble<br>$1 = 800 Tajik rubles | Tajik | **Tajikistan** |
| 30,608,769 | Shilling<br>$1 = 680 shillings | Swahili,<br>English | **Tanzania** |
| 60,037,366 | Baht<br>$1 = 36 bahts | Thai | **Thailand** |
| 4,905,827 | CFA franc<br>$1 = 560 CFA francs | French | Togo |
| 108,207 | Pa'anga<br>$1 = 1$\frac{5}{8}$ pa'angas | Tongan,<br>English | **Tonga** |

| COUNTRY | CAPITAL | LOCATION OF COUNTRY | AREA |
|---|---|---|---|
| Trinidad and Tobago | Port-of-Spain | Islands off the north coast of South America | 2,000 sq. mi. (5,130 sq. km.) |
| Tunisia | Tunis | North Africa, on the Mediterranean, between Algeria and Libya | 63,200 sq. mi. (163,610 sq. km.) |
| Turkey | Ankara | On the southern shore of the Black Sea, partly in Europe and partly in Asia | 301,400 sq. mi. (780,580 sq. km.) |
| Turkmenistan | Ashgabat | Western Asia, north of Afghanistan and Iran | 188,500 sq. mi. (488,100 sq. km.) |
| Tuvalu | Funafuti | Chain of islands in the South Pacific Ocean | 10 sq. mi. (26 sq. km.) |
| Uganda | Kampala | East Africa, south of Sudan | 91,100 sq. mi. (236,040 sq. km.) |
| Ukraine | Kiev | Eastern Europe, south of Belarus and Russia | 233,100 sq. mi. (603,700 sq. km.) |
| United Arab Emirates | Abu Dhabi | Arabian Peninsula, on the Persian Gulf | 32,000 sq. mi. (82,880 sq. km.) |
| United States | Washington, D.C. | Most of the country (48 of 50 states) in North America, between Canada and Mexico | 3,787,319 sq. mi. (9,629,091 sq. km.) |
| Uruguay | Montevideo | South America, on the Atlantic Ocean, south of Brazil | 68,000 sq. mi. (176,220 sq. km.) |
| Uzbekistan | Tashkent | Central Asia, south of Kazakhstan | 172,700 sq. mi. (447,400 sq. km.) |
| Vanuatu | Port-Vila | Islands in the South Pacific Ocean | 5,700 sq. mi. (14,760 sq. km.) |
| Vatican City | | Surrounded by the city of Rome, Italy | 1/5 sq. mi. (1/2 sq. km.) |
| Venezuela | Caracas | On the northern coast of South America, east of Colombia | 352,100 sq. mi. (912,050 sq. km.) |
| Vietnam | Hanoi | Southeast Asia, south of China, on the eastern coast | 127,200 sq. mi. (329,560 sq. km.) |
| Yemen | Sanaa | Asia, on the southern coast of the Arabian Peninsula | 203,800 sq. mi. (527,970 sq. km.) |
| Yugoslavia | Belgrade | Europe, on Balkan Peninsula, west of Romania and Bulgaria, north of Albania | 39,500 sq. mi. (102,350 sq. km.) |
| Zambia | Lusaka | Southern Africa, east of Angola | 290,600 sq. mi. (752,610 sq. km.) |
| Zimbabwe | Harare | Southern Africa, south of Zambia | 150,800 sq. mi. (390,580 sq. km.) |

| POPULATION | CURRENCY | LANGUAGE | COUNTRY |
|---:|---|---|---|
| 1,116,595 | Trinidad and Tobago dollar<br>$1 = 6\frac{1}{4}$ Trinidad dollars | English | Trinidad and Tobago |
| 9,380,404 | Dinar<br>$1 = 1\frac{1}{10}$ dinar | Arabic | Tunisia |
| 64,566,511 | Turkish lira<br>$1 = 300,000$ Turkish liras | Turkish | Turkey |
| 4,297,629 | Manat<br>$1 = 5,250$ manats | Turkmen | Turkmenistan |
| 10,444 | Tuvaluan dollar<br>$ 1= 1\frac{5}{8}$ Tuvaluan dollars | Tuvaluan, English | Tuvalu |
| 22,167,195 | Shilling<br>$1 = 1,200$ shillings | English | Uganda |
| 50,125,108 | Hryvna<br>$1 = 4$ hryvna | Ukranian | Ukraine |
| 2,303,088 | Dirham<br>$1 = 3\frac{2}{3}$ dirhams | Arabic | United Arab Emirates |
| 270,311,758 | U.S. dollar | English | United States |
| 3,284,841 | Peso<br>$1 = 10$ pesos | Spanish | Uruguay |
| 23,784,321 | Som<br>$1 = 100$ soms | Uzbek | Uzbekistan |
| 185,204 | Vatu<br>$1 = 130$ vatus | French, English, Bislama | Vanuatu |
| 840 | Vatican lira, Italian lira<br>$1 = 1,700$ lire | Italian, Latin | Vatican City |
| 22,803,409 | Bolivar<br>$1 = 550$ bolivares | Spanish | Venezuela |
| 76,236,259 | Dong<br>$1 = 14,000$ dong | Vietnamese | Vietnam |
| 16,387,963 | Rial<br>$1 = 140$ rials | Arabic | Yemen |
| 11,206,039 | New dinar<br>$1 = 10$ new dinars | Serbo-Croatian | Yugoslavia |
| 9,460,736 | Kwacha<br>$1 = 2,500$ kwacha | English | Zambia |
| 11,044,147 | Zimbabwe dollar<br>$1 = 37$ Zimbabwe dollars | English | Zimbabwe |

# A QUICK VISIT to Some COUNTRIES of the WORLD

Suppose you got a free round-trip ticket to visit any spot in the whole world. Where would you like to go? Here are a few sights you might want to see.

## AUSTRALIA

In Australia is **Ayers Rock**, the biggest exposed rock in the world. Located in a remote desert, it is about $1\frac{1}{2}$ miles long and shines bright red when the sun sets. Australia's first people, the Aborigines, thought it was sacred.

## CANADA

Want to feel like you're in France without leaving North America? Visit **Quebec City**. You'll see a high, walled fortress (the Citadel), a hotel that looks like a French castle (Château Frontenac), and people who speak French. In **Toronto**, however, English is the main language. You can get a view of that fast-growing city by going to the top of the **CN Tower**, the tallest free-standing structure in the world.

## CANADA—UNITED STATES

On the border between Canada and the United States is the famous waterfall **Niagara Falls**. About 20,000 bathtubs of water pour over the falls every second. You can put on a slicker and look at the falls from an observation deck—or ride by in a boat.

## CHINA

Some 2,400 years ago, workers started putting up the **Great Wall**. It became the world's longest structure, with a main section 2,150 miles long. It was built to keep out invaders, but it didn't stop Genghis Khan from conquering much of China in the 1200s.

## DENMARK

One of the world's oldest and most charming amusement parks is Denmark's **Tivoli Gardens**. There you will find everything from a mouse circus to the world's oldest roller coaster.

## ECUADOR

The **Galapagos Islands**, which belong to Ecuador, are remote islands in the Pacific Ocean, about 600 miles off South America. They are filled with wildlife (such as cormorants and penguins, giant tortoises and lizards) and odd plants.

## EGYPT

In Egypt you can see the **Great Sphinx**, a stone figure with a man's head and a lion's body. Carved in the desert 4,500 years ago, it's still there, despite wear and tear. Nearby, at Giza, are the great **pyramids** of ancient Egyptian pharaohs.

## FRANCE

A high point of a trip to France would be the **Eiffel Tower**. You get to the top of this open, cast-iron tower in four elevators, one after another. Then you can look down 1,000 feet on the beautiful city of Paris below.

## GERMANY

Though it was built in the 1800s, the mad King Ludwig II planned **Neuschwanstein Castle** to look just like a fairy-tale castle from the Middle Ages, complete with turrets and drawbridges.

*Eiffel Tower*

## GREAT BRITAIN

The regular London home of the queen of England is **Buckingham Palace**. When she's there a royal flag is flying. Outside you can see the Changing of the Guard. Another attraction is the **Tower of London**, where many famous people were jailed, tortured, and killed. The crown jewels are shown there.

## GREECE

On the **Acropolis**, you will find the ruins of the **Parthenon** and other public buildings from ancient Athens. The remains of the buildings, some partly rebuilt, stand high on a hill overlooking the city.

## INDIA

One of the world's biggest and richest tombs is the **Taj Mahal**, which took about 20,000 workers to build. A ruler of India had the Taj Mahal built for his wife after her death in 1631.

## IRELAND

If you kiss the **Blarney Stone**, which is in the tower of Blarney Castle, legends say you'll be able to throw words around and get people to agree with you—even if what you say is nonsense.

## ISRAEL

In Israel you can visit **Jerusalem**—a Holy City for three faiths. You can see the **Dome of the Rock**, built over the rock where Muhammad, founder of Islam, is said to have risen to heaven. You can stop at the **Western Wall**, where Jews pray; it is said to contain stones from Solomon's Temple. And you can see the **Church of the Holy Sepulcher**, built where it is said that Jesus was crucified and buried.

## ITALY

The **Leaning Tower of Pisa** is proof that kids aren't the only ones who make mistakes. Long before it was finished, the bell tower began sinking into the soft ground and leaning to one side. Every year, it leans $\frac{1}{20}$ of an inch more.

*The Parthenon in Greece*

## KENYA

Here and in other countries of East Africa, you can visit **National Parks**. You can go on safaris to see lions, zebras, giraffes, elephants, and other animals in their natural home.

## MEXICO

On the Yucatán peninsula, you can visit remains of the city of **Chichén Itzá**, where the Mayan people settled in the sixth century. Abandoned before the Spanish came, it's now partly rebuilt. You can see stone pyramids and temples and a Mayan ballfield.

## RUSSIA

A famous place to visit here is the **Kremlin**, a walled fortress in Moscow, with old churches, palaces, and towers with onion-shaped gold domes, dating back to the Middle Ages. Today the Kremlin is the headquarters for the Russian government.

## UNITED STATES

**Yellowstone National Park** was the world's first national park and is one of the best. (See page 280 for more details.) There are many other places to visit in Washington, D.C., and the 50 states. (See FACTS ABOUT THE STATES in the UNITED STATES chapter for further information.)

# NATIONS PUZZLE

**F**ind the hidden nations in this crossword puzzle.
The first letter of each NATION is already given. Can you fill in the others?
What two letters are not the first letters of any nation?

## ACROSS

**3** The capital of this nation is Cairo.

**4** This nation next to France is under 1 square mile in size.

**9** It takes up most of the southern part of South America.

**10** Some of the people here speak Quechua.

**11** It is on the same island as the Dominican Republic.

**14** Its capital is Nairobi.

**15** It is on the southern coast of West Africa.

**16** It lies between Jordan and the Mediterranean Sea.

**18** Its capital is Bridgetown.

**23** Its capital is Doha.

**24** It is surrounded by the city of Rome.

## DOWN

**1** Its people spend rials.

**2** A nation of islands with Tokyo as its capital.

**5** Two African countries use this as part of their name.

**6** Its capital is Copenhagen.

**7** The people in this South Pacific island country speak English.

**8** It is a small country on the Arabian peninsula.

**9** Its capital is Canberra.

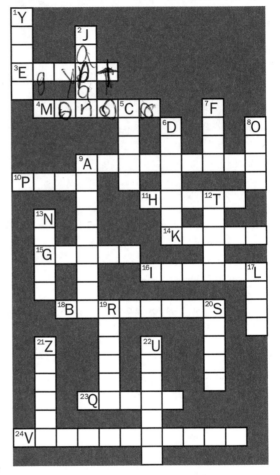

**12** Its currency is called Pa'anga.

**13** It is bigger than Nigeria and north of it.

**17** It is between Vietnam and Thailand.

**19** A huge nation, it stretches from Europe to Asia.

**20** Many of its people speak Castilian Spanish.

**21** Lusaka is its capital.

**22** You can find it south of Belarus and Russia.

*Answers are on pages 317–320.*

# MAPS and FLAGS
## of the
## NATIONS of the WORLD

Maps showing the continents and nations of the world appear on pages 161 through 172. Flags of the nations appear on pages 173 through 176.

A map of the United States appears on pages 270–271.

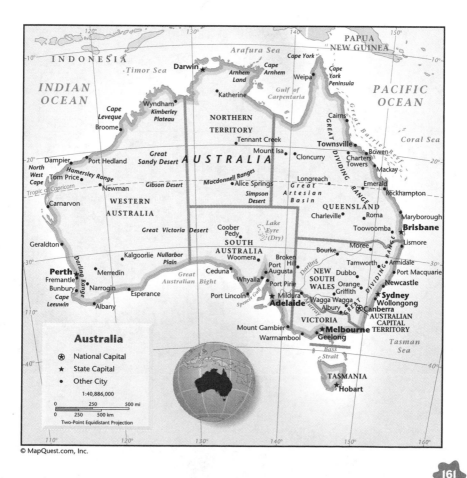

© MapQuest.com, Inc.

SWEDEN

NORWAY

GREAT BRITAIN

ICELAND

Arctic Circle

Denmark Strait

Greenland Sea

Cape Farewell

Ammassalik

Spitsbergen

GREENLAND (KALAALLIT NUNAAT) (Den.)

Nuuk (Godthaab)

Labrador Sea

NEWFOUNDLAND

St. Anthony Island of Newfoundland

St. John's

Corner Brook

St. Pierre & Miquelon Is. (Fr.)

Sydney

Antcosti I.

NEW P.E.I.

BRUNS.

Happy Valley-Goose Bay

Hebron

Schefferville

Labrador City

Sep-Iles

QUÉBEC

Chicoutimi

Chibougamau

Davis Strait

Baffin Bay

Pangnirtung

Iqaluit

Hudson Strait

Ungava Peninsula

Povungnituk

Belcher Is.

James Bay

CANADIAN

Moosonee

SHIELD

ONTARIO

Nord

0°

Cape Morris Jessup

North Pole

Arctic Ocean

Knud Rasmussen Land

Qaanaaq (Thule)

Gise Fiord

Ellesmere I.

Alert

Arctic Bay

Pond Inlet

Baffin Island

Repulse Bay

Southampton I.

Hudson Bay

Churchill

York Factory

L. Winnipeg

Winnipeg

Queen Elizabeth Islands

Resolute

Cambridge Bay

Victoria I.

Holman

Banks I.

NUNAVUT

CANADA

Uranium City

MANITOBA

Thompson

Flin Flon

La Ronge

SASK.

Prince Albert

Saskatoon

Regina

Beaufort Sea

Sachs Harbour

Yellowknife

Ft. Simpson

Great Slave Lake

Great Bear L.

Fort Smith

Ft. Resolution

Hay River

NORTHWEST TERRITORIES

Déline

Inuvik

Fort McPherson

Mackenzie

La Loche

Ft. McMurray

ALBERTA

Edmonton

Peace River

GREAT

ROCKY

Calgary

Athabasca

Athabasca L.

Saskatchewan

Point Barrow

Barrow

BROOKS RANGE

Fort Yukon

Dawson

Mayo

Carmacks

YUKON

Whitehorse

Watson Lake

BRITISH COLUMBIA

Prince George

Jasper

Williams Lake

Columbia

Fraser

RANGE

Fairbanks

Yukon

ALASKA

Point Hope

Kotzebue

Nome

Bering Strait

Arctic Circle

Mt. McKinley 6,194 m. (20,320 ft.)

ALASKA RANGE

Anchorage

Valdez

Kenai

Seward

Kodiak

Bethel

Mt. Logan 5,951 m (19,524 ft)

Yakutat

Skagway

Juneau

Sitka

COAST MOUNTAINS

Ketchikan

Prince Rupert

Kitimat

Queen Charlotte Is.

Vancouver I.

Vancouver

Victoria

Gulf of Alaska

Bering Sea

RUSSIA

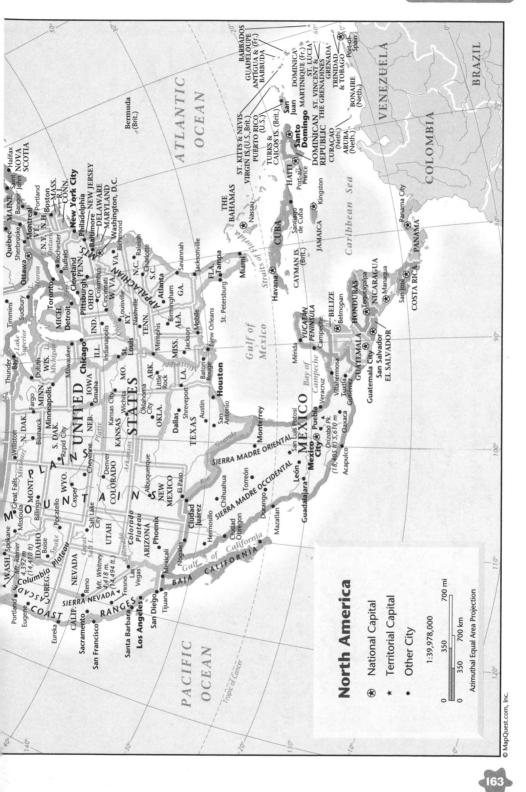

**North America**

⊛ National Capital
★ Territorial Capital
• Other City

1:39,978,000

0   350   700 mi
0   350   700 km

Azimuthal Equal Area Projection

ATLANTIC OCEAN

PACIFIC OCEAN

UNITED STATES

MEXICO

CANADA

VENEZUELA

BRAZIL

COLOMBIA

Caribbean Sea

Gulf of Mexico

CUBA

THE BAHAMAS

BARBADOS
GUADELOUPE (Fr.)
ANTIGUA & BARBUDA
DOMINICA
MARTINIQUE (Fr.)
ST. LUCIA
ST. VINCENT & THE GRENADINES
GRENADA
TRINIDAD & TOBAGO

ST. KITTS & NEVIS
VIRGIN IS. (U.S., Brit.)
PUERTO RICO (U.S.)
TURKS & CAICOS IS. (Brit.)

DOMINICAN REPUBLIC
HAITI
Santo Domingo
San Juan
Port-au-Prince
Port-of-Spain

BONAIRE (Neth.)
CURAÇAO (Neth.)
ARUBA (Neth.)

Santiago de Cuba
Havana
Nassau

JAMAICA
Kingston
CAYMAN IS. (Brit.)

BELIZE
Belmopan
GUATEMALA
Guatemala City
HONDURAS
Tegucigalpa
EL SALVADOR
San Salvador
NICARAGUA
Managua
COSTA RICA
San José
PANAMA
Panama City

Bermuda (Brit.)

© MapQuest.com, Inc.

163

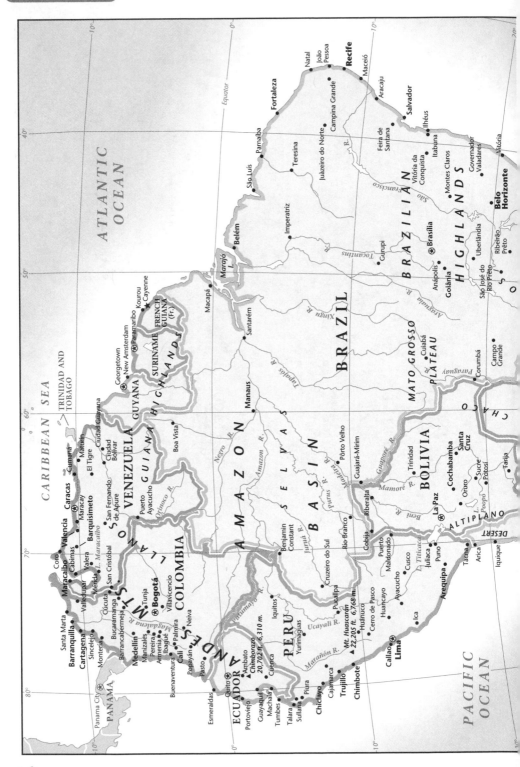

ATLANTIC OCEAN

Equator

Recife
João Pessoa
Natal
Campina Grande
Fortaleza
Maceió
Aracaju
Salvador
Ilhéus
Itabuna
Feira de Santana
Vitória da Conquista
Governador Valadares
Vitória
Montes Claros
Belo Horizonte
Juàzeiro do Norte
Teresina
Parnaíba
São Luís
Imperatriz
Belém

BRAZILIAN HIGHLANDS

São Francisco R.

Brasília
Anápolis
Goiânia
Uberlândia
São José do Rio Prêto
Ribeirão Prêto
Curupi

CARIBBEAN SEA

TRINIDAD AND TOBAGO

Georgetown
New Amsterdam
Paramaribo
Cayenne
Kourou
FRENCH GUIANA (Fr.)
SURINAME
GUYANA
GUIANA HIGHLANDS

Marajó I.
Macapá
Santarém
Manaus
Negro R.
Amazon R.
Tapajós R.
Xingu R.
Tocantins R.
Araguaia R.

BRAZIL

MATO GROSSO PLATEAU
Cuiabá
Corumbá
Campo Grande
Paraguay R.
CHACO

AMAZON BASIN

SELVAS

Pôrto Velho
Guajará-Mirim
Madeira R.
Guaporé R.
Mamoré R.
Beni R.
Trinidad
Riberalta
Cobija
Puerto Maldonado

BOLIVIA
Santa Cruz
Cochabamba
Sucre
Potosí
Oruro
La Paz
Tarija
ALTIPLANO
L. Poopó
L. Titicaca
DESERT

VENEZUELA
Caracas
Valencia
Maracay
Barquisimeto
Cumaná
Maturín
El Tigre
Ciudad Guayana
Ciudad Bolívar
Boa Vista
San Fernando de Apure
Puerto Ayacucho
Orinoco R.

Coro
Maracaibo
Cabimas
Valera
L. Maracaibo
Mérida
San Cristóbal
Cúcuta
Bucaramanga
Barrancabermeja
Magdalena R.
LLANOS
ANDES MTS.

COLOMBIA
Bogotá
Villavicencio
Tunja

Santa Marta
Barranquilla
Cartagena
Sincelejo
Montería
Medellín
Manizales
Pereira
Armenia
Ibagué
Cali
Palmira
Neiva
Popayán
Pasto
Buenaventura

PANAMA

Esmeraldas
ECUADOR
Quito
Portoviejo
Ambato
Chimborazo 20,702 ft. 6,310 m.
Cuenca
Guayaquil
Machala
Tumbes
Talara
Sullana
Piura
Chiclayo
Trujillo
Chimbote
Mt. Huascarán 22,205 ft. 6,768 m.
Cajamarca
Chachapoyas
Putumayo R.
Iquitos
Yurimaguas
Marañón R.
Ucayali R.
Huánuco
Cerro de Pasco
Huancayo
Ayacucho
Cusco
Puno
Juliaca
Arequipa
Tacna
Arica
Iquique
Ica
Callao
Lima

PERU
Cruzeiro do Sul
Rio Branco
Benjamin Constant
Juruá R.
Purus R.
Pucallpa
Amazon R.

PACIFIC OCEAN

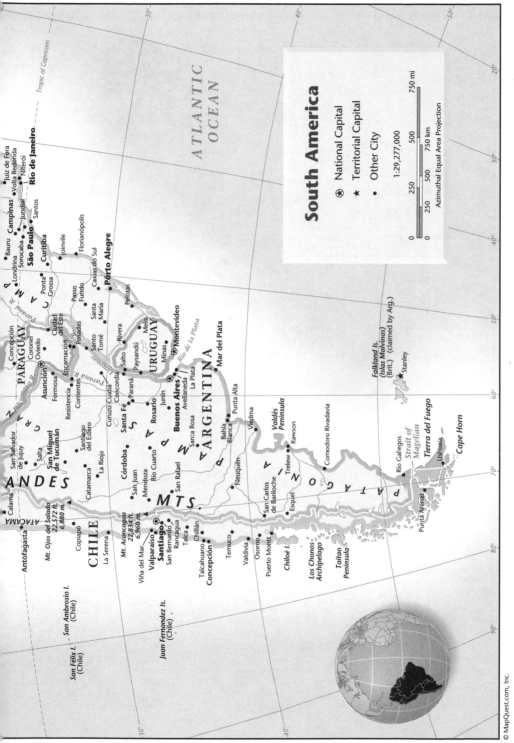

## South America

- ⊛ National Capital
- ★ Territorial Capital
- • Other City

1:29,277,000

| 0 | 250 | 500 | 750 mi |
| 0 | 250 500 | 750 km |

Azimuthal Equal Area Projection

ATLANTIC OCEAN

Tropic of Capricorn

Luiz de Fora
Volta Redonda
Niterói
**Rio de Janeiro**
Bauru • Campinas • Jundiaí
Londrina • Sorocaba • Santos
**São Paulo** • **Curitiba**
Joinvile
Ponta Grossa
Florianópolis
Passo Fundo
Santa Maria
Caxias do Sul
Pelotas
**Pôrto Alegre**

PARAGUAY
Concepción
Coronel Oviedo
Ciudad del Este
Posadas
Encarnación
**Asunción** ⊛
Formosa
Resistencia
Corrientes
Curuzú Cuatiá
Concordia
Santa
Santo Tomé
Rivera
Salto
Paysandú

URUGUAY
Minas
Melo
⊛ **Montevideo**
Rio de la Plata
**Mar del Plata**
La Plata
Avellaneda
⊛ **Buenos Aires**
**Rosario**
**Santa Fe**
Paraná
Junín
Santa Rosa
Punta Alta
Bahía Blanca
Viedma

**ARGENTINA**

Paraná R.
Paraguay R.
Pilcomayo R.
Uruguay R.

G R A N   C H A C O

San Salvador de Jujuy
Salta
**San Miguel de Tucumán**
Santiago del Estero
Catamarca
La Rioja
**Córdoba**
San Juan
Río Cuarto
Mendoza
San Rafael
Neuquén

**A N D E S**
Calama
Antofagasta
ATACAMA
**Mt. Ojos del Salado**
22,572 ft.
6,880 m.
Copiapó
San Félix I. (Chile)
San Ambrosio I. (Chile)
Juan Fernández Is. (Chile)

**CHILE**
La Serena
**Mt. Aconcagua**
22,834 ft.
6,960 m.
Viña del Mar
**Valparaíso**
**Santiago** ⊛
San Bernardo
Rancagua
Talca
Chillán
Talcahuano
**Concepción**
Temuco
Valdivia
Osorno
Puerto Montt
Chiloé I.
Los Chonos Archipelago
Taitao Peninsula
San Carlos de Bariloche
Esquel
Rawson
Trelew
**Valdés Peninsula**
Comodoro Rivadavia

**M T S.**

**P A T A G O N I A**

Río Gallegos
Strait of Magellan
Punta Arenas
Ushuaia
**Tierra del Fuego**
"Cape Horn"

Falkland Is. (Islas Malvinas) (Brit.) (claimed by Arg.)
★ Stanley

© MapQuest.com, Inc.

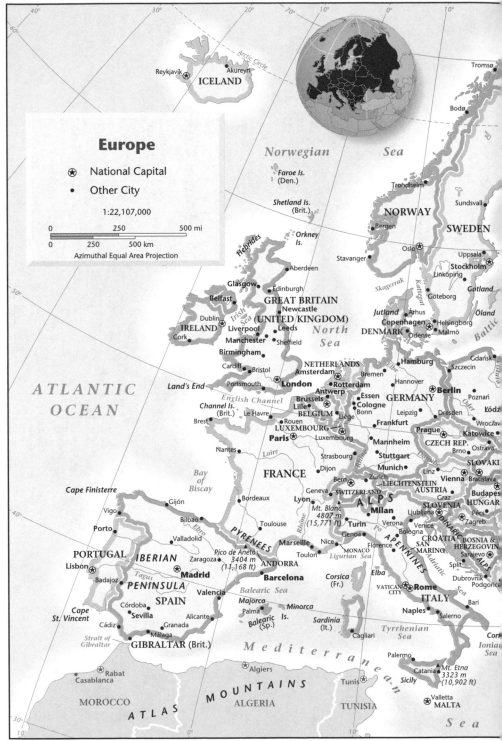

## Europe

⊛ National Capital

• Other City

1:22,107,000

| 0 | 250 | 500 mi |

| 0 | 250 | 500 km |

Azimuthal Equal Area Projection

Reykjavík • Akureyri
ICELAND

*Norwegian* *Sea*

Tromsø
Bodø

Faroe Is.
(Den.)

Trondheim

Shetland Is.
(Brit.)

Sundsvall

NORWAY
Bergen

SWEDEN
Uppsala
Stockholm
Linköping

Orkney
Is.

Oslo ⊛

Stavanger

*Skagerrak* *Kattegat*
Göteborg
Gotland
Öland

*Hebrides*
Aberdeen

Glasgow • Edinburgh
Belfast
GREAT BRITAIN
Newcastle

Jutland • Århus
Copenhagen ⊛
DENMARK • Helsingborg
Odense • Malmö

Dublin ⊛
IRELAND • Liverpool
(UNITED KINGDOM)
Leeds
Sheffield

*Irish Sea*

*North Sea*

*Baltic*
Gdańsk
Szczecin

Cork
Manchester •
Birmingham

Cardiff • Bristol

NETHERLANDS
Amsterdam ⊛
Bremen

Hamburg

*Elbe*

Hannover

Berlin ⊛
Poznań
Łódź

ATLANTIC
OCEAN

Land's End
Portsmouth • London ⊛ • Rotterdam
Antwerp
Brussels ⊛
Lille
BELGIUM
Liège
Bonn

Essen
Cologne
GERMANY
Leipzig
Dresden

Dortmund

Wrocław

*English Channel*

Channel Is.
(Brit.)

Le Havre

Brest

Rouen
LUXEMBOURG
Paris ⊛
Luxembourg

Frankfurt
Mannheim

Prague ⊛
Katowice
CZECH REP.
Brno • Ostrava

Nantes
*Loire*

Strasbourg
Dijon

Stuttgart
Munich

SLOVAKI
Linz
Vienna ⊛ Bratislava

*Bay of Biscay*

FRANCE
Bordeaux

Bern ⊛
Zürich
Geneva
SWITZERLAND

LIECHTENSTEIN
AUSTRIA
Graz
Budapest ⊛
HUNGAR
Pécs

Cape Finisterre
Vigo
Porto

Gijón
Bilbao
Valladolid

Lyon
Toulouse
*Rhône*
Mt. Blanc
4807 m
(15,771 ft)

ALPS
Milan • Turin
Verona
Venice
Bologna

Ljubljana ⊛
SLOVENIA
DINARIC
CROATIA
Zagreb ⊛

*Ebro*

PYRENEES

Marseille
Nice
Toulon
Genoa •
Florence

*APENNINES*
SAN MARINO
BOSNIA &
HERZEGOVIN

PORTUGAL
Lisbon ⊛
Badajoz

IBERIAN
PENINSULA

Pico de Aneto
3404 m
(11,168 ft)
Zaragoza
*Tagus*
Madrid ⊛

ANDORRA
Barcelona
Valencia

Marseille

Corsica
(Fr.)

Elba
VATICAN
CITY ⊛ Rome
ITALY
Sarajevo ⊛
Split
Dubrovnik
Podgorica
Bari

Cape
St. Vincent
Cádiz

Córdoba
Sevilla
Granada
SPAIN
Alicante
Málaga

*Balearic Sea*
Majorca
Palma
Minorca
Balearic Is.
(Sp.)

Sardinia
(It.)

Naples
Salerno

*Tyrrhenian Sea*
Cagliari

Cor
*Ionia
Sea*

*Strait of
Gibraltar*
GIBRALTAR (Brit.)

Palermo

Rabat ⊛
Casablanca

Algiers •

*M e d i t e r r a n e a n*

Tunis •

Catania
Sicily
Mt. Etna
3323 m
(10,902 ft)

MOROCCO
ATLAS MOUNTAINS
ALGERIA
TUNISIA

Valletta ⊛
MALTA

*Sea*

© MapQuest.com, Inc.

North Cape
Hammerfest
Barents Sea
Nar'yan-Mar
Ob
LAPLAND
Murmansk
KOLA PENINSULA
Apatity
Kiruna
Pechora
Pechora
Irtysh
Arctic Circle
Ukhta
Luleå
Oulu
White Sea
Arkhangel'sk
RUSSIA
Serov
Syktyvkar
Berezniki
Petropavl
Umeå
FINLAND
Vaasa
Kotlas
Yekaterinburg
Divina
Belomorsk
Chelyabinsk
Petrozavodsk
Lake Onega
Kirov
Perm'
Qostanay
Tampere
Lahti
Lake Ladoga
Izhevsk
Kama
Ufa
Turku
Helsinki
PLAIN
Vologda
Naberezhnyye Chelny
Magnitogorsk
Åland
St. Petersburg
Cherepovets
Kazan
MOUNTAINS
Sea
Tallinn
Novgorod
Yaroslavl'
Nizhniy Novgorod
ESTONIA
Tartu
Ivanovo
Ul'yanovsk
Tol'yatti
Orenburg
Orsk
Rīga
LATVIA
Pskov
EUROPEAN
Tver
Moscow
Saransk
Samara
Aqtöbe
Daugavpils
Penza
50°
LITHUANIA
Vitsyebsk
Ryazan'
Oral
Kaunas
Vilnius
Smolensk
Tula
Tambov
Volga
Ural
KAZAKHSTAN
RUSSIA
Kaliningrad
Mahilyow
Lipetsk
Saratov
Aral Sea
NORTHERN
Hrodna
BELARUS
Bryansk
Voronezh
Atyraū
Minsk
Homyel'
Kursk
Warsaw
Brest
Volgograd
UZBEKISTAN
POLAND
Kiev
Kharkiv
Don
Astrakhan
Aqtaū
Kraków
L'viv
UKRAINE
Dnieper
Luhans'k
Donets'k
CARPATHIAN
Dniester
Dnipropetrovs'k
Caspian
Košice
Chernivtsi
Zaporizhzhia
Rostov na Donu
MTS.
MOLDOVA
Kryyyy Rih
Mariupol'
TURKMENISTAN
Debrecen
Iaşi
Chişinău
Mykolaiv
Sea of Azov
Stavropol'
Groznyy
Makhachkala
Sea
Odesa
Krasnodar
40°
ROMANIA
CRIMEA
Simferopol'
CAUCASUS
Türkmenbashi
Timişoara
Sevastopol'
GEORGIA
Novi Sad
Ploieşti
T'bilisi
Baku
Bucharest
Constanţa
Black Sea
ARMENIA
AZERBAIJAN
Belgrade
Danube
Varna
Trabzon
Yerevan
YUGOSLAVIA
BULGARIA
Burgas
Tabriz
Sofia
MACEDONIA
Skopje
Plovdiv
Istanbul
Tehran
Tiranë
Thessaloníki
Ankara
TURKEY
ALBANIA
BALKAN PENINSULA
IRAN
Lárisa
GREECE
Izmir
Adana
Pátrai
IRAQ
Athens
PELOPONNESUS
Cyclades
Rhodes
SYRIA
Baghdad
Sea of Crete
Nicosia
Euphrates
Crete
Iráklion
CYPRUS
LEBANON
Beirut
Damascus
Persian Gulf

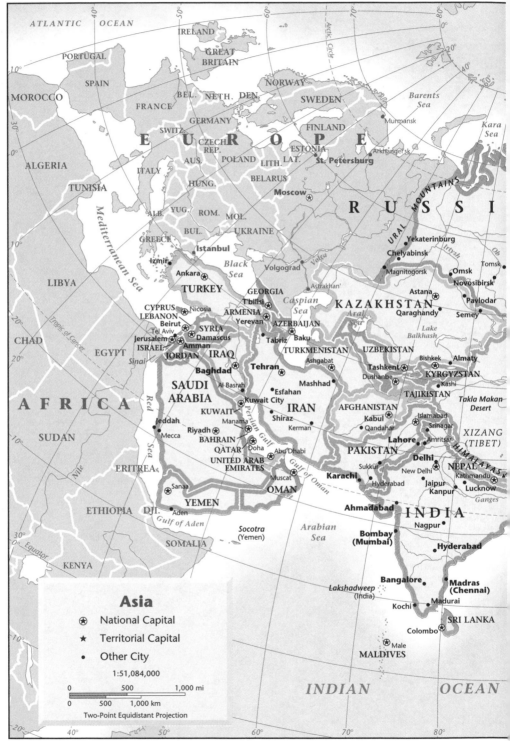

ATLANTIC OCEAN

IRELAND
GREAT BRITAIN

PORTUGAL
SPAIN

MOROCCO

FRANCE
BEL. NETH. DEN.
GERMANY
SWITZ.
CZECH REP.
AUS. POLAND LITH. LAT.
ITALY
HUNG.
ALB. YUG. ROM. MOL.
BUL. UKRAINE
GREECE
Izmir
Ankara
Black Sea

NORWAY
SWEDEN
FINLAND
ESTONIA
Barents Sea
Murmansk
Arkhangel'sk
St. Petersburg
BELARUS
Moscow

Kara Sea

R U S S I

E U R O P E

ALGERIA

TUNISIA

LIBYA

Mediterranean Sea

Tropic of Cancer

CHAD

EGYPT

Sinai

AFRICA

SUDAN

Nile

ERITREA

Red Sea

ETHIOPIA DJI.

KENYA

Equator

TURKEY
CYPRUS
LEBANON
Beirut
Tel Aviv
Jerusalem
ISRAEL
JORDAN
Amman

Nicosia
Damascus
SYRIA

Istanbul
GEORGIA
T'bilisi
ARMENIA
Yerevan
AZERBAIJAN
Tabriz
Baku

Volgograd
Astrakhan'
Caspian Sea
Aral Sea

URAL MOUNTAINS
Yekaterinburg
Chelyabinsk
Magnitogorsk
Astana
Qaraghandy

Irtysh
Omsk
Tomsk
Novosibirsk
Pavlodar
Semey

KAZAKHSTAN

Lake Balkhash

Volga

IRAQ
Baghdad
Al-Basrah

SAUDI ARABIA
KUWAIT
Kuwait City
Manama
BAHRAIN
QATAR
Doha
Abu Dhabi
UNITED ARAB EMIRATES

Jeddah
Mecca
Riyadh

Sanaa

YEMEN
Aden
Gulf of Aden

SOMALIA

Tehran
Esfahan
Mashhad
IRAN
Shiraz
Kerman

TURKMENISTAN
Ashgabat
Dushanbe
Tashkent

UZBEKISTAN
Bishkek
KYRGYZSTAN
Kashi
TAJIKISTAN
Almaty

Takla Makan Desert

AFGHANISTAN
Kabul
Qandahar
Islamabad
Srinagar
XIZANG (TIBET)

PAKISTAN
Lahore
Amritsar
Delhi
New Delhi
Sukkur
Hyderabad
Karachi
Jaipur
Kanpur

HIMALAYAS
NEPAL
Kathmandu
Lucknow
Ganges

Muscat
OMAN

Gulf of Oman

Arabian Sea

Socotra (Yemen)

Lakshadweep (India)
Kochi

Ahmadabad
Nagpur
INDIA
Bombay (Mumbai)
Hyderabad

Bangalore
Madras (Chennai)
Madurai

SRI LANKA
Colombo

Male
MALDIVES

Persian Gulf

## Asia

⊛ National Capital

★ Territorial Capital

• Other City

1:51,084,000

| 0 | 500 | 1,000 mi |

| 0 | 500 | 1,000 km |

Two-Point Equidistant Projection

INDIAN OCEAN

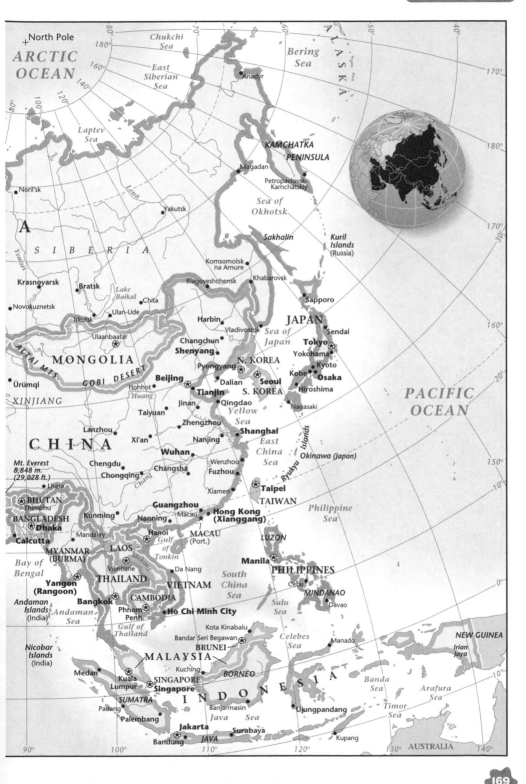

North Pole

ARCTIC OCEAN

180°
160°
140°
120°
100°
80°

Chukchi Sea

East Siberian Sea

Bering Sea

ALASKA

170°

Anadyr

Laptev Sea

KAMCHATKA PENINSULA

180°

Magadan

Petropavlovsk-Kamchatskiy

Noril'sk

Yakutsk

Sea of Okhotsk

170°

Sakhalin

Kuril Islands (Russia)

30°

A

Yenisey

S I B E R I A

Komsomolsk na Amure

Krasnoyarsk

Bratsk

Lake Baikal

Chita

Blagoveshchensk

Khabarovsk

Sapporo

160°

Novokuznetsk

Irkutsk

Ulan-Ude

Harbin

Vladivostok

Sea of Japan

JAPAN

Sendai

Ulaanbaatar

Changchun

Tokyo

MONGOLIA

Shenyang

N. KOREA

Yokohama

Kyoto

Osaka

20°

Ürümqi

GOBI DESERT

Pyongyang

Kobe

ALTAI MTS.

Hohhot

Beijing

Dalian

Seoul

XINJIANG

Huang

Tianjin

S. KOREA

Hiroshima

Jinan

Qingdao

Nagasaki

PACIFIC OCEAN

Lanzhou

Taiyuan

Zhengzhou

Yellow Sea

Xi'an

Nanjing

Shanghai

C H I N A

Wuhan

East China Sea

Islands

Mt. Everest 8,848 m. (29,028 ft.)

Chengdu

Changsha

Wenzhou

Okinawa (Japan)

150°

Chongqing

Chang

Fuzhou

Ryukyu

Lhasa

Xiamen

Taipei

10°

BHUTAN

Thimphu

Guangzhou

Macau

TAIWAN

BANGLADESH

Kunming

Nanning

Hong Kong (Xianggang)

Philippine Sea

Dhaka

Mandalay

Hanoi

MACAU

Calcutta

Gulf of Tonkin

(Port.)

LUZON

MYANMAR (BURMA)

LAOS

Vientiane

Da Nang

Manila

Bay of Bengal

Yangon (Rangoon)

THAILAND

VIETNAM

South China Sea

PHILIPPINES

Cebu

MINDANAO

Andaman Islands (India)

Andaman Sea

Bangkok

CAMBODIA

Phnom Penh

Ho Chi Minh City

Sulu Sea

Davao

Kota Kinabalu

Nicobar Islands (India)

Gulf of Thailand

Bandar Seri Begawan

Celebes Sea

Manado

NEW GUINEA

Irian Jaya

BRUNEI

MALAYSIA

Kuching

BORNEO

Banda Sea

Arafura Sea

Medan

Kuala Lumpur

SINGAPORE

Singapore

I N D O N E S I A

SUMATRA

Padang

Banjarmasin

Java Sea

Ujungpandang

Timor Sea

Palembang

Jakarta

Surabaya

Kupang

AUSTRALIA

Bandung

JAVA

90°
100°
110°
120°
130°
140°

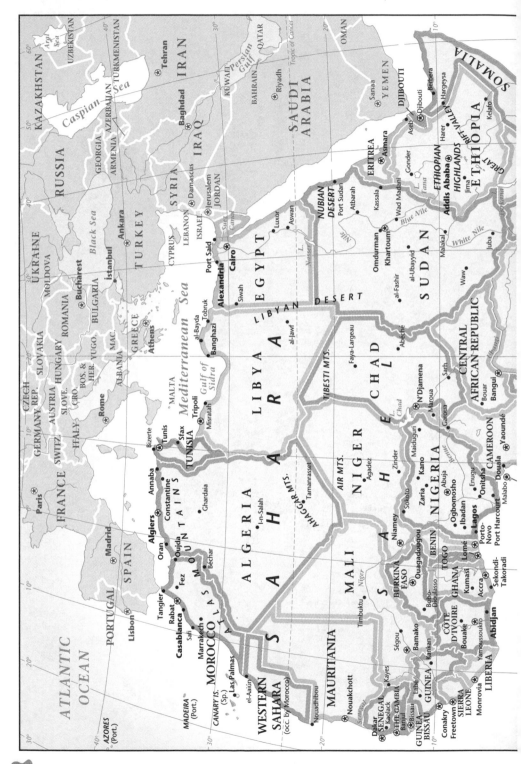

KAZAKHSTAN

UZBEKISTAN

TURKMENISTAN

Aral Sea

Caspian Sea

RUSSIA

GEORGIA

ARMENIA AZERBAIJAN

Tehran

IRAN

Baghdad

IRAQ

KUWAIT

Persian Gulf

QATAR

BAHRAIN

Riyadh

SAUDI ARABIA

OMAN

YEMEN

Sanaa

DJIBOUTI

Djibouti

Berbera

Hargeysa

SOMALIA

UKRAINE

MOLDOVA

Black Sea

Bucharest

BULGARIA

ROMANIA

Ankara

TURKEY

istanbul

GREECE

Athens

CYPRUS

SYRIA

Damascus

LEBANON

ISRAEL

Jerusalem

JORDAN

Port Said

Suez Canal

ERITREA

Asmara

Gonder

Aseb

ETHIOPIAN HIGHLANDS

Addis Ababa

Jima

GREAT RIFT VALLEY

ETHIOPIA

Harer

Kelafo

Tropic of Cancer

NUBIAN DESERT

Port Sudan

Atbarah

Kassala

Wad Madani

Blue Nile

L. Tana

SLOVAKIA

HUNGARY

AUSTRIA

CZECH

GERMANY REP.

SWITZ.

SLOVE.

CRO.

BOS.& HER.

YUGO. MAC.

ALBANIA

ITALY

Rome

Alexandria

Cairo

EGYPT

Siwah

Luxor

Aswan

NILE

L. Nasser

Omdurman

Khartoum

al-Ubayyid

al-Fashir

Malakal

SUDAN

White Nile

Waw

Juba

Mediterranean Sea

MALTA

Gulf of Sidra

Tripoli

Misratah

al-Bayda

Tobruk

Banghazi

LIBYA

LIBYAN DESERT

al-Jawf

SAHARA

TIBESTI MTS.

Faya-Largeau

CHAD

Abeche

CENTRAL AFRICAN REPUBLIC

Bouar

Bangui

FRANCE

SPAIN

Paris

Madrid

Lisbon

PORTUGAL

ATLANTIC OCEAN

MADEIRA (Port.)

AZORES (Port.)

CANARY IS. (Sp.)

Las Palmas

Bizerte

Tunis

Sfax

TUNISIA

Annaba

Algiers

Constantine

Oran

Oujda

Ghardaia

I-n-Salah

ALGERIA

SAHARA

AHAGGAR MTS.

Tamanrasset

AIR MTS.

Agadez

NIGER

Zinder

N'Djamena

L. Chad

Maroua

Garoua

Sarh

CAMEROON

Yaoundé

Douala

Malabo

Enugu

Onitsha

Port Harcourt

NIGERIA

Kano

Zaria

Maiduguri

Sokoto

Abuja

Ibadan

Ogbomosho

Lagos

Porto-Novo

BENIN

TOGO

Lomé

Cotonou

Niamey

Ouagadougou

BURKINA FASO

Bobo-Dioulasso

GHANA

Kumasi

Accra

Sekondi-Takoradi

CÔTE D'IVOIRE

Bouake

Yamoussoukro

Abidjan

LIBERIA

Monrovia

SIERRA LEONE

Freetown

GUINEA

Conakry

Kankan

Kindia

Labé

GUINEA-BISSAU

Bissau

SENEGAL

Dakar

Kaolack

Banjul

THE GAMBIA

MAURITANIA

Nouakchott

Nouadhibou

WESTERN SAHARA (occ. by Morocco)

el-Aaiún

MOROCCO

ATLAS MOUNTAINS

Casablanca

Rabat

Tangier

Fez

Marrakech

Safi

Béchar

Tangier

MALI

Bamako

Ségou

Kayes

Timbuktu

Niger

SENEGAL

Mediterranean Sea

Benue

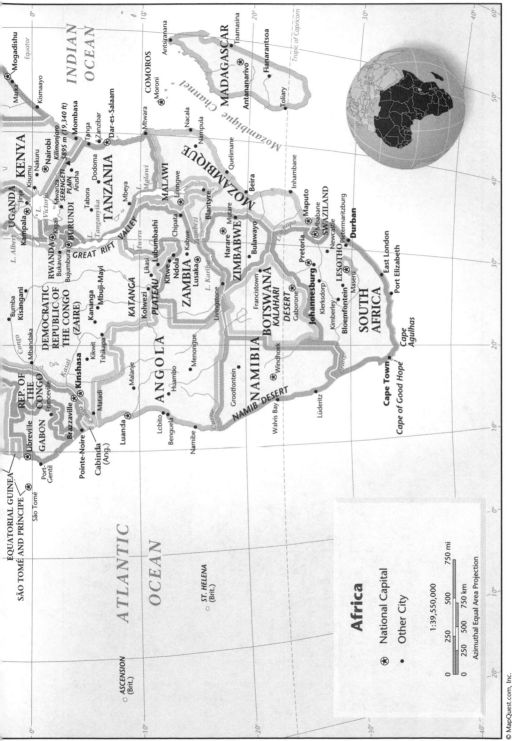

**Africa**

⊛ National Capital

• Other City

1:39,550,000

0    250    500    750 mi

0    250    500    750 km

Azimuthal Equal Area Projection

MADAGASCAR

INDIAN OCEAN

KENYA

UGANDA

RWANDA

BURUNDI

TANZANIA

MALAWI

MOZAMBIQUE

ZAMBIA

DEMOCRATIC REPUBLIC OF THE CONGO (ZAIRE)

ANGOLA

NAMIBIA

BOTSWANA

ZIMBABWE

SOUTH AFRICA

LESOTHO

SWAZILAND

GABON

REP. OF THE CONGO

EQUATORIAL GUINEA

SÃO TOMÉ AND PRÍNCIPE

COMOROS

KATANGA

PLATEAU

KALAHARI DESERT

NAMIB DESERT

GREAT RIFT VALLEY

SERENGETI PLAIN

Kilimanjaro 5895 m (19,340 ft)

ATLANTIC OCEAN

Mogadishu

Merka

Kismaayo

Nairobi

Nakuru

Kisumu

Kampala

Jinja

L. Albert

L. Victoria

Kigali

Bukavu

Bujumbura

Mombasa

Tanga

Zanzibar

Dar-es-Salaam

Mtwara

Nacala

Nampula

Quelimane

Dodoma

Arusha

Tabora

Mbeya

L. Tanganyika

L. Malawi

Lilongwe

Chipata

Blantyre

Beira

Inhambane

Maputo

Mbabane

Pietermaritzburg

Durban

East London

Port Elizabeth

Harare

Mutare

Bulawayo

Pretoria

Johannesburg

Newcastle

Klerksdorp

Kimberley

Bloemfontein

Maseru

Gaborone

Francistown

Windhoek

Walvis Bay

Lüderitz

Grootfontein

Menongue

Huambo

Malanje

Benguela

Lobito

Namibe

Luanda

Matadi

Kinshasa

Brazzaville

Pointe-Noire

Cabinda (Ang.)

Libreville

Port-Gentil

São Tomé

Franceville

Mbandaka

Bumba

Kisangani

Kikwit

Tshikapa

Kananga

Mbuji-Mayi

Likasi

Lubumbashi

Kolwezi

Kitwe

Ndola

Kabwe

Lusaka

Livingstone

L. Kariba

L. Mweru

Zambezi

Zambezi

Limpopo

Orange

Congo

Kasai

Cuango

Cunene

Okavango

Cape Town

Cape of Good Hope

Cape Agulhas

Antsiranana

Toamasina

Antananarivo

Fianarantsoa

Toliary

Moroni

Antsiranana

Mozambique Channel

Equator

Tropic of Capricorn

ST. HELENA (Brit.)

ASCENSION (Brit.)

© MapQuest.com, Inc.

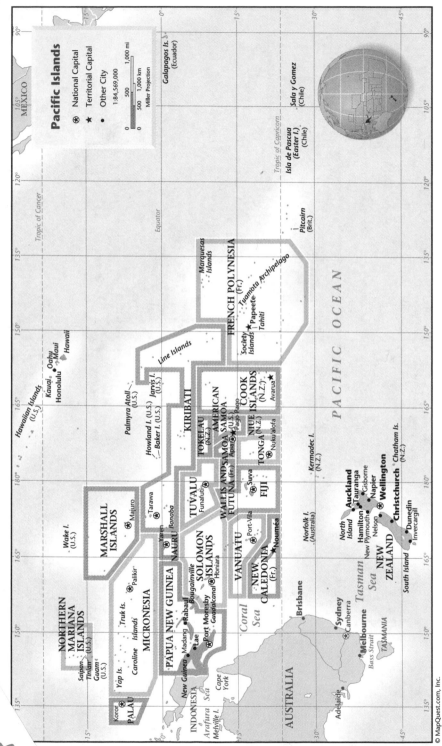

## Pacific Islands

⊛ National Capital
★ Territorial Capital
• Other City

1:84,569,000

0    500    1,000 mi
0    500 1,000 km
Miller Projection

MÉXICO

Galapagos Is.
(Ecuador)

Sala y Gomez
(Chile)

Tropic of Capricorn

Isla de Pascua
(Easter I.)
(Chile)

Pitcairn
(Brit.)

Equator

Tropic of Cancer

PACIFIC OCEAN

Marquesas
Islands

FRENCH POLYNESIA
(Fr.)

Tuamotu Archipelago

Society ★Papeete
Islands   Tahiti

Hawaiian Islands
(U.S.)

Kauai• Oahu•
Honolulu  ▲Maui
•Hawaii

Line Islands

Palmyra Atoll
(U.S.)

Howland I. (U.S.)
Baker I. (U.S.)

Jarvis I.
(U.S.)

KIRIBATI

AMERICAN
SAMOA
★Pago Pago
(U.S.)

COOK
ISLANDS
(N.Z.)
★Avarua

Wake I.
(U.S.)

MARSHALL
ISLANDS

⊛Majuro

Tarawa

TOKELAU
(N.Z.)

WALLIS AND SAMOA
FUTUNA (Fr.)   ★Apia

NIUE
(N.Z.)

TONGA
⊛Nuku'alofa

TUVALU
Funafuti•

Yaren
Banaba

NAURU ⊛

NORTHERN
MARIANA
ISLANDS

Saipan•
Tinian (U.S.)
Guam•
(U.S.)

Yap Is.    Truk Is.
Caroline  Islands

MICRONESIA

Koror⊛
PALAU

⊛Palikir

PAPUA NEW GUINEA

New Guinea• Madang
•Lae
⊛Port Moresby

Rabaul•
Bougainville

SOLOMON
ISLANDS
⊛Honiara
Guadalcanal•

VANUATU

Port-Vila•

•Suva

FIJI

Kermadec I.
(N.Z.)

NEW
CALEDONIA
(Fr.)
★Nouméa

Norfolk I.
(Australia)

North
Island

Auckland•
Hamilton•  •Tauranga
New Plymouth•  •Gisborne
•Napier
Nelson•   Wellington⊛

Christchurch•   Chatham Is.
(N.Z.)

South Island

Dunedin•
Invercargill•

NEW
ZEALAND

Brisbane•

Sydney•
•Canberra

Melbourne•

AUSTRALIA

•Adelaide

Coral
Sea

Cape
York

Arafura Sea

Melville I.

INDONESIA

Tasman
Sea

Bass Strait

TASMANIA

© MapQuest.com, Inc.

# FLAGS of the NATIONS of the WORLD

## (Afghanistan-Dominican Republic)

AFGHANISTAN ALBANIA ALGERIA ANDORRA ANGOLA

ANTIGUA AND BARBUDA ARGENTINA ARMENIA AUSTRALIA AUSTRIA

AZERBAIJAN THE BAHAMAS BAHRAIN BANGLADESH BARBADOS

BELARUS BELGIUM BELIZE BENIN BHUTAN

BOLIVIA BOSNIA AND HERZEGOVINA BOTSWANA BRAZIL BRUNEI

BULGARIA BURKINA FASO BURUNDI CAMBODIA CAMEROON

CANADA CAPE VERDE CENTRAL AFRICAN REPUBLIC CHAD CHILE

CHINA COLOMBIA COMOROS CONGO, DEM. REP. OF THE CONGO, REP. OF THE

COSTA RICA COTE D'IVOIRE CROATIA CUBA CYPRUS

CZECH REPUBLIC DENMARK DJIBOUTI DOMINICA DOMINICAN REPUBLIC

# FLAGS of the
# NATIONS of the WORLD
## (Ecuador-Lithuania)

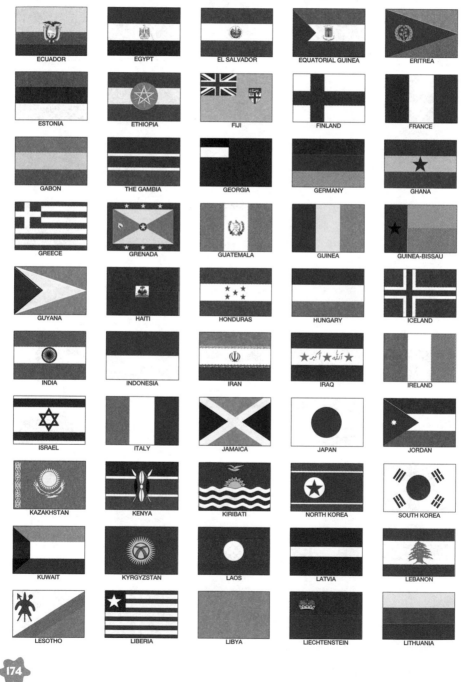

ECUADOR · EGYPT · EL SALVADOR · EQUATORIAL GUINEA · ERITREA

ESTONIA · ETHIOPIA · FIJI · FINLAND · FRANCE

GABON · THE GAMBIA · GEORGIA · GERMANY · GHANA

GREECE · GRENADA · GUATEMALA · GUINEA · GUINEA-BISSAU

GUYANA · HAITI · HONDURAS · HUNGARY · ICELAND

INDIA · INDONESIA · IRAN · IRAQ · IRELAND

ISRAEL · ITALY · JAMAICA · JAPAN · JORDAN

KAZAKHSTAN · KENYA · KIRIBATI · NORTH KOREA · SOUTH KOREA

KUWAIT · KYRGYZSTAN · LAOS · LATVIA · LEBANON

LESOTHO · LIBERIA · LIBYA · LIECHTENSTEIN · LITHUANIA

# FLAGS of the NATIONS of the WORLD

## (Luxembourg-Senegal)

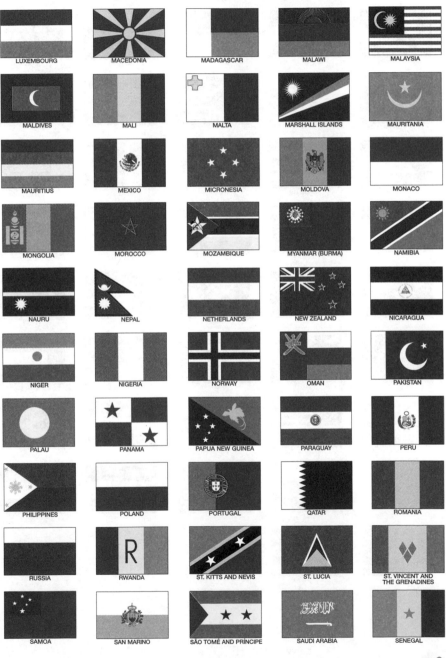

| | | | | |
|---|---|---|---|---|
| LUXEMBOURG | MACEDONIA | MADAGASCAR | MALAWI | MALAYSIA |
| MALDIVES | MALI | MALTA | MARSHALL ISLANDS | MAURITANIA |
| MAURITIUS | MEXICO | MICRONESIA | MOLDOVA | MONACO |
| MONGOLIA | MOROCCO | MOZAMBIQUE | MYANMAR (BURMA) | NAMIBIA |
| NAURU | NEPAL | NETHERLANDS | NEW ZEALAND | NICARAGUA |
| NIGER | NIGERIA | NORWAY | OMAN | PAKISTAN |
| PALAU | PANAMA | PAPUA NEW GUINEA | PARAGUAY | PERU |
| PHILIPPINES | POLAND | PORTUGAL | QATAR | ROMANIA |
| RUSSIA | RWANDA | ST. KITTS AND NEVIS | ST. LUCIA | ST. VINCENT AND THE GRENADINES |
| SAMOA | SAN MARINO | SÃO TOMÉ AND PRÍNCIPE | SAUDI ARABIA | SENEGAL |

# FLAGS of the NATIONS of the WORLD

## (Seychelles-Zimbabwe)

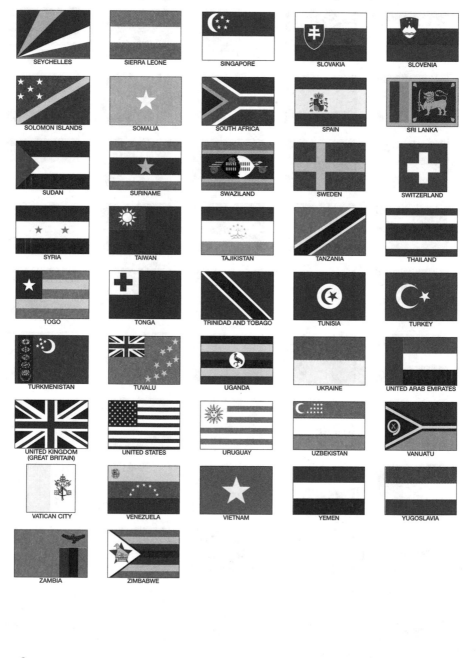

SEYCHELLES

SIERRA LEONE

SINGAPORE

SLOVAKIA

SLOVENIA

SOLOMON ISLANDS

SOMALIA

SOUTH AFRICA

SPAIN

SRI LANKA

SUDAN

SURINAME

SWAZILAND

SWEDEN

SWITZERLAND

SYRIA

TAIWAN

TAJIKISTAN

TANZANIA

THAILAND

TOGO

TONGA

TRINIDAD AND TOBAGO

TUNISIA

TURKEY

TURKMENISTAN

TUVALU

UGANDA

UKRAINE

UNITED ARAB EMIRATES

UNITED KINGDOM
(GREAT BRITAIN)

UNITED STATES

URUGUAY

UZBEKISTAN

VANUATU

VATICAN CITY

VENEZUELA

VIETNAM

YEMEN

YUGOSLAVIA

ZAMBIA

ZIMBABWE

**? How many zeros are in a googol?**
*You can find the answer on page 178.*

# Numerals in ANCIENT CIVILIZATIONS

People have been counting since the earliest of times. This is what some early numerals looked like.

| Modern | 1 | 2 | 3 | 4 | 5 | 6 | 7 | 8 | 9 | 10 | 20 | 50 | 100 |
|---|---|---|---|---|---|---|---|---|---|---|---|---|---|
| Egyptian | I | II | III | IIII | III/II | III/III | IIII/III | IIII/IIII | IIII/IIIII | ∩ | ∩∩ | ∩∩∩∩∩ | ⌐ |
| Babylonian | Y | YY | YYY | YYY/Y | YYY/YY | YYY/YYY | YYYY/YYY | YYYY/YYYY | YYYY/YYYYY | < | << | <<< | Y<<< |
| Greek | A | B | Γ | Δ | E | F | Z | H | θ | I | K | N | P |
| Mayan | • | •• | ••• | •••• | — | •/— | ••/— | •••/— | ••••/— | = | •/= | ••/= | ◎ |
| Chinese | 一 | 二 | 三 | 四 | 五 | 六 | 七 | 八 | 九 | 十 | 二十 | 五十 | 百 |
| Hindu | I | ২ | ३ | ૪ | ५ | ६ | ७ | ८ | ९ | 10 | ২0 | ૪0 | 100 |
| Arabic | I | ٢ | ٣ | ۴ | ۵ | ۶ | ٧ | ٨ | ٩ | ١٥ | ٢٥ | ۴٥ | ١٥٥ |

# Roman NUMERALS

Roman numerals are still used today. The symbols used to represent different numbers are the letters I (1), V (5), X (10), L (50), C (100), D (500), and M (1,000). If one Roman numeral is followed by a larger one, the first is subtracted from the second. For example, the numeral IX means 10 – 1 = 9. Think of it as "one less than ten." On the other hand, if one Roman numeral is followed by another that is equal or smaller, add them together. Therefore, VII means 5 + 1 + 1 = 7.

| | | | |
|---|---|---|---|
| 1 | I | 20 | XX |
| 2 | II | 30 | XXX |
| 3 | III | 40 | XL |
| 4 | IV | 50 | L |
| 5 | V | 60 | LX |
| 6 | VI | 70 | LXX |
| 7 | VII | 80 | LXXX |
| 8 | VIII | 90 | XC |
| 9 | IX | 100 | C |
| 10 | X | 200 | CC |
| 11 | XI | 300 | CCC |
| 12 | XII | 400 | CD |
| 13 | XIII | 500 | D |
| 14 | XIV | 600 | DC |
| 15 | XV | 700 | DCC |
| 16 | XVI | 800 | DCCC |
| 17 | XVII | 900 | CM |
| 18 | XVIII | 1,000 | M |
| 19 | XIX | | |

Can you write the year on the front cover of this book in Roman numerals? The answer is on pages 317–320.

# The PREFIX Tells the Number

**E**ach number listed below has one or more prefixes used to form words that include that number. Knowing which number the prefix stands for may help you to understand the meaning of the word. For example, a unicycle has one wheel. A triangle has three sides. An octopus has eight tentacles. Next to the prefixes are some examples of words that use these prefixes.

| 1 | uni-, mon-, mono- | unicycle, unicorn, monarch, monotone |
|---|---|---|
| 2 | bi- | bicycle, binary, binoculars, bifocals |
| 3 | tri- | tricycle, triangle, trilogy, triplet |
| 4 | quadr-, tetr- | quadrangle, quadruplet, tetrahedron |
| 5 | pent-, penta- | pentagon, pentathlon |
| 6 | hex-, hexa- | hexagon |
| 7 | hepta- | heptathlon |
| 8 | oct-, octa-, octo- | octave, octet, octopus, octagon |
| 9 | nona- | nonagon |
| 10 | dec-, deca- | decade, decibel, decimal |
| 100 | cent- | centipede, century |
| 1000 | kilo- | kilogram, kilometer |
| million | mega- | megabyte, megahertz |
| billion | giga- | gigabyte, gigawatt |

## Reading and Writing LARGE NUMBERS

**B**elow is the name of a number and the number of zeros that would follow it when the number is written out.

| ten: | 1 zero | 10 |
|---|---|---|
| hundred: | 2 zeros | 100 |
| thousand: | 3 zeros | 1,000 |
| ten thousand: | 4 zeros | 10,000 |
| hundred thousand: | 5 zeros | 100,000 |
| million: | 6 zeros | 1,000,000 |
| ten million: | 7 zeros | 10,000,000 |
| hundred million: | 8 zeros | 100,000,000 |
| billion: | 9 zeros | 1,000,000,000 |
| trillion: | 12 zeros | 1,000,000,000,000 |
| quadrillion: | 15 zeros | 1,000,000,000,000,000 |
| quintillion: | 18 zeros | 1,000,000,000,000,000,000 |
| sextillion: | 21 zeros | 1,000,000,000,000,000,000,000 |
| septillion: | 24 zeros | 1,000,000,000,000,000,000,000,000 |

Look below to see how numbers larger than these would be written:

octillion has 27 zeros     decillion has 33 zeros
nonillion has 30 zeros     googol has 100 zeros

# How Many SIDES and FACES Do They Have?

**W**hen a figure is flat (two-dimensional), it is a **plane** figure. When a figure takes up space (three-dimensional), it is a **solid figure**. The flat surface of a solid figure is called a **face**. Plane and solid figures come in many different shapes.

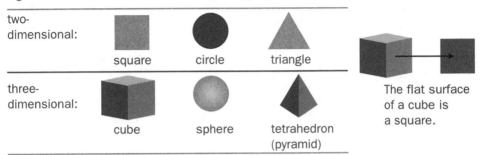

two-dimensional:

square    circle    triangle

three-dimensional:

cube    sphere    tetrahedron (pyramid)

The flat surface of a cube is a square.

## WHAT ARE POLYGONS?

A polygon is a two-dimensional figure with three or more straight sides (called line segments). A square is a polygon. Polygons have different numbers of sides—and each has a different name. If the sides are all the same length and all the angles between the sides are equal, the polygon is called regular. If the sides are of different lengths or the angles are not equal, the polygon is called irregular. Below are some regular and irregular polygons.

| NAME AND NUMBER OF SIDES | REGULAR | IRREGULAR |
|---|---|---|
| triangle - 3 | | |
| quadrilateral or tetragon - 4 | | |
| pentagon - 5 | | |
| hexagon - 6 | | |
| heptagon - 7 | | |
| octagon - 8 | | |
| nonagon - 9 | | |
| decagon - 10 | | |

## WHAT ARE POLYHEDRONS?

A polyhedron is a three-dimensional figure with four or more faces. Each face on a polyhedron is a polygon. Below are some polyhedrons with many faces.

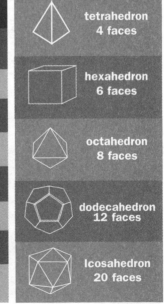

tetrahedron
4 faces

hexahedron
6 faces

octahedron
8 faces

dodecahedron
12 faces

Icosahedron
20 faces

# NUMBERS PUZZLES

## Square 1

What do these numbers have in common?

| | | |
|---|---|---|
| 15 | 55 | 100 |
| 75 | 10 | 40 |
| 50 | 60 | 90 |

## Square 2

On your mark . . . get set . . . time yourself. How many squares can you draw by connecting the dots in two minutes . . . in one minute? Each corner of each square must touch a dot.

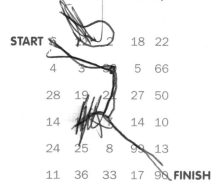

## Magic Square

The numbers in each row—across, up or down, and diagonally—must add up to 18. Fill in the boxes, using numbers from 1 to 11. You can only use each number once, and 6 is already used.

| | | |
|---|---|---|
| | | |
| | 6 | |
| | | |

## Through the Threes

Find your way from Start to Finish in this mini-maze by drawing a line to connect all the numbers that are multiples of 3.

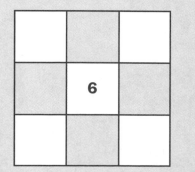

| START | | | | |
|---|---|---|---|---|
| | 2 | 18 | 22 |
| 4 | 3 | 5 | 66 |
| 28 | 19 | 27 | 50 |
| 14 | | 14 | 10 |
| 24 | 25 | 8 | 99 | 13 |
| 11 | 36 | 33 | 17 | 90 FINISH |

*Answers are on pages 317–320.*

# NUMBERS PUZZLES

## Know Your Numbers

Numbers in parentheses after each clue tell you what page you'll find the answer on.

### ACROSS

1. The length of the world's largest animal: _____ feet (page 35)
3. This number is an important part of Veterans Day (page 101)
7. Ten million in numerals (page 178)
9. Number of species of human beings (page 72)
10. Number of nations in the world (page 138)
13. Number of wonders in the ancient world (page 54)
16. How many billions of years ago Earth was formed (The answer has a decimal point between the two numerals) (page 40)
17. Length of a person's small intestine: _____ feet (page 93)
18. Kids between 7 and _____ years old need about 2,400 calories a day (page 94)

### DOWN

2. Its Roman numeral is M (page 177)
4. A box turtle lives about _____ years (page 37)
5. Its Roman numeral is D (page 177)
6. The number of miles per hour a cheetah can run (page 35)
8. The only two digits in a computer's binary code (page 62)
10. The number of muscles it takes to smile (page 93)
11. The Triassic period was as long as _____ million years ago (page 41)
12. Weight of the largest reptile: _____ pounds (page 35)
14. The lowest point in Europe is _____ feet below sea level (page 82)
15. Number of teeth most adults have (page 93)

*Answers are on pages 317–320.*

❷ **When did an Eagle land on the moon?**
*You can find the answer on page 189.*

# The SOLAR SYSTEM

**N**ine planets, including Earth, travel around the sun. These planets, together with the sun, form the solar system.

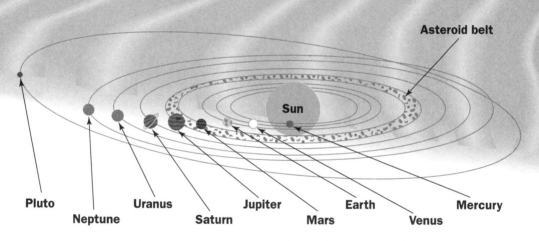

Asteroid belt

Sun

Pluto
Neptune
Uranus
Saturn
Jupiter
Mars
Earth
Venus
Mercury

## THE SUN IS A STAR

Did you know that the sun is a star, like the other stars you see at night? It is a typical, medium-size star. But because the sun is much closer to our planet than any other star, we can study it in great detail. The diameter of the sun is 864,000 miles—more than 100 times Earth's diameter. The gravity of the sun is nearly 28 times the gravity of Earth.

**How Hot Is the Sun?** The temperature of the sun's surface is close to 10,000°F, and it is believed that the sun's inner core may reach temperatures near 35 million degrees! The sun provides enough light and heat energy to support all forms of life on our planet.

## THE PLANETS ARE IN MOTION

The planets move around the sun along oval-shaped paths called **orbits**. One complete path around the sun is called a **revolution**. Earth takes one year, or 365 ¼ days, to make one revolution around the sun. Planets that are farther away from the sun take longer. Some planets have one or more **moons**. A moon orbits a planet in much the same way that the planets orbit the sun.

Each planet also spins (or rotates) on its axis. An **axis** is an imaginary line running through the center of a planet. The time it takes for of the planet Earth to rotate one time on its axis equals one day. Here are some other facts about the planets and the symbol for each planet.

# The PLANETS

## ① MERCURY

**Average distance from the sun:**
36 million miles
**Diameter:** 3,032 miles
**Time to revolve around the sun:**
88 days
**Time to rotate on its axis:**
58 days, 15 hours, 30 minutes
**Number of moons:** 0

**DID YOU KNOW?** *Like Earth's moon, Mercury is covered with craters. Astronomers have named the craters after famous writers, artists, and composers.*

## ② VENUS

**Average distance from the sun:**
67 million miles
**Diameter:** 7,521 miles
**Time to revolve around the sun:**
224.7 days
**Time to rotate on its axis:**
243 days
**Number of moons:** 0

**DID YOU KNOW?** *The surface of Venus is covered with thick clouds. Its atmosphere of carbon dioxide traps heat. The temperature of Venus can reach close to 900°F.*

## ③ EARTH

**Average distance from the sun:**
93 million miles
**Diameter:** 7,926 miles
**Time to revolve around the sun:**
365 ¼ days
**Time to rotate on its axis:**
23 hours, 56 minutes,
4.2 seconds
**Number of moons:** 1

**DID YOU KNOW?** *Earth's path around the sun is nearly 600 million miles long. To make the trip in one year, Earth travels more than 66,000 miles per hour.*

## ④ MARS

**Average distance from the sun:**
142 million miles
**Diameter:** 4,213 miles
**Time to revolve around the sun:**
687 days
**Time to rotate on its axis:**
24 hours, 37 minutes,
22 seconds
**Number of moons:** 2

**DID YOU KNOW?** *There may be water and traces of life in the polar regions of Mars. The Mars Polar Lander, launched in 1999, is trying to find out.*

## ⑤ JUPITER

**Average distance from the sun:**
484 million miles
**Diameter:** 88,732 miles
**Time to revolve around the sun:**
11.9 years
**Time to rotate on its axis:** 9 hours,
55 minutes, 30 seconds
**Number of moons:** 16

**DID YOU KNOW?** *Observations from the Galileo spacecraft suggest that there is an ocean beneath the icy surface of Callisto, one of Jupiter's known moons.*

## ⑥ SATURN

**Average distance from the sun:**
888 million miles
**Diameter:** 74,975 miles
**Time to revolve around the sun:**
29.5 years
**Time to rotate on its axis:**
10 hours, 30 minutes
**Number of moons:** at least 18

**DID YOU KNOW?** *Saturn's rings are made of billions of chunks of ice. The Cassini spacecraft will fly through the rings in 2004 and give us information about them.*

*Saturn ▶*

## ❼ URANUS

**Average distance from the sun:**
1.8 billion miles
**Diameter:** 31,763 miles
**Time to revolve around the sun:** 84 years
**Time to rotate on its axis:** 17 hours, 14 minutes
**Number of moons:** at least 17

### DID YOU KNOW?

*Uranus was the first planet discovered with a telescope, by William Herschel in 1781. Its surface is covered with greenish clouds of gas.*

## ❽ NEPTUNE

**Average distance from the sun:**
2.8 billion miles
**Diameter:** 30,603 miles
**Time to revolve around the sun:** 164.8 years
**Time to rotate on its axis:** 16 hours, 6 minutes
**Number of moons:** 8

### DID YOU KNOW?

*Neptune's largest moon is called Triton. At about −390°F, Triton is the coldest place in the solar system.*

## ❾ PLUTO

**Average distance from the sun:**
3.6 billion miles
**Diameter:** 1,413 miles
**Time to revolve around the sun:** 247.7 years
**Time to rotate on its axis:** 6 days, 9 hours, 18 minutes
**Number of moons:** 1

### DID YOU KNOW?

*In 1999, Pluto again became the farthest planet. It had been closer to the sun than Neptune for 20 years. Pluto is an oddball among planets, partly because it is so small.*

# FACTS ABOUT THE PLANETS

**Largest planet: Jupiter**
**Smallest planet: Pluto**
**Planet closest to the sun: Mercury**
**Planet that comes closest to Earth:**
 **Venus (Every 19 months, Venus gets closer to Earth than any other planet.)**

**Fastest-moving planet: Mercury (107,000 miles per hour)**
**Slowest-moving planet: Pluto (10,600 miles per hour)**
**Warmest planet: Venus**
**Coldest planet: Pluto**
**Planet with the most moons: Saturn**

# The MOON

The moon is about 238,900 miles from Earth. It is 2,160 miles in diameter and has no atmosphere. Its dusty surface is covered with deep craters. It takes the same amount of time for the moon to rotate on its axis as it does to orbit Earth (27 days, 7 hours, 43 minutes). This is why one side of the moon is always facing Earth. The moon has no light of its own, but reflects light from the sun. The lighted part of the moon that we see from Earth is called a **phase**. It takes the moon about 29½ days to go through all of its phases.

### PHASES OF THE MOON

| New Moon | Crescent Moon | First Quarter | Full Moon | Last Quarter | Crescent Moon | New Moon |

**DID YOU KNOW?** *In 1998 the Lunar Prospector, a U.S. spacecraft, found strong evidence of some water, in the form of ice, at the moon's poles.*

# EXPLORING the SOLAR SYSTEM

American space exploration began in January 1958, when the Explorer I satellite was launched into orbit. In 1958, NASA (The National Aeronautics and Space Administration) was formed. To the right are some unmanned space missions launched by NASA.

## The Search for LIFE BEYOND EARTH

For years scientists have tried to discover if there is life on other planets in our solar system or elsewhere. They look for signs of what is needed for life on Earth—basics like water and proper temperature.

### WHAT SCIENTISTS HAVE LEARNED

**Mars and Jupiter.** In 1996, two teams of scientists examined two meteorites that may have come from **Mars** and found evidence that some form of life may have existed on Mars billions of years ago. In 1997 and 1998, photographs of Europa, a moon of **Jupiter**, showed areas of water. Europa may have had an ocean, and perhaps life, in the far-distant past.

**New Planets.** Since 1996, astronomers have found evidence of several planets around stars other than the sun. In 1999, astronomers reported the first evidence of a group of planets orbiting one star, a star not very different from our sun. Perhaps there could be a form of life on one of those planets, or on a planet we have not found yet.

### SPACECRAFT ON THE GO

**NASA** is searching for signs of life on Mars. The search will continue until 2013. Some spacecraft will fly around Mars taking pictures. Others will land there to study soil and rocks and look for living things. *Mars Pathfinder* and *Mars Global Surveyor,* launched in 1996, reached Mars in 1997. *Mars Climate Orbiter,* launched in 1998, and *Mars Polar Lander,* launched in January 1999, were scheduled to reach the planet in late 1999.

Another program that searches for life on other worlds is called SETI (Search for Extraterrestrial Intelligence). Most often it uses powerful radio telescopes to detect signs of life. Recently, however, astronomers began searching for light signals as signs of extraterrestrial life.

**1962–Mariner 2**
*First successful flyby of Venus.*

**1964–Mariner 4**
*First probe to reach Mars, 1965.*

**1972–Pioneer 10**
*First probe to reach Jupiter, 1973.*

**1973–Mariner 10**
*Only U.S. probe to Mercury, 1974.*

**1975–Viking 1 and 2**
*Landed on Mars in 1976.*

**1977–Voyager 1**
*Reached Jupiter in 1979 and Saturn in 1980.*

**1977–Voyager 2**
*Reached Jupiter in 1979, Saturn in 1981, Uranus in 1986, Neptune in 1989.*

**1978–Pioneer Venus 1**
*Operated in Venus orbit 14 years.*

**1989–Magellan**
*Orbited and mapped Venus.*

**1989–Galileo**
*Reached Jupiter, 1995; studied its moons.*

**1996–Mars Pathfinder**
*Landed on Mars, sent a roving vehicle (Sojourner) to explore the surface.*

**1997–Cassini**
*Expected to reach Saturn in 2004.*

**1998–Lunar Prospector**
*Began yearlong orbit just a few miles above the moon's surface.*

**1998–Mars Climate Orbiter**
*Expected to reach Mars September 1999, to study surface and climate.*

**1999–Mars Polar Lander**
*Expected to reach Mars December 1999, to search for ice.*

# COMETS, ASTEROIDS, and SATELLITES

Comets, asteroids, and satellites, in addition to the planets and their moons, are also in the solar system.

## COMETS

Comets are fast-moving chunks of ice, dust, and rock that form huge gaseous heads as they move nearer to the sun. One of the most well-known is **Halley's Comet**. It can be seen about every 76 years and will appear in the sky again in the year 2061.

## ASTEROIDS

Asteroids (or minor planets) are solid chunks of rock or metal that range in size from very small, like grains of sand, to very large. **Ceres**, the largest, is about 600 miles across. Thousands of asteroids orbit the sun between Mars and Jupiter.

## SATELLITES

Satellites are objects that move in an orbit around a planet. Moons are natural satellites. Satellites made by humans are used as space stations and astronomical observatories. They are also used to photograph Earth's surface and to transmit communications signals.

**DID YOU KNOW?** In addition to planets, moons, satellites, and comets, about 10,000 scraps of debris float in the solar system. This space garbage includes dead spacecraft, used-up rockets, and pieces of broken satellites. It can be a danger to space travelers. The U.S. Space Surveillance Network is tracking the garbage, and attempts may be made in the future to "sweep" it up.

## WHAT IS AN ECLIPSE?

A **solar eclipse** occurs when the moon moves between the sun and Earth, casting a shadow over part of Earth. When the moon completely blocks out the sun, it is called a total solar eclipse. When this happens, a halo of gas can be seen around the sun. This halo of gas is called the corona.

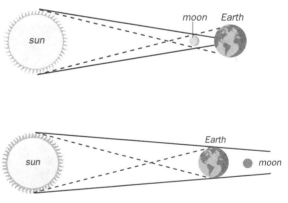

Sometimes Earth casts a shadow on the moon. This is called a **lunar eclipse**. Usually, a lunar eclipse lasts longer than a solar eclipse. The moon remains visible, but becomes dark, often with a reddish tinge (from sunlight that is bent through Earth's atmosphere).

## UPCOMING TOTAL SOLAR ECLIPSES AND WHERE THEY CAN BE SEEN

**June 21, 2001**
Will be seen over the Atlantic Ocean, Africa, and Madagascar.

**December 4, 2002**
Will be seen in southern Africa, over the Indian Ocean, and in Australia.

**November 23, 2003**
Will be seen in Antarctica.

# CONSTELLATIONS

Thousands of years ago, ancient astronomers grouped stars together to form pictures. These groupings, or the areas of sky that they cover, are known as **constellations**. Astronomers all over the world named the constellations after animals or mythological figures or tools. Many of the constellations we know today were named by the people living in ancient Greece and Rome. But the southernmost parts of the sky could not be seen from that part of the world. Constellations in this part of the sky were not named until later, when Europeans began traveling more in Earth's southern hemisphere.

In 1930, the International Astronomical Union established a standard set of 88 constellations, which cover the entire sky that is visible from Earth. Astronomers use constellations as a quick way to locate other objects. For example, from Earth, the other planets moving around the sun appear in different constellations at different times.

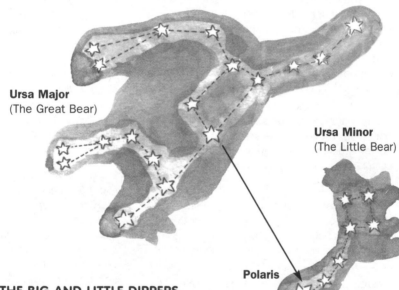

**Ursa Major**
(The Great Bear)

**Ursa Minor**
(The Little Bear)

Polaris

## THE BIG AND LITTLE DIPPERS

The picture above shows stars in the constellations thought to resemble bears—**Ursa Major** (Great Bear) and **Ursa Minor** (Little Bear). The tail and hips of the Great Bear are also known as the Big Dipper. Ursa Minor is also known as the Little Dipper.

## THE NORTH STAR

Throughout history, the stars have guided people in their travels. **Polaris**, the last star in the handle of the Little Dipper, shines to the north and is called the North Star. The two stars at the end of the bowl of the Big Dipper always point in the direction of Polaris, making it easy to find.

# Heavenly QUESTIONS and ANSWERS

## WHAT IS A GALAXY?

A **galaxy** is a group of billions of stars held together by gravity. Galaxies also contain interstellar gas and dust. The universe may have about 50 billion galaxies. The one we live in is called the **Milky Way**. The sun and the stars we see at night are just a few of the 200 billion stars in the Milky Way. Light from a star along one edge of the galaxy would take about 100,000 years to reach the other edge. Astronomers measure the distance between stars and between galaxies in light-years. One **light-year** is the distance light travels in one year—about 5.9 trillion miles.

## WHAT ARE METEORS, METEORITES, AND METEOR SHOWERS?

On a clear night, you may see a sudden streak of light in the sky. It may be caused by chunks of rock or metal called **meteoroids** speeding through space. When a meteoroid enters Earth's atmosphere, friction with air molecules causes it to burn brightly. The streak we see is called a **meteor**, or **shooting star**.

Many meteoroids follow in the path of a comet as it orbits the sun. As these meteoroids enter Earth's atmosphere, large numbers can be seen coming from about the same area. These streaks are called **meteor showers**. If a meteoroid is big enough to land without burning up completely, it is called a **meteorite**.

## WHAT IS A BLACK HOLE?

Stars have limited life spans. Our sun, which is a star, is about five billion years old. It is expected to last another five billion years. **Black holes** cannot be seen, but astronomers believe they are what remain at the end of the life of certain stars.

Some stars merely stop shining, but others explode. Many astronomers believe that when a star explodes it may leave behind a chunk of matter as heavy as our sun yet only a few miles across. The force of gravity of this chunk is so strong that nothing close to it can escape its pull, not even light. These stars are called black holes.

## HOW DID THE UNIVERSE BEGIN?

Most astronomers believe that the universe began in a huge explosion 10 to 20 billion years ago and has been expanding ever since. This is the **big bang theory**.

**DID YOU KNOW?**

▶ *In August 1998, astronomers at Hawaii's Mauna Kea Observatory discovered a galaxy over 20 billion light-years away. This was the most far-away object ever observed in the universe.*

▶ *The largest known meteorite was found in Namibia in 1920. It is 9 feet long, 8 feet wide, and weighs around 65 tons. The biggest meteorite that can be seen in a museum is at the American Museum of Natural History in New York City. It weighs over 68,000 pounds and was found in Greenland in 1897.*

▶ *In February 1999, NASA launched* Stardust, *a space probe to collect samples of comet and interstellar dust from deep space. After seven years,* Stardust *will come back toward Earth and release its dust collection capsule, which will descend by parachute to a site in Utah. This dust may tell us more about the origin of solar systems, planets, and life.*

# ASTRONAUTS in OUTER SPACE

The rapid entry of the United States into space in 1958 was in response to the Soviet Union's launching of its satellite *Sputnik I* into orbit on October 4, 1957. In 1961, three years after NASA was formed, President John F. Kennedy promised Americans that the United States would land a person on the moon by the end of the 1960s. As promised, NASA landed the first person on the moon in July 1969. Since then, many astronauts have made trips into outer space. This time line gives some of the major flights of astronauts into space.

**1961** — On April 12, Soviet cosmonaut Yuri Gagarin, in *Vostok 1*, became the **first human to orbit Earth**. On May 5, U.S. astronaut Alan B. Shepard Jr. of the *Mercury 3* mission became the **first American in space**.

**1962** — On February 20, U.S. astronaut John H. Glenn Jr. of *Mercury 6* became the **first American to orbit Earth**.

**1963** — From June 16 to 19, the Soviet spacecraft *Vostok 6* carried the **first woman in space**, Valentina V. Tereshkova.

**1965** — On March 18, Soviet cosmonaut Aleksei A. Leonov became the **first person to walk in space**. He spent 10 minutes outside the spaceship. On December 15, U.S. *Gemini 6A* and *7* (with astronauts) became the **first vehicles to rendezvous** (approach and see each other) **in space**.

**1966** — On March 16, U.S. *Gemini 8* became the **first craft to dock with** (become attached to) **another vehicle** (an unmanned Agena rocket).

**1967** — On January 27, a fire in a U.S. *Apollo* spacecraft on the ground killed astronauts Virgil I. Grissom, Edward H. White, and Roger B. Chaffee. On April 23, *Soyuz 1* crashed to the Earth, killing Soviet cosmonaut Vladimir Komarov.

**1969** — On July 20, after successful flights of *Apollo 8, 9,* and *10*, **U.S. *Apollo 11*'s lunar module Eagle landed on the moon's surface** in the area known as the Sea of Tranquility. Neil Armstrong became the **first person ever to walk on the moon**.

**1970** — In April, *Apollo 13* astronauts returned safely to Earth after an explosion damaged their spacecraft and prevented them from landing on the moon.

**1971** — In July and August, U.S. *Apollo 15* astronauts tested the **Lunar Rover** on the moon.

**1972** — In December, *Apollo 17* was the sixth and **final U.S. space mission to land successfully on the moon**.

**1973** — On May 14, the U.S. put its **first space station, Skylab, into orbit**. Crews worked in Skylab until January 1974, when the last crew left.

**1975** — On July 15, the U.S. launched *Apollo 18* and the U.S.S.R. launched *Soyuz 19*. Two days later, the **American and Soviet spacecraft docked**, and for several days their crews worked and spent time together in space. This was NASA's last space mission with astronauts until the space shuttle.

# SHUTTLES and SPACE STATIONS

In an effort to reduce costs, NASA developed the space shuttle program during the 1970s. The U.S. space shuttle became the first reusable spacecraft. Earlier space capsules could not be used again after returning to Earth, but the space shuttle lands on a runway like an airplane and can be launched again at a later date. On space shuttle missions, astronauts perform many experiments, test equipment, and sometimes place satellites into orbit.

The European Space Agency, which was formed by some European countries in 1975, constructed the Spacelab scientific laboratory. Spacelab first rode a space shuttle in 1983. In 1986, the Soviet Union launched its successful *Mir* space station. By the mid-1990s, the United States and Russia were sharing projects in space.

**1977** — On August 12, the first shuttle, **Enterprise**, took off from the back of a 747 jet airliner.

**1981** — On April 12, **Columbia** was launched and became the first shuttle to reach Earth's orbit.

**1983** — In April, NASA began using a third shuttle, **Challenger**. Two more **Challenger** flights in 1983 included astronauts Sally K. Ride and Guion S. Bluford Jr., the first American woman and African-American man in space. On November 28, **Columbia** was launched carrying the scientific laboratory Spacelab.

**1984** — In August, the shuttle **Discovery** was launched for the first time.

**1985** — In October, the shuttle **Atlantis** was launched for the first time.

**1986** — On January 28, after 24 successful shuttle missions, **Challenger** exploded 73 seconds after takeoff. Astronauts Dick Scobee, Michael Smith, Ellison Onizuka, Judith Resnik, Greg Jarvis, and Ron McNair, and teacher Christa McAuliffe all died. In February, the Soviet space station **Mir** was launched into orbit.

**1988** — In September, more than two years after the **Challenger** disaster, new safety procedures led to the successful launch of **Discovery**.

**1990** — On April 24, the **Hubble Space Telescope** was launched from **Discovery**, but the images sent back to Earth were fuzzy.

**1992** — In May, NASA launched a new shuttle, **Endeavour**.

**1993** — In December, a crew aboard **Endeavour** repaired the Hubble telescope.

**1995** — In March, astronaut Norman Thagard became the first American to travel in a Russian spacecraft; he joined cosmonauts on **Mir**. In June, **Atlantis** docked with **Mir** for the first time, and they orbited Earth while joined together.

**1996** — In March, Shannon Lucid joined the **Mir** crew. She spent 188 days in space, setting the record for all American and all female astronauts.

**1998** — Astronaut Andrew Thomas in January became the last U.S. astronaut to join the **Mir** crew. In October astronaut John Glenn was launched into space a second time, aboard the shuttle **Discovery.**

# INTERNATIONAL SPACE STATION

After many years of research and planning, a permanent space research laboratory is being built in orbit around the Earth. Three astronauts are expected to go to the station in 2000 to help build it. The United States, Russia, and 14 other countries hope to complete this International Space Station by 2004. At that time, seven crew members will call the station home. They will figure out how people can live and work safely in space for long periods. Their experiments will also help scientists plan future space travel to the moon, to Mars, and beyond.

When completed, the space station will have a mass of about 500 tons. It will be as long as a football field, including the end zones. The living space for the crew will match the inside of a 747 jumbo jet. Four windows will allow the crew to observe the Earth and other objects in space. A solar array with a surface area of about half an acre will provide electricity for the station. Fifty-two computers will control the systems and the six scientific laboratories on the station.

# The ZODIAC

**Aries** (Ram)
March 21 - April 19

**Taurus** (Bull)
April 20 - May 20

**Gemini** (Twins)
May 21 - June 21

**Cancer** (Crab)
June 22 - July 22

**Leo** (Lion)
July 23 - August 22

**Virgo** (Maiden)
August 23 - Sept. 22

**Libra** (Balance)
Sept. 23 - Oct. 23

**Scorpio** (Scorpion)
Oct. 24 - Nov. 21

**Sagittarius** (Archer)
Nov. 22 - Dec. 21

**Capricorn** (Goat)
Dec. 22 - Jan. 19

**Aquarius** (Water Bearer)
Jan. 20 - Feb. 18

**Pisces** (Fishes)
Feb. 19 - March 20

The zodiac is an imaginary belt (or path) that goes around the sky. The orbits of the sun, the moon, and most of the planets are within the zodiac. The zodiac crosses 26 different constellations. Above are the symbols for the 12 constellations most commonly associated with the zodiac.

**DID YOU KNOW?** *Astronomers* are scientists who study the sky, including stars, planets, moons, comets, asteroids, and meteors, to discover what they are made of, and how they behave. *Astrologers* are not scientists. They believe that the positions and movements of the sun, moon, and planets influence the lives of people on Earth.

# PLANTS

❷ Can you name some plants that eat bugs?
*You can find the answer on page 195.*

**DID YOU KNOW?**

*You can grow plants from some common foods, such as a sweet potato, an avocado pit, grapefruit seeds, or the tops of carrots.*

## Record Breaking Plants

**World's Oldest Living Plants:** Bristlecone pine trees in California (4,700 years old)

**World's Tallest Plants:** The tallest tree ever measured was a eucalyptus tree in Victoria, Australia, measuring 435 feet in 1872. The tallest tree now standing is a giant sequoia tree in Redwood National Park, California, standing at 365 feet.

# What Makes a Plant a Plant?

Plants were the first living things on Earth. They appeared around three billion years ago, long before there were any animals. The first plants, called algae, grew in or near water. Years later—about 300 or 400 million years ago—the first land plants appeared. These were ferns, club mosses, and horsetails. After these came plants that had cones (conifers) and trees that were ancestors of the palm trees we see today.

Flowers, grass, weeds, oak trees, palm trees, and poison ivy have certain things in common with one another and with every other plant. The following facts are true about all plants:

They can create their own food from air, sunlight, and water.

They are rooted in one place—they don't move around.

Their cells contain cellulose, a substance that keeps plants standing upright.

Plants need air, water, light, and warmth to grow. Not all plants need soil or the same climate, or the same amount of light, warmth, and water. A cactus plant needs a lot of heat and light but not much water, while a fir tree will grow in a northern forest where it is cold much of the year and light is limited. Water lilies really have roots in the soil underwater, while water hyacinths just float on the water's surface and grow to about two feet above it.

**DID YOU KNOW?** *You can tell how old a tree is by looking at its rings. Rings are the irregularly shaped circles you see on the stump of a tree that has been cut down. As a tree gets taller, it also gets wider, and each year that a tree grows outward is marked by a ring. A year with a good growing season leaves a thicker ring than a year that is too dry or cold.*

# PLANT TALK

**agronomy**

The growing of plants for food.

**annual**

A plant that grows, flowers, and dies in one year. Most annuals produce seeds that can be planted the following spring.

**biennial**

A plant that takes two years to mature. The first year the plant produces a stem and leaves, and the second year it produces flowers and seeds.

**deciduous**

A tree that loses its leaves in autumn and gets new ones in the spring.

**evergreen**

A tree that keeps its leaves or needles all year long.

**fertilizer**

A natural or chemical substance applied to the soil to help plants grow bigger and faster.

**herb**

A plant used for flavoring or seasoning, for its scent, or as medicine. Mint, lavender, and rosemary are all herbs.

**horticulture**

The growing of plants for beauty.

**house plant**

A plant that is grown indoors. Many plants that are grown outdoors in tropical and desert regions have become popular as house plants.

**hybrid**

A plant that has been scientifically combined with another plant or has been changed to make it more beautiful, larger, stronger, or better in some other way. Many roses are hybrids.

**hydroponics**

A way of growing plants in a nutritional liquid rather than in soil.

**mulch**

A covering of bark, compost (decomposed garbage), hay, or other substance used to conserve water and control weeds. Mulch can also provide nutrients for plants and keep plants warm in winter.

**native**

A plant that has always grown in a certain place, rather than being brought there from somewhere else. Corn is native to North America.

**perennial**

A plant that stops growing and may look dead in the fall, but comes back year after year.

**photosynthesis**

The process that allows plants to make their own food from air, sunlight, and water.

**phototropism**

The turning of plants toward the light.

**propagation**

The reproduction of plants. Plants can be reproduced from seeds, or by dividing the roots of a plant, or sometimes by simply placing a piece of the leaf on soil.

**terrarium**

A glass box containing small plants and animals, such as moss, ferns, lizards, and turtles.

**transplant**

A plant that is dug up and moved from one place to another.

**wildflower**

A flowering plant that grows on its own in the wild, rather than being planted by a person.

# WHERE DO PLANTS GROW?

**P**lants grow nearly everywhere except near the South and North Poles.

## FORESTS

**Where Evergreens Grow.** Forests cover much of Earth's land surface. Evergreens, such as pines, hemlocks, firs, and spruces, grow in the cool forest regions farthest from the equator. These trees are called **conifers** because they produce cones.

**Temperate Forests.** Temperate forests have warm, rainy summers and cold, snowy winters. Here **deciduous trees** (which lose their leaves in the fall and grow new ones in the spring) join the evergreens. Temperate forests are home to maple, oak, beech, and poplar trees, and to wildflowers and shrubs. These forests are found in eastern United States, southeastern Canada, northern Europe and Asia, and southern Australia.

**Tropical Rain Forests.** Still closer to the equator are the tropical rain forests, home to the greatest variety of plants on Earth. The temperature never falls below freezing except on the mountain slopes. About 60 to 100 inches of rain fall each year. Tropical trees stay green all year. They grow close together, shading the ground. There are several layers of trees. The top, **emergent layer** has trees that can reach 200 feet in height. The **canopy,** which gets lots of sun, comes next, followed by the **understory**. The **forest floor,** covered with roots, gets little sun, and many plants cannot grow there.

Tropical rain forests are found mainly in Central America, South America, Asia, and Africa. They once covered more than 8 million square miles. Today, because of destruction by humans, fewer than 3.4 million square miles remain. More than half the plant and animal species in the world live there. Foods such as bananas and pineapples first grew there. Woods such as mahogany and teak also come from rain forests. Many kinds of plants there are used to make medicines.

When rain forests are burned, carbon dioxide is released into the air. This adds to the greenhouse effect (see page 77). As forests are destroyed, the soil also slowly wears away, so there is nothing to keep heavy rain from flooding the ground.

Emergent Layer

Canopy

Understory

Forest floor

## TUNDRA AND ALPINE REGION

The northernmost regions of North America, Europe, and Asia surrounding the Arctic Ocean are called the **tundra**. The temperature rarely rises above 45 degrees Fahrenheit, and it is too cold for trees to grow there. Most tundra plants are mosses and lichens that hug the ground for warmth. A few wildflowers and small shrubs also grow where the soil thaws for about two months of the year. This kind of climate and plant life also exists on top of the highest mountains (the Himalayas, Alps, Andes, Rockies), where small Alpine flowers also grow.

**What Is the Tree Line?** On mountains in the north (such as the Rockies) and in the far south (such as the Andes), there is an altitude above which trees will not grow. This is the **tree line** or **timberline**. Above the tree line, you can see low shrubs and small plants, like Alpine flowers. As you move farther from the poles to the edge of the tundra, small dwarfed and twisted trees begin to appear. This is the start of the forest region.

## DESERTS

The driest areas of the world are the **deserts**. They can be hot or cold, but they also contain an amazing number of plants. Cactuses and sagebrush are native to dry regions of North and South America. The deserts of Africa and Asia contain plants called euporbias. Dates have grown in the deserts of the Middle East and North Africa for thousands of years. In the southwestern United States and northern Mexico, there are many types of cactuses, including prickly pear, barrel, and saguaro.

## GRASSLAND

The areas of the world that are too dry to have green forests, but not dry enough to be deserts, are called **grasslands**. The most common plants found there are grasses. Cooler grasslands are found in the Great Plains of the United States and Canada, in the steppes of Europe and Asia, and in the pampas of Argentina. The drier grasslands are used for grazing cattle and sheep. In the **prairies**, where there is a little more rain, important grains, such as wheat, rye, oats, and barley are grown. The warmer grasslands, called **savannas**, are found in central and southern Africa, Venezuela, southern Brazil, and Australia. Most savannas have moist summers and cool, dry winters.

*A rain forest*

# Fascinating Plants

## PLANTS THAT EAT BUGS

Bugs sometimes eat plants. But did you know that some plants trap insects and eat them? These are "carnivorous plants." The pitcher-plant, Venus's-flytrap, and sundew are three examples. Most carnivorous plants live in poor soils, where they don't get enough nourishment. They digest their prey very slowly over a long period of time.

## FLOWERING STONES

Plants have ways of protecting themselves. For example, Lithops (or flowering stones) are plants in the South African desert that look like small, gray stones. They are much less likely to be eaten by animals than something that looks green and delicious.

# LEAVES ARE TREE-MENDOUS!

**Here is an activity you can do. It will remind you that leaves are truly tree-mendous.**

## WATER WATCH

Did you know that leaves put fresh water and oxygen back into the air?

**You need**
- a pebble
  - a clear plastic bag
- a twist tie
  - a living tree leaf (still attached to the tree branch)

**What to do**

❶ Put the pebble inside the plastic bag and slip the bag over the living tree leaf. (Choose a leaf that gets a lot of sun.)

❷ Seal the bag to the stem with the twist tie.

❸ After several hours, check the leaf. You should notice droplets of water beginning to form.

❹ After a week, remove the plastic bag and measure the water with a measuring spoon. (How much water did your leaf produce? During a sunny week, a small leaf may produce about $\frac{1}{2}$ teaspoon of water.)

## COLOR WATCH

In the fall, leaves change color because there are fewer hours of sunlight each day. When leaves get less sun, chlorophyll, which makes leaves green, breaks down. Watch how leaves change color with this experiment.

**You need**
- black construction paper
  - a paper clip
- scissors
  - a living tree leaf

**What to do**

❶ Cut a small circle from the black construction paper.

❷ Then paper clip it to a living tree leaf in sunlight.

❸ After two hours, remove the circle. (What do you notice? The leaf under the circle gets less sun. When this happens, the leaf turns color, just as it does in the fall.)

## CONTEST! For Fifth Graders Only

The National Arbor Day Foundation, a group that educates people around the world about the importance of trees, sponsors an annual poster contest about trees, for fifth-graders. One national winner will receive a $1,000 savings bond, a free trip to an awards ceremony in Nebraska, and a lifetime membership in the foundation. The winner's teacher gets $200 to help buy classroom materials. To participate, students must live in a state that has a contest coordinator. Arbor Day is always the last Friday in April.

**WEB SITE** To learn more about the contest, go to
*http://www.arborday.org/teaching/poster_contest.html*

**❷ What is the world's smallest country?**
*You can find the answer below.*

# The Largest and Smallest Places in the World

If someone asks you for the largest nation in the world, you would have to ask that person another question before you could answer: Do you mean the one with the largest area or the one with the biggest population (most people)? The world's largest country in area is Russia. The world's biggest country in population is China. Vatican City is the smallest country in both area and population. Here are lists of the world's largest and smallest countries and largest cities, with their populations.

**Total Population of the World in 1998: 5,927,000,000**

## Largest Cities (Most People)

Here are the 10 cities in the world that have the most people. Numbers include people from the whole built-up area around each city (the metropolitan area).

| City, Country | Population |
|---|---|
| Tokyo, Japan | 26,959,000 |
| Mexico City, Mexico | 16,562,000 |
| São Paulo, Brazil | 16,533,000 |
| New York City, U.S. | 16,332,000 |
| Bombay (Mumbai), India | 15,138,000 |
| Shanghai, China | 13,584,000 |
| Los Angeles, U.S. | 12,410,000 |
| Calcutta, India | 11,923,000 |
| Buenos Aires, Argentina | 11,802,000 |
| Seoul, South Korea | 11,609,000 |

## LARGEST COUNTRIES (Most People)

| POPULATION | COUNTRY |
|---|---|
| 1,236,915,000 | China |
| 984,004,000 | India |
| 270,299,000 | United States |
| 212,942,000 | Indonesia |
| 169,807,000 | Brazil |
| 146,861,000 | Russia |
| 135,135,000 | Pakistan |
| 127,567,000 | Bangladesh |
| 125,932,000 | Japan |
| 110,532,000 | Nigeria |
| 98,553,000 | Mexico |
| 82,079,000 | Germany |
| 77,726,000 | Philippines |
| 76,236,000 | Vietnam |
| 68,960,000 | Iran |
| 66,050,000 | Egypt |
| 64,563,000 | Turkey |
| 60,037,000 | Thailand |
| 58,970,000 | Great Britian |
| 58,805,000 | France |
| 58,390,000 | Ethiopia |
| 56,783,000 | Italy |
| 50,125,000 | Ukraine |
| 49,001,000 | Congo Republic |
| 47,305,000 | Myanmar |

## SMALLEST COUNTRIES (Fewest People)

| POPULATION | COUNTRY |
|---|---|
| 840 | Vatican City |
| 10,000 | Tuvalu |
| 11,000 | Naura |
| 18,000 | Palau |
| 25,000 | San Marino |
| 32,000 | Liechtenstein |
| 32,000 | Monaco |

# Population of the United States

## Total Population of the United States in April 1998: 270,298,524

### POPULATION OF THE STATES AND DISTRICT OF COLUMBIA IN 1998

| Rank & State Name | Population | Rank & State Name | Population |
|---|---|---|---|
| 1 California | 32,666,550 | 27 Oklahoma | 3,346,713 |
| 2 Texas | 19,759,614 | 28 Oregon | 3,281,974 |
| 3 New York | 18,175,301 | 29 Connecticut | 3,274,069 |
| 4 Florida | 14,915,980 | 30 Iowa | 2,862,447 |
| 5 Illinois | 12,045,326 | 31 Mississippi | 2,752,092 |
| 6 Pennsylvania | 12,001,451 | 32 Kansas | 2,629,067 |
| 7 Ohio | 11,209,493 | 33 Arkansas | 2,538,303 |
| 8 Michigan | 9,817,242 | 34 Utah | 2,099,758 |
| 9 New Jersey | 8,115,011 | 35 West Virginia | 1,811,156 |
| 10 Georgia | 7,642,207 | 36 Nevada | 1,746,898 |
| 11 North Carolina | 7,546,493 | 37 New Mexico | 1,736,931 |
| 12 Virginia | 6,791,345 | 38 Nebraska | 1,662,719 |
| 13 Massachusetts | 6,147,132 | 39 Maine | 1,244,250 |
| 14 Indiana | 5,899,195 | 40 Idaho | 1,228,684 |
| 15 Washington | 5,689,263 | 41 Hawaii | 1,193,001 |
| 16 Missouri | 5,438,559 | 42 New Hampshire | 1,185,048 |
| 17 Tennessee | 5,430,621 | 43 Rhode Island | 988,480 |
| 18 Wisconsin | 5,223,500 | 44 Montana | 880,453 |
| 19 Maryland | 5,134,808 | 45 Delaware | 743,603 |
| 20 Minnesota | 4,725,419 | 46 South Dakota | 738,171 |
| 21 Arizona | 4,668,631 | 47 North Dakota | 638,244 |
| 22 Louisiana | 4,368,967 | 48 Alaska | 614,010 |
| 23 Alabama | 4,351,999 | 49 Vermont | 590,883 |
| 24 Colorado | 3,970,971 | 50 District of Columbia | 523,124 |
| 25 Kentucky | 3,936,499 | 51 Wyoming | 480,907 |
| 26 South Carolina | 3,835,962 | | |

## LARGEST CITIES IN THE UNITED STATES

Cities grow and shrink in population. At right is a list of the largest cities in the United States in 1996 compared with their populations in 1950. Can you find the six cities that increased in population? The four that decreased?

| Rank & City | 1996 | 1950 |
|---|---|---|
| 1 New York, NY | 7,380,906 | 7,891,957 |
| 2 Los Angeles, CA | 3,553,638 | 1,970,358 |
| 3 Chicago, IL | 2,721,547 | 3,620,962 |
| 4 Houston, TX | 1,744,058 | 596,163 |
| 5 Philadelphia, PA | 1,478,002 | 2,071,605 |
| 6 San Diego, CA | 1,171,121 | 334,387 |
| 7 Phoenix, AZ | 1,159,014 | 106,818 |
| 8 San Antonio, TX | 1,067,816 | 408,442 |
| 9 Dallas, TX | 1,053,292 | 434,462 |
| 10 Detroit, MI | 1,000,272 | 1,849,568 |

# Taking the Census: Everyone Counts

## WHAT IS A CENSUS?

Every 10 years the United States government counts the people who live in the United States. This is called taking the census. The census is taken to find out how many people there are, where they live, how old they are, what they do, how much money they earn, the number of children in families, and other information about them.

## WHEN WAS THE FIRST U.S. CENSUS TAKEN?

The first census was taken in 1790, after the American Revolution. That year there were 3,929,200 people in the United States. Most of the people then lived in the eastern part of the country, on farms or in small towns.

## WHEN WILL THE NEXT CENSUS TAKE PLACE?

The next census will begin on April 1, 2000. Census 2000 will be the 22nd decennial (every 10 years) counting of the U.S. population. For the first time ever, computers that read handwriting will be used to read the completed census forms.

## WHY DO WE NEED TO BE COUNTED?

▶ **Congress**
The number of representatives from each state in the U.S. House of Representatives depends on the population of each state.

▶ **National government**
Census information helps the national government make plans to provide public services such as health care, highways, and parks.

▶ **State and local governments**
Census information helps state and local governments decide local questions, such as whether to build more schools for children or homes for elderly people.

▶ **Private companies**
The census gives companies information that helps them—such as how many people use cars, baby food, refrigerators, and other products; how many people read newspapers; and where these people live.

## WHAT DID THE LAST CENSUS TELL US ABOUT THE UNITED STATES?

▶ By 1990, the population increased to 248,709,873.

▶ More than half of the people in the United States live in the south or west.

▶ About 8 out of every 10 Americans live in cities or suburbs.

▶ The United States is known for a large population that includes people of different races and nationalities.

The list below shows how many Americans called themselves white, black, Asian, American Indian, and Hispanic in the 1990 census. The percentages add up to more than 100% because most Hispanics also count themselves as white, black, or some other race.

**White,** 199,686,070 .............................80%

**Black,** 29,986,060 ...............................12%

**Hispanic,** 22,354,059 ............................9%

**Asian,** 7,276,662....................................3%
(including the Pacific Islands)

**American Indian,** 1,959,234....................1%
(including Eskimo, or Aleut)

**Other race,** 9,804,847 ............................4%
(people who said "other race")

# Counting the FIRST AMERICANS

### WHERE DID THEY COME FROM?

American Indians, also called Native Americans, lived in North and South America long before the first European explorers arrived. Their ancestors are thought to have come from northeast Asia more than 20,000 years ago. American Indians are not one people, but many different peoples, each with their own traditions.

### HOW MANY WERE THERE IN THE BEGINNING?

It is believed that many millions of Indians lived in the Americas before Columbus came. About 850,000 Native Americans lived in what is now the United States.

### HOW MANY ARE THERE NOW?

During the 17th, 18th, and 19th centuries, disease and wars with white settlers and soldiers caused the deaths of thousands of American Indians. By 1910 there were only about 220,000 left in the United States. Since then, the American Indian population has increased dramatically. By 1990, the total number of Native Americans was close to two million.

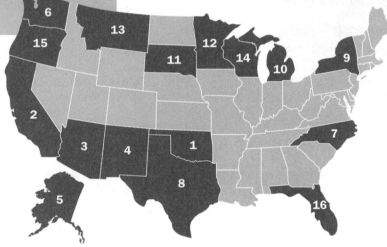

## WHERE DO NATIVE AMERICANS LIVE?

Below are the states with the largest Native American populations.
They are numbered in the map above.

| | | | | | |
|---|---|---|---|---|---|
| **1.** Oklahoma | 252,420 | | **9.** New York | 62,651 |
| **2.** California | 242,164 | | **10.** Michigan | 55,638 |
| **3.** Arizona | 203,527 | | **11.** South Dakota | 50,575 |
| **4.** New Mexico | 134,355 | | **12.** Minnesota | 49,909 |
| **5.** Alaska | 85,698 | | **13.** Montana | 47,679 |
| **6.** Washington | 81,483 | | **14.** Wisconsin | 39,387 |
| **7.** North Carolina | 80,155 | | **15.** Oregon | 38,496 |
| **8.** Texas | 65,877 | | **16.** Florida | 36,335 |

# The MANY FACES of America: IMMIGRATION

You have probably heard it said that America is a nation of immigrants. Many Americans are descended from Europeans, Africans, or Asians. Do you know someone who was born in another country?

## WHY DO PEOPLE COME TO THE UNITED STATES?

Have you ever wondered why so many people leave their native lands and come and live in the United States? It usually isn't because they don't love their own country. Most people are very attached to the place where they were born. Immigrants come to America for many reasons: to live in freedom, to worship as they choose, to escape poverty, to make a better life for themselves and their children.

Millions of people have immigrated to the United States from all over the world—more than 40 million since 1820. Much of the art we see or the music we hear, and many of the scientific discoveries, inventions we use, foods we eat, and languages we speak were introduced to us by people who came from other countries.

## WHAT COUNTRIES DO IMMIGRANTS COME FROM?

Immigrants come to the United States from many countries. Below are some of the countries immigrants came from in 1997. The name of the country is followed by the number of immigrants. In 1997, immigration from all countries to the United States totaled 798,378.

| | |
|---|---|
| Mexico | 146,865 |
| Philippines | 49,117 |
| China | 41,147 |
| Vietnam | 38,519 |
| India | 38,071 |
| Cuba | 33,587 |
| Dominican Republic | 27,053 |
| El Salvador | 17,969 |
| Jamaica | 17,840 |
| Russia | 16,632 |
| Ukraine | 15,696 |
| Haiti | 15,057 |
| North and South Korea | 14,239 |
| Colombia | 13,004 |
| Pakistan | 12,967 |
| Poland | 12,038 |

## WHERE DO IMMIGRANTS SETTLE?

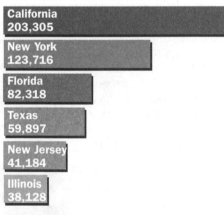

California 203,305

New York 123,716

Florida 82,318

Texas 59,897

New Jersey 41,184

Illinois 38,128

The bar chart shows the states that received the highest number of immigrants in 1997.

More than two-thirds of the immigrants from Mexico went to live in California or Texas, while over half of the immigrants from China went to two states: California and New York. Nearly 85 percent of the immigrants from Cuba went to live in Florida.

201

# Becoming an American Citizen: Naturalization

When a foreign-born person becomes a citizen of the United States, we say the person has become naturalized. To apply for American citizenship, a person:

Must be at least 18 years old.

Must have lived legally in the United States for at least five years.

Must be able to understand English if under the age of 55.

Must be of good moral character.

Must show knowledge of the history and form of government of the United States.

## ELLIS ISLAND AND THE STATUE OF LIBERTY

### ELLIS ISLAND: THE GATEWAY TO AMERICA

Many immigrants have crossed the Atlantic Ocean to the United States. They piled on to ships and came, hoping to find a better life. Between 1892 and 1924, more than 12 million people arrived by passing through Ellis Island, a huge immigration center in New York Harbor. There they were screened for certain contagious diseases and some sick people were sent back, but most immigrants were allowed to stay.

Immigrants who passed through Ellis Island came from many places, including Italy, Russia, Hungary, Austria, Germany, England, Ireland, Sweden, Greece, Norway, Turkey, Scotland, the West Indies, Poland, Portugal, and France.

### ELLIS ISLAND AS A MUSEUM

As an immigration center, Ellis Island was closed in 1954. But in 1990, it reopened as a museum to tell the story of the immigrants who helped make the United States a great country. The names of many who came through Ellis Island are carved on a wall in their memory.

### THE STATUE OF LIBERTY

Many of the immigrants who steamed into New York Harbor passed by the Statue of Liberty. Set on her own island, the "Lady With the Lamp" was given to the United States by France and has served as a welcome to Americans-to-be since she was erected in 1886. In 1903, a poem by the U.S. poet Emma Lazarus was inscribed at the base of the statue. Two of its lines read: "Give me your tired, your poor, your huddled masses yearning to breathe free...."

*Thousands of immigrants entered through this hall at Ellis Island.*

❓ **Who won the Grammy for Best New Artist of 1998?**
*You can find the answer on page 204.*

# ENTERTAINMENT AWARDS

Who is your favorite movie actor or actress? What is your all-time favorite film? If you are interested in the movies, you probably know that an Oscar is a golden statuette that is awarded for the year's best actor, best actress, best movies, and so on. The Oscar presentations are watched on TV by millions of people all over the world. Among other awards given every year for the best in entertainment are the Grammys, the Emmys, and the Tonys.

## ACADEMY AWARDS: THE OSCARS

The Oscars are given every year by the Academy of Motion Picture Arts and Sciences for the best in movies. Here are some of the films and people that won Oscars for 1998.

**Best Picture:** *Shakespeare in Love*

**Best Actor:** Roberto Benigni in *Life Is Beautiful*

**Best Actress:** Gwyneth Paltrow in *Shakespeare in Love*

**Best Supporting Actor:** James Coburn in *Affliction*

**Best Supporting Actress:** Judi Dench in *Shakespeare in Love*

**Best Director:** Steven Spielberg for *Saving Private Ryan*

**Best Original Screenplay:** Marc Norman and Tom Stoppard for *Shakespeare in Love*

**Best Original Song:** "When You Believe," from *The Prince of Egypt*

**Best Original Musical Score:** *Shakespeare in Love*

**Best Visual Effects:** *What Dreams May Come*

**Best Costume Design:** *Shakespeare in Love*

**Best Makeup:** *Elizabeth*

▲ Scene from *The Prince of Egypt*

**DID YOU KNOW?**

Walt Disney won 20 Oscars during his career—more than anyone else.

The youngest person ever to receive an Oscar was Shirley Temple. She won an honorary Oscar in 1934 at the age of five.

The oldest was Jessica Tandy. In 1990, at the age of 80, she won an Oscar for Best Actress in *Driving Miss Daisy*.

## THE GRAMMYS

Grammys are awards given out each year by the National Academy of Recording Arts and Sciences for the best in popular music. Some of the winners for 1998:

Lauryn Hill

**Best Record and Best Song:** "My Heart Will Go On," Celine Dion

**Best Album:** *The Miseducation of Lauryn Hill,* Lauryn Hill

**Best New Artist:** Lauryn Hill

**Best Performance by a Rock Group:** "Pink," Aerosmith

**Best Rock Album:** *The Globe Sessions,* Sheryl Crow

**Best Rock Song:** "Uninvited," Alanis Morissette

**Best Pop Album:** *Ray of Light,* Madonna

**Best Rhythm-and-Blues Song:** "Doo Wop (That Thing)," Lauryn Hill

**Best Rap Solo Performance**: "Gettin' Jiggy Wit It," Will Smith

**Best Rap Album:** *Vol. 2 . . . Hard Knock Life,* Jay-Z

**Best Performance by a Country Group:** "There's Your Trouble," Dixie Chicks

**Best Country Album:** *Wide Open Spaces,* Dixie Chicks

**Best Contemporary Folk Album:** *Car Wheels on a Gravel Road,* Lucinda Williams

**Best Musical Album for Children:** *Elmopalooza!,* the Sesame Street Muppets with various artists

**Best Spoken Word Album for Children:** *The Children's Shakespeare,* various artists

## THE EMMYS

The Emmy Awards are given each year by the Academy of Television Arts and Sciences. Here are some of the major winners for the 1997-1998 season for primetime (the evening from 8 PM to 11 PM).

**Best Drama Series:** *The Practice* (ABC)

**Best Actor in a Drama Series:** Andre Braugher in *Homicide: Life on the Street* (NBC)

**Best Actress in a Drama Series:** Christine Lahti in *Chicago Hope* (CBS)

**Best Comedy Series:** *Frasier* (NBC)

**Best Actor in a Comedy Series:** Kelsey Grammer in *Frasier* (NBC)

**Best Actress in a Comedy Series:** Helen Hunt in *Mad About You* (NBC)

**Best Miniseries:** *From Earth to the Moon* (HBO)

## THE TONYS

The Antoinette Perry Awards, known as the "Tonys," are annual awards given to the best Broadway plays and to those who write them, act in them, and direct them. Winners for the 1997-1998 season were:

**Best Play:** *Art*

**Best Musical:** *The Lion King*

**Best Musical Revival:** *Cabaret*

**Leading Actor in a Play:** Anthony LaPaglia

**Leading Actress in a Play:** Marie Mullen

**Leading Actor in a Musical:** Alan Cumming

**Leading Actress in a Musical:** Natasha Richardson

# Other PRIZES and AWARDS

## NOBEL PRIZES

The Nobel Prizes are named after Alfred B. Nobel (1833–1896), a Swedish scientist who left money to be given every year to people who have helped humankind. Albert Einstein, the world-famous German-born physicist, won the physics prize in 1921. The Polish-French scientist Marie Curie won two Nobel Prizes—one in physics in 1903 (with Pierre Curie, her husband, and Henry Becquerel) and one in chemistry in 1911. Prizes are also given for medicine-physiology, literature, economics, and peace.

The Nobel Peace Prize goes to people that the judges think did the most during the past year to help achieve peace. In 1998, the prize went to John Hume and David Trimble, two political leaders who worked for peace in Northern Ireland.

## PULITZER PRIZES

The Pulitzer Prizes are named after Joseph Pulitzer (1847–1911), a journalist and publisher, who gave the money to set them up. The prizes are given yearly in the United States for journalism, drama, literature, and music.

## Spingarn Medal

The Spingarn Medal was set up in 1914 by Joel Elias Spingarn, leader of the National Association for the Advancement of Colored People (NAACP). It is awarded every year by the NAACP for achievement by a black American. Here are some winners.

**1999: Publisher Earl Graves**

**1998: Civil rights activist Myrlie Evers-Williams**

**1994: Writer and poet Maya Angelou**

**1991: General Colin Powell**

**1985: Actor Bill Cosby**

**1979: Civil rights activist Rosa Parks**

**1975: Baseball player Hank Aaron**

**1957: Civil rights leader Martin Luther King, Jr.**

## THE MEDAL OF HONOR

The Medal of Honor is given by the United States government for bravery in war against an enemy. The first medals were awarded in 1863. Since that time, nearly 3,400 people have received the award.

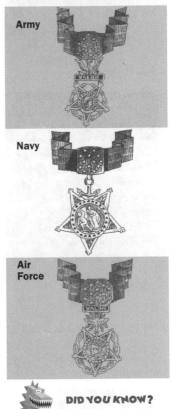

Army

Navy

Air Force

**DID YOU KNOW?**

*Dr. Mary E. Walker, a surgeon during the Civil War, was the only woman to receive the Medal of Honor. She got it in 1865 for her medical treatment of Union soldiers.*

# CONTESTS

Putting your best foot forward—that's what contests are all about. If you have a special talent and you like to compete, why not consider entering a contest. From making posters and writing stories to creating thrilling science projects, contests can be challenging and fun, and you can choose from many kinds. Some appear in books, magazines, or newspapers and you can enter on your own. Others are run only through schools; you need to ask your teacher about these.

So go ahead—enter. The next winner could be you!

## TWO MAGAZINE CONTESTS

**Do you like history?**
The *American History Magazine for Young People* runs an annual contest asking readers (ages 8–14) to create a short video, poster, or essay telling why they think a particular person played an important role in history. For details, take a look at the December issue of the magazine.
**WEB SITE**
*http://www.cobblestonepub.com*

**If you think science is a blast,**
check out the magazine *Odyssey: Adventures in Science*. It holds contests in which kids (ages 10–16) do artwork, write science fiction stories, or design science projects.
**WEB SITE**
*http://www.odysseymagazine.com*

For more information about the above contests, visit their Web sites or write to: Cobblestone Publishing, 30 Grove St., Peterborough, NH 03458.

## CHANCES TO GET PUBLISHED AND WIN PRIZES!

Kids, here's your chance to actually get your book published! You can enter an original book on any topic in *The National Written & Illustrated By . . . Awards Contest for Students*. Each contestant must write and illustrate his or her own book. Winners in three age categories—6–9, 10–13, and 14–19—will get publishing contracts and receive money (royalties) from the sales of their books. For information, send a self-addressed business size No. 10 envelope stamped with 66 cents postage to Contest/Landmark Editions, P.O. Box 270169, Kansas City, MO 64127.
**WEB SITE**
*http://www.landmarkeditions.com*

**The NewsCurrents Editorial Cartoon Contest** invites kids in grades K–12 to send in their original and creative editorial cartoons. You can enter as many cartoons as you wish. Winners will receive U.S. savings bonds and their entry will be published in the book *Editorial Cartoons by Kids*.
**WEB SITE**
*http://www.ku.com/carcontest.html*

**Read magazine offers annual writing contests.** Who's your favorite author? Kids in two grade categories—4–7 and 8–12—can write a letter to an author—living or dead—describing how the author's work has changed your life. Send it to the Letters About Literature Program. Winners will receive cash awards.

**WEB SITE**
http://www.weeklyreader.com/features/readct.html

# CONTESTS THROUGH SCHOOLS

**National Spelling Bee.** Twelve-year-old Jody-Anne Maxwell, from Kingston, Jamaica, was the 1998 winner of the National Spelling Bee. If you're a good speller, you could follow in her footsteps. A company named Scripps Howard runs spelling bees for kids ages 15 years old and under. Winners go to regional contests, and then possibly to the National Spelling Bee in Washington, D.C. The competition is usually held in late May or early June. For information, ask your school principal to contact The Scripps Howard National Spelling Bee, P.O. Box 371541, Pittsburgh, PA 15251. Phone: (513) 977-3040.

**WEB SITE** http://www.spellingbee.com

**Contests in Literature, Musical Composition, Photography, and Visual Arts.** Do you like to take photographs, write stories or poems, compose music, or create art? If so, the National PTA (Parent Teacher Association) Reflections Program may interest you. It's based on a different theme each year. Entries may be in literature, musical composition, photography, or visual arts. Students must enter through a local PTA or PTSA (Parent Teacher Student Association) in good standing and will be recognized at the local, council, district, and national levels. For information, a school PTA or PTSA may contact: National PTA Reflections Program, 330 North Wabash Ave., Suite 2100, Chicago, IL 60611. Phone: (800) 307-4782.

**WEB SITE** http://www.pta.org

**National Geography Bee.** Test your knowledge of geography with The National Geography Bee sponsored by The National Geographic Society. In this contest, students in grades 4–8 compete on local, state, and national levels by answering oral and written questions about geography. For information, a school principal may write to: National Geography Bee, National Geographic Society, 1145 17th St., N.W., Washington, D.C. 20036. The registration deadline is October 15 of every year.

**WEB SITE**
http://www.nationalgeographic.com

## CHECK IT OUT!

A number of magazines also hold contests not mentioned in these pages, or print kids' original stories, poems, opinions, artwork, photographs, and even jokes and riddles. Some of them are: *Contact, Highlights for Children, Sports Illustrated for Kids, Stone Soup: The Magazine by Young Writers and Artists,* and *Zillions.* Look for these magazines and others in your local library. Good luck!

❓ **Which is the world's largest religion?**
*You can find the answer below.*

# WORLD RELIGIONS

How did the universe begin? Why are we here on Earth? What happens to us after we die? For many people, religion is a way of answering questions like these. Believing in a God or gods, or in a Divine Being, is one way of making sense of the world around us. Religions can also help guide people's lives.

About five billion people all over the world belong to some group. Different religions have different beliefs. For example, Christians, Jews, and Muslims all believe in one God, while Hindus believe in many gods. On this page and the next are some facts about the world's major religions.

## CHRISTIANITY

**Who Started Christianity?** Jesus Christ, in the first century. He was born in Bethlehem between 8 B.C. and 4 B.C. and died about A.D. 29.

**What Do Christians Believe?** That there is one God. That Jesus Christ is the Son of God, who came on Earth, died to save humankind, and rose from the dead.

**How Many Are There?** Christianity is the world's biggest religion. In 1998 there were almost two billion Christians, in nearly all parts of the world. More than one billion of the Christians were **Roman Catholics**, who follow the leadership of the pope in Rome. Other groups of Christians include **Orthodox Christians**, who accept most of the same teachings as Roman Catholics but do not follow the pope as their leader, and **Protestants**, who often disagree with Catholic teachings. Protestants rely especially on the Bible itself. They belong to many different groups.

## JUDAISM

**Who Started Judaism?** Abraham is considered to be the founder of Judaism. He lived around 1300 B.C.

**What Do Jews Believe?** That there is one God who created the universe and rules over it. That they should be faithful to God and carry out God's commandments.

**How Many Are There?** In 1998, there were about 14 million Jews living around the world. Many live in Israel or the United States.

**What Kinds Are There?** In the United States there are three main kinds: **Orthodox, Conservative**, and **Reform**. Orthodox Jews are the most traditional. Traditional means that they follow strict laws about how they dress, what they can eat, and how they conduct their lives. Conservative Jews follow many of the traditions. Reform Jews are the least traditional.

## ISLAM

**Who Started Islam?**
Muhammad, the Prophet, in A.D. 610.

**What Do Muslims Believe?**
People who believe in Islam are known as Muslims. The word "Islam" means submission to God. Muslims believe that there is no other god than God; that Muhammad is the prophet and lawgiver of his community; that they should pray five times a day, fast during the month of Ramadan, give to the poor, and once during their life make a pilgrimage to Mecca in Saudi Arabia if they can afford it.

**How Many Are There?** In 1998, there were about one billion Muslims, mostly in parts of Africa and Asia. The two main branches are: **Sunni Muslims**, who make up over 80 percent of all Muslims today, and **Shiite Muslims**, who broke away in a dispute over leadership after Muhammad died in 632.

## HINDUISM

**Who Started Hinduism?**
No one person. Aryan invaders of India, around 1500 B.C., brought their own beliefs with them, which were mixed with the beliefs of the people who already lived in India.

**What Do Hindus Believe?**
That there are many gods and many ways of worshipping. That people die and are reborn many times as other living things. That there is a universal soul or principle known as *Brahman*. That the goal of life is to escape the cycle of birth and death and become part of the *Brahman*. This is achieved by leading a pure and good life.

**How Many Are There?** In 1998, there were nearly 800 million Hindus, mainly in India and places where people from India have gone to live.

**What Kinds Are There?**
There are many kinds of Hindus, who worship different gods or goddesses.

## BUDDHISM

**Who Started Buddhism?**
Gautama Siddhartha (the Buddha), around 525 B.C.

**What Do Buddhists Believe?** Buddha taught that life is filled with suffering. In order to be free of that suffering, believers have to give up worldly possessions and worldly goals and try to achieve a state of perfect peace known as *nirvana*.

**How Many Are There?**
In 1998, there were more than 350 million Buddhists, mostly in Asia.

**What Kinds Are There?**
There are two main kinds of Buddhists. **Theravada** ("Path of the Elders") **Buddhism,** the older kind, is more common in the southern part of Asia. **Mahayana** ("Great Vessel") **Buddhism** is more common in northern Asia.

# RELIGIOUS MEMBERSHIP
# in the United States

**D**id you know that Protestants are the largest religious group in the United States, and that Catholics are the second largest? The pie chart below shows how many people belong to the major religious groups. These numbers are recent estimates; no one knows exactly how many people belong to each group.

Protestants

Roman Catholics

**More than 100 million**
*Including:*

| | | | |
|---|---|---|---|
| Baptists | 32 million | Methodists | 14 million |
| Pentacostals | 10 million | Lutherans | 8 million |
| Mormons | 6 million | Presbyterians | 4 million |
| Episcopalians | 2 million | Reformed Churches | 2 million |

**Muslims....................4 million**

**Jews........................6 million**

**Orthodox Christians...6 million**

**60 million**

## RELIGIOUS Writings

**E**very religion has its writings or sacred texts that set out its laws and beliefs. Among them are:

**THE BIBLE**

**The Old Testament.** Also known as the Hebrew Bible, this is a collection of laws, history, and other writings that are holy books for Jews and also for Christians. The first five books of the Old Testament are known by Jews as the Torah. These contain the stories of creation and the beginnings of human life, as well as the laws handed down by the prophet Moses.

**The New Testament.** A collection of Gospels (stories about Jesus), epistles (letters written to guide the early Christians), and other writings. The Old Testament and New Testament together make up the Bible that is read by Christians.

**THE KORAN**

The Koran (al-Qur'an in Arabic) sets out the main beliefs and practices of Islam, the religion of Muslims. Muslims believe that the Koran was revealed by God to the prophet Muhammad through the angel Gabriel.

**THE BHAGAVAD GHITA**

The Bhagavad Ghita is one of several Hindu religious writings. Part of a long poem about war, it is familiar to almost every Hindu. In it the god Krishna, in the form of a man, drives the chariot of Prince Arjuna into battle and teaches him about how to live.

# Major HOLY DAYS
# for Christians, Jews, and Muslims

## CHRISTIAN HOLY DAYS

|  | 1999 | 2000 | 2001 |
|---|---|---|---|
| Ash Wednesday | February 17 | March 8 | February 28 |
| Good Friday | April 2 | April 21 | April 13 |
| Easter Sunday | April 4 | April 23 | April 15 |
| Easter for Orthodox Churches | April 11 | April 30 | April 15 |
| Christmas | December 25 | December 25 | December 25 |

## JEWISH HOLY DAYS  The Jewish holy days begin at sundown the previous night. The dates listed below are the first full day of the observance.

|  | 1999 (5759–60) | 2000 (5760–5761) | 2001 (5761–5762) |
|---|---|---|---|
| Passover | April 1 | April 20 | April 8 |
| Rosh Hashanah (New Year) | September 11 | September 30 | September 18 |
| Yom Kippur | September 20 | October 9 | September 27 |
| Hanukkah | December 4 | December 22 | December 10 |

## ISLAMIC (MUSLIM) HOLY DAYS

|  | 1999–2000 (1420) | 2000–2001 (1421) | 2001–2002 (1422) |
|---|---|---|---|
| Muharram 1 (New Year) | April 17 | April 6 | March 26 |
| Mawlid (Birthday of Muhammad) | June 26 | June 14 | June 4 |
| Ramadan 1 | December 9 | November 27 | November 16 |
| Id al-Adha Dhu al-Hijjah 10 | March 16 | March 5 | February 22 |

# SCIENCE

❷ **What do you call the process that kills the germs in milk?**
*You can find the answer on page 216.*

# WHAT THINGS ARE MADE OF

People, dogs, butterflies, flowers, rocks, air, water, CDs, baseball cards, telephones—everything we see and use is made up of "basic ingredients" called elements. There are at least 112 elements. Most have been found in nature. Some have been created in laboratories. (Scientists are now struggling to create more elements.)

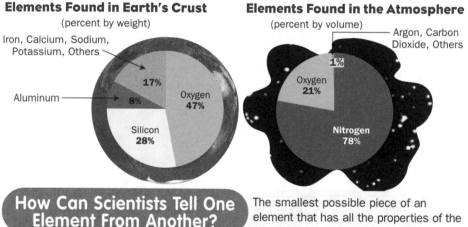

**Elements Found in Earth's Crust**
(percent by weight)

Iron, Calcium, Sodium, Potassium, Others

Aluminum

17%

8%

Oxygen 47%

Silicon 28%

**Elements Found in the Atmosphere**
(percent by volume)

Argon, Carbon Dioxide, Others

1%

Oxygen 21%

Nitrogen 78%

## How Can Scientists Tell One Element From Another?

The smallest possible piece of an element that has all the properties of the original element is called an **atom**. Each tiny atom is made up of even smaller particles called **protons**, **neutrons**, and **electrons**.

To tell one element from another, scientists count the number of protons in an atom. The total number of protons is called the element's **atomic number**. All of the atoms of an element have the same number of protons and electrons, but some atoms have a different number of neutrons. For example, carbon-12 has six protons and six neutrons, and carbon-13 has six protons and seven neutrons.

We call the amount of matter in an atom its **atomic mass**. Carbon-13 has a greater atomic mass than carbon-12. The average atomic mass of all of the different atoms of the same element is called the element's **atomic weight**. Every element has a different atomic number and a different atomic weight.

**Chemical Symbols Are Scientific Shorthand.** When scientists write the names of elements, they often use a symbol instead of spelling out the full name. The symbol for each element is one or two letters. Scientists write O for oxygen and He for helium. The symbols usually come from the English name for the element (C for carbon). The symbols for some of the elements come from the element's Latin name. For example, the symbol for gold is Au, which is short for *Aurum*, the Latin word for gold.

# Some COMMON ELEMENTS

The table below shows some common elements with their symbol, atomic number, atomic weight, the year they were discovered, and some of their common uses.

| NAME OF ELEMENT | SYMBOL | ATOMIC NUMBER | ATOMIC WEIGHT | YEAR FOUND | COMMON USE |
|---|---|---|---|---|---|
| Hydrogen | H | 1 | 1.01 | 1766 | in welding |
| Helium | He | 2 | 4.00 | 1868 | inflate balloons |
| Carbon | C | 6 | 12.01 | B.C. | pencils, diamonds |
| Nitrogen | N | 7 | 14.01 | 1772 | fertilizers |
| Oxygen | O | 8 | 16.00 | 1774 | breathing |
| Fluorine | F | 9 | 19.00 | 1771 | toothpastes |
| Neon | Ne | 10 | 20.18 | 1898 | electric signs |
| Sodium | Na | 11 | 22.99 | 1807 | in salt |
| Aluminum | Al | 13 | 26.98 | 1825 | soda cans |
| Silicon | Si | 14 | 28.09 | 1823 | in sand |
| Sulfur | S | 16 | 32.06 | B.C. | matches |
| Chlorine | Cl | 17 | 35.45 | 1774 | purifies water, in salt |
| Calcium | Ca | 20 | 40.08 | 1808 | in bones |
| Iron | Fe | 26 | 55.85 | B.C. | steel, magnets |
| Copper | Cu | 29 | 63.55 | B.C. | water pipes, wire |
| Silver | Ag | 47 | 107.87 | B.C. | jewelry, dental fillings |
| Gold | Au | 79 | 196.97 | B.C. | jewelry, coins |
| Mercury | Hg | 80 | 200.59 | B.C. | in thermometers |
| Lead | Pb | 82 | 207.19 | B.C. | in car batteries |

## ELEMENTS Are All Around Us

Neon signs light up store windows. Car batteries contain lead. Soda cans are made from aluminum. Chips using silicon are found in computers. Jewelry is made from gold and silver.

When elements join together, they form **compounds**. Water is a compound made up of hydrogen and oxygen. Salt is a compound made up of sodium and chlorine. Many things we use at home or in school are compounds.

| Common Name | Contains the Compound | Contains the Elements |
|---|---|---|
| Vinegar | Acetic acid | carbon, hydrogen, oxygen |
| Chalk | Calcium carbonate | calcium, carbon, oxygen |
| Soda bubbles | Carbon dioxide | carbon, oxygen |
| Rust | Iron oxide | iron, oxygen |
| Baking soda | Sodium bicarbonate | sodium, hydrogen, carbon, oxygen |
| Toothpaste | Sodium fluoride | sodium, fluorine |

# MINERALS, ROCKS, and GEMS

## What Are Minerals?

Minerals are solid materials in the soil that were never alive. All the land on our planet—even the ocean floor—rests on a layer of rock made up of minerals. Minerals have also been found on other planets, on our moon, and in meteorites that landed on Earth. Some minerals, such as **gold** and **silver,** are made up entirely of one element. But most are formed from two or more elements joined together.

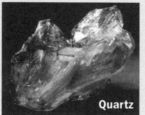

Quartz

The most common mineral is **quartz,** which is made of silicon and oxygen and is found all over the world. **Sand** is made up mostly of quartz. **Graphite,** which is used in pencils, is another common mineral. Other minerals, like **diamonds,** are very rare and valuable. Oddly enough, diamonds and graphite are different forms of the same element—carbon.

## What Are Rocks?

Rocks are combinations of minerals. The three kinds of rocks are:

❶ Igneous rocks—rocks that form from melted minerals in the Earth that cool and become solid. Granite is an igneous rock made from quartz, feldspar, and mica.

❷ Sedimentary rocks— rocks that usually form in sea and river beds from tiny pieces of other rocks, sand, and shells packed together. It takes millions of years for these pieces to form sedimentary rocks. Limestone is a kind of sedimentary rock.

❸ Metamorphic rock. Over millions of years, the heat and pressure inside Earth can change the minerals in igneous and sedimentary rocks. When the minerals in a rock change, the new rock is called a **metamorphic rock**. Marble is a metamorphic rock formed from limestone.

## What Are Gems?

Most **gems** are minerals that have been cut and polished to be used as jewelry or other kinds of decoration. Some gems are not minerals. A pearl is a gem that is not a mineral, because it comes from an oyster, which is a living thing. The most valued gems—diamonds, emeralds, rubies, and sapphires—are minerals called **precious stones**. Below are some popular gems, the kind of mineral each one is, the elements each is made up of, and the usual colors for the gem.

| Gem Name | Mineral | Element It Is Made Of | Usual Colors |
|---|---|---|---|
| Amethyst | quartz | silicon, oxygen | purple |
| Diamond | carbon | carbon | bluish white |
| Emerald | beryl | beryllium, silicon, aluminum, oxygen | green |
| Opal | opal | silicon, oxygen | red, green, blue |
| Ruby | corundum | aluminum, oxygen | red |
| Sapphire | corundum | aluminum, oxygen | blue |

 **DID YOU KNOW?**  *Some minerals glow in the dark. Those that change color under ultraviolet light—like diamonds, opals, and rubies—are called **fluorescent minerals.** Fluorescent minerals that glow in the dark even after ultraviolet light is taken away are called **phosphorescent minerals.***

# BUILDING BLOCKS of LIFE

## What Is DNA?

DNA (deoxyribonucleic acid) contains the information that shapes all living things (organisms). Lengths of DNA, called genes, determine what each organism is like. Genes are like tiny pieces of a secret code. They are passed on from parents to children. They determine how we look and grow. Many things about us, from the color of our eyes to the size of our feet, depend on the genes we inherited from our parents.

### How Is DNA Used To Identify People?

Each person's DNA is distinctly different from that of other people. That makes DNA useful for identifying people.

DNA traces at a crime scene can be used to convict a suspect or show that the suspect is not guilty.

DNA tests can also show whether people are related. They can be used to identify a baby's parents and prevent mix-ups.

*DNA*

# WHAT DO MAGNETS DO?
## What Is a Magnet?

Have you ever seen paper clips or pins sliding toward a magnet and then sticking to it? Magnets have two areas, called **poles**, where magnetic effects are strongest. A bar magnet has a pole at each end. Around each pole is a region called a **magnetic field**. A magnetic field cannot be seen, but it can be felt when another magnet enters the field or when something with iron in it, such as a paper clip or a pin, enters the magnetic field. Such an object will then become attracted to one of the magnet's poles.

## How Do Magnets React to Other Magnets?

Magnets have two poles. One is called the north pole and the other is called the south pole. The north pole of one magnet will attract the south pole of another magnet—in other words, opposites attract.

But when the north poles of two magnets are brought near each other, they will push away (repel) each other. Magnets can have different shapes and can be made of different materials.

### DID YOU KNOW?

▶ *Do you know that Earth is a giant magnet whose magnetic field exists at all locations? Like a bar magnet, Earth has two magnetic poles. One of them is near the geographical North Pole and the other is near the geographical South Pole.*

▶ *If you have ever used a compass, you have seen that the compass needle always points in the same direction—toward the north—no matter which way you turn. The needle is a small bar magnet that can rotate easily. It points north because the north pole of the magnet is attracted to the magnetic north pole of Earth.*

# Some FAMOUS SCIENTISTS

**Archimedes** (about 287 B.C.–212 B.C.), a Greek mathematician who discovered that heavy objects could be moved with little force. Archimedes was one of the first people ever to test his ideas with experiments.

**Nicolaus Copernicus** (1473–1543), a Polish scientist known as the founder of modern astronomy. He believed that Earth and other planets revolved around the sun.

**Galileo Galilei** (1564–1642), an Italian astronomer who, like Copernicus, believed that the sun was at the center of the solar system, and that the planets revolved around it. He also proved that all objects, whether heavy or light, fall at the same rate.

**Sir Isaac Newton** (1642–1727), a British scientist famous for discovering the laws of gravity. He also discovered that sunlight is made up of all the colors of the rainbow.

**Edward Jenner** (1749–1823), a British doctor who discovered a way to prevent smallpox by injecting healthy people with cowpox vaccine. Today's vaccines work in a similar way.

**Michael Faraday** (1791–1867), a British scientist who discovered that magnets can be used to create electricity in copper wires. Faraday's discoveries enable us to produce massive amounts of electricity.

**Charles Darwin** (1809–1882), a British scientist best known for his theory of evolution. According to this theory, living creatures slowly develop over millions of years.

**Gregor Johann Mendel** (1822–1884), an Austrian monk who discovered the laws of heredity by showing how characteristics are passed from one generation of plants to the next.

**Louis Pasteur** (1822–1895), a French chemist who discovered a process called pasteurization, in which heat is used to kill germs in milk.

**Marie Curie** (1867–1934), a Polish-French physical chemist known for discovering radium, which is used to treat certain diseases.

**Albert Einstein** (1879–1955), a German-American physicist who developed a revolutionary theory about the relationships between time, space, matter, and energy.

**Francis Crick** (born 1916) and **Maurice Wilkins** (born 1916) of England and **James D. Watson** (born 1928) of the United States, worked out the structure of DNA, the basic chemical that controls inheritance in all living cells.

**DID YOU KNOW?** *Emily Rosa of Loveland, Colorado, recently designed a science experiment that was described in an important medical journal. She did the project for her fourth-grade science fair when she was only nine years old. People called healers say they can heal some ailments by changing a body's energy field through "therapeutic touch." But the healers she tested could not tell whether her hand was hidden behind a screen or not. This showed that they could not detect a body's energy field.*

# LIGHT and SOUND

## WHAT IS LIGHT?

Light is a form of energy that travels in **rays**. Light rays generally move in straight lines, at a speed of 186,000 miles per second through empty space. It takes more than eight minutes for the light from the sun to reach Earth. Light also moves through materials like water and glass, but more slowly.

## WHAT IS A RAINBOW?

The light we usually see (visible light) is made up of colors called the **spectrum**. The colors of the spectrum are red, orange, yellow, green, blue, indigo, and violet. White light is formed from a mixture of all the colors of the spectrum. A prism can separate the colors in a beam of white light. When you see a rainbow, the tiny water droplets in the air are separating the white light into the spectrum.

## WHERE DOES SOUND COME FROM?

When objects vibrate quickly back and forth in the air, they create **sound**. The vibrating objects cause the molecules in the air around the objects to move. As the molecules move, the vibrations travel through the air in **waves**. These sound waves move outward in every direction from the place where they started—like ripples in a pond moving away from the point where a pebble is dropped.

## WHAT CAN YOU HEAR IN OUTER SPACE?

Sound waves have to have a medium to move through. Usually air serves as the medium. But sounds can also travel through water, wood, glass, and other materials. In outer space, where there is no air or other medium for sound waves to travel through, there is no sound. Astronauts in space communicate with Earth over radio waves, not sound waves.

## HOW LOUD ARE THOSE SOUNDS?

The loudness of a sound (called volume) is measured in **decibels**. The volume depends on how many air molecules are vibrating and how strongly they are vibrating. The quietest sound that can be heard has a value of zero decibels.

**0 decibels**
*faintest sound heard*

**10-20 decibels**
*rustling leaves*

**20-30 decibels**
*whispering*

**50-70 decibels**
*conversation*

**80-100 decibels**
*heavy traffic and trains*

**100-120 decibels**
*loud music*

**140-150 decibels**
*nearby jet engine*

# SCIENCE MUSEUMS

If you like hands-on exhibits and like to learn about science, here are a few museums that you might visit. Look in the INDEX under Museums to find out about museums with exhibits on natural history and computers.

**CALIFORNIA MUSEUM OF SCIENCE AND INDUSTRY,** Los Angeles, California. Includes a giant electromagnet activated by visitors, plus exhibits on electricity, earthquakes, computer-assisted design, aerospace, and health sciences.
**WEB SITE** http://www.casciencectr.org

**EXPLORATORIUM,** San Francisco, California. Has interactive hands-on exhibits.
**WEB SITE** http://www.exploratorium.edu

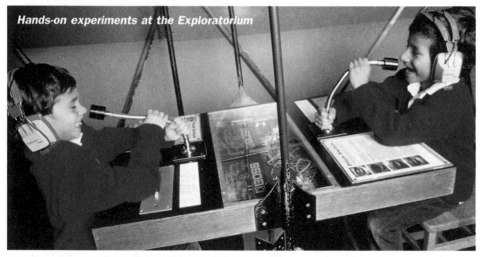

*Hands-on experiments at the Exploratorium*

**THE FRANKLIN INSTITUTE SCIENCE MUSEUM,** Philadelphia, Pennsylvania. Includes an exhibit on the environment called Earth Quest, a giant heart people can walk through, and many hands-on exhibits.
**WEB SITE** http://www.sln.fi.edu

**LIBERTY SCIENCE CENTER,** Liberty State Park, Jersey City, New Jersey. Features more than 250 interactive exhibits and an OMNIMAX theater.
**WEB SITE** http://www.libertystatepark.com/libertys.htm

**MUSEUM OF SCIENCE AND INDUSTRY,** Chicago, Illinois. Features a reproduction of a coal mine, as well as displays to help visitors learn more about health, human intelligence, and how people live.
**WEB SITE** http://www.msichicago.org

**NATIONAL AIR AND SPACE MUSEUM,** Washington, D.C. Has the Wright brothers' plane, Charles Lindbergh's *Spirit of St. Louis*, *Skylab*, and many other planes and rockets.
**WEB SITE** http://www.nasm.si.edu

**THE SCIENCE PLACE AND TI FOUNDERS IMAX THEATER,** Dallas, Texas. Includes hands-on science exhibits, water and sound experiments, an exhibit on special effects in movies, mathematical puzzles, and a planetarium.
**WEB SITE** http://www.scienceplace.org

# MAGIC ICE CUBE

**D**o you know how and why you can pick up an ice cube without touching it? Try this simple experiment to find out.

## YOU NEED

▶ one ice cube

▶ a small bowl of water

▶ a foot-long piece of heavy string or twine

▶ some salt

## WHAT TO DO

1. Place the ice cube in a shallow bowl of water so that the water comes just to the top of the ice cube.
2. Make a lasso–like loop at the end of the string.
3. Make the loop lie flat on top of the ice cube.
4. Sprinkle salt on the loop and the cube so that the string is completely covered.
5. Slowly count to 10.
6. Holding the other end of the string, lift the ice cube out of the water.

Can you guess what happened? Try figuring it out before you read the answer. It's upside down on the bottom of the page.

**Answer:** Salt lowers the melting point of ice, which is why people sprinkle salt on their driveways and sidewalks after a snow or ice storm. So your ice cube started to melt. The lasso stuck to the ice cube, however. This is because the coldness of the ice made the melted top of the ice cube refreeze around the string.

# SIGNS AND SYMBOLS

❷ **What are four ways to make up a secret cipher?**
You can find the answer on page 223.

SIGNS AND SYMBOLS

**S**igns and symbols give us information at a glance. Many signs indicate where something is located, such as a hospital or rest rooms. Others give commands, such as Stop or Yield. Still others warn us of danger. Long ago, when most people did not know how to read, simple pictures and symbols were used on signs to help strangers find the shops in a town.

| | | | | |
|---|---|---|---|---|
|  | |  | |  |
| Telephone | Gasoline | Hospital | First Aid | Drug Store |

| | | | | |
|---|---|---|---|---|
| |  | |  |  |
| Handicapped Access | Men's Rest Room | Women's Rest Room | Food | Lodging |

| | | |
|---|---|---|
|  | | |
| Airport | Information | Library |

| | | | | |
|---|---|---|---|---|
|  |  | |  |  |
| Picnic Area | Camping | Swimming | Fishing | Hiking Trail |

| | | | | |
|---|---|---|---|---|
| |  | |  |   |
| No Smoking | Flammable | Poison | Radioactive | Explosives | No Bicycles |

# Road Signs

**STOP** — Stop

**One Way**

**No Entry**

**No U-Turn**

**No Parking**

**Right Turn**

**No Left Turn**

**Hill**

**Signal Ahead**

**School Zone**

**Pedestrian Crossing**

**Deer Crossing**

**Railroad Crossing**

**Road Work Ahead**

**Cross Road**

**Winding Road**

**Slippery Road**

**Divided Highway**

**Yield**

**Merging Traffic**

# Some Useful Symbols

$ — Dollar

¢ — Cent

% — Percent

& — Ampersand (and)

℞ — Prescription

© — Copyright

® — Registered Trademark

♂ — Male

♀ — Female

± — Plus or Minus

= — Is Equal To

≠ — Is Not Equal To

< — Is Less Than

> — Is Greater Than

( ) — Parentheses

# BRAILLE

Blind people read with their fingers using a system of raised dots called Braille. Braille was developed by Louis Braille (1809-1852) in France in 1826, when he was a teenager.

The Braille alphabet, numbers, punctuation, and speech sounds are represented by 63 different combinations of 6 raised dots arranged in a grid like this:

|  |  |
|---|---|
| ❶ | ❹ |
| ❷ | ❺ |
| ❸ | ❻ |

All the letters in the basic Braille alphabet are lowercase. Special symbols are added to show that what follows is a capital letter or a number. The light circles on the grid below show the raised dots.

a  b  c  d  e  f  g  h  i  j  k  l  m

n  o  p  q  r  s  t  u  v  w  x  y  z

cap  #  1  2  3  4  5  6  7  8  9  0

**BRAILLE ALPHABET AND NUMBERS**

# SIGN LANGUAGE

Many people who are deaf or hearing-impaired, and cannot hear spoken words, talk with their fingers instead of their voices. To do this, they use a system of manual signs (the manual alphabet), or finger spelling, in which the fingers are used to form letters and words. Originally developed in France by Abbe Charles Michel De l'Epee in the late 1700s, the manual alphabet was later brought to the United States by Laurent Clerc (1785-1869), a Frenchman who taught people who were deaf.

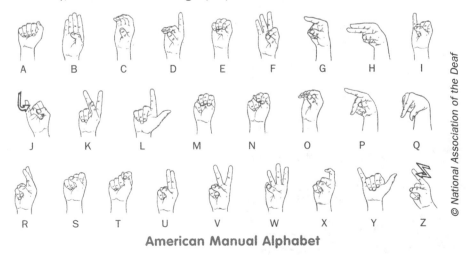

© National Association of the Deaf

**American Manual Alphabet**

# SEGASSEM TERCES GNIDIH

Can you guess what the title of this page says? If you look closely, you will see that it is "hiding secret messages" written backward. This is one simple way to create a secret code. Different kinds of codes have been used since ancient times to keep military plans secret. Secret codes are still used today by the military, by banks for ATM machines, and in many other places. The science of writing and reading secret messages is called **cryptography**.

## CIPHERS

One system of cryptography is called **ciphers**. In this system, letters are rearranged in different ways or may be switched for other letters. In the examples below, you can see four ways ciphers are used to hide the same sentence. Can you figure out what the message is?

➊ Changing the spaces: MEE TME ATT HEB IGO AKT REE.

➋ Writing the sentence backward: EERT KAO GIB EHT TA EM TEEM.

➌ Writing the sentence using the alphabet from Z to A instead of A to Z, so that A=Z, B=Y, C=X, D=W, and so on: NVVG NV ZG GSV YRT LZP GIVV.

➍ Writing the sentence using an alphabet with the letters rearranged, for example, MQPUWXRDBSVAECNTZFIHOUGKJL ( M=A, Q=B, P=C, U=D, and so on): EWWH EW MH HDW QBR NMV HFWW.

## NUMBERS FOR LETTERS

Numbers can also be used in place of some or all of the letters of the alphabet. If you know that 2=W, 3=T, 4=E, 5=H, 6=L, 7=N, 8=C, 9=I, 10=M, 11=O, 12=U, you can read the message below.

2 4 6 8 11 10 4   3 11   3 5 4   7 4 2   10 9 6 6 4 7 7 9 12 10.

*Answers are on pages 317–320.*

# SECRET MESSAGE PUZZLE

To decipher (figure out) this message, look at the telephone buttons. Notice that most buttons contain one number and three letters.
**Let A=2, B=2, and C=(2).** Do the same thing with the other buttons, so that **D=3, E=3, and F=(3)**, and so on. If you need Q and Z,
**let Q=\* and Z=#.** Now can you crack the code for this sentence?

4 3 (5) (5) (6)   FROM   8 4 3   9 (6) 7 (5) 3

2 (5) 6 2 6 2 (2)   (3) (6) R   5 (4) 3 (7)

| 1 | ABC 2 | DEF 3 |
|---|---|---|
| GHI 4 | JKL 5 | MNO 6 |
| PRS 7 | TUV 8 | WXY 9 |
| \* | OPER 0 | # |

*Answers are on pages 317–320.*

❓ **What college football player won the 1998 Heisman Trophy?**
*You can find the answer on page 231.*

# BASEBALL

The 1998 baseball season was the most exciting one in years. Mark McGwire of the St. Louis Cardinals set a new single-season home run record by blasting an incredible 70 homers. Sammy Sosa of the Chicago Cubs was close behind with 66, also breaking the old mark of 61 set by Roger Maris in 1961. The New York Yankees won 114 games, an American League record for a regular season, and swept the San Diego Padres in four straight games to win their second World Series in three years. Their total of 125 victories—regular and post-season —was yet another major league mark. And in September, the Baltimore Orioles' Cal Ripken, Jr., sat out a game, ending his playing streak at 2,632 games. The last game he missed was in May 1982. What a streak! What a year for baseball!

## FINAL 1998 STANDINGS

| AMERICAN LEAGUE | | | NATIONAL LEAGUE | | |
|---|---|---|---|---|---|
| **Eastern Division** | **Won** | **Lost** | **Eastern Division** | **Won** | **Lost** |
| New York Yankees | 114 | 48 | Atlanta Braves | 106 | 56 |
| Boston Red Sox* | 92 | 70 | New York Mets | 88 | 74 |
| Toronto Blue Jays | 88 | 74 | Philadelphia Phillies | 75 | 87 |
| Baltimore Orioles | 79 | 83 | Montreal Expos | 65 | 97 |
| Tampa Bay Devil Rays | 63 | 99 | Florida Marlins | 54 | 108 |
| **Central Division** | **Won** | **Lost** | **Central Division** | **Won** | **Lost** |
| Cleveland Indians | 89 | 73 | Houston Astros | 102 | 60 |
| Chicago White Sox | 80 | 82 | Chicago Cubs*[1] | 90 | 73 |
| Kansas City Royals | 72 | 89 | St. Louis Cardinals | 83 | 79 |
| Minnesota Twins | 70 | 92 | Cincinnati Reds | 77 | 85 |
| Detroit Tigers | 65 | 97 | Milwaukee Brewers | 74 | 88 |
| | | | Pittsburgh Pirates | 69 | 93 |
| **Western Division** | **Won** | **Lost** | **Western Division** | **Won** | **Lost** |
| Texas Rangers | 88 | 74 | San Diego Padres | 98 | 64 |
| Anaheim Angels | 85 | 77 | San Francisco Giants[1] | 89 | 74 |
| Seattle Mariners | 76 | 85 | Los Angeles Dodgers | 83 | 79 |
| Oakland Athletics | 74 | 88 | Colorado Rockies | 77 | 85 |
| | | | Arizona Diamondbacks | 65 | 97 |

(1) Chicago beat San Francisco (5-3) in a one game playoff to win the wild card spot.
* Wild card team.

## PLAYOFF RESULTS

**Division Series**
  New York defeated Texas, 3-0
  Cleveland defeated Boston, 3-1
**Championship Series**
  New York defeated Cleveland, 4-2

**Division Series**
  Atlanta defeated Chicago, 3-0
  San Diego defeated Houston, 3-1
**Championship Series**
  San Diego defeated Atlanta, 4-2

**1998 WORLD SERIES** - NEW YORK DEFEATED SAN DIEGO, 4 GAMES TO 0

## 1998 MAJOR LEAGUE LEADERS

**Most Valuable Players**
American League: Juan Gonzalez,
Texas Rangers
National League: Sammy Sosa, Chicago Cubs

**Cy Young Award Winners** (top pitcher)
American League: Roger Clemens, Toronto Blue
Jays (joined New York Yankees, 1999)
National League: Tom Glavine, Atlanta Braves

**Rookies of the Year**
American League: Ben Grieve, Oakland Athletics
National League: Kerry Wood, Chicago Cubs

**Batting Champs**
American League: Bernie Williams,
New York Yankees, .339
National League: Larry Walker,
Colorado Rockies, .363

**Home Run Leaders**
American League: Ken Griffey, Jr.,
Seattle Mariners, 56
National League: Mark McGwire,
St. Louis Cardinals, 70 (new record)

**Runs Batted In (RBI) Leaders**
American League: Juan Gonzalez,
Texas Rangers, 157
National League: Sammy Sosa, Chicago Cubs, 158

**Most Pitching Victories**
American League: Roger Clemens,
Toronto Blue Jays, 20
    David Cone, New York Yankees, 20
    Rick Helling, Texas Rangers, 20
National League: Tom Glavine, Atlanta Braves, 20

Roger Clemens ▲

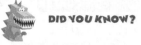

DID YOU KNOW?

*1998 was a year for hitters in more ways than one. In the American League, Juan Gonzalez of Texas drove in 157 runs. That was the most RBIs in the A.L. since Ted Williams and his Red Sox teammate Vern Stephens tied for the league lead with 159 in 1949. In the National League, Sammy Sosa drove home 158 runs. That was the most in the National League since another Cub, Hack Wilson, set the all-time record with 190, back in 1930. It's no surprise that both Gonzalez and Sosa were voted as Most Valuable Players in their leagues.*

*By stealing 66 bases in 1998, 39-year-old Rickey Henderson of the Oakland Athletics became the oldest player in major league history to win a stolen base crown. Henderson was baseball's all-time stolen base king, with 1,297 thefts at the end of the 1998 season.*

WEB SITE *http://www. majorleaguebaseball.com*

## BASEBALL HALL OF FAME

The National Baseball Hall of Fame and Museum opened in 1939, in Cooperstown, New York. To be nominated for membership, players must be retired from baseball for five years. **Address:** PO Box 590, Cooperstown, NY 13326.
**Phone:** (607) 547-7200; toll-free: (888) 425-5633

WEB SITE

*www.baseballhalloffame.org*

## LITTLE LEAGUE

Little League Baseball is the largest youth sports program in the world. It began in 1939 in Williamsport, Pennsylvania, with 30 boys playing on 3 teams. By 1998, 3 million boys and girls ages 5 to 18 were playing on 200,000 Little League teams in 90 countries. For more information go to

WEB SITE

*http:// www.littleleague.org*

# BASKETBALL

**B**asketball began in 1891 in Springfield, Massachusetts, when Dr. James Naismith invented it, using peach baskets as hoops. At first, each team had nine players instead of five. Big-time professional basketball was born in 1949, when the National Basketball Association (NBA) was formed. In the 1998-1999 season, there were 29 NBA teams.

## Professional Basketball

### FINAL 1998-1999 NBA STANDINGS

| EASTERN CONFERENCE | | | WESTERN CONFERENCE | | |
| --- | --- | --- | --- | --- | --- |
| **Atlantic Division** | **Won** | **Lost** | **Midwest Division** | **Won** | **Lost** |
| Miami Heat | 33 | 17 | San Antonio Spurs | 37 | 13 |
| Orlando Magic | 33 | 17 | Utah Jazz | 37 | 13 |
| Philadelphia 76ers | 28 | 22 | Houston Rockets | 31 | 19 |
| New York Knicks | 27 | 23 | Minnesota Timberwolves | 25 | 25 |
| Boston Celtics | 19 | 31 | Dallas Mavericks | 19 | 31 |
| Washington Wizards | 18 | 32 | Denver Nuggets | 14 | 36 |
| New Jersey Nets | 16 | 34 | Vancouver Grizzlies | 8 | 42 |
| **Central Division** | **Won** | **Lost** | **Pacific Division** | **Won** | **Lost** |
| Indiana Pacers | 33 | 17 | Portland Trail Blazers | 35 | 15 |
| Atlanta Hawks | 31 | 19 | Los Angeles Lakers | 31 | 19 |
| Detroit Pistons | 29 | 21 | Sacramento Kings | 27 | 23 |
| Milwaukee Bucks | 28 | 22 | Phoenix Suns | 27 | 23 |
| Charlotte Hornets | 26 | 24 | Seattle SuperSonics | 25 | 25 |
| Toronto Raptors | 23 | 27 | Golden State Warriors | 21 | 29 |
| Cleveland Cavaliers | 22 | 28 | Los Angeles Clippers | 9 | 41 |
| Chicago Bulls | 13 | 37 | | | |

**Note:** Because of a labor dispute that delayed the 1998-1999 NBA season, the season was shortened to 50 games.

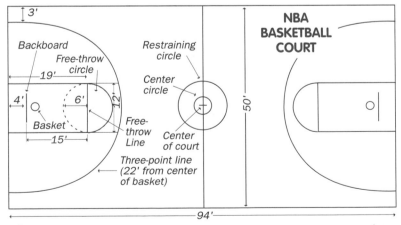

**WEB SITE** You can have fun and find out more facts about basketball at the Web site for the National Basketball Association: *http://www.nba.com*

## HIGHLIGHTS OF THE 1998-1999 BASKETBALL SEASON

**Scoring Leader:** Allen Iverson, Philadelphia 76ers
**Games:** 48          **Points:** 1,284          **Average:** 26.8

**Rebounding Leader:** Chris Webber, Sacramento Kings
**Games:** 42          **Rebounds:** 545          **Average:** 13.0

**Assists Leader:** Jason Kidd, Phoenix Suns
**Games:** 50          **Assists:** 539          **Average:** 10.8

**Steals Leader:** Kendall Gill, New Jersey Nets
**Games:** 50          **Steals:** 134          **Average:** 2.68

**Blocked Shots Leader:** Alonzo Mourning, Miami Heat
**Games:** 46          **Blocks:** 180          **Average:** 3.91

**DID YOU KNOW?**

In the 1998-1999 season, Toronto Raptor rookie Vince Carter led his team, as well as all NBA rookies, in scoring, with 18.3 points per game. Carter made an immediate impact in the NBA with his spectacular slam dunks. He also finished first among the rookies in blocked shots, field goals, and free throws.

▲ *Vince Carter*

## WOMEN'S BASKETBALL

The Women's National Basketball Association (WNBA) completed its second season in 1998. The Houston Comets won their second straight WNBA championship, defeating the Phoenix Mercury in the final game of a best of three series, 80-71. Cynthia Cooper, the Houston star, scored 23 points in the victory. She was named Most Valuable Player for the second straight year and won her second WNBA scoring championship in a row. Cooper also became the first-ever WNBA player to score 1,000 career points. In 1999, the WNBA will add two teams, in Minnesota and Florida, bringing the league total to 12.

The other women's pro league, the American Basketball League (ABL), had big money problems and closed in the middle of the third season.

## LAST OF A LEGEND

Sports fans everywhere were saddened when Michael Jordan announced his retirement from the NBA before the start of the 1998-1999 season. The game lost its greatest player and the greatest gate attraction in all of sports. Jordan, a five-time Most Valuable Player and record 10-time NBA scoring champion, led the Chicago Bulls to six NBA titles in eight years. Jordan missed all or part of two seasons when he left the game temporarily to pursue a baseball career. He retired as the NBA's third all-time leading scorer, had the highest regular season and playoff scoring averages ever, and will be remembered as the game's greatest clutch player. His final NBA basket was the winning shot in the Bulls' sixth NBA championship.

## BASKETBALL HALL OF FAME

The Naismith Memorial Basketball Hall of Fame was founded in 1959 to honor great basketball players, coaches, referees, and others important to the history of the game. **Address:** 1150 W. Columbus Ave., Springfield, MA 01105. **Phone:** (413) 781-6500.
**WEB SITE** *http://www.hoophall.com*

# College Basketball

College basketball has become a huge sport. The National Collegiate Athletic Association (NCAA) Tournament began in 1939. Today, it is a spectacular 64-team extravaganza. The Final Four weekend, when the semi-finals and finals are played, is one of the most watched sports events in the United States. The NCAA Tournament for women's basketball began in 1982. Since then, the popularity of the women's game has grown by leaps and bounds.

## THE 1998 NCAA TOURNAMENT RESULTS

**MEN'S FINAL FOUR RESULTS**

**Semi-Finals:**
    Connecticut 64, Ohio State 58
    Duke 68, Michigan State 62
**Championship Game:**
    Connecticut 77, Duke 74

**WOMEN'S FINAL FOUR RESULTS**

**Semi-Finals:**
    Duke 81, Georgia 69
    Purdue 77, Louisiana Tech 63
**Championship Game:**
    Purdue 62, Duke 45

 **DID YOU KNOW?** *Up to its 68-62 semi-final win against Michigan State, Duke had beaten its NCAA tournament opponents by an average of 30 points a game. During the regular season, the once-beaten Blue Devils won by an average of more than 25 points a game. On the brink of being considered one of the greatest college teams ever, they only had to win the national championship to firm up their place in history. But it didn't happen. The University of Connecticut Huskies, who lost just twice during the regular season, played 40 minutes of great basketball to upset Duke, 77-74, for their first title. Led by Richard Hamilton (the Final Four MVP), Kahlid El-Amin, and Ricky Moore, the Huskies just wouldn't let Duke take over and outplayed their rivals at crunch time to ensure the win.*

**DID YOU KNOW?** *The Lady Boilermakers of Purdue University won their first national championship ever by showing the grit of a number one team. In the championship game, they were trailing Duke University, 22-17, at the half. But after intermission, senior guards Stephanie White-McCarty and Ukari Figgs took over. White-McCarty ran the offense with poise while Figgs, held scoreless in the first half, exploded for 18 points to key the victory. Purdue, which began the season with an upset over three-time defending champion Tennessee, finished at 34-1, winning the last 32 games in a row. Said Figgs, named Outstanding Player of the Final Four, "I had 20 minutes to be a winner or a loser, and I wanted to go out a winner."*

**Elton Brand**

## NAISMITH AWARD WINNERS
## 1998-1999

**MEN**
**Player of the Year:** Elton Brand, Duke ▶
**Coach of the Year:** Mike Krzyzewski, Duke

**WOMEN**
**Player of the Year:** Chamique Holdsclaw, Tennessee
**Coach of the Year:** Carolyn Peck, Purdue

# FOOTBALL

American football began as a college sport. The first game that was like today's football took place between Yale and Harvard in New Haven, Connecticut, on November 13, 1875. The sport was largely shaped by Walter Camp in the 1880s. He reduced the number of players to 11 on each side and had each play begin from the line of scrimmage. He also introduced "downs" and was the first to have the field lined with chalk every 5 yards.

## Professional Football

The 1998 National Football League season was marked by outstanding individual performances, with a great team repeating as Super Bowl champs. In the regular season, Denver running back Terrell Davis became the fourth player in NFL history to rush for over 2,000 yards, and was named the league's Most Valuable Player. Rookie wide receiver Randy Moss of Minnesota proved almost unstoppable with 69 catches for 1,313 yards, and an NFL-best 17 touchdowns. Veteran quarterback John Elway led the Broncos to a second straight Super Bowl victory over the Atlanta Falcons.

It was a year of quarterback comebacks. Buffalo's Doug Flutie made his mark on the NFL after stardom in the Canadian Football League. Randall Cunningham, who had retired and then returned to football, quarterbacked the Minnesota Vikings to a 15-1 record and the NFC championship game. Vinny Testeverde, after years of disappointing seasons, joined the New York Jets and led them to an AFC Eastern Division title.

### FINAL NFL STANDINGS FOR THE 1998 SEASON

| National Football Conference | | | | American Football Conference | | | |
|---|---|---|---|---|---|---|---|
| **Eastern Division** | **Won** | **Lost** | **Tied** | **Eastern Division** | **Won** | **Lost** | **Tied** |
| Dallas Cowboys | 10 | 6 | 0 | New York Jets | 12 | 4 | 0 |
| Arizona Cardinals* | 9 | 7 | 0 | Miami Dolphins* | 10 | 6 | 0 |
| New York Giants | 8 | 8 | 0 | Buffalo Bills* | 10 | 6 | 0 |
| Washington Redskins | 6 | 10 | 0 | New England Patriots* | 9 | 7 | 0 |
| Philadelphia Eagles | 3 | 13 | 0 | Indianapolis Colts | 3 | 13 | 0 |
| **Central Division** | **Won** | **Lost** | **Tied** | **Central Division** | **Won** | **Lost** | **Tied** |
| Minnesota Vikings | 15 | 1 | 0 | Jacksonville Jaguars | 11 | 5 | 0 |
| Green Bay Packers* | 11 | 5 | 0 | Tennessee Oilers | 8 | 8 | 0 |
| Tampa Bay Buccaneers | 8 | 8 | 0 | Pittsburgh Steelers | 7 | 9 | 0 |
| Detroit Lions | 5 | 11 | 0 | Baltimore Ravens | 6 | 10 | 0 |
| Chicago Bears | 4 | 12 | 0 | Cincinnati Bengals | 3 | 13 | 0 |
| **Western Division** | **Won** | **Lost** | **Tied** | **Western Division** | **Won** | **Lost** | **Tied** |
| Atlanta Falcons | 14 | 2 | 0 | Denver Broncos | 14 | 2 | 0 |
| San Francisco 49ers* | 12 | 4 | 0 | Oakland Raiders | 8 | 8 | 0 |
| New Orleans Saints | 6 | 10 | 0 | Seattle Seahawks | 8 | 8 | 0 |
| Carolina Panthers | 4 | 12 | 0 | Kansas City Chiefs | 7 | 9 | 0 |
| St. Louis Rams | 4 | 12 | 0 | San Diego Chargers | 5 | 11 | 0 |
| *Wild card team | | | | *Wild card team | | | |

### 1998 CONFERENCE CHAMPIONSHIP GAMES
**National Football Conference:** Atlanta Falcons 30, Minnesota Vikings 27 (OT)
**American Football Conference:** Denver Broncos 23, New York Jets 10

### SUPER BOWL XXXIII, JANUARY 31, 1999, PRO PLAYER STADIUM, MIAMI, FLORIDA
Denver Broncos 34, Atlanta Falcons 19

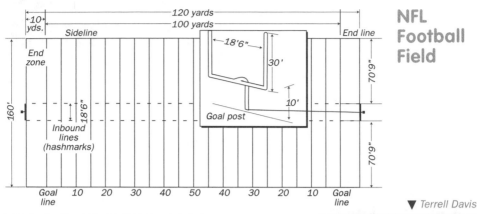

**NFL Football Field**

120 yards
100 yards
10 yds.
Sideline
End line
End zone
18'6"
30'
70'9"
160'
18'6"
10'
Goal post
70'9"
Inbound lines (hashmarks)
Goal line  10  20  30  40  50  40  30  20  10  Goal line

▼ *Terrell Davis*

# TOP NFL PLAYERS, 1998

**Rushing Leader:** Terrell Davis, Denver Broncos
  **Carries:** 392 **Yards:** 2,008 **Average:** 5.1
**Passing Leader:** Randall Cunningham,
    Minnesota Vikings
  **Passing Attempts:** 425 **Passing Completions:** 259
  **Passing Yards:** 3,704
  **Passing Completion Percentage:** 60.9
  **Touchdown Passes:** 34 **Passes Intercepted:** 10
  **Quarterback Rating:** 106.0
**Pass Receiving Leader:** O.J. McDuffie, Miami Dolphins
  **Catches:** 90 **Yards:** 1,050 **Average:** 11.7

**The following awards were all chosen by the Associated Press**
  **Most Valuable Player:** Terrell Davis, Denver Broncos
  **Offensive Player of the Year:** Terrell Davis,
    Denver Broncos
  **Defensive Player of the Year:** Reggie White,
    Green Bay Packers
  **Coach of the Year:** Dan Reeves, Atlanta Falcons
  **Offensive Rookie of the Year:** Randy Moss,
    Minnesota Vikings
  **Defensive Rookie of the Year:** Charles Woodson,
    Oakland Raiders
  **Comeback Player of the Year:** Doug Flutie,
    Buffalo Bills
  **Super Bowl Most Valuable Player:** John Elway,
    Denver Broncos

 **DID YOU KNOW?**

*A football is 11 to 11¼ inches long and weighs 14-15 ounces. It is oval in shape and somewhat pointed at the ends. It is made up of an inflated bladder covered with pebbled grain leather.*

**WEB SITE** You can reach the NFL at *http://www.nfl.com*

## PRO FOOTBALL HALL OF FAME

Football's Hall of Fame was founded in 1963 by the National Football League to honor outstanding players, coaches, and contributors. To be nominated, players must be retired for five years.
**Address:** Pro Football Hall of Fame, 2121 George Halas Drive, Canton, OH 44708. **Phone:** (330) 456-8207.
**WEB SITE** http://www.profootballhof.com

# COLLEGE FOOTBALL

College football is one of America's most colorful and exciting sports. The National Collegiate Athletic Association (NCAA), founded in 1906, oversees college football today.

On January 4, 1999, the Tennessee Volunteers became the national champions by defeating the Florida State Seminoles 23–16 in the Fiesta Bowl.

### THE BOWL GAMES

The Bowl Championship Series (BCS) now determines the national champion. The BCS consists of the Fiesta, Rose, Sugar, and Orange Bowls. After the 1998 regular season, the winner of the Fiesta Bowl became national champion. The Sugar Bowl will determine the national champion after the 1999 regular season, followed by the Orange Bowl after the 2000 season. After the 2001 regular season, the Rose Bowl, the oldest bowl game (first played in 1902), will decide the champion.

### SOME 1998 SEASON BOWL RESULTS

**Rose Bowl** (Pasadena, California): Wisconsin 38, UCLA 31

**Orange Bowl** (Miami, Florida): Florida 31, Syracuse 10

**Cotton Bowl** (Dallas, Texas): Texas 38, Mississippi State 11

**Sugar Bowl** (New Orleans, Louisiana): Ohio State 24, Texas A&M 14

**Fiesta Bowl** (Tempe, Arizona): Tennessee 23, Florida State 16

## 1998 TOP 10 COLLEGE TEAMS
### Chosen by the Associated Press Poll and the USA Today/ESPN Poll

| Rank | AP | USA Today/ESPN |
|------|-----|----------------|
| ① | Tennessee | Tennessee |
| ② | Ohio State | Ohio State |
| ③ | Florida State | Florida State |
| ④ | Arizona | Arizona |
| ⑤ | Florida | Wisconsin |
| ⑥ | Wisconsin | Florida |
| ⑦ | Tulane | Tulane |
| ⑧ | UCLA | UCLA |
| ⑨ | Georgia Tech | Kansas State |
| ⑩ | Kansas State | Air Force |

## HEISMAN TROPHY

The Heisman Trophy is given to the most outstanding college football player in the United States. It was first presented in 1935. The 1998 winner was senior running back Ricky Williams of the University of Texas. He tied or set 16 NCAA records, including a new all-time career rushing record of 6,279 yards, breaking the old mark held by Tony Dorsett. As a senior, the 6-foot, 225-pound Williams ran for 2,124 yards and scored 27 touchdowns. Besides winning the Heisman, Williams was a consensus All-America selection and won nearly every other individual college football award.

*Ricky Williams* ▼

### COLLEGE FOOTBALL HALL OF FAME

The College Football Hall of Fame was established in 1955 by the National Football Foundation. To be nominated, a player must be out of college 10 years and must have been a first team All-American pick by a major selector. Coaches must be retired 3 years. **Address:** 111 South St. Joseph Street, PO Box 11146, South Bend, IN 46601. **Phone:** (219) 235-9999.

**WEB SITE** *http://collegefootball.org*

231

# GAMES: CHESS and Other BOARD GAMES

**C**hess is a game of skill for two players. The aim is to checkmate, or trap, the opponent's king. Chess was probably invented around the 6th or 7th century A.D. in India. From there it moved into Persia (now Iran); the word chess comes from the Persian word shah, which means king. Today, there are national chess contests for children, and many schools have chess clubs. For further information, contact the U.S. Chess Federation, 3054 NYS Route 9W, New Windsor, NY 12553. Phone: 914-562-8350.

**WEB SITE** ▶ *http://www.uschess.org*

## THE BOARD AND THE CHESSMEN

Chess is played on a chessboard divided into 64 squares, alternately light and dark in color, arranged in 8 rows of 8. No matter what colors the squares and chessmen really are, they are always called white and black. White always moves first, then white and black take turns, moving only one chessman at a time. Each player begins the game with 16 chessmen: 8 pieces (the king, the queen, 2 bishops, 2 knights, and 2 rooks) and 8 pawns. When a chessman lands on a space occupied by an opponent's piece or pawn, that piece or pawn is captured and removed from the board.

## THE MOVES

Each piece or pawn has particular moves it can make, as are described below. The number (or point value) after each chessman gives an idea of how powerful it is.

*queen*

*rook*

*knight*

*bishop*

*pawn*

*king*

**queen** (9): moves any number of squares in any direction—forward or backward, side to side, or diagonally

**rook** (5): moves any number of squares forward or backward, or side to side

**knight** (3): moves two squares forward or backward and one square to either side, or one forward or backward and two to the side(the knight is the only chessman that can jump over others)

**bishop** (3): moves any number of squares diagonally forward or diagonally backward

**pawn** (1): first moves one or two squares; otherwise, moves one square straight ahead, except when it moves diagonally forward to capture another chessman

**king:** moves one square in any direction; is not given a point value

When a player moves a chessman into position to capture the opponent's king, he or she says "check" and the opponent must block the move or must move the king to safety; otherwise, the king is "checkmated" and the game is over.

**DID YOU KNOW?**

▶ In 1851, Adolf Anderssen of Germany became the first world chess champion.

▶ In 1958, 14-year-old Bobby Fischer became the youngest-ever grandmaster, one of the world's top players. He was world champion from 1972 to 1975.

# Some Other Board Games

**W**e play board games to have fun, but they also sharpen our mental skills. Games can teach us how to win without gloating and how to lose without being too disappointed. Some games are based on skill. Others depend only on the throw of dice. For most, winning takes a mixture of skill and luck.

Games like chess, checkers, Monopoly, and Scrabble are played all over the world by both kids and adults. Many board games can also be played on the computer. And remember, even in games of skill you can get lucky if your opponent makes a bad move!

**Backgammon**, a game for two players, was played in ancient Egypt, Greece, and Rome. Each player has 15 pieces to move around the board, and the skill is in deciding which pieces to move. Getting the right numbers when you throw the dice can also help make you a winner. To win the game, you must be the first to get all your pieces off the board.

**Checkers** is a game of skill. A form of checkers was played in ancient Egypt and Greece. The game is played by two players on a board with alternating light and dark squares. The goal is to capture all the opponent's pieces by jumping. To do so, you have to think ahead and take advantage of your opponent's mistakes.

**Parcheesi,** a game for two, three, or four players, is based on pachisi, a game played thousands of years ago in India. It is a mixture of skill and luck. Each player has four counters, and the one who gets them all into the center of the board first wins.

**Monopoly**, a game for two or more players, is one of the best-selling games of the 20th century. It involves both skill and luck. The skill is in making choices. Should you buy Water Works? How many houses should you put on Boardwalk? The luck is in throwing the dice and landing on the right places.

Monopoly was created in the 1930s by Charles P. Darrow, who took the names for places in the game from streets in Atlantic City, New Jersey.

**Scrabble** is a crossword game for two, three, or four players, played on a board with tiles that are letters. It had its beginnings in the 1930s with a game called Criss-Cross Words, which was invented by Alfred Butts.

To win at Scrabble, it helps to be a good speller and have a big vocabulary. The lucky part is picking up the letters you need at the right time. Scrabble is also available in Braille for blind players.

▶ *Current world champions are Garry Kasparov and Anatoly Karpov, both of Russia.*

▶ *In 1999, Maurice Ashley was the first African-American player to become a chess grandmaster.*

▶ *Irina Krush, U.S. women's champion, won a bronze medal in the women's division of the 1998 World Junior Championship. She was 14 at the time.*

Se Ri Pak ▲

# GOLF

Golf began in Scotland as early as the 1400s. The first golf course in the United States opened in 1888. Since then, the sport has grown to include both men's and women's professional tours. And millions play golf just for fun.

The men's tour is guided by the Professional Golf Association (PGA). The four major championships, with the year they were first played, are:

DID YOU KNOW?

▶ In 1998, Korean-born golfer Se Ri Pak turned 21, and made the same kind of impact on women's golf that Tiger Woods had on the men's game the year before. New to the LPGA tour, Pak won the first major tournament she entered, the McDonald's LPGA. She added three more wins before the year ended. She was just the third golfer to win the LPGA Championship and U.S. Women's Open the same year, and was the youngest to win four tournaments in a year.

▶ José María Olazábal won the 1999 Masters Tournament. He also won in 1994. In between, he had health problems that made it very hard for him to walk. "I thought I would never play golf again," he said. Was he ever wrong!

WEB SITE▶ For more information: http://www.pga.com

| British Open (1860) |
| United States Open (1895) |
| PGA Championship (1916) |
| Masters Tournament (1934) |

The women's tour is guided by the Ladies Professional Golf Association (LPGA). The major championships are:

| United States Open (1946) |
| McDonalds LPGA Championship (1955) |
| Nabisco Dinah Shore Championship (1972) |
| Du Maurier Classic (1973) |

# GYMNASTICS

It takes strength, coordination, and grace to become a top gymnast. Although the sport goes back to ancient Greece, modern-day gymnastics began in Sweden in the early 1800s. The sport has been part of the Olympics since 1896. There is also an annual World Gymnastics Championship meet.

## GYMNASTIC EVENTS

| FOR WOMEN | FOR MEN |
|---|---|
| ① All-Around | ① All-Around |
| ② Side Horse Vault | ② Horizontal Bar |
| ③ Asymmetrical (Uneven) Bars | ③ Parallel Bars |
| ④ Balance Beam | ④ Rings |
| ⑤ Floor Exercises | ⑤ Long Horse Vault |
| ⑥ Team Combined Exercises | ⑥ Side Horse (Pommel Horse) |
| ⑦ Rhythmic All-Around | ⑦ Floor Exercises |
| | ⑧ Team Combined Exercises |

# ICE HOCKEY

Ice hockey began in Canada in the mid-1800s. The National Hockey League (NHL) was formed in 1916. In the 1998–1999 season, the NHL had 27 teams, 21 in the United States and 6 in Canada.

WEB SITE For more information: *http://www.nhl.com*

## Final 1998–1999 Standings

### EASTERN CONFERENCE

| Northeast Division | W | L | T | Pts |
|---|---|---|---|---|
| Ottawa Senators | 44 | 23 | 15 | 103 |
| Toronto Maple Leafs | 45 | 30 | 7 | 97 |
| Boston Bruins | 39 | 30 | 13 | 91 |
| Buffalo Sabres | 37 | 28 | 17 | 91 |
| Montreal Canadiens | 32 | 39 | 11 | 75 |

| Atlantic Division | W | L | T | Pts |
|---|---|---|---|---|
| New Jersey Devils | 47 | 24 | 11 | 105 |
| Philadelphia Flyers | 37 | 26 | 19 | 93 |
| Pittsburgh Penguins | 38 | 30 | 14 | 90 |
| New York Rangers | 33 | 38 | 11 | 77 |
| New York Islanders | 24 | 48 | 10 | 58 |

| Southeast Division | W | L | T | Pts |
|---|---|---|---|---|
| Carolina Hurricanes | 34 | 30 | 18 | 86 |
| Florida Panthers | 30 | 34 | 18 | 78 |
| Washington Capitols | 31 | 45 | 6 | 68 |
| Tampa Bay Lightning | 19 | 54 | 9 | 47 |

### WESTERN CONFERENCE

| Central Division | W | L | T | Pts |
|---|---|---|---|---|
| Detroit Red Wings | 43 | 32 | 7 | 93 |
| St. Louis Blues | 37 | 32 | 13 | 87 |
| Chicago Blackhawks | 29 | 41 | 12 | 70 |
| Nashville Predators | 28 | 47 | 7 | 63 |

| Northwest Division | W | L | T | Pts |
|---|---|---|---|---|
| Colorado Avalanche | 44 | 28 | 10 | 98 |
| Edmonton Oilers | 33 | 37 | 12 | 78 |
| Calgary Flames | 30 | 40 | 12 | 72 |
| Vancouver Canucks | 23 | 47 | 12 | 58 |

| Pacific Division | W | L | T | Pts |
|---|---|---|---|---|
| Dallas Stars | 51 | 19 | 12 | 114 |
| Phoenix Coyotes | 39 | 31 | 12 | 90 |
| Anaheim Mighty Ducks | 35 | 34 | 13 | 83 |
| San Jose Sharks | 31 | 33 | 18 | 80 |
| Los Angeles Kings | 32 | 45 | 5 | 69 |

**The league's leading scorer was Jaromir Jagr of Pittsburgh, with 127 points.**

**DID YOU KNOW?**

*When Wayne Gretzky announced his retirement from hockey at the end of the 1998–1999 season, he was cheered as the greatest ever to play the game. In 20 NHL seasons, he scored 894 goals and had 1,963 assists for 2,857 points, all records. He holds or shares 61 NHL scoring records—including the single season mark for goals (92), assists (163), and points (215). The Great One, as he is known, played with grace and dignity in a game sometimes known for its rough and unsportsmanlike play. Early in his career, he led the Edmonton Oilers to four Stanley Cup championships. He later played with the Los Angeles Kings and the St. Louis Blues. He finished his spectacular career with the New York Rangers. Holder of nine MVP awards, he is a shoo-in for the Hockey Hall of Fame.*

Wayne Gretzky
▼

### HOCKEY HALL OF FAME

The Hockey Hall of Fame was opened in 1961 to honor hockey greats.
**Address:** BCE Place, 30 Yonge Street, Toronto, Ontario, Canada M5E 1X8.
**Phone:** (416) 360-7735
WEB SITE http://www.hhof.com

# The OLYMPIC GAMES

The first Olympic Games were played in Greece more than 2,500 years ago. They began in 776 B.C. and featured just one event—a footrace. The ancient Greeks later added boxing, wrestling, chariot racing, and the pentathlon (which consists of five different events). The ancient Olympic Games were held every four years for more than 1,000 years, until A.D. 393, when a Roman Emperor stopped them. The modern Olympic Games were organized by a French educator named Baron Pierre de Coubertin. In 1894, he helped set up the International Olympic Committee, which organized the Games.

## SOME OLYMPIC FIRSTS

1896 — **The first modern Olympic Games were held in Athens, Greece.** Thirteen countries and 311 athletes took part.

1900 — **Women competed in the Olympic Games for the first time.**

1908 — **For the first time, medals were awarded to the first three people to finish each event**—a gold medal for first place, a silver medal for second, and a bronze medal for third.

1920 — **The Olympic flag was raised for the first time, and the Olympic oath was introduced.** The five interlaced rings of the flag represent: Africa, America, Europe, Asia, and Australia.

1924 — **The Winter Olympics, featuring skiing and skating events, were held for the first time.**

1928 — **The Olympic flame was introduced at the Olympic Games.** The flame is carried by runners in a relay, from Olympia in Greece to the site of where the Games are played.

1994 — **Starting with the 1994 Winter Olympics, the winter and summer Games have been held two years apart,** instead of in the same year.

## SYDNEY AT THE TURN OF THE CENTURY

Sydney, Australia, will be the host city for the games of the 27th Olympiad from September 15 to October 1, 2000. That time of year is early spring in Australia. Temperatures in the daytime range from 60 to 68 degrees Fahrenheit, and the weather is usually good. Two new medal sports will be added—Taekwondo and the Triathlon. The sport of taekwondo will have four men's and four women's weight classes. Both men and women will also compete in the grueling triathlon. Other new events include trampoline, added to the gymnastics program, and women's water polo. Women will also be competing in the modern pentathlon for the first time. In total, there will be 296 events—166 for men, 118 for women, and 12 mixed. The Sydney Olympics will feature three official mascots. They are Olly, the kockaburra bird; Syd, the duck-billed platypus; and Millie, the spiny anteater.

### SITES OF UPCOMING OLYMPIC GAMES

**WINTER GAMES:**
2002—Salt Lake City, Utah

**SUMMER GAMES:**
2000—Sydney, Australia
2004—Athens, Greece

# Olympic Sports

## 2000 SUMMER OLYMPIC SPORTS

| | | |
|---|---|---|
| Archery | Football (Soccer) | Table Tennis |
| Badminton | Gymnastics | Taekwondo |
| Baseball | Judo | Team Handball |
| Basketball | Modern Pentathlon (show jumping, running, fencing, pistol shooting, swimming—one event per day for 5 days) | Tennis |
| Boxing | Rowing | Track and Field |
| Canoe/Kayak | Sailing | Triathlon |
| Cycling | Shooting | Volleyball |
| Diving | Softball | Water Polo |
| Equestrian (dressage, jumping, 3-day event) | Swimming | Weight Lifting |
| Fencing | Synchronized Swimming | Wrestling |
| Field Hockey | | |

## 2002 WINTER OLYMPIC SPORTS

| | | |
|---|---|---|
| Biathlon (cross-country skiing, rifle marksmanship) | Luge (Toboggan) | Freestyle Skating |
| Bobsled | Figure Skating | Nordic Skiing Cross-Country Ski Jumping Nordic Combined |
| Curling | Speed Skating | |
| Ice Hockey | Alpine Skiing | Snowboarding |

Carl Lewis ▲

**DID YOU KNOW?**

*The 2000 Olympic Games at Sydney will be missing a legend. Carl Lewis of the United States retired from competition in 1997 after winning nine gold medals (and one silver) in four different Olympics. Lewis won gold in the 100-meter dash (twice), the 200-meter dash (once), and the 4x100 meters relay (twice), as well as a record-tying four gold medals in four straight Olympics in the long jump. He is an all-time great in his sport.*

# SKATING

**P**eople have enjoyed ice skating for centuries. The first ice skates were made from animal bones ground to a smooth, flat surface. Wooden skates with iron blades appeared in the Netherlands around the 1200s or 1300s. Steel skating blades appeared around 1860. They let skaters move quickly and with more control.

## FIGURE SKATING

The two types of competitive ice skating are figure skating and speed skating. Figure skating, which is almost like ballet, is judged by the way the skaters perform certain turns and jumps and by the creative difficulty of their programs. There are singles competitions for both men and women, pairs skating, and ice dancing.

### 1999 World Championships

|  | WOMEN'S SINGLES | MEN'S SINGLES |
|---|---|---|
| **Gold Medal:** | Maria Butyrskaya, Russia | Alexei Yagudin, Russia |
| **Silver Medal:** | Michelle Kwan, United States | Evgeny Plushenko, Russia |
| **Bronze Medal:** | Julia Soldatova, Russia | Michael Weiss, United States |

 **DID YOU KNOW?**

*Michelle Kwan won the World Championships for the first time in 1996, when she was just 15. Since then, she has continued to captivate fans. At the 1998 U.S. Championships, Michelle got 15 perfect scores out of a total of 36 marks to take the title. At the 1998 Winter Olympics, Michelle had to settle for the silver medal when Tara Lipinski edged past her in the final freeskating program. But she won the U.S. Championships in 1999. Despite a bad head cold, she finished second at the 1999 World Championships.*

*Michelle Kwan* ▶

## America's Olympic Champions

(for skating in singles competition)

**Men:** Dick Button (1948, 1952), Hayes Alan Jenkins (1956), David Jenkins (1960), Scott Hamilton (1984), Brian Boitano (1988).

**Women:** Tenley Albright (1956), Carol Heiss (1960), Peggy Fleming (1968), Dorothy Hamill (1976), Kristi Yamaguchi (1992), Tara Lipinski (1998).

## SPEED SKATING

Speed skating is a race around an oval track. The skaters go two at a time, racing the clock. The winner is the skater with the fastest time of all. Speed skating for men became part of the Winter Olympics in 1924, for women in 1960. Men compete in five events: the 500, 1,000, 1,500, 5,000, and 10,000 meters. Women compete in five events: the 500, 1,000, 1,500, 3,000, and 5,000 meters.

# SOCCER

Soccer, which is called football in many countries, is the number one sport worldwide. It is estimated that soccer is played by more than 100 million people in over 150 countries. The first rules for the game were published in 1863 by the London Football Association. Since then, the sport has spread rapidly from Europe to almost every part of the world.

More than 18 million children (6 years old and up) and adults play soccer in the United States, according to the 1998 Soccer Industry Council of America survey. More than 13 million are under the age of 18—the sport is growing very fast among young people. Among children between the age of 6 and 11, soccer is now the second most popular sport, after basketball.

## MAJOR LEAGUE SOCCER

Major League Soccer finished its third successful season in 1998. The Chicago Fire, in its first year, won the league championship in a 2-0 upset of the defending two-time champion, Washington D.C. United. The title game was watched by more than 51,000 fans at the Rose Bowl in Pasadena, California. Marco Etcheverry of D.C. United was the league's Most Valuable Player, while John Stern of the Columbus Crew was the leading scorer with 57 points. Zach Thornton of the Chicago Fire was MLS's goalkeeper. Major League Soccer was also seen on network TV for the first time, and the league expanded to 12 teams. The 1999 season began on March 20 and ends with the championship game on November 21, 1999.

*Zach Thornton* ▲

## THE WORLD CUP

The biggest soccer tournament in the world, the World Cup, was held in France in 1998. Thirty-two qualifying teams competed. To the delight of millions of French, the team from the host country won! Playing at Le Stade de France in St. Denis, before 80,000 fans, France defeated four-time champion Brazil, 3-0, in the final game. The French gave up just two goals in seven matches, the lowest number ever for a winner. France also became the seventh national team to win the World Cup. The others have been Brazil (4 times), Germany and Italy (3 each), Uruguay and Argentina (2 each), and England. The next World Cup will be held in 2002, hosted by Japan and South Korea.

 **DID YOU KNOW?**

▶ Major League Soccer set the all-time attendance record for a U.S. professional soccer game at the Rose Bowl in Pasadena, California, on June 16, 1996. That day, 92,216 fans watched the Los Angeles Galaxy win a 3–2 shootout victory over the Tampa Bay Mutiny.

▶ His real name is Edson Arantes do Nascimento, but the soccer world knows him as Pele. A native of Brazil, Pele retired as a player in 1977. He is still considered by many the greatest soccer player who ever lived. He was the only player to play on three World Cup champion teams, in 1958, 1962, and 1970.

# SPECIAL OLYMPICS

The Special Olympics is the world's largest program of sports training and athletic competition for children and adults with mental retardation. Founded in 1968, Special Olympics International has offices in all 50 U.S. states and Washington, D.C., and in many countries throughout the world. The organization offers year-round training and competition to nearly 1.5 million athletes in 150 countries.

The first Special Olympics competition was held in Chicago in 1968. After holding national events in individual countries, Special Olympics International holds World Games. The World Games alternate between summer and winter sports every two years. The 1999 World Summer Games were held in North Carolina in June and July. More than 7,000 athletes competed in 19 sports.

## SPECIAL OLYMPICS OFFICIAL SPORTS

**Winter:** alpine and cross-country skiing, figure and speed skating, floor hockey

**Summer:** aquatics, athletics (track and field), basketball, bowling, cycling, equestrian, golf, gymnastics, powerlifting, roller skating, soccer, softball, tennis, volleyball

**Demonstration sports:** badminton, bocce, sailing

For more information on the Special Olympics, contact Special Olympics International Headquarters, 1325 G Street, Washington, D.C. 20005. Phone: (202) 628-3630.

**WEB SITE** *http://www.specialolympics.org*

*Amy Van Dyken* ▼

# SWIMMING

Competitive swimming as an organized sport began in the second half of the 19th century. When the modern Olympic Games began in Athens, Greece, in 1896, the only racing stroke was the breaststroke. Today, men and women at the Olympics swim the backstroke, breaststroke, butterfly, and freestyle, in events ranging from 50 meters to 1,500 meters.

**OLYMPIC GOLD FOR THE U.S.** At the 1996 Olympic Games in Atlanta, U.S. men and women swimmers won 13 gold medals. The biggest story was unheralded Amy Van Dyken, who became the first American woman in history to win four gold medals in a single Olympics. Van Dyken was first in the 50-meter freestyle and 100-meter butterfly, and took two more gold medals as part of two American relay teams.

## SOME GREAT U.S. OLYMPIC SWIMMERS

▶ **Johnny Weissmuller** won three gold medals at the 1924 and 1928 Games. He later became even more famous playing Tarzan in movies.

▶ **Mark Spitz** won two gold medals in relays at the 1968 Games. He returned in 1972 to make Olympic swimming history by winning seven gold medals.

▶ **Matt Biondi** won seven medals at the 1988 Olympics, including five golds.

▶ **Janet Evans**, at age 17, won three gold medals at the 1988 Olympics in Seoul, South Korea. In 1992, she won another gold and a silver in Barcelona, Spain.

# TENNIS

The modern game of tennis began in 1873 when a Britsh officer, Major Walter Wingfield, developed it from the earlier game of court tennis. In 1877, the first championships were held at the old Wimbledon Grounds near London, England. In 1881 the first United States men's championships were held at Newport, Rhode Island. Six year later the first women's championships took place, in Philadelphia, Pennsylvania.

## GRAND SLAM TOURNAMENTS

Today, professional tennis players from all over the world compete in dozens of tournaments. The four most important, called the grand slam tournaments, are the Australian Open, the French Open, the All-England (Wimbledon) Championships, and the United States Open. There are separate competitions for men and women in singles and doubles. There are also mixed doubles, where men and women team together.

## MEN'S and WOMEN'S Singles Champions

### 1999 Australian Open Finals
Men: Evgeny Kafelnikov (Russia) defeated Thomas Enqvist (Sweden), 4-6, 6-0, 6-3, 7-6.
Women: Martina Hingis (Switzerland) defeated Amelie Mauresmo (France), 6-2, 6-3.

### 1998 United States Open Finals
Men: Patrick Rafter (Australia) defeated Mark Philippoussis (Australia), 6-3, 3-6, 6-2, 6-0.
Women: Lindsay Davenport (U.S.) defeated Martina Hingis (Switzerland), 6-3, 7-5.

### 1998 Wimbledon Finals
Men: Pete Sampras (U.S.) defeated Goran Ivanisevic (Croatia), 6-7, 7-6, 6-4, 3-6, 6-2.
Women: Jana Novotna (Czech Republic) defeated Nathalie Tauziat (France), 6-4, 7-6.

### 1998 French Open Finals
Men: Carlos Moya (Spain) defeated Alex Corretja (Spain) 6-3, 7-5, 6-3.
Women: Arantxa Sanchez-Vicario (Spain) defeated Monica Seles (U.S.), 7-6, 0-6, 6-2.

**RANKINGS for 1998** The Association of Tennis Professionals (ATP) and the Women's Tennis Association (WTA) now keep computer rankings of all the players on the tour. The top five men and women at the end of 1998 were:

### Men
1. **Pete Sampras**, United States
2. **Marcelo Rios**, Chile
3. **Alex Corretja**, Spain
4. **Patrick Rafter**, Australia
5. **Carlos Moya**, Spain

### Women
1. **Lindsay Davenport**, United States
2. **Martina Hingis**, Switzerland
3. **Jana Novotna**, Czech Republic
4. **Arantxa Sanchez-Vicario**, Spain
5. **Venus Williams**, United States

*Pete Sampras* ▼

**DID YOU KNOW?**

When Pete Sampras ended the 1998 season as the player ranked number one on the men's tour, it marked a record sixth straight year he finished on top. His 1998 Wimbledon title was his eleventh grand slam title since he won the U.S. Open as a 19-year-old in 1990. Having won Wimbledon five times, the United States Open four times, and the Australian Open twice by the age of 27, Sampras was already considered one of the greatest players of all time.

# UNITED NATIONS

❓ What is unusual about the land on which the United Nations stands? You can find the answer on page 243.

# A COMMUNITY of NATIONS

The United Nations (UN) was established in 1945 after World War II to promote world peace and cooperation. The UN conducts its business in six official languages: Arabic, Chinese, English, French, Russian, and Spanish. The first members of the UN were the 50 nations that met and signed its charter. The charter was approved on October 24, 1945. By 1999, 185 countries—all nations except Kiribati, Nauru, Switzerland, Taiwan, Tonga, Tuvalu, and Vatican City—were UN members.

**The UN has set these goals. Not all of them have been reached.**

| | |
|---|---|
| To keep worldwide peace and security. | To promote respect for human rights and basic freedoms. |
| To develop friendly relations among countries. | |
| To help countries cooperate in solving economic, social, cultural, and humanitarian problems. | To be a center that helps countries to achieve these goals. |

**DID YOU KNOW?**

*The headquarters for the UN is located in New York City, but the land and the buildings are not part of the United States. The United Nations is an international zone, with its own flag, post office, stamps, and security.*

To get more information about the United Nations, you can write to the Public Inquiries Unit, Room GA-57, United Nations, NY 10017, or call the UN at (212) 963-4475. Information can be found on-line at:

**WEB SITE** ➤ http://www.pbs.org/tal/un

## UN SECRETARIES-GENERAL AND THEIR TERMS IN OFFICE

The Secretary-General is the chief officer of the United Nations and is appointed by the General Assembly for a five-year term. Seven people have had this job:

| | |
|---|---|
| 1997– Kofi Annan, Ghana | 1961–1971 U Thant, Burma (Myanmar) |
| 1992–1996 Boutros Boutros-Ghali, Egypt | 1953–1961 Dag Hammarskjold, Sweden |
| 1982–1991 Javier Perez de Cuellar, Peru | |
| 1972–1981 Kurt Waldheim, Austria | 1945–1952 Trygve Lie, Norway |

# How the UN Is ORGANIZED

The work of the United Nations is carried out almost all over the world. It is done through six main organs, each with a different purpose. The Secretary-General is the chief officer of the UN.

## General Assembly

The General Assembly can discuss any problem important to the world. The Assembly admits new members to the UN, appoints the Secretary-General, and decides the UN's budget. It meets once a year for three months, but emergency meetings can be called at any time.

**Who Are Its Members?** All members of the UN are represented in the General Assembly.

**How Do Members Vote?** When the General Assembly votes, each country—whether large or small, rich or poor—has one vote. Two thirds of the members must agree for a resolution to be decided.

## International Court of Justice

The International Court of Justice, or World Court, is the highest court of law for legal disputes between countries. When countries have a dispute, they can take their case before the International Court of Justice, which is located at The Hague, Netherlands. Countries that come before the Court must promise to obey the decision of the judges.

**Who Are Its Members?** There are 15 judges on the Court, each from a different country, elected by the General Assembly and the Security Council.

## Secretariat

The Secretariat is the UN staff that carries out the day-to-day operations of the United Nations. Its head is the Secretary-General, currently Kofi Annan. Members of the Secretariat collect background information for the delegates to study and help carry out UN decisions.

## Security Council

The Security Council discusses questions of peace and security.

**Who Are Its Members?** The Security Council is made up of 5 permanent members (China, France, Great Britain, Russia, and the United States) and 10 members that are elected by the General Assembly for two-year terms.

**How Do Members Vote?** To pass a resolution, at least 9 of the 15 members, including all the permanent members, must vote "yes." If any permanent member vetoes (votes "no" on) the resolution, it is not passed.

## Economic and Social Council

The Economic and Social Council deals with world problems such as trade, economic development, industry, population, children, food, education, health, and human rights. The Council works closely with many commissions and special agencies, such as FAO (Food and Agriculture Organization), UNICEF (United Nations International Children's Fund), and WHO (World Health Organization).

**Who Are Its Members?** It has 54 member countries elected by the General Assembly for three-year terms.

## Trusteeship Council

The Trusteeship Council was formed to watch over the people living in territories that were placed under UN trust until they could become independent.

**Who Are Its Members?** Its members are the permanent members of the Security Council.

# UNITED STATES

❓ Which state was the first to agree to the Constitution?
*You can find the answer on page 275.*

## United States: FACTS & FIGURES

| AREA: | Land | Water | Total |
|---|---|---|---|
| | 3,536,278 square miles | 251,041 square miles | 3,787,319 square miles |

**POPULATION** (1998): 270,311,758    **CAPITAL:** Washington, D.C.

### LARGEST, HIGHEST, AND OTHER STATISTICS

| | |
|---|---|
| Largest state: | Alaska (615,230 square miles) |
| Smallest state: | Rhode Island (1,231 square miles) |
| Northernmost city: | Barrow, Alaska (71°17' north latitude) |
| Southernmost city: | Hilo, Hawaii (19°44' north latitude) |
| Easternmost city: | Eastport, Maine (66°59'05" west longitude) |
| Westernmost city: | Atka, Alaska (174°12' west longitude) |
| Highest town: | Climax, Colorado (11,360 feet) |
| Lowest town: | Calipatria, California (184 feet below sea level) |
| Oldest national park: | Yellowstone National Park (Idaho, Montana, Wyoming), 2,219,791 acres, established 1872 |
| Largest national park: | Wrangell-St. Elias, Alaska (8,323,618 acres) |
| Longest river system: | Mississippi-Missouri-Red Rock (3,710 miles) |
| Deepest lake: | Crater Lake, Oregon (1,932 feet) |
| Highest mountain: | Mount McKinley, Alaska (20,320 feet) |
| Lowest point: | Death Valley, California (282 feet below sea level) |
| Rainiest spot: | Mount Waialeale, Hawaii (average annual rainfall, 460 inches) |
| Tallest building: | Sears Tower, Chicago, Illinois (1,450 feet) |
| Tallest structure: | TV tower, Blanchard, North Dakota (2,063 feet) |
| Longest bridge span: | Verrazano-Narrows Bridge, New York (4,260 feet) |
| Highest bridge: | Royal Gorge, Colorado (1,053 feet above water) |

### INTERNATIONAL BOUNDARY LINES OF THE U.S.

U.S.-Canadian border ....................................3,987 miles (excluding Alaska)
Alaska-Canadian border ...............................1,538 miles
U.S.-Mexican border (Rio Grande)..................1,933 miles
Atlantic coast................................................2,069 miles
Gulf of Mexico coast .....................................1,631 miles
Pacific coast.................................................7,623 miles
Arctic coast, Alaska......................................1,060 miles

**TERRITORIAL SEA OF THE U.S.** The territorial sea of the United States is the surrounding waters that the country claims as its own. A proclamation made by President Ronald Reagan on December 27, 1988, said that the territorial sea of the United States extends 12 nautical miles from the shores of the country.

# SYMBOLS of the United States

## THE MOTTO

The U.S. motto, "In God We Trust," was originally put on coins during the Civil War (1861-1865). It disappeared and reappeared on various coins until 1955, when Congress ordered it placed on all paper money and coins.

## THE GREAT SEAL OF THE UNITED STATES

The Great Seal of the United States shows an American bald eagle with a ribbon in its mouth bearing the Latin words "e pluribus unum" (one out of many). In its talons are the arrows of war and an olive branch of peace. On the back of the Great Seal is an unfinished pyramid with an eye (the eye of Providence) above it. The seal was approved by Congress on June 20, 1782.

## THE FLAG

1777

The flag of the United States has 50 stars (one for each state) and 13 stripes (one for each of the original 13 states). It is called unofficially the "Stars and Stripes." The first U.S. flag was commissioned by the Second Continental Congress in 1777 but did not exist until 1783, after the American Revolution. Historians are not certain who designed the Stars and Stripes. Many different flags are believed to have been used during the American Revolution.

1795

The flag of 1777 was used until 1795. In that year President George Washington ordered that a new flag have 15 stripes, alternate red and white, and 15 stars on a blue field. In 1818, Congress directed that the flag have 13 stripes and that a new star be added for each new state of the Union. The last star was added in 1960 for the state of Hawaii.

1818

## PLEDGE OF ALLEGIANCE TO THE FLAG

"I pledge allegiance to the flag of the United States of America and to the republic for which it stands, one nation under God, indivisible, with liberty and justice for all."

## NATIONAL ANTHEM: "THE STAR-SPANGLED BANNER"

"The Star-Spangled Banner" was a poem written in 1814 by Francis Scott Key as he watched British ships bombard Fort McHenry, Maryland, during the War of 1812. It became the National Anthem by an act of Congress in 1931. Although it has four stanzas, the one most commonly sung is the first stanza. The music to "The Star-Spangled Banner" was originally a tune called "Anacreon in Heaven."

# THE U.S. CONSTITUTION:
## The Foundation of American Government

The Constitution is the document that created the present government of the United States. It was written in 1787 and went into effect in 1789. It establishes the three branches of the U.S. government, which are the executive (headed by the president), the legislative (the Congress), and the judicial (the Supreme Court and other federal courts). The first 10 amendments to the Constitution (the **Bill of Rights**) explain the basic rights of all American citizens.

**WEB SITE** You can find the Constitution on-line at:
http://www.usia.gov/usa/infousa/facts/aboutusa/consteng.htm

## THE PREAMBLE TO THE CONSTITUTION

The Constitution begins with a short statement called the **Preamble**. The Preamble states that the government of the United States was established by the people.

> "We, the people of the United States, in order to form a more perfect Union, establish justice, insure domestic tranquility, provide for the common defense, promote the general welfare, and secure the blessings of liberty to ourselves and our posterity do ordain and establish this Constitution for the United States of America."

## THE ARTICLES

The original Constitution contained seven articles. The first three articles of the Constitution establish the three branches of the U.S. government.

**Article 1, Legislative Branch**
Creates the Senate and House of Representatives and describes their functions and powers.

**Article 2, Executive Branch**
Creates the office of the President and the Electoral College and lists their powers and responsibilities.

**Article 3, Judicial Branch**
Creates the Supreme Court and gives Congress the power to create lower courts. The powers of the courts and certain crimes are defined.

**Article 4, The States**
Discusses the relationship of the states to one another and to the citizens. Defines the states' powers.

**Article 5, Amending the Constitution**
Describes how the Constitution can be amended (changed).

**Article 6, Federal Law**
Makes the Constitution the supreme law of the land over state laws and constitutions.

**Article 7, Ratifying the Constitution**
Establishes how to ratify (approve) the Constitution.

# AMENDMENTS TO THE CONSTITUTION

The writers of the Constitution understood that the Constitution might need to be amended, or changed, in the future. Article 5 describes how the Constitution can be amended. In order to pass, an amendment must be approved by a two-thirds majority in the House of Representatives and a two-thirds majority in the Senate. The amendment must then be approved by three-fourths of the states (38 states). Since 1791 the Constitution has been amended 27 times.

## The Bill of Rights: The First Ten Amendments

The first 10 amendments were adopted in 1791 and contain the basic freedoms Americans enjoy as a people. These amendments are known as the Bill of Rights. They are summarized below.

❶ Guarantees freedom of religion, speech, and the press

❷ Guarantees the right of the people to have firearms

❸ Guarantees that soldiers cannot be lodged in private homes unless the owner agrees

❹ Protects citizens against being searched or having their property searched or taken away by the government without a good reason

❺ Protects rights of people on trial for crimes

❻ Guarantees people accused of crimes the right to a speedy public trial by jury

❼ Guarantees people the right to a trial by jury for other kinds of cases

❽ Prohibits cruel and unusual punishments

❾ States that specific rights listed in the Constitution do not take away rights that may not be listed

❿ Establishes that any powers not given specifically to the federal government belong to state governments or the people

## Other Important Amendments

**13 (1865):** Ends slavery in the United States

**14 (1868):** Establishes the Bill of Rights as protection against actions by a state government; guarantees equal protection under the law for all citizens

**15 (1870):** Guarantees that a person cannot be denied the right to vote because of race or color

**19 (1920):** Gives women the right to vote

**22 (1951):** Limits the president to two four-year terms of office

**24 (1964):** Outlaws the poll tax (a tax people had to pay before they could vote) in federal elections. (The poll tax had been used to keep African-Americans in the South from voting.)

**25 (1967):** Gives the president the power to appoint a new vice president, with the approval of Congress, if a vice president dies or leaves office in the middle of a term

**26 (1971):** Lowers the voting age to eighteen

# The Executive Branch:
# The PRESIDENT and the CABINET

The executive branch of the federal government is headed by the president of the United States. It also includes the vice president, people who work for the president or vice president, the major departments of the federal government, and special agencies. The cabinet is made up of the vice president, heads of the major departments, and other important officials. It meets when the president asks for its advice. As head of the executive branch, the president is responsible for enforcing the laws passed by Congress. The president is also commander in chief of U.S. armed forces. The chart below shows how the executive branch is organized.

## President

### Vice President

▲ The White House, home of the U.S. president.

| CABINET DEPARTMENTS | |
|---|---|
| State | Health and Human |
| Treasury | Services |
| Defense | Housing and Urban |
| Justice | Development |
| Interior | Transportation |
| Agriculture | Energy |
| Commerce | Education |
| Labor | Veterans Affairs |

## How Long Does the President Serve?

The president serves a four-year term, starting on January 20. No president can be elected more than twice.

## What Happens If the President Dies?

If the president dies in office or cannot complete the term, the vice president becomes president. If the president is disabled, the vice president can become acting president until the president is able to work again. The next person to become president after the vice president would be the Speaker of the House of Representatives. A person who finishes more than two years of a president's term can be elected to only one more term.

**WEB SITE** The White House has an address on the World Wide Web especially for kids. It is: *http://www.whitehouse.gov/WH/kids/html/home.html*

**DID YOU KNOW?** *You can use that site to "tour" the White House and learn about the First Family.*

**E-MAIL** You can send e-mail to the president at: *president@whitehouse.gov*

# The Judicial Branch:
# The SUPREME COURT

The highest court in the United States is the Supreme Court. It has nine justices who are appointed for life by the president with the approval of the Senate. Eight of the nine members are called associate justices. The ninth is the chief justice, who presides over the Court's meetings.

**What Does the Supreme Court Do?** The Supreme Court's major responsibilities are to review federal laws, actions of the president, treaties of the United States, and laws passed by state governments to be sure that they do not conflict in any way with the U.S. Constitution. The Supreme Court carries out these responsibilities by deciding cases that come before it. This process is known as **judicial review**. If the Supreme Court finds that a law or action violates the Constitution, the justices declare it **unconstitutional**.

**The Supreme Court's Decision Is Final.** Most cases must go through other federal courts or state courts before they go to the Supreme Court. The Supreme Court is the final court for a case, and the justices usually decide which cases they will review. After the Supreme Court hears a case, it may agree or disagree with the decision by an earlier court. When the Supreme Court makes a ruling, its decision is final, and all people involved in the case must abide by it.

**DID YOU KNOW?**

*In 1967, Thurgood Marshall became the first African-American to serve on the Supreme Court. He served until 1991. In 1981, Sandra Day O'Connor became the first woman on the Court.*

**Who Is on the Supreme Court?** Below are the nine justices who were on the Supreme Court at the beginning of its 1998–1999 session.

**Back row** *(from left to right): Ruth Bader Ginsburg, David H. Souter, Clarence Thomas, Stephen Breyer.*
**Front row** *(from left to right): Antonin Scalia, John Paul Stevens, Chief Justice William H. Rehnquist, Sandra Day O'Connor, Anthony M. Kennedy.*

# The Legislative Branch: CONGRESS

The Congress of the United States is the legislative branch of the federal government. Congress's major responsibility is to pass the laws that govern the country. It is the president's responsibility to enforce them. Congress consists of two parts—the Senate and the House of Representatives.

*The Capitol, where Congress meets* ▶

## The Senate

The Senate has 100 members, two from each state. The Constitution says that the Senate will have equal representation (the same number of representatives) from each state. Thus, large states have the same number of senators as small states. Senators are elected for six-year terms. There is no limit on the number of terms a senator can serve.

The Senate also has the responsibility of approving people the president appoints for certain jobs, for example, cabinet members and Supreme Court justices. The Senate must approve all treaties by at least a two-thirds vote. It also has the responsibility under the Constitution of putting on trial high-ranking federal officials who have been impeached (see box below) by the House of Representatives.

## The House of Representatives

The House of Representatives has 435 members. The number of representatives a state has is set by the state's population. For example: California has many more representatives than Wyoming. Each state has at least one representative—no matter how small its population. The first House of Representatives in 1789 had 65 members. As the country's population grew, the number of representatives increased. The total membership has been fixed at 435 since the 1910 census.

**WEB SITE**
*You can reach the Senate and the House on-line at:*
*http://www.senate.gov*
*http://www.house.gov*

# The House of Representatives, by State
### Each state has the following number of representatives in the House:

| State | Reps | State | Reps |
|---|---|---|---|
| Alabama | 7 | Montana | 1 |
| Alaska | 1 | Nebraska | 3 |
| Arizona | 6 | Nevada | 2 |
| Arkansas | 4 | New Hampshire | 2 |
| California | 52 | New Jersey | 13 |
| Colorado | 6 | New Mexico | 3 |
| Connecticut | 6 | New York | 31 |
| Delaware | 1 | North Carolina | 12 |
| Florida | 23 | North Dakota | 1 |
| Georgia | 11 | Ohio | 19 |
| Hawaii | 2 | Oklahoma | 6 |
| Idaho | 2 | Oregon | 5 |
| Illinois | 20 | Pennsylvania | 21 |
| Indiana | 10 | Rhode Island | 2 |
| Iowa | 5 | South Carolina | 6 |
| Kansas | 4 | South Dakota | 1 |
| Kentucky | 6 | Tennessee | 9 |
| Louisiana | 7 | Texas | 30 |
| Maine | 2 | Utah | 3 |
| Maryland | 8 | Vermont | 1 |
| Massachusetts | 10 | Virginia | 11 |
| Michigan | 16 | Washington | 9 |
| Minnesota | 8 | West Virginia | 3 |
| Mississippi | 5 | Wisconsin | 9 |
| Missouri | 9 | Wyoming | 1 |

The District of Columbia (Washington, D.C.), Puerto Rico, American Samoa, Guam, and the Virgin Islands each have one nonvoting member of the House of Representatives.

## What Impeachment Means

"Impeachment" means charging a high-ranking United States government official (such as a president, vice president, or federal judge) with serious crimes in order to possibly remove the person from office. Under the Consititution, only the House of Representatives can impeach officials for crimes. Once the House votes to impeach the person, a trial takes place in the Senate.The chief justice of the Supreme Court presides over the trial. In order to remove the person from office, two-thirds of the senators (67 senators) must find the person guilty of the crimes.

In 1868, President Andrew Johnson (above) was impeached. He was acquitted (found not guilty) by one vote in a Senate trial. In 1974, a committee of the House of Representatives recommended the impeachment of President Richard Nixon (right), but President Nixon resigned before the whole House could vote. On December 19, 1998, the House voted to impeach President Bill Clinton. On February 12, 1999, after a trial in the Senate, he was found not guilty.

# How a Bill Becomes a Law

### Step 1. Senators and Representatives Propose a Bill.

A proposed law is called a bill. Any member of Congress may propose (introduce) a bill. A bill is introduced in each house of Congress. The House of Representatives and the Senate consider a bill separately. A member of Congress who introduces a bill is known as the bill's *sponsor.*

### Step 2. House and Senate Committees Consider the Bill.

The bill is then sent to appropriate committees for consideration. A committee is made up of a small number of members of the House or Senate. A bill relating to agriculture, for example, would be sent to the agriculture committees in the House and in the Senate. When committees are considering a bill, they hold hearings at which people can speak for or against it.

### Step 3. Committees Change the Bill.

The committees consider the bill and change it as they see fit. Then they vote on the bill.

### Step 4. The Bill Is Debated in the House and Senate.

If the committees vote in favor of the bill, it goes to the full House and Senate, where it is debated and may be changed further. The House and Senate then vote on the bill.

### Step 5. From the House and Senate to Conference Committee.

If the House and the Senate pass different versions of the same bill, the bill must go to a "conference committee," where differences between the two versions must be worked out. A conference committee is a special committee made up of Senate and House members who meet to settle the differences in versions of the same bill.

### Step 6. Final Vote in the House and Senate.

The House and the Senate then vote on by the conference committee version. In order for a bill to become a law, it must be approved in exactly the same form by a majority of members of both houses of Congress and signed by the president.

### Step 7. The President Signs the Bill Into Law.

If the bill passes both houses of Congress, it goes to the president for his signature. Once the president signs a bill, it becomes law.

### Step 8. What If the President Doesn't Sign the Bill?

Sometimes the president does not approve of a bill and decides not to sign it. This is called vetoing the bill. A bill that has been vetoed goes back to Congress, where the members can vote on it again. If the House and the Senate pass the bill again with a two-thirds majority vote, the bill becomes law. This is called overriding the president's veto.

# Major GOVERNMENT AGENCIES

Government agencies have a variety of functions. Some set rules and regulations or enforce laws. Others investigate or gather information. Some major agencies are listed below, along with what they try to do.

## Central Intelligence Agency (CIA)

Gathers secret information on other countries and their leaders.

## Consumer Product Safety Commission

Examines the products that people buy to see that they are safe.

## Environmental Protection Agency (EPA)

Enforces laws on clean air and water and is responsible for cleaning up hazardous waste sites.

## Equal Employment Opportunity Commission (EEOC)

Makes sure that people are not discriminated against when they apply for a job and when they are at work.

## Federal Aviation Administration (FAA)

Watches over the airline industry and establishes safety rules.

## Federal Bureau of Investigation (FBI)

Investigates federal crimes and collects statistics on crime in the United States.

## Federal Communications Commission (FCC)

Gives out licenses to radio and TV stations and makes broadcasting rules.

## Federal Emergency Management Agency (FEMA)

Helps local communities recover from disasters such as hurricanes, earthquakes, and floods.

## Federal Trade Commission (FTC)

Makes sure that businesses operate fairly and that they obey the law.

## Library of Congress

The main library of the United States. Collects most of the books published in the United States. It also has many historic documents and photographs.

## National Foundation on the Arts and the Humanities

Gives government money to museums and artists.

## Occupational Safety and Health Administration (OSHA)

Makes sure that places where people work are safe and will not harm their health.

## Peace Corps

Sends American volunteers to foreign countries for two years to help with special projects such as teaching and farming.

## Securities and Exchange Commission (SEC)

Makes sure that the stock market operates fairly and obeys the laws.

# ELECTIONS

## Electing the President and Vice President

You may be amazed to learn that the president and vice president of the United States are not really elected in November on Election Day. They are officially elected in December by 538 people called the Electoral College.

## What Is the Electoral College?

The Electoral College is a group of people, called "electors," that officially elect the president and vice president. Electors are usually members of political parties. Their votes are counted at a joint session of the Senate and the House of Representatives. The U.S. Constitution says that each state and the District of Columbia must choose a group of electors equal to the total number of senators and representatives it has in Congress. For example, Missouri has 9 representatives and 2 senators for a total of 11 electors.

**The Electoral College State by State**

## How Are the President and Vice President Elected?

Every four years on Election Day in November, the names of the candidates for president and vice president appear on the voting machine or ballot. Voters select the people they prefer. When a voter pulls the lever for president, he or she is really choosing a group of electors who have promised to support (are "pledged to") the voter's presidential candidate. The names of the electors are not usually shown on the voting machine.

After the election polls close, each state begins counting the votes cast for each presidential and vice presidential candidate. The electors in the Electoral College, who are pledged to the candidate with the most votes in each state, meet in their home state in December. There, they officially cast their ballots for president and vice president. To be elected, a candidate must receive a majority of the Electoral College votes, or 270 votes. The results are announced in Congress the following January. If no candidate receives 270 electoral votes, the election goes to the House of Representatives, where the president is selected from the top three candidates. In the 1996 presidential election, the Electoral College cast 379 votes for Bill Clinton and 159 votes for Bob Dole.

# PRESIDENTS and VICE PRESIDENTS
## of the UNITED STATES

| PRESIDENT / VICE PRESIDENT | YEARS IN OFFICE | PRESIDENT / VICE PRESIDENT | YEARS IN OFFICE |
|---|---|---|---|
| ❶ George Washington | 1789–1797 | ㉒ Grover Cleveland | 1885–1889 |
| John Adams | 1789–1797 | Thomas A. Hendricks | 1885 |
| ❷ John Adams | 1797–1801 | ㉓ Benjamin Harrison | 1889–1893 |
| Thomas Jefferson | 1797–1801 | Levi P. Morton | 1889–1893 |
| ❸ Thomas Jefferson | 1801–1809 | ㉔ Grover Cleveland | 1893–1897 |
| Aaron Burr | 1801–1805 | Adlai E. Stevenson | 1893–1897 |
| George Clinton | 1805–1809 | ㉕ William McKinley | 1897–1901 |
| ❹ James Madison | 1809–1817 | Garret A. Hobart | 1897–1899 |
| George Clinton | 1809–1812 | Theodore Roosevelt | 1901 |
| Elbridge Gerry | 1813–1814 | ㉖ Theodore Roosevelt | 1901–1909 |
| ❺ James Monroe | 1817–1825 | Charles W. Fairbanks | 1905–1909 |
| Daniel D. Tompkins | 1817–1825 | ㉗ William Howard Taft | 1909–1913 |
| ❻ John Quincy Adams | 1825–1829 | James S. Sherman | 1909–1912 |
| John C. Calhoun | 1825–1829 | ㉘ Woodrow Wilson | 1913–1921 |
| ❼ Andrew Jackson | 1829–1837 | Thomas R. Marshall | 1913–1921 |
| John C. Calhoun | 1829–1832 | ㉙ Warren G. Harding | 1921–1923 |
| Martin Van Buren | 1833–1837 | Calvin Coolidge | 1921–1923 |
| ❽ Martin Van Buren | 1837–1841 | ㉚ Calvin Coolidge | 1923–1929 |
| Richard M. Johnson | 1837–1841 | Charles G. Dawes | 1925–1929 |
| ❾ William H. Harrison | 1841 | ㉛ Herbert Hoover | 1929–1933 |
| John Tyler | 1841 | Charles Curtis | 1929–1933 |
| ❿ John Tyler | 1841–1845 | ㉜ Franklin D. Roosevelt | 1933–1945 |
| No Vice President | | John Nance Garner | 1933–1941 |
| ⓫ James Knox Polk | 1845–1849 | Henry A. Wallace | 1941–1945 |
| George M. Dallas | 1845–1849 | Harry S. Truman | 1945 |
| ⓬ Zachary Taylor | 1849–1850 | ㉝ Harry S. Truman | 1945–1953 |
| Millard Fillmore | 1849–1850 | Alben W. Barkley | 1949–1953 |
| ⓭ Millard Fillmore | 1850–1853 | ㉞ Dwight D. Eisenhower | 1953–1961 |
| No Vice President | | Richard M. Nixon | 1953–1961 |
| ⓮ Franklin Pierce | 1853–1857 | ㉟ John F. Kennedy | 1961–1963 |
| William R. King | 1853 | Lyndon B. Johnson | 1961–1963 |
| ⓯ James Buchanan | 1857–1861 | ㊱ Lyndon B. Johnson | 1963–1969 |
| John C. Breckinridge | 1857–1861 | Hubert H. Humphrey | 1965–1969 |
| ⓰ Abraham Lincoln | 1861–1865 | ㊲ Richard M. Nixon | 1969–1974 |
| Hannibal Hamlin | 1861–1865 | Spiro T. Agnew | 1969–1973 |
| Andrew Johnson | 1865 | Gerald R. Ford | 1973–1974 |
| ⓱ Andrew Johnson | 1865–1869 | ㊳ Gerald R. Ford | 1974–1977 |
| No Vice President | | Nelson A. Rockefeller | 1974–1977 |
| ⓲ Ulysses S. Grant | 1869–1877 | ㊴ Jimmy Carter | 1977–1981 |
| Schuyler Colfax | 1869–1873 | Walter F. Mondale | 1977–1981 |
| Henry Wilson | 1873–1875 | ㊵ Ronald Reagan | 1981–1989 |
| ⓳ Rutherford B. Hayes | 1877–1881 | George Bush | 1981–1989 |
| William A. Wheeler | 1877–1881 | ㊶ George Bush | 1989–1993 |
| ⓴ James A. Garfield | 1881 | Dan Quayle | 1989–1993 |
| Chester A. Arthur | 1881 | ㊷ Bill Clinton | 1993– |
| ㉑ Chester A. Arthur | 1881–1885 | Al Gore | 1993– |
| No Vice President | | | |

# PRESIDENTS of the UNITED STATES

**GEORGE WASHINGTON**   Federalist Party                1789-1797
**Born:** Feb. 22, 1732, at Wakefield, Westmoreland County, Virginia
**Married:** Martha Dandridge Custis (1731-1802); no children
**Died:** Dec. 14, 1799; buried at Mount Vernon, Fairfax County, Virginia
**Early Career:** Soldier; head of the Virginia militia; commander in chief of the Continental Army; chairman of Constitutional Convention (1787)

**JOHN ADAMS**   Federalist Party                1797-1801
**Born:** Oct. 30, 1735, in Quincy, Massachusetts
**Married:** Abigail Smith (1744-1818); 3 sons, 2 daughters
**Died:** July 4, 1826; buried in Quincy, Massachusetts
**Early Career:** Lawyer; delegate to Continental Congress; signer of the Declaration of Independence; first vice president

**THOMAS JEFFERSON**   Democratic-Republican Party      1801-1809
**Born:** Apr. 13, 1743, at Shadwell, Albemarle County, Virginia
**Married:** Martha Wayles Skelton (1748-1782); 1 son, 5 daughters
**Died:** July 4, 1826; buried at Monticello, Albemarle County, Virginia
**Early Career:** Lawyer; member of the Continental Congress; author of the Declaration of Independence; governor of Virginia; first secretary of state; author of the Virginia Statute on Religious Freedom

**JAMES MADISON**   Democratic-Republican Party      1809-1817
**Born:** Mar. 16, 1751, at Port Conway, King George County, Virginia
**Married:** Dolley Payne Todd (1768-1849); no children
**Died:** June 28, 1836; buried at Montpelier, Orange County, Virginia
**Early Career:** Member of the Virginia Constitutional Convention (1776); member of the Continental Congress; major contributor to the U.S. Constitution; writer of the *Federalist Papers*; secretary of state

**JAMES MONROE**   Democratic-Republican Party      1817-1825
**Born:** Apr. 28, 1758, in Westmoreland County, Virginia
**Married:** Elizabeth Kortright (1768-1830); 2 daughters
**Died:** July 4, 1831; buried in Richmond, Virginia
**Early Career:** Soldier; lawyer; U.S. senator; governor of Virginia; secretary of state

**JOHN QUINCY ADAMS**   Democratic-Republican Party      1825-1829
**Born:** July 11, 1767, in Quincy, Massachusetts
**Married:** Louisa Catherine Johnson (1775-1852); 3 sons, 1 daughter
**Died:** Feb. 23, 1848; buried in Quincy, Massachusetts
**Early Career:** Diplomat; U.S. senator; secretary of state

**ANDREW JACKSON**   Democratic Party                     **1829-1837**
   **Born:** Mar. 15, 1767, in New Lancaster County, South Carolina
   **Married:** Rachel Donelson Robards (1767-1828); no children
   **Died:** June 8, 1845; buried in Nashville, Tennessee
   **Early Career:** Lawyer; U.S. representative and senator; Indian
   fighter; general in the U.S. Army

**MARTIN VAN BUREN**   Democratic Party                   **1837-1841**
   **Born:** Dec. 5, 1782, at Kinderhook, New York
   **Married:** Hannah Hoes (1783-1819); 4 sons
   **Died:** July 24, 1862; buried at Kinderhook, New York
   **Early Career:**  Governor of New York; secretary of state; vice
   president

**WILLIAM HENRY HARRISON**   Whig Party                         **1841**
   **Born:** Feb. 9, 1773, at Berkeley, Charles City County, Virginia
   **Married:** Anna Symmes (1775-1864); 6 sons, 4 daughters
   **Died:** Apr. 4, 1841; buried in North Bend, Ohio
   **Early Career:** First governor of Indiana Territory; superintendent of
   Indian affairs; U.S. representative and senator

**JOHN TYLER**   Whig Party                               **1841-1845**
   **Born:** Mar. 29, 1790, in Greenway, Charles City County, Virginia
   **Married:** Letitia Christian (1790-1842); 3 sons, 5 daughters
            Julia Gardiner (1820-1889); 5 sons, 2 daughters
   **Died:** Jan. 18, 1862; buried in Richmond, Virginia
   **Early Career:** U.S. representative and senator; vice president

**JAMES KNOX POLK**   Democratic Party                    **1845-1849**
   **Born:** Nov. 2, 1795, in Mecklenburg County, North Carolina
   **Married:** Sarah Childress (1803-1891); no children
   **Died:** June 15, 1849; buried in Nashville, Tennessee
   **Early Career:** U.S. representative; Speaker of the House; governor
   of Tennessee

**ZACHARY TAYLOR**   Whig Party                           **1849-1850**
   **Born:** Nov. 24, 1784, in Orange County, Virginia
   **Married:** Margaret Smith (1788-1852); 1 son, 5 daughters
   **Died:** July 9, 1850; buried in Louisville, Kentucky
   **Early Career:** Indian fighter; general in the U.S. Army

**MILLARD FILLMORE**   Whig Party                         **1850-1853**
   **Born:** Jan. 7, 1800, in Cayuga County, New York
   **Married:** Abigail Powers (1798-1853); 1 son, 1 daughter
            Caroline Carmichael McIntosh (1813-1881); no children
   **Died:** Mar. 8, 1874; buried in Buffalo, N.Y.
   **Early Career:** Teacher; lawyer; U.S. representative; vice president

**FRANKLIN PIERCE**   Democratic Party                    **1853-1857**
  **Born:** Nov. 23, 1804, in Hillsboro, New Hampshire
  **Married:** Jane Means Appleton (1806-1863); 3 sons
  **Died:** Oct. 8, 1869, in Concord, New Hampshire
  **Early Career:** U.S. representative, senator

**JAMES BUCHANAN**   Democratic Party                    **1857-1861**
  **Born:** Apr. 23, 1791, near Mercersburg, Pennsylvania
  Never Married
  **Died:** June 1, 1868, in Lancaster, Pennsylvania
  **Early Career:** U.S. representative; secretary of state

**ABRAHAM LINCOLN**   Republican Party                   **1861-1865**
  **Born:** Feb. 12, 1809, in Larue, Kentucky
  **Married:** Mary Todd (1818-1882); 4 sons
  **Died:** Apr. 15, 1865; buried in Springfield, Illinois
  **Early Career:** Lawyer; U.S. representative

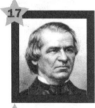

**ANDREW JOHNSON**   Democratic Party                    **1865-1869**
  **Born:** Dec. 29, 1808, in Raleigh, North Carolina
  **Married:** Eliza McCardle (1810-1876); 3 sons, 2 daughters
  **Died:** July 31, 1875; buried in Greeneville, Tennessee
  **Early Career:** State representative and senator; U.S. representative;
  governor of Tennessee; U.S. senator; vice president

**ULYSSES S. GRANT**   Republican Party                  **1869-1877**
  **Born:** Apr. 27, 1822, in Point Pleasant, Ohio
  **Married:** Julia Dent (1826-1902); 3 sons, 1 daughter
  **Died:** July 23, 1885; buried in New York City
  **Early Career:** Army officer; commander of Union forces during Civil War

**RUTHERFORD B. HAYES**   Republican Party               **1877-1881**
  **Born:** Oct. 4, 1822, in Delaware, Ohio
  **Married:** Lucy Ware Webb (1831-1889); 7 sons, 1 daughter
  **Died:** Jan. 17, 1893; buried in Fremont, Ohio
  **Early Career:** Lawyer; general in Union Army; U.S. representative;
  governor of Ohio

**JAMES A. GARFIELD**   Republican Party                    **1881**
  **Born:** Nov. 19, 1831, in Orange, Cuyahoga County, Ohio
  **Married:** Lucretia Rudolph (1832-1918); 4 sons, 1 daughter
  **Died:** Sept. 19, 1881; buried in Cleveland, Ohio
  **Early Career:** Teacher; Ohio state senator; general in Union Army;
  U.S. representative

**CHESTER A. ARTHUR**   Republican Party                21                **1881-1885**
**Born:** Oct. 5, 1829, in Fairfield, Vermont
**Married:** Ellen Lewis Herndon (1837-1880); 2 sons, 1 daughter
**Died:** Nov. 18, 1886; buried in Albany, New York
**Early Career:** Lawyer; vice president

**GROVER CLEVELAND**   Democratic Party                22                **1885-1889**
**Born:** Mar. 18, 1837, in Caldwell, New Jersey
**Married:** Frances Folsom (1864-1947); 2 sons, 3 daughters
**Died:** June 24, 1908; buried in Princeton, New Jersey
**Early Career:** Lawyer; mayor of Buffalo; governor of New York

**BENJAMIN HARRISON**   Republican Party                23                **1889-1893**
**Born:** Aug. 20, 1833, in North Bend, Ohio
**Married:** Caroline Lavinia Scott (1832-1892); 1 son, 1 daughter
            Mary Scott Lord Dimmick (1858-1948); 1 daughter
**Died:** Mar. 13, 1901; buried in Indianapolis, Indiana
**Early Career:** Lawyer; general in Union Army; U.S. senator

24

**GROVER CLEVELAND**                                **1893-1897** See 22, above.

**WILLIAM MCKINLEY**   Republican Party                25                **1897-1901**
**Born:** Jan. 29, 1843, in Niles, Ohio
**Married:** Ida Saxton (1847-1907); 2 daughters
**Died:** Sept. 14, 1901; buried in Canton, Ohio
**Early Career:** Lawyer; U.S. representative; governor of Ohio

**THEODORE ROOSEVELT**   Republican Party                26                **1901-1909**
**Born:** Oct. 27, 1858, in New York City
**Married:** Alice Hathaway Lee (1861-1884); 1 daughter
            Edith Kermit Carow (1861-1948); 4 sons, 1 daughter
**Died:** Jan. 6, 1919; buried in Oyster Bay, New York
**Early Career:** Assistant secretary of the navy; cavalry leader in
Spanish-American War; governor of New York; vice president

**WILLIAM HOWARD TAFT**   Republican Party                27                **1909-1913**
**Born:** Sept. 15, 1857, in Cincinnati, Ohio
**Married:** Helen Herron (1861-1943); 2 sons, 1 daughter
**Died:** Mar. 8, 1930; buried in Arlington National Cemetery, Virginia
**Early Career:** Lawyer; judge; secretary of war

**WOODROW WILSON**   Democratic Party                28                **1913-1921**
**Born:** Dec. 28, 1856, in Staunton, Virginia
**Married:** Ellen Louise Axson (1860-1914); 3 daughters
            Edith Bolling Galt (1872-1961); no children
**Died:** Feb. 3, 1924; buried in Washington, D.C.
**Early Career:** Lawyer; college professor; governor of New Jersey

**WARREN G. HARDING**   Republican Party                   **1921-1923**
   **Born:** Nov. 2, 1865, near Blooming Grove, Ohio
   **Married:** Florence Kling De Wolfe (1860-1924); no children
   **Died:** Aug. 2, 1923; buried in Marion, Ohio
   **Early Career:** Ohio state senator; U.S. senator

**CALVIN COOLIDGE**   Republican Party                   **1923-1929**
   **Born:** July 4, 1872, in Plymouth, Vermont
   **Married:** Grace Anna Goodhue (1879-1957); 2 sons
   **Died:** Jan. 5, 1933; buried in Plymouth, Vermont
   **Early Career:** Massachusetts state senator, lieutenant governor,
   and governor; vice president

**HERBERT HOOVER**   Republican Party                   **1929-1933**
   **Born:** Aug. 10, 1874, in West Branch, Iowa
   **Married:** Lou Henry (1875-1944); 2 sons
   **Died:** Oct. 20, 1964; buried West Branch, Iowa
   **Early Career:** Mining engineer; secretary of commerce

**FRANKLIN DELANO ROOSEVELT**   Democratic Party       **1933-1945**
   **Born:** Jan. 30, 1882, in Hyde Park, New York
   **Married:** Anna Eleanor Roosevelt (1884-1962); 4 sons, 1 daughter
   **Died:** Apr. 12, 1945; buried in Hyde Park, New York
   **Early Career:** Lawyer; New York state senator; assistant secretary
   of the navy; governor of New York

**HARRY S. TRUMAN**   Democratic Party                   **1945-1953**
   **Born:** May 8, 1884, in Lamar, Missouri
   **Married:** Elizabeth Virginia "Bess" Wallace (1885-1982); 1 daughter
   **Died:** Dec. 26, 1972; buried in Independence, Missouri
   **Early Career:** Haberdasher (ran men's clothing store); judge; U.S.
   senator; vice president

**DWIGHT D. EISENHOWER**   Republican Party              **1953-1961**
   **Born:** Oct. 14, 1890, in Denison, Texas
   **Married:** Mamie Geneva Doud (1896-1979); 1 son
   **Died:** Mar. 28, 1969; buried in Abilene, Kansas
   **Early Career:** Commander, Allied landing in North Africa and later
   Supreme Allied Commander in Europe during World War II;
   president of Columbia University

**JOHN FITZGERALD KENNEDY**   Democratic Party          **1961-1963**
   **Born:** May 29, 1917, in Brookline, Massachusetts
   **Married:** Jacqueline Lee Bouvier (1929-1994); 1 son, 1 daughter
   **Died:** Nov. 22, 1963; buried in Arlington National Cemetery, Virginia
   **Early Career:** U.S. naval commander; U.S. representative and senator

**36** **LYNDON BAINES JOHNSON**  Democratic Party          **1963-1969**
**Born:** Aug. 27, 1908, in Stonewall, Texas
**Married:** Claudia "Lady Bird" Alta Taylor (b. 1912); 2 daughters
**Died:** Jan. 22, 1973; buried in Stonewall, Texas
**Early Career:** U.S. representative and senator; vice president

**37** **RICHARD MILHOUS NIXON**  Republican Party          **1969-1974**
**Born:** Jan. 9, 1913, in Yorba Linda, California
**Married:** Patricia Ryan (1912-1993); 2 daughters
**Died:** Apr. 22, 1994; buried in Yorba Linda, California
**Early Career:** Lawyer; U.S. representative and senator; vice president

**38** **GERALD R. FORD**  Republican Party          **1974-1977**
**Born:** July 14, 1913, in Omaha, Nebraska
**Married:** Elizabeth Bloomer Warren (b. 1918);
          3 sons, 1 daughter
**Early Career:** Lawyer; U.S. representative; vice president

**39** **JIMMY (JAMES EARL) CARTER**  Democratic Party          **1977-1981**
**Born:** Oct. 1, 1924, in Plains, Georgia
**Married:** Rosalynn Smith (b. 1927); 3 sons, 1 daughter
**Early Career:** Peanut farmer; Georgia state senator; governor
of Georgia

**40** **RONALD REAGAN**  Republican Party          **1981-1989**
**Born:** Feb. 6, 1911, in Tampico, Illinois
**Married:** Jane Wyman (b. 1914); 1 son, 1 daughter
          Nancy Davis (b. 1921); 1 son, 1 daughter
**Early Career:** Film and television actor; governor of California

**41** **GEORGE BUSH**  Republican Party          **1989-1993**
**Born:** June 12, 1924, in Milton, Massachusetts
**Married:** Barbara Pierce (b. 1925); 4 sons, 2 daughters
**Early Career:** U.S. navy pilot; businessman; U.S. representative;
U.S. ambassador to the United Nations; vice president

**42** **BILL (WILLIAM JEFFERSON) CLINTON**  Democratic Party          **1993-**
**Born:** Aug. 19, 1946, in Hope, Arkansas
**Married:** Hillary Rodham (b. 1947); 1 daughter
**Early Career:** Arkansas state attorney general;
governor of Arkansas

# Presidential Facts, Families, and First Ladies

## PRESIDENTIAL FACTS

**Youngest president:** Theodore Roosevelt, who was 42 when he was sworn in

**Oldest president:** Ronald Reagan, who was 77 when he left office

**Only president to serve more than two terms:** Franklin Delano Roosevelt

**Only president to serve two terms that were not back to back:** Grover Cleveland

**Only president who was unmarried:** James Buchanan. His niece acted as White House hostess for her uncle.

**Presidents who died in office:** Eight U.S. presidents have died while they served as president. Four of them were assassinated: Abraham Lincoln, James Garfield, William McKinley, and John F. Kennedy. The other four who died in office were William Henry Harrison, Zachary Taylor, Warren G. Harding, and Franklin D. Roosevelt.

## FAMOUS FIRST FAMILIES

**Adams family:** John Adams was the 2nd president, and his son, John Quincy Adams, became the 6th president.

**Harrison family:** Benjamin Harrison, the 23rd president, was the great-grandson of Benjamin Harrison, a signer of the Declaration of Independence, and the grandson of William Henry Harrison, the 9th president of the United States.

**Roosevelt family:** Theodore Roosevelt was the 26th president and his 5th cousin, Franklin Delano Roosevelt, the 32nd. Franklin's wife, Eleanor Roosevelt, was also Theodore Roosevelt's niece.

## FAMOUS FIRST LADIES

**Martha Washington** was the first First Lady. A wealthy widow when she married George Washington, she helped his position as a Virginia planter.

**Abigail Adams,** the wife of John Adams, was a thoughtful, outspoken woman. She wrote hundreds of letters in which she clearly expressed her opinions on the issues of the day.

**Dolley Madison,** James Madison's wife, was famous as a hostess and for saving a portrait of George Washington during the War of 1812, when the British were about to burn the White House.

**Eleanor Roosevelt,** wife of Franklin D. Roosevelt, was an important public figure. She urged her husband to support civil rights and the rights of workers. After his death she served as a delegate to the United Nations.

**Jacqueline Kennedy,** wife of John F. Kennedy, known for her elegance and style, restored the White House and made it a symbol the country could be proud of.

**Hillary Rodham Clinton,** wife of Bill Clinton, is a successful lawyer and outspoken defender of women's and children's rights. She won a Grammy in 1997 for a recording of her book about children, *It Takes a Village*.

# United States History TIME LINE

## The First People in North America: Before 1492

**40,000 B.C.-11,000 B.C.**
First people (called Paleo-Indians) cross from Siberia to Alaska and begin to move into North America.

**14,000 B.C.-11,000 B.C.**
Paleo-Indians use stone points attached to spears to hunt big mammoths in northern parts of North America.

**11,000 B.C.**
Big mammoths disappear and Paleo-Indians begin to gather plants for food.

**8000 B.C.-1000 B.C.**
North American Indians begin using stone to grind food and to hunt bison and smaller animals.

**1000 B.C.-A.D. 500**
Woodland Indians, who lived east of the Mississippi River, bury people who have died under large burial mounds (which can still be seen today).

**After A.D. 500**
Anasazi peoples in the Southwestern United States live in homes on cliffs, called cliff dwellings. Anasazi pottery and dishes are well known for their beautiful patterns.

**After A.D. 700**
Mississippian Indian people in Southeastern United States develop farms and build burial mounds.

**700-1492**
Many different Indian cultures develop throughout North America.

## Colonial America and the American Revolution: 1492-1783

**1492**
Christopher Columbus sails across the Atlantic Ocean and reaches an island in the Bahamas in the Caribbean Sea.

**1513**
Juan Ponce de León explores the Florida coast.

**1524**
Giovanni da Verrazano explores the coast from Carolina north to Nova Scotia, enters New York harbor.

**1540**
Francisco Vásquez de Coronado explores the Southwest.

**1565**
St. Augustine, Florida, the first town established by Europeans in United States, is founded by the Spanish. Later burned by the English in 1586.

**1607**
Jamestown, Virginia, the first English settlement in North America, is founded by Captain John Smith.

**1609**
Henry Hudson sails into New York Harbor, explores Hudson River. Spaniards settle Santa Fe, New Mexico.

**1619**
The first African slaves are brought to Jamestown. (Slavery is made legal in 1650.)

**1620**
Pilgrims from England arrive at Plymouth, Massachusetts, on the *Mayflower*.

**1626**
Peter Minuit buys Manhattan island for the Dutch from Man-a-hat-a Indians for goods worth $24. The island is renamed New Amsterdam.

**1630**
Boston is founded by Massachusetts colonists led by John Winthrop.

**1634**
Maryland is founded as a Catholic colony with religious freedom for all its settlers.

**1644**
The English seize New Amsterdam from the Dutch. The city is renamed New York.

**1699**
French settlers move into Mississippi and Louisiana.

**1732**
Benjamin Franklin begins publishing *Poor Richard's Almanack.*

**1754-1763**
French and Indian War between England and France. The French are defeated and lose their lands in Canada and the American Midwest.

**1764-1767**
England places taxes on sugar that comes from their North American colonies. England also requires colonists to purchase stamps to raise money to pay for the French and Indian War. Colonists protest and meet in the Stamp Act Congress.

**1770**
Boston Massacre: English troops fire on a group of people protesting English taxes.

**1773**
Boston Tea Party: English tea is thrown into the harbor to protest a tax on tea.

**1775**
Fighting at Lexington and Concord, Massachusetts, marks the beginning of the American Revolution.

**1776**
The Declaration of Independence is approved July 4 by the Continental Congress (made up of representatives from the American colonies).

**1781**
British General Cornwallis surrenders to the Americans at Yorktown, Virginia, ending the fighting in the Revolutionary War.

**Benjamin Franklin (1706-1790)**
was a great American leader, printer, scientist, and writer. In 1732, he began publishing a magazine called *Poor Richard's Almanack.* Poor Richard was a make-believe person who gave advice about common sense and honesty. Many of Poor Richard's sayings are still known today. Among the most famous are "God helps them that help themselves" and "Early to bed, early to rise, makes a man healthy, wealthy, and wise."

**Portion of
The Declaration of Independence, July 4, 1776**
"We hold these truths to be self-evident, that all men are created equal, that they are endowed by their Creator with certain unalienable rights, that among these are life, liberty, and the pursuit of happiness."

## Who Attended the Convention?

The Constitutional Convention met in Philadelphia in the hot summer of 1787. Most of the great founders of America attended. Among those present were George Washington, James Madison, and John Adams. They met to form a new government that would be strong and, at the same time, protect the liberties that were fought for in the American Revolution. The Constitution they created is still the law of the United States.

Louisiana Purchase

## The New Nation: 1783–1900

**1783**
The Treaty of Paris ending the Revolutionary War is signed by the United States and England. The English recognize U.S. independence.

**1784**
The first successful daily newspaper, the *Pennsylvania Packet & General Advertiser,* is published.

**1787**
The Constitutional Convention meets to write a Constitution for the U.S.

**1789**
The new Constitution is approved by the states. George Washington is chosen as the first president.

**1800**
The federal government moves to a new capital, Washington, D.C.

**1803**
The U.S. makes the Louisiana Purchase from France. Millions of square miles of territory are added to the U.S.

**1804**
Lewis and Clark explore what is now the northwestern United States.

**1812–1814**
War of 1812 with Great Britain: British forces burn the Capitol and White House. Francis Scott Key writes "The Star-Spangled Banner."

**1820**
The Missouri Compromise bans slavery west of the Mississippi River and north of line 36°30' north latitude, except in Missouri.

**1823**
The Monroe Doctrine warns European countries not to interfere in the Americas.

**1825**
The Erie Canal opens and links New York City with the Great Lakes.

**1831**
*The Liberator*, a newspaper opposing slavery, is published in Boston.

**"The Trail of Tears"**
The Cherokee Indians living in Georgia were forced, by the state government of Georgia, to leave in 1838. They were sent to Oklahoma. On the long march, thousands died because of disease and the cold weather.

The Trail of Tears

*Uncle Tom's Cabin*
Harriet Beecher Stowe's novel about the sufferings of slaves was an instant bestseller in the North and banned in most of the South. When President Abraham Lincoln met Stowe, he called her "the little lady who started this war" (the Civil War).

**The Bloodiest War in U.S. History**
The U.S. Civil War between the North and South lasted four years (1861-1865) and resulted in the deaths of more than 600,000 people — more than all other U.S. wars combined. Little was known at the time about the spread of diseases. As a result, many casualties were also the result of illnesses such as influenza, measles, and infections from battle wounds.

**1836**
Texans fighting for independence from Mexico are defeated at the Alamo.

**1838**
Cherokee Indians are forced to move to Oklahoma, along "The Trail of Tears."

**1844**
The first telegraph line connects Washington and Baltimore.

**1846–1848**
U.S. war with Mexico: Mexico is defeated and the United States takes control of the Republic of Texas and of Mexican territories in the West.

**1848**
The discovery of gold in California leads to a "rush" of more than 80,000 people to the West in search of gold.

**1852**
*Uncle Tom's Cabin* is published.

**1858**
Abraham Lincoln and Stephen Douglas debate about slavery during their Senate campaign in Illinois.

**1860**
Abraham Lincoln is elected president.

**1861**
The Civil War begins.

**1863**
President Lincoln issues the Emancipation Proclamation, freeing most slaves.

**1865**
The Civil War ends as the South surrenders. President Lincoln is assassinated.

**1869**
The first railroad connecting the East and West coasts is completed.

**1890**
Battle of Wounded Knee is fought in South Dakota—the last major battle between Indians and U.S. troops.

**1898**
Spanish-American War: The United States defeats Spain, gains control of the Philippines and Puerto Rico.

## World War I

In World War I the United States fought with Great Britain, France, and Russia (the Allies) against Germany and Austria-Hungary. The Allies won the war in 1918.

## The Great Depression

The stock market crash of October 1929 led to a period of severe hardship for the American people—the Great Depression. As many as 25 percent of all workers could not find jobs. The Depression lasted until the early 1940s. The Depression also led to a great change in politics. In 1932, Franklin D. Roosevelt, a Democrat, was elected president. He served as president for 12 years, longer than any other president.

## United States in the 20th Century

**1903**
The United States begins digging the Panama Canal. The canal opens in 1914, connecting the Atlantic and Pacific oceans.

**1908**
Henry Ford introduces the Model T car, the first auto bought by thousands of people.

**1916**
Jeanette Rankin of Montana becomes the first woman elected to Congress.

**1917-1918**
The United States joins World War I on the side of the Allies against Germany.

**1927**
Charles A. Lindbergh becomes the first person to fly alone nonstop across the Atlantic Ocean.

**1929**
A stock market crash marks the beginning of the Great Depression.

**1933**
President Franklin D. Roosevelt's New Deal increases government help to people hurt by the Depression.

**1941**
Japan attacks Pearl Harbor, Hawaii. The United States enters World War II.

**1945**
Germany and Japan surrender, ending World War II. Japan's surrender comes after the United States drops atomic bombs on Hiroshima and Nagasaki.

**1950-1953**
U.S. armed forces fight in the Korean War.

**1954**
The U.S. Supreme Court forbids racial segregation in public schools.

**1958**
The first U.S. space satellite, *Explorer I,* goes into orbit.

**1962**
The U.S. forces the Soviet Union to pull its missiles out of Cuba.

**1963**
President John Kennedy is assassinated.

**1964**
Congress passes the Civil Rights Act, which outlaws discrimination in voting and jobs.

**1965**
The United States sends large numbers of soldiers to fight in the Vietnam War.

**1968**
Civil rights leader Martin Luther King, Jr., is assassinated in Memphis. Senator Robert F. Kennedy is assassinated in Los Angeles.

**1969**
U.S. astronaut Neil Armstrong becomes first person to walk on the moon.

**1973**
U.S. participation in the Vietnam War ends.

**1974**
President Richard Nixon resigns because of the Watergate scandal.

**1979**
U.S. hostages are taken in Iran, beginning a 444-day crisis until their release in 1981.

**1981**
Sandra Day O'Connor becomes the first woman on the U.S. Supreme Court.

**1985**
U.S. President Ronald Reagan and Soviet leader Mikhail Gorbachev begin working together to improve relations between their countries.

**1991**
The Persian Gulf War: The United States and its allies defeat Iraq.

**1992**
Bill Clinton, a Democrat, is elected president, defeating George Bush.

**1994**
The Republican Party wins majorities in both houses of Congress for the first time in 40 years.

**1998**
The federal government announces that, for the first time in many years, it will begin receiving more money than it spends

**1999**
The Senate finds President Clinton not guilty, after an impeachment trial.

**Watergate**
In June 1972, five men were arrested in the Watergate building in Washington, D.C., for trying to bug the telephones in the offices of the Democratic National Committee. Some of the men worked for the committee to reelect President Richard Nixon. In 1973, it was discovered that President Nixon had tape-recorded his conversations in the Oval Office of the White House. One of the tapes revealed that Nixon knew about a plan to hide information about "Watergate." Facing impeachment, Nixon resigned the presidency.

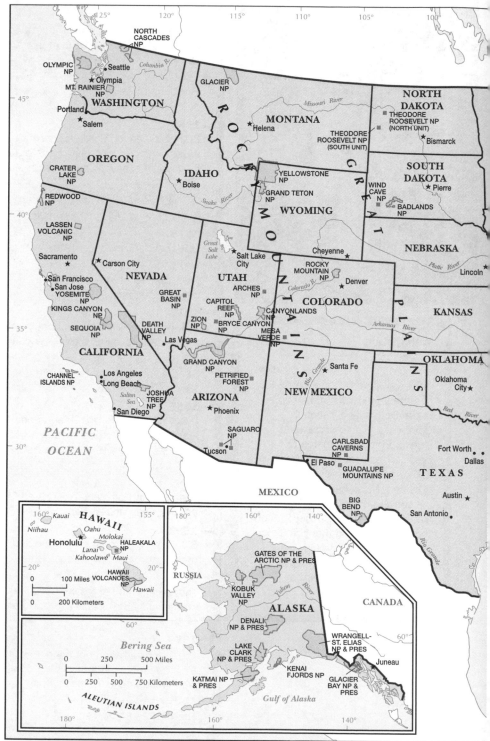

125°  120°  115°  110°  105°  100°

NORTH CASCADES NP

OLYMPIC NP
Seattle
Olympia
MT. RAINIER NP
Portland
WASHINGTON
Salem

Columbia R.

GLACIER NP

ROCKY

Missouri River

NORTH DAKOTA
THEODORE ROOSEVELT NP (NORTH UNIT)
Bismarck

45°

MONTANA
Helena

THEODORE ROOSEVELT NP (SOUTH UNIT)

OREGON

CRATER LAKE NP

IDAHO
Boise

Snake River

YELLOWSTONE NP

GRAND TETON NP

WYOMING

GREAT

SOUTH DAKOTA
Pierre

WIND CAVE NP

BADLANDS NP

REDWOOD NP

40°

LASSEN VOLCANIC NP

Sacramento

Great Salt Lake

Salt Lake City

Cheyenne

NEBRASKA

Platte River

Lincoln

Carson City

NEVADA

UTAH

ROCKY MOUNTAIN NP

Denver

San Francisco
San Jose
YOSEMITE NP
KINGS CANYON NP

GREAT BASIN NP

ARCHES NP

CAPITOL REEF NP

COLORADO

Colorado R.

MOUNTAINS

35°

SEQUOIA NP

DEATH VALLEY NP

Las Vegas

ZION NP

BRYCE CANYON NP

CANYONLANDS NP

MESA VERDE NP

KANSAS

Arkansas River

CALIFORNIA

CHANNEL ISLANDS NP

Los Angeles
Long Beach

Salton Sea

JOSHUA TREE NP

GRAND CANYON NP

PETRIFIED FOREST NP

Santa Fe

OKLAHOMA

Oklahoma City

ARIZONA
Phoenix

NEW MEXICO

San Diego

30°

PACIFIC OCEAN

SAGUARO NP

Tucson

Rio Grande

CARLSBAD CAVERNS NP

El Paso

GUADALUPE MOUNTAINS NP

Fort Worth
Dallas

TEXAS

MEXICO

BIG BEND NP

Austin
San Antonio

Red River

Rio Grande

HAWAII

160°  Kauai  155°
Niihau  Oahu
Honolulu  Molokai
HALEAKALA NP
Lanai  Maui
Kahoolawe

20°  20°

HAWAII VOLCANOES NP

Hawaii

0   100 Miles
0   200 Kilometers

180°  160°  140°

RUSSIA

GATES OF THE ARCTIC NP & PRES

KOBUK VALLEY NP

Yukon River

ALASKA

CANADA

DENALI NP & PRES

WRANGELL-ST. ELIAS NP & PRES

60°  60°

Bering Sea

LAKE CLARK NP & PRES

Juneau

KENAI FJORDS NP

GLACIER BAY NP & PRES

KATMAI NP & PRES

0   250   500 Miles
0   250   500   750 Kilometers

ALEUTIAN ISLANDS

Gulf of Alaska

180°  160°  140°

© MapQuest.com, Inc.

270

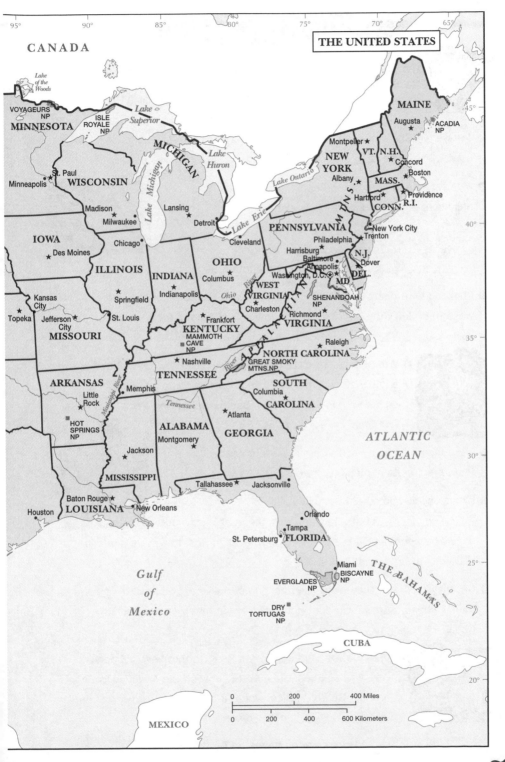

THE UNITED STATES

CANADA

95° 90° 85° 80° 75° 70° 65°

Lake
of the
Woods

VOYAGEURS NP

MINNESOTA

ISLE ROYALE NP

Lake Superior

MICHIGAN

Lake Huron

Lake Michigan

MAINE

Augusta ★

ACADIA NP

45°

Montpelier ★

VT. N.H.

Concord

NEW YORK

Albany ★

MASS.

Boston

Lake Ontario

Hartford ★ Providence

CONN. R.I.

St. Paul

Minneapolis ★

WISCONSIN

Madison ★

Milwaukee ★

Lansing ★

Detroit

PENNSYLVANIA

New York City

Trenton ★

40°

Cleveland

Philadelphia ★

IOWA

Chicago

Des Moines ★

ILLINOIS

INDIANA

OHIO

Columbus ★

Harrisburg ★

Baltimore

N.J.

Dover ★

Springfield ★

Indianapolis ★

WEST VIRGINIA

Ohio River

Washington, D.C. ⊛ Annapolis

DEL.

MD

Kansas City ★

Topeka ★

Jefferson City ★

St. Louis ★

Frankfort ★

Charleston ★

SHENANDOAH NP

Richmond ★

VIRGINIA

35°

MISSOURI

KENTUCKY

MAMMOTH CAVE NP

Raleigh ★

Nashville ★

GREAT SMOKY MTNS. NP

NORTH CAROLINA

ARKANSAS

Little Rock ★

Memphis

TENNESSEE

Tennessee River

SOUTH CAROLINA

Columbia ★

Mississippi River

HOT SPRINGS NP

Atlanta ★

ALABAMA

Montgomery ★

GEORGIA

ATLANTIC OCEAN

30°

Jackson ★

MISSISSIPPI

Tallahassee ★

Jacksonville

Houston

Baton Rouge ★

LOUISIANA

New Orleans

Orlando

Tampa

St. Petersburg

FLORIDA

Gulf
of
Mexico

Miami

BISCAYNE NP

THE BAHAMAS

25°

EVERGLADES NP

DRY TORTUGAS NP

CUBA

MEXICO

20°

APPALACHIAN MTNS

0    200    400 Miles

0    200    400    600 Kilometers

# Tour with Teri

**T**eri Terrific is touring the western United States to promote her new album, *I Am Terrific*. She's keeping track of all the places she visits. You can use the map on pages 270–271 to help you fill in the blanks.

❶ Today I left California and went to the state on its southeast border. The state is _____ and they just love me there.

❷ My next stop is right to the east. This state has four neighbors (not counting Utah). The state is _____ and its neighbors are _____, _____, _____, and _____. I hope they like one another as much as they like me.

❸ I hopped on a plane and flew to the state that's farthest north in the western United States (not counting Alaska). It's named for a president. The state is _____.

❹ Wow! I'm getting dizzy. (Some people might say dizzier, but that's another story.) I'm heading southeast again, to a state that's bordered by Idaho, Montana, South Dakota, Nebraska, Colorado, and Utah. I'm going to _____.

❺ From there, I'm going southwest to a state nearby that has four letters in its name. The state is _____.

❻ Where should I go now? I could go south to _____, but I've already been there. Another state should have the benefit of seeing me. Maybe I'll go west to a state that's in between California and Utah. It is _____.

❼ Oh, they liked me. They really liked me. Time to give another state a treat. I think I'll head northwest to a neighbor of Nevada that's on the Pacific Ocean. I'm going to _____.

❽ I need a rest; I'm saying "so long" to the West. I'll head way, way southeast to a state between the Atlantic Ocean and the Gulf of Mexico, where it's nice and warm. Look out, _____, here I come!

**Answers are on pages 317–320.**

# FACTS About the STATES

After every state name is the postal abbreviation for the state. The Area includes both land and water. It is given in square miles (sq. mi.) and square kilometers (sq. km.). Numbers in parentheses after Population, Area, and Entered Union show the state's rank compared with other states. For example, Alabama is the 23rd largest state in population.

## ALABAMA (AL)

*Heart of Dixie, Camellia State*

**Population** (1998): 4,351,999 (23rd)
**Area:** 52,237 sq. mi. (30th) (135,294 sq. km.)
**Entered Union:** December 14, 1819 (22nd)
**Flower:** Camellia          **Bird:** Yellowhammer
**Tree:** Southern pine       **Song:** "Alabama"
**Capital:** Montgomery
**Largest Cities** (with population): Birmingham, 258,543;
Mobile, 202,581; Montgomery, 196,363; Huntsville, 170,424
**Important Products:** clothing and textiles, metal products, transportation equipment, paper, industrial machinery, food products, lumber, coal, oil, natural gas, livestock, peanuts, cotton
**Places to Visit:** Alabama Space and Rocket Center, Huntsville; DeSoto State Park, near Fort Payne
**WEB SITE** *http://alaweb.asc.edu*

**DID YOU KNOW?** *Montgomery, Alabama, was the first capital of the Confederate States of America (1861). Alabama is a major center for rocket and space research.*

## ALASKA (AK)

*The Last Frontier*

**Population** (1998): 614,010 (48th)
**Area:** 615,230 sq. mi. (1st) (1,593,444 sq. km.)
**Entered Union:** January 3, 1959 (49th)
**Flower:** Forget-me-not      **Bird:** Willow ptarmigan
**Tree:** Sitka spruce         **Song:** "Alaska's Flag"
**Capital:** Juneau (population, 29,756)
**Largest Cities** (with population): Anchorage, 250,505; Fairbanks, 32,960
**Important Products:** oil, natural gas, fish, food products, lumber and wood products, fur
**Places to Visit:** Glacier Bay and Denali national parks, Mendenhall Glacier, Mount McKinley
**WEB SITE** *http://www.state.ak.us*

**DID YOU KNOW?** *Mount McKinley is the highest mountain in the United States. Alaska is the biggest and coldest state in the United States.*

## ARIZONA (AZ)

*Grand Canyon State*

**Population** (1998): 4,668,631 (21st)
**Area:** 114,006 sq. mi. (6th) (295,276 sq. km.)
**Entered Union:** February 14, 1912 (48th)
**Flower:** Blossom of the Saguaro cactus  **Bird:** Cactus wren
**Tree:** Paloverde                         **Song:** "Arizona"
**Capital and Largest City:** Phoenix (population, 1,159,014)
**Other Large Cities** (with population): Tucson, 449,002; Mesa, 344,764; Glendale, 182,219; Scottsdale, 179,012; Tempe, 162,701
**Important Products:** electronic equipment, transportation and industrial equipment, instruments, printing and publishing, copper, and other metals
**Places to Visit:** Grand Canyon, Painted Desert, Petrified Forest, Hoover Dam
**WEB SITE** *http://www.state.az.us*

**DID YOU KNOW?** *The Grand Canyon is the largest land gorge in the world and one of the world's natural wonders. It is 217 miles long and from 4 to 18 miles wide at the rim.*

## ARKANSAS (AR)

*Land of Opportunity*

**Population** (1998): 2,538,303 (33rd)
**Area:** 53,182 sq. mi. (28th) (137,741 sq. km.)
**Flower:** Apple blossom    **Bird:** Mockingbird
**Tree:** Pine    **Song:** "Arkansas"
**Entered Union:** June 15, 1836 (25th)
**Capital and Largest City:** Little Rock (population, 175,752)
**Other Large Cities** (with population): North Little Rock, 60,468; Pine Bluff, 54,165
**Important Products:** food products, paper, electronic equipment, industrial machinery, metal products, lumber and wood products, livestock, soybeans, rice, cotton, natural gas
**Places to Visit:** Hot Springs National Park, Fort Smith National Historic Site
**WEB SITE** *http://www.state.ar.us*

**DID YOU KNOW?** *Arkansas has the only working diamond mine in North America. President Bill Clinton was born in Arkansas and served as one of its governors.*

## CALIFORNIA (CA)

*Golden State*

**Population** (1998): 32,666,550 (1st)
**Area:** 158,869 sq. mi. (3rd) (411,471 sq. km.)
**Flower:** Golden poppy    **Bird:** California valley quail
**Tree:** California redwood    **Song:** "I Love You, California"
**Entered Union:** September 9, 1850 (31st)
**Capital:** Sacramento (population, 376,243)
**Largest Cities** (with population): Los Angeles, 3,553,638; San Diego, 1,171,121; San Jose, 838,744; San Francisco, 735,315
**Important Products:** transportation and industrial equipment, electronic equipment, oil, natural gas, motion pictures, milk, cattle, fruit, vegetables
**Places to Visit:** Yosemite Valley, Lake Tahoe, Palomar Observatory, Disneyland, San Diego Zoo, Hollywood, Sequoia National Park
**WEB SITE** *http://www.state.ca.us*

**DID YOU KNOW?** *California has more people, more cars, more schools, and more businesses than any other state in the United States. The oldest living things on earth are believed to be the Bristlecone pine trees in California's Inyo National Forest, estimated to be 4,700 years old. The world's tallest tree, 365 feet tall and 44 feet around, is a redwood tree in Humboldt County.*

## COLORADO (CO)

*Centennial State*

**Population** (1998): 3,970,971 (24th)
**Area:** 104,100 sq. mi. (8th) (269,619 sq. km.)
**Flower:** Rocky Mountain columbine    **Bird:** Lark bunting
**Tree:** Colorado blue spruce    **Song:** "Where the Columbines
**Entered Union:** August 1, 1876 (38th)    Grow"
**Capital and Largest City:** Denver (population, 497,840)
**Other Large Cities** (with population): Colorado Springs, 345,127; Aurora, 252,341; Lakewood, 134,999
**Important Products:** instruments and industrial machinery, food products, printing and publishing, metal products, electronic equipment, oil, coal, cattle
**Places to Visit:** Rocky Mountain National Park, Mesa Verde National Park, Dinosaur National Monument, old mining towns
**WEB SITE** *http://www.state.co.us*

**DID YOU KNOW?** *The Grand Mesa in Colorado is the world's largest flat-top mountain. The highest bridge in the world (1,053 feet) is in Colorado—it is the suspension bridge over the Royal Gorge of the Arkansas River. Colorado has more mountains over 14,000 feet and more elk than any other state.*

## CONNECTICUT (CT)

**Constitution State, Nutmeg State**

**Population** (1998): 3,274,069 (28th)
**Area:** 5,544 sq. mi. (48th) (14,359 sq. km.)
**Flower:** Mountain laurel     **Bird:** American robin
**Tree:** White oak     **Song:** "Yankee Doodle"
**Entered Union:** January 9, 1788 (5th)
**Capital:** Hartford
**Largest Cities** (with population): Bridgeport, 137,990; Hartford, 133,086; New Haven, 124,665; Waterbury, 106,412; Stamford, 110,056
**Important Products:** aircraft parts and helicopters, industrial machinery, metals and metal products, electronic equipment, printing and publishing, instruments, chemicals, dairy products, stone
**Places to Visit:** Mystic Seaport and Marine Life Aquarium, in Mystic; P. T. Barnum Circus Museum, Bridgeport; Peabody Museum, New Haven
**WEB SITE** *http://www.state.ct.us*

**DID YOU KNOW?** *The first library for children opened in Salisbury, in 1803, and the first permanent school for the deaf opened in Hartford in 1817. The first woman to receive an American patent was Mary Kies of South Killingly, in 1809, for a machine to weave straw and silk or thread.*

## DELAWARE (DE)

**First State, Diamond State**

**Population** (1998): 743,603 (45th)
**Area:** 2,396 sq. mi. (49th) (6,206 sq. km.)
**Flower:** Peach blossom     **Bird:** Blue hen chicken
**Tree:** American holly     **Song:** "Our Delaware"
**Entered Union:** December 7, 1787 (1st)
**Capital:** Dover
**Largest Cities** (with population): Wilmington, 69,490; Dover, 30,414; Newark, 27,870
**Important Products:** chemicals, food products, instruments, chickens
**Places to Visit:** Rehoboth Beach, Henry Francis du Pont Winterthur Museum near Wilmington
**WEB SITE** *http://www.state.de.us*

**DID YOU KNOW?** *Delaware was the first state to agree to the Constitution and thus became the first state of the United States. Delaware had the first log cabins in America.*

## FLORIDA (FL)

**Sunshine State**

**Population** (1998): 14,915,980 (4th)
**Area:** 59,928 sq. mi. (23rd) (155,213 sq. km.)
**Flower:** Orange blossom     **Bird:** Mockingbird
**Tree:** Sabal palmetto palm     **Song:** "Old Folks at Home"
**Entered Union:** March 3, 1845 (27th)
**Capital:** Tallahassee (population, 136,812)
**Largest Cities** (with population): Jacksonville, 679,792; Miami, 365,127; Tampa, 285,206; Saint Petersburg, 235,988
**Important Products:** electronic and transportation equipment, instruments, printing and publishing, food products, citrus fruits, vegetables, livestock, phosphates, fish
**Places to Visit:** Walt Disney World and Universal Studios, near Orlando; Sea World, Orlando; Busch Gardens, Tampa; Spaceport USA, at Kennedy Space Center, Cape Canaveral; Everglades National Park
**WEB SITE** *http://www.state.fl.us*

**DID YOU KNOW?** *St. Augustine, Florida, is the oldest permanent European settlement in the United States. Florida grows more citrus fruit than any other state. Also, Florida's warm, sunny climate attracts people from all over the country who are retired from their jobs. One out of every five people there is over the age of 65.*

# GEORGIA (GA)

*Empire State of the South, Peach State*

**Population** (1998): 7,642,207 (10th)
**Area:** 58,977 sq. mi. (24th) (152,750 sq. km.)
**Flower:** Cherokee rose    **Bird:** Brown thrasher
**Tree:** Live oak    **Song:** "Georgia on My Mind"
**Entered Union:** January 2, 1788 (4th)
**Capital and Largest City:** Atlanta (population, 401,907)
**Other Large Cities** (with population): Columbus, 182,828;
Savannah, 136,262; Macon, 113,352
**Important Products:** clothing and textiles, transportation equipment, food products, paper, chickens, peanuts, peaches, clay
**Places to Visit:** Stone Mountain Park, Six Flags Over Georgia, New Echota State Historic Site (eastern Cherokee capital) in Calhoun
**WEB SITE** *http://www.state.ga.us*

**DID YOU KNOW?** *Georgia has more woods than any other state. The first U.S. gold rush took place in Georgia. The first American Indian newspaper was published in Georgia by a Cherokee in 1828. The first radio station owned and operated by African-Americans started in Atlanta in 1949. Civil rights leader Martin Luther King, Jr. (1929-1968) and baseball player Jackie Robinson (1919-1972) were born in Georgia.*

# HAWAII (HI)

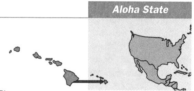
*Aloha State*

**Population** (1998): 1,193,001 (41st)
**Area:** 6,459 sq. mi. (47th) (16,728 sq. km.)
**Flower:** Yellow hibiscus    **Bird:** Hawaiian goose
**Tree:** Kukui    **Song:** "Hawaii Ponoi"
**Entered Union:** August 21, 1959 (50th)
**Capital and Largest City:** Honolulu (population, 423,475)
**Other Large Cities** (with population): Hilo, 37,808; Kailua, 36,818; Kaneohe, 35,448
**Important Products:** food products, pineapples, sugarcane, printing and publishing, fish, stone
**Places to Visit:** Hawaii Volcanoes National Park; Haleakala National Park, Maui; Iolani Palace, Honolulu; U.S.S. *Arizona* Memorial, Pearl Harbor
**WEB SITE** *http://www.state.hi.us*

**DID YOU KNOW?** *Hawaii is the only state made up entirely of islands, 122 of them. (People live on seven of the islands.) Hawaii's Mauna Loa is the biggest active volcano in the United States.*

# IDAHO (ID)

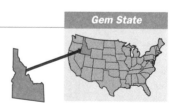
*Gem State*

**Population** (1998): 1,228,684 (40th)
**Area:** 83,574 sq. mi. (14th) (216,456 sq. km.)
**Flower:** Syringa    **Bird:** Mountain bluebird
**Tree:** White pine    **Song:** "Here We Have Idaho"
**Entered Union:** July 3, 1890 (43rd)
**Capital and Largest City:** Boise (population, 152,737)
**Other Large Cities** (with population): Pocatello, 51,344; Idaho Falls, 48,079
**Important Products:** potatoes, hay, wheat, cattle, milk, lumber and wood products, food products
**Places to Visit:** Sun Valley; Hells Canyon; Craters of the Moon, near Arco; Nez Percé National Historical Park, near Lewiston; ghost towns
**WEB SITE** *http://www2.state.id.us*

**DID YOU KNOW?** *The first hydroelectric power plant built by the federal government was the Minidoka Dam on the Snake River in Idaho; the first unit started in 1909. Two-thirds of all potatoes grown in the United States are grown in Idaho.*

# ILLINOIS (IL)

**Prairie State**

**Population** (1998): 12,045,326 (5th)
**Area:** 57,918 sq. mi. (25th) (150,007 sq. km.)
**Flower:** Native violet **Bird:** Cardinal
**Tree:** White oak **Song:** "Illinois"
**Entered Union:** December 3, 1818 (21st)
**Capital:** Springfield
**Largest Cities** (with population): Chicago, 2,721,547;
Rockford, 143,531; Peoria, 112,306; Aurora, 116,405; Springfield, 112,921
**Important Products:** industrial machinery, metals and metal products, printing and publishing, electronic equipment, food products, corn, soybeans, hogs
**Places to Visit:** Lincoln Park Zoo, Adler Planetarium, Field Museum of Natural History, and Museum of Science and Industry, all in Chicago; Abraham Lincoln's home and tomb, Springfield; New Salem Village
**WEB SITE** *http://www.state.il.us*

**DID YOU KNOW?** *Illinois has one of the world's busiest airports (O'Hare) and the tallest building in the U.S. (the Sears Tower in Chicago). The world's first skyscraper was built in Chicago, in 1885. Abraham Lincoln lived and worked in Illinois and is buried there.*

# INDIANA (IN)

**Hoosier State**

**Population** (1998): 5,899,195 (14th)
**Area:** 36,420 sq. mi. (38th) (94,328 sq. km.)
**Flower:** Peony **Bird:** Cardinal
**Tree:** Tulip poplar **Song:** "On the Banks of the Wabash, Far Away"
**Entered Union:** December 11, 1816 (19th)
**Capital and Largest City:** Indianapolis (population, 746,737)
**Other Large Cities** (with population): Fort Wayne, 184,783; Evansville, 123,456; Gary, 110,975; South Bend, 102,100
**Important Products:** transportation equipment, electronic equipment, industrial machinery, iron and steel, metal products, corn, soybeans, livestock, coal
**Places to Visit:** Children's Museum, Indianapolis; Conner Prairie Pioneer Settlement, Noblesville; Lincoln Boyhood Memorial, Lincoln City; Wyandotte Cave
**WEB SITE** *http://www.state.in.us*

**DID YOU KNOW?** *The first city to be lit with electricity was Wabash. Indiana's Lost River travels 22 miles underground. Indiana is the biggest basketball state and home of the famous Indianapolis 500 auto race.*

# IOWA (IA)

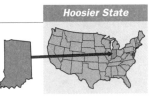

**Hawkeye State**

**Population** (1998): 2,862,447 (30th)
**Area:** 56,276 sq. mi. (26th) (145,754 sq. km.)
**Flower:** Wild rose **Bird:** Eastern goldfinch
**Tree:** Oak **Song:** "The Song of Iowa"
**Entered Union:** December 28, 1846 (29th)
**Capital and Largest City:** Des Moines (population, 193,422)
**Other Large Cities** (with population): Cedar Rapids, 113,482; Davenport, 97,010; Sioux City, 83,791
**Important Products:** corn, soybeans, hogs, cattle, industrial machinery, food products
**Places to Visit:** Effigy Mounds National Monument, Marquette; Herbert Hoover Birthplace, West Branch; Living History Farms, Des Moines; Adventureland; the Amana Colonies; Fort Dodge Historical Museum
**WEB SITE** *http://www.state.ia.us*

**DID YOU KNOW?** *The bridge built in 1856 between Davenport and Rock Island was the first bridge to span the Mississippi River. Buffalo Bill Cody (1846-1917), who was a frontiersman and the head of a famous Wild West show, was born in Iowa.*

## KANSAS (KS)

*Sunflower State*

Population (1998): 2,629,067 (32nd)
**Area:** 82,282 sq. mi. (15th) (213,110 sq. km.)
**Flower:** Native sunflower    **Bird:** Western meadowlark
**Tree:** Cottonwood    **Song:** "Home on the Range"
**Entered Union:** January 29, 1861 (34th)
**Capital:** Topeka
**Largest Cities** (with population): Wichita, 320,395;
Kansas City, 142,654; Overland Park, 131,053; Topeka, 119,658
**Important Products:** cattle, aircraft and other transportation equipment, industrial machinery, food products, wheat, corn, hay, oil, natural gas
**Places to Visit:** Dodge City; Fort Scott and Fort Larned national historical sites; Dwight D. Eisenhower Museum and Home, Abilene; Kansas Cosmosphere and Space Discovery Center, Hutchinson
**WEB SITE** *http://www.state.ks.us*

**DID YOU KNOW?** *Kansas is at the geographical center of the United States (excluding Alaska and Hawaii). It is one of the two biggest U.S. wheat-growing states (the other is North Dakota). The carousel with jumping horses was invented in Kansas in 1898.*

## KENTUCKY (KY)

*Bluegrass State*

Population (1998): 3,936,499 (25th)
**Area:** 40,411 sq. mi. (37th) (104,665 sq. km.)
**Flower:** Goldenrod    **Bird:** Cardinal
**Tree:** Tulip poplar    **Song:** "My Old Kentucky Home"
**Entered Union:** June 1, 1792 (15th)
**Capital:** Frankfort (population, 26,695)
**Largest Cities** (with population): Louisville, 260,689; Lexington 239,942
**Important Products:** coal, industrial machinery, electronic equipment, transportation equipment, metals, tobacco, cattle
**Places to Visit:** Mammoth Cave National Park; Lincoln Birthplace, Hodgenville; Cumberland Gap National Historical Park, Middlesboro
**WEB SITE** *http://www.state.ky.us*

**DID YOU KNOW?** *Kentucky has the longest group of caves in the world (Mammoth Caves). Abraham Lincoln was born in Kentucky. Kentucky is also the home of the Kentucky Derby, the most famous horse race in America.*

## LOUISIANA (LA)

*Pelican State*

Population (1998): 4,368,967 (22nd)
**Area:** 49,651 sq. mi. (31st) (128,596 sq. km.)
**Flower:** Magnolia    **Bird:** Eastern brown pelican
**Tree:** Cypress    **Songs:** "Give Me Louisiana";
     "You Are My Sunshine"
**Entered Union:** April 30, 1812 (18th)
**Capital:** Baton Rouge
**Largest Cities** (with population): New Orleans, 476,625; Baton Rouge, 215,882; Shreveport, 191,558
**Important Products:** natural gas, oil, chemicals, transportation equipment, paper, food products, cotton, fish
**Places to Visit:** French quarter in New Orleans; Jean Lafitte National Historical Park
**WEB SITE** *http://www.state.la.us*

**DID YOU KNOW?** *The busiest port in the United States is located in Louisiana. It's the second-biggest mining state (after Alaska). Louisiana is the home of New Orleans, known for its jazz and the colorful Mardi Gras festival.*

# MAINE (ME)

Pine Tree State

**Population** (1998): 1,244,250 (39th)
**Area:** 33,741 sq. mi. (39th) (87,389 sq. km.)
**Flower:** White pine cone and tassel    **Bird:** Chickadee
**Tree:** Eastern white pine                **Song:** "State of Maine
**Entered Union:** March 15, 1820 (23rd)        Song"
**Capital:** Augusta (population, 20,441)
**Largest Cities** (with population): Portland, 63,123; Lewiston, 36,830; Bangor, 31,649
**Important Products:** paper, transportation equipment, wood and wood products, electronic equipment, footwear, clothing, potatoes, milk, eggs, fish, and seafood
**Places to Visit:** Acadia National Park, Bar Harbor; Booth Bay Railway Museum; Portland Headlight Lighthouse, near Portland
**WEB SITE** *http://www.state.me.us*

**DID YOU KNOW?** *Maine is known for its lobsters, rocky seacoast, fishing villages, and the highest tides in the United States. Mount Katahdin, the highest spot in Maine (5,267 feet), is the first place in the United States that the sun hits in the morning.*

# MARYLAND (MD)

Old Line State, Free State

**Population** (1998): 5,134,808 (19th)
**Area:** 12,297 sq. mi. (42nd) (31,849 sq. km.)
**Flower:** Black-eyed susan    **Bird:** Baltimore oriole
**Tree:** White oak            **Song:** "Maryland, My Maryland"
**Entered Union:** April 28, 1788 (7th)
**Capital:** Annapolis (population, 33,234)
**Largest Cities** (with population): Baltimore, 675,401;
Frederick, 46,227; Rockville, 46,019; Gaithersburg, 45,361
**Important Products:** instruments, printing and publishing, food products, transportation equipment, electronic equipment, chickens, milk, corn, stone
**Places to Visit:** Antietam National Battlefield; Fort McHenry National Monument, in Baltimore Harbor; U.S. Naval Academy in Annapolis
**WEB SITE** *http://www.state.md.us*

**DID YOU KNOW?** *Maryland is the narrowest state—near the town of Hancock, Maryland is only about one mile wide. The American flag on Fort McHenry during the War of 1812 inspired Francis Scott Key to write "The Star-Spangled Banner," the national anthem.*

# MASSACHUSETTS (MA)

Bay State, Old Colony

**Population** (1998): 6,147,132 (13th)
**Area:** 9,241 sq. mi. (45th) (23,934 sq. km.)
**Flower:** Mayflower    **Bird:** Chickadee
**Tree:** American elm    **Song:** "All Hail to Massachusetts"
**Entered Union:** February 6, 1788 (6th)
**Capital and Largest City:** Boston (population: 558,394)
**Other Large Cities** (with population): Worcester, 166,350;
Springfield, 149,948; Lowell, 100,973
**Important Products:** industrial machinery, electronic equipment, instruments, printing and publishing, metal products, clothing and textiles, fish, flowers and shrubs, cranberries
**Places to Visit:** Plymouth Rock, historical sites in Boston, and Minute Man National Historical Park; Children's Museum, Boston; Basketball Hall of Fame, Springfield; Old Sturbridge Village; Martha's Vineyard; Cape Cod
**WEB SITE** *http://www.state.ma.us*

**DID YOU KNOW?** *The Pilgrims settled in Massachusetts and celebrated the first Thanksgiving. Massachusetts had America's first printing press (1639) and first college (Harvard, 1636). The American Revolution began in Massachusetts.*

## MICHIGAN (MI)

*Great Lakes State, Wolverine State*

**Population** (1998): 9,817,242 (8th)
**Area:** 96,705 sq. mi. (11th) (250,465 sq. km.)
**Flower:** Apple blossom      **Bird:** Robin
**Tree:** White pine      **Song:** "Michigan, My Michigan"
**Entered Union:** January 26, 1837 (26th)
**Capital:** Lansing (population, 125,736)
**Largest Cities** (with population): Detroit, 1,000,272;
Grand Rapids, 188,242; Warren, 138,078; Flint, 134,881
**Important Products:** automobiles, industrial machinery, metal products, printing and publishing, plastic products, chemicals, food products, milk, corn, natural gas, iron ore
**Places to Visit:** Greenfield Village and Henry Ford Museum, Dearborn; Detroit's "Art Center"; Isle Royal National Park; Pictured Rocks and Sleeping Bear Dunes national lakeshores; Mackinac Island
**WEB SITE** *http://www.migov.state.mi.us*

**DID YOU KNOW?** *Michigan is known for manufacturing automobiles. Lake Michigan is the largest lake entirely in the United States.*

## MINNESOTA (MN)

*North Star State, Gopher State*

**Population** (1998): 4,725,419 (20th)
**Area:** 86,943 sq. mi. (12th) (225,182 sq. km.)
**Flower:** Pink and white lady's-slipper  **Bird:** Common loon
**Tree:** Red pine      **Song:** "Hail! Minnesota"
**Entered Union:** May 11, 1858 (32nd)
**Capital:** St. Paul
**Largest Cities** (with population): Minneapolis, 358,785; St. Paul, 259,606
**Important Products:** industrial machinery, metal products, printing and publishing, food products, instruments, milk, hogs, cattle, corn, soybeans, iron ore
**Places to Visit:** Voyageurs National Park; Grand Portage National Monument; Minnesota Zoo; Fort Snelling; U.S. Hockey Hall of Fame, Eveleth
**WEB SITE** *http://www.state.mn.us*

**DID YOU KNOW?** *Minnesota is sometimes called the Land of 10,000 Lakes—it actually has more than 15,000 lakes. Minnesota is the second coldest state (Alaska is the coldest). The Mall of America, in Bloomington, is the largest shopping mall in the United States; it has space for 12,750 cars.*

## MISSISSIPPI (MS)

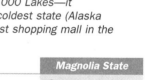
*Magnolia State*

**Population** (1998): 2,752,092 (31st)
**Area:** 48,286 sq. mi. (32nd) (125,061 sq. km.)
**Flower:** Magnolia      **Bird:** Mockingbird
**Tree:** Magnolia      **Song:** "Go, Mississippi!"
**Entered Union:** December 10, 1817 (20th)
**Capital and Largest City:** Jackson (population, 192,923)
**Other Large Cities** (with population): Biloxi, 48,414; Greenville, 42,933
**Important Products:** transportation equipment, clothing and textiles, furniture, electronic equipment, wood and wood products, cotton, chickens, cattle, oil
**Places to Visit:** Vicksburg National Military Park; Natchez Trace Parkway; Old Capitol, Jackson; Old Spanish Fort and Museum, Pascagoula
**WEB SITE** *http://www.state.ms.us*

**DID YOU KNOW?** *Mississippi was the first state to celebrate Memorial Day (originally called Decoration Day) as a holiday, in 1866. Mississippi opened the first state-run college for women in Columbus in 1884. Jefferson Davis, president of the Confederate States of America, was born in Mississippi.*

# MISSOURI (MO)

*Show Me State*

**Population** (1998): 5,438,559 (16th)
**Area:** 69,709 sq. mi. (21st) (180,546 sq. km.)
**Flower:** Hawthorn          **Bird:** Bluebird
**Tree:** Dogwood          **Song:** "Missouri Waltz"
**Entered Union:** August 10, 1821 (24th)
**Capital:** Jefferson City (population, 36,143)
**Largest Cities** (with population): Kansas City, 441,259; St. Louis, 351,565; Springfield, 143,407; Independence, 110,303
**Important Products:** transportation equipment, metal products, printing and publishing, food products, cattle, hogs, milk, soybeans, corn, hay, lead
**Places to Visit:** Gateway Arch, St. Louis; Mark Twain Home and Museum, Hannibal; Harry S. Truman Museum, Independence; George Washington Carver Birthplace, Diamond
**WEB SITE** *http://www.state.mo.us*

**DID YOU KNOW?** *Missouri is a major center for shipping and railroads. President Harry S. Truman, agricultural scientist George Washington Carver, and poet Langston Hughes were born in Missouri. It has been said that the ice cream cone was first sold at a World's Fair in St. Louis, in 1904. Gateway Arch, in St. Louis, is the tallest monument (630 feet high) in the United States.*

# MONTANA (MT)

*Treasure State*

**Population** (1998): 880,453 (44th)
**Area:** 147,046 sq. mi. (4th) (380,850 sq. km.)
**Flower:** Bitterroot          **Bird:** Western meadowlark
**Tree:** Ponderosa pine          **Song:** "Montana"
**Entered Union:** November 8, 1889 (41st)
**Capital:** Helena (population, 27,982)
**Largest Cities** (with population): Billings, 91,195; Great Falls, 57,758; Missoula, 51,204; Butte, 34,051
**Important Products:** cattle, coal, oil, gold, wheat, hay, wood and wood products
**Places to Visit:** Yellowstone and Glacier national parks; Little Bighorn Battlefield National Monument, in Crow Agency; Museum of the Rockies, Bozeman
**WEB SITE** *http://www.mt.gov*

**DID YOU KNOW?** *Montana is the fourth-biggest state, after Alaska, Texas, and California. The most famous Indian battle in history took place in Montana, at Little Bighorn in 1876.*

# NEBRASKA (NE)

*Cornhusker State*

**Population** (1998): 1,662,719 (38th)
**Area:** 77,358 sq. mi. (16th) (200,358 sq. km.)
**Flower:** Goldenrod          **Bird:** Western meadowlark
**Tree:** Cottonwood          **Song:** "Beautiful Nebraska"
**Entered Union:** March 1, 1867 (37th)
**Capital:** Lincoln
**Largest Cities** (with population): Omaha, 364,253; Lincoln, 209,192
**Important Products:** cattle, hogs, milk, corn, soybeans, hay, wheat, sorghum, food products, industrial machinery
**Places to Visit:** Oregon Trail landmarks; Stuhr Museum of the Prairie Pioneer, Grand Island; Agate Fossil Beds National Monument; Boys Town, near Omaha
**WEB SITE** *http://www.state.ne.us*

**DID YOU KNOW?** *Nebraska is not only a cattle state; it is the biggest meat-packing center in the world. It is also a farm state. Nebraska is the only state whose nickname comes from a college football team—the popular University of Nebraska Cornhuskers.*

# NEVADA (NV)

*Sagebrush State, Battle Born State, Silver State*

**Population** (1998): 1,746,898 (36th)
**Area:** 110,567 sq. mi. (7th) (286,368 sq. km.)
**Flower:** Sagebrush  **Bird:** Mountain bluebird
**Trees:** Single-leaf piñon, bristlecone pine  **Song:** "Home Means
**Entered Union:** October 31, 1864 (36th)  Nevada"
**Capital:** Carson City (population, 47,237)
**Largest Cities** (with population): Las Vegas, 376,906;
Reno, 155,499; Henderson, 122,339
**Important Products:** gold, silver, cattle, hay, food products, plastics, chemicals
**Places to Visit:** Great Basin National Park; Nevada State Museum, Carson City; Lake Mead
National Recreation Area; ghost towns
**WEB SITE** *http://www.state.nv.us*

**DID YOU KNOW?** *It usually rains less in Nevada than in any other state. Between 1980 and 1990 the population of Nevada increased by more than one half, making it the fastest-growing state. It also has the most wild horses.*

# NEW HAMPSHIRE (NH)

*Granite State*

**Population** (1998): 1,185,048 (42nd)
**Area:** 9,283 sq. mi. (44th) (24,043 sq. km.)
**Flower:** Purple lilac  **Bird:** Purple finch
**Tree:** White birch  **Song:** "Old New Hampshire"
**Entered Union:** June 21, 1788 (9th)
**Capital:** Concord
**Largest Cities** (with population): Manchester, 100,967; Nashua, 81,094; Concord, 37,021
**Important Products:** industrial machinery, electric and electronic equipment, metal products,
plastic products, dairy products, maple syrup and maple sugar
**Places to Visit:** White Mountain National Forest; Mount Washington; Fort at Number 4 Living
History Museum, Charlestown; Old Man in the Mountain, Franconia Notch; Canterbury
Shaker Village
**WEB SITE** *http://www.state.nh.us*

**DID YOU KNOW?** *Mount Washington is the highest mountain in the northeast. Its peak is said to be the windiest spot on Earth. The first town-supported, free public library in the United States opened in New Hampshire in 1833.*

# NEW JERSEY (NJ)

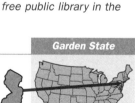

*Garden State*

**Population** (1998): 8,115,011 (9th)
**Area:** 8,215 sq. mi. (46th) (21,277 sq. km.)
**Flower:** Purple violet  **Bird:** Eastern goldfinch
**Tree:** Red oak  **Song:** none
**Entered Union:** December 18, 1787 (3rd)
**Capital:** Trenton (population, 85,437)
**Largest Cities** (with population): Newark, 268,510; Jersey City, 229,039;
Paterson, 150,270; Elizabeth, 110,149
**Important Products:** chemicals, pharmaceuticals/drugs, electronic equipment, nursery and
greenhouse products, food products, tomatoes, blueberries and peaches
**Places to Visit:** ocean beaches; Edison National Historical Site, West Orange; Liberty State
Park; Pine Barrens wilderness area; Great Adventure amusement park
**WEB SITE** *http://www.state.nj.us*

**DID YOU KNOW?** *The electric light bulb was invented in New Jersey by Thomas Edison in 1879. The first ferryboat just for cars was built in New Jersey and placed in service in 1926. New Jersey manufactures more flags than any other state.*

# NEW MEXICO (NM)

*Land of Enchantment*

**Population** (1998): 1,736,931 (37th)
**Area:** 121,598 sq. mi. (5th) (314,939 sq. km.)
**Flower:** Yucca          **Bird:** Roadrunner
**Tree:** Piñon          **Song:** "O, Fair New Mexico"
**Entered Union:** January 6, 1912 (47th)
**Capital:** Santa Fe
**Largest Cities** (with population): Albuquerque, 419,681; Las Cruces, 74,779; Santa Fe, 66,522
**Important Products:** electronic equipment, foods, machinery, clothing, lumber, transportation equipment, hay, onions, chiles
**Places to Visit:** Carlsbad Caverns National Park; Palace of the Governors and Mission of San Miguel, Santa Fe; Chaco Canyon National Monument; cliff dwellings
**WEB SITE** *http://www.state.nm.us*

**DID YOU KNOW?** *The oldest capital city in the United States is Santa Fe, New Mexico. Pueblo Indians had an advanced civilization in New Mexico a thousand years ago. The deepest cave in the United States is in New Mexico's Carlsbad Caverns. The first atom bomb was exploded in New Mexico, in a test on July 16, 1945.*

# NEW YORK (NY)

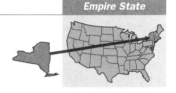

*Empire State*

**Population** (1998): 18,175,301 (3rd)
**Area:** 53,989 sq. mi. (27th) (139,831 sq. km.)
**Flower:** Rose          **Bird:** Bluebird
**Tree:** Sugar maple          **Song:** "I Love New York"
**Entered Union:** July 26, 1788 (11th)
**Capital:** Albany (population, 103,564)
**Largest Cities** (with population): New York, 7,380,906; Buffalo, 310,548; Rochester, 221,594; Yonkers, 190,316
**Important Products:** books and magazines, automobile and airplane parts, toys and sporting goods, electronic equipment, machinery, clothing and textiles, metal products, milk, cattle, hay, apples
**Places to Visit:** *In New York City, museums, Empire State Building, United Nations, Bronx Zoo, Statue of Liberty and Ellis Island; Niagara Falls; National Baseball Hall of Fame, Cooperstown; Fort Ticonderoga; Franklin D. Roosevelt National Historical Site, Hyde Park*
**WEB SITE** *http://www.state.ny.us*

**DID YOU KNOW?** *New York City is the largest city in the United States and was the nation's first capital. The first pizza restaurant in the United States opened in New York City in 1895.*

# NORTH CAROLINA (NC)

*Tar Heel State, Old North State*

**Population** (1998): 7,546,493 (11th)
**Area:** 52,672 sq. mi. (29th) (136,420 sq. km.)
**Flower:** Dogwood          **Bird:** Cardinal
**Tree:** Pine          **Song:** "The Old North State"
**Entered Union:** November 21, 1789 (12th)
**Capital:** Raleigh
**Largest Cities** (with population): Charlotte, 441,297; Raleigh, 243,835; Greensboro, 195,426; Winston-Salem, 153,541; Durham, 149,799
**Important Products:** clothing and textiles, tobacco and tobacco products, industrial machinery, electronic equipment, furniture, cotton, soybeans, peanuts
**Places to Visit:** Great Smoky Mountains National Park; Cape Hatteras National Seashore; Wright Brothers National Memorial, at Kitty Hawk
**WEB SITE** *http://www.state.nc.us*

**DID YOU KNOW?** *The Wright Brothers took the first airplane ride in history, in North Carolina. The first U.S. school of forestry was opened in North Carolina.*

# NORTH DAKOTA (ND)

*Peace Garden State*

**Population** (1998): 638,244 (47th)
**Area:** 70,704 sq. mi. (18th) (183,123 sq. km.)
**Flower:** Wild prairie rose     **Bird:** Western meadowlark
**Tree:** American elm     **Song:** "North Dakota Hymn"
**Entered Union:** November 2, 1889 (39th)
**Capital:** Bismarck
**Largest Cities** (with population): Fargo, 83,778; Grand Forks, 50,675; Bismarck, 53,514; Minot, 35,926
**Important Products:** wheat, barley, hay, sunflowers, sugar beets, cattle, sand and gravel, food products, farm equipment, high-tech electronics
**Places to Visit:** Theodore Roosevelt National Park; Bonanzaville, near Fargo; Dakota Dinosaur Museum, Dickinson; International Peace Garden
**WEB SITE** *http://www.ndtourism.com*

**DID YOU KNOW?** *North Dakota is one of the two biggest wheat-growing states in the United States (the other is Kansas). Theodore Roosevelt was a rancher here before he became president.*

# OHIO (OH)

*Buckeye State*

**Population** (1998): 11,209,493 (7th)
**Area:** 44,828 sq. mi. (34th) (116,103 sq. km.)
**Flower:** Scarlet carnation     **Bird:** Cardinal
**Tree:** Buckeye     **Song:** "Beautiful Ohio"
**Entered Union:** March 1, 1803 (17th)
**Capital and Largest City:** Columbus (population, 657,053)
**Other Large Cities** (with population): Cleveland, 498,246; Cincinnati, 345,818; Toledo, 317,606; Akron, 216,882; Dayton, 172,947
**Important Products:** metal and metal products, transportation equipment, industrial machinery, rubber and plastic products, electronic equipment, printing and publishing, chemicals, food products, corn, soybeans, livestock, milk
**Places to Visit:** Mound City Group National Monuments, Indian burial mounds; Neil Armstrong Air and Space Museum; Cedar Point and King's Island amusement parks
**WEB SITE** *http://www.state.oh.us*

**DID YOU KNOW?** *Seven American presidents were born in Ohio (Garfield, Grant, Harding, B. Harrison, Hayes, McKinley, Taft). Ohio was the home of the first professional baseball team, the Cincinnati Red Stockings, and the birthplace of the hot dog.*

# OKLAHOMA (OK)

*Sooner State*

**Population** (1998): 3,346,713 (27th)
**Area:** 69,903 sq. mi. (20th) (181,049 sq. km.)
**Flower:** Mistletoe     **Bird:** Scissor-tailed flycatcher
**Tree:** Redbud     **Song:** "Oklahoma!"
**Entered Union:** November 16, 1907 (46th)
**Capital and Largest City:** Oklahoma City (population, 469,852)
**Other Large Cities** (with population): Tulsa, 378,491; Norman, 90,228; Lawton, 82,582
**Important Products:** natural gas, oil, cattle, nonelectrical machinery, transportation equipment, metal products, wheat, hay
**Places to Visit:** Indian City U.S.A., near Anadarko; Fort Gibson Stockade; National Cowboy Hall of Fame; White Water Bay and Frontier City theme parks; Cherokee Heritage Center
**WEB SITE** *http://www.oklaosf.state.ok.us*

**DID YOU KNOW?** *The American Indian nations called The Five Civilized Tribes (Cherokee, Chickasaw, Choctaw, Creek, and Seminole) settled in Oklahoma. Today, more Native Americans live in Oklahoma than in any other state.*

# OREGON (OR)

**Beaver State**

**Population** (1998): 3,281,974 (28th)
**Area:** 97,132 sq. mi. (10th) (251,572 sq. km.)
**Flower:** Oregon grape    **Bird:** Western meadowlark
**Tree:** Douglas fir    **Song:** "Oregon, My Oregon"
**Entered Union:** February 14, 1859 (33rd)
**Capital:** Salem
**Largest Cities** (with population): Portland, 480,824; Eugene, 123,718; Salem, 122,566
**Important Products:** wood and wood products, industrial machinery, food products, paper, cattle, hay, vegetables, Christmas trees
**Places to Visit:** Crater Lake National Park; Oregon Caves National Monument; Astoria Column and Fort Clatsop National Memorial, Astoria
**WEB SITE** *http://www.state.or.us*

**DID YOU KNOW?** *Oregon produces more timber than any other state. Oregon's Hells Canyon, 7,900 feet deep at its maximum, is one of the deepest canyons in the world, and Crater Lake, which gets as deep as 1,932 feet, is the deepest lake in the United States.*

# PENNSYLVANIA (PA)

**Keystone State**

**Population** (1998): 12,001,451 (6th)
**Area:** 46,058 sq. mi. (33rd) (119,290 sq. km.)
**Flower:** Mountain laurel    **Bird:** Ruffled grouse
**Tree:** Hemlock    **Song:** "Pennsylvania"
**Entered Union:** December 12, 1787 (2nd)
**Capital:** Harrisburg (population, 50,886)
**Largest Cities** (with population): Philadelphia, 1,478,002; Pittsburgh, 350,363; Erie, 105,270; Allentown, 102,211
**Important Products:** iron and steel, coal, industrial machinery, printing and publishing, food products, electronic equipment, transportation equipment, stone, clay and glass products
**Places to Visit:** Independence Hall and other historic sites in Philadelphia; Franklin Institute Science Museum, Philadelphia; Valley Forge; Gettysburg; Hershey; Pennsylvania Dutch country, Lancaster County
**WEB SITE** *http://www.state.pa.us*

**DID YOU KNOW?** *Pennsylvania is known for the Liberty Bell in Philadelphia, which first rang after the signing of the Declaration of Independence. Philadelphia was also the U.S. capital for 10 years. The first hospital in the United States was built there.*

# RHODE ISLAND (RI)

**Little Rhody, Ocean State**

**Population** (1998): 988,480 (43rd)
**Area:** 1,231 sq. mi. (50th) (3,188 sq. km.)
**Flower:** Violet    **Bird:** Rhode Island red
**Tree:** Red maple    **Song:** "Rhode Island"
**Entered Union:** May 29, 1790 (13th)
**Capital and Largest City:** Providence (population, 152,558)
**Other Large Cities** (with population): Warwick, 84,514; Cranston, 74,324; Pawtucket, 69,068
**Important Products:** costume jewelry, toys, textiles, machinery, electronic equipment, fish
**Places to Visit:** Block Island; mansions, old buildings, and harbor in Newport; International Tennis Hall of Fame, Newport
**WEB SITE** *http://www.state.ri.us*

**DID YOU KNOW?** *Rhode Island is the smallest state. The bluffs and islands of Rhode Island attract many tourists who like fishing and swimming. The oldest synagogue in the United States (Touro Synagogue, 1763) is in Newport.*

## SOUTH CAROLINA (SC)

*Palmetto State*

**Population** (1998): 3,835,962 (26th)
**Area:** 31,189 sq. mi. (40th) (80,779 sq. km.)
**Flower:** Yellow jessamine    **Bird:** Carolina wren
**Tree:** Palmetto    **Song:** "Carolina"
**Entered Union:** May 23, 1788 (8th)
**Capital and Largest City:** Columbia (population, 112,773)
**Other Large Cities** (with population): Charleston, 71,052; North Charleston, 59,923;
Greenville, 57,064
**Important Products:** clothing and textiles, chemicals, industrial machinery, metal products,
livestock, tobacco, portland cement
**Places to Visit:** Grand Strand and Hilton Head Island beaches; Revolutionary War
battlefields; historic sites in Charleston; Fort Sumter; Historic Camden
**WEB SITE** *http://www.state.sc.us*

**DID YOU KNOW?** *More battles of the American Revolution took place in South Carolina
than in any other state. The first shots of the Civil War were fired in South Carolina.
Charleston Museum, opened in 1773, is the oldest U.S. museum.*

## SOUTH DAKOTA (SD)

*Mt. Rushmore State,
Coyote State*

**Population** (1998): 738,171 (46th)
**Area:** 77,121 sq. mi. (17th) (199,743 sq. km.)
**Flower:** Pasqueflower    **Bird:** Ring-necked pheasant
**Tree:** Black Hills spruce    **Song:** "Hail, South Dakota"
**Entered Union:** November 2, 1889 (40th)
**Capital:** Pierre (population, 13,422)
**Largest Cities** (with population): Sioux Falls, 113,223; Rapid City, 57,642
**Important Products:** food and food products, machinery, electric and electronic equipment,
corn, soybeans
**Places to Visit:** Mount Rushmore National Memorial; Crazy Horse Memorial; Jewel Cave;
Badlands and Wind Caves national parks; Wounded Knee battlefield; Homestake Gold Mine
**WEB SITE** *http://www.state.sd.us*

**DID YOU KNOW?** *South Dakota is best known for the faces of presidents carved on Mount
Rushmore (Presidents Washington, Jefferson, Lincoln, and T. Roosevelt). Famous South
Dakotans include Crazy Horse, Sitting Bull, and Wild Bill Hickok.*

## TENNESSEE (TN)

*Volunteer State*

**Population** (1998): 5,430,621 (17th)
**Area:** 42,146 sq. mi. (36th) (109,158 sq. km.)
**Flower:** Iris    **Bird:** Mockingbird
**Tree:** Tulip poplar    **Song:** "The Tennessee Waltz"
**Entered Union:** June 1, 1796 (16th)
**Capital:** Nashville
**Largest Cities** (with population): Memphis, 596,725; Nashville, 511,263;
Knoxville, 167,535; Chattanooga, 150,425
**Important Products:** chemicals, machinery, vehicles, food products, metal products,
publishing, electronic equipment, paper products, rubber and plastic products, tobacco
**Places to Visit:** Great Smoky Mountains National Park; the Hermitage, home of President
Andrew Jackson, near Nashville; Civil War battle sites; Grand Old Opry and Opryland, USA
theme park, Nashville; Graceland, home of Elvis Presley, in Memphis
**WEB SITE** *http://www.state.tn.us*

**DID YOU KNOW?** *Tennessee can claim Nashville as country music capital of the world.
Frontiersman Davy Crockett was born in Tennessee. Elvis Presley and President Andrew
Jackson are among the famous people who lived in Tennessee.*

## TEXAS (TX)

Lone Star State

**Population** (1998): 19,759,614 (2nd)
**Area:** 267,277 sq. mi. (2nd) (692,247 sq. km.)
**Flower:** Bluebonnet          **Bird:** Mockingbird
**Tree:** Pecan                 **Song:** "Texas, Our Texas"
**Entered Union:** December 29, 1845 (28th)
**Capital:** Austin
**Largest Cities** (with population): Houston, 1,744,058; Dallas, 1,053,292; San Antonio, 1,067,816; El Paso, 599,865; Austin, 541,278; Fort Worth, 479,716
**Important Products:** oil, natural gas, cattle, milk, eggs, transportation equipment, chemicals, clothing, industrial machinery, electrical and electronic equipment, cotton, grains
**Places to Visit:** Guadalupe and Big Bend national parks; the Alamo, in San Antonio; Lyndon Johnson National Historic Site, near Johnson City; Six Flags Over Texas amusement park, Arlington
**WEB SITE** *http://www.state.tx.us*

**DID YOU KNOW?** *Texas is the largest of the contiguous 48 states (the states that border each other) and is second in size only to Alaska. Texas has more oil and natural gas than any other state and the most farmland. It is the only state with five major ports, and has the country's busiest airport (Dallas-Fort Worth).*

## UTAH (UT)

Beehive State

**Population** (1998): 2,009,758 (34th)
**Area:** 84,904 sq. mi. (13th) (219,902 sq. km.)
**Flower:** Sego lily           **Bird:** Seagull
**Tree:** Blue spruce           **Song:** "Utah, We Love Thee"
**Entered Union:** January 4, 1896 (45th)
**Capital and Largest City:** Salt Lake City (population, 172,575)
**Other Large Cities** (with population): Provo, 99,606; West Valley City, 99,136
**Important Products:** transportation equipment, metal products, medical instruments, electronic parts, food products, steel, copper, cattle, corn, hay
**Places to Visit:** Arches, Canyonlands, Bryce Canyon, Zion, and Capitol Reef national parks; Great Salt Lake; Temple Square (Mormon Church headquarters) in Salt Lake City, Indian cliff dwellings
**WEB SITE** *http://www.state.ut.us*

**DID YOU KNOW?** *Utah's Great Salt Lake, which contains 6 billion tons of salt, is the largest lake in the United States outside of the Great Lakes. Rainbow Bridge in Utah is the largest natural arch or rock bridge in the world; it is 200 feet high and 270 feet wide.*

## VERMONT (VT)

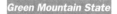

Green Mountain State

**Population** (1998): 590,883 (49th)
**Area:** 9,615 sq. mi. (43rd) (24,903 sq. km.)
**Flower:** Red clover          **Bird:** Hermit thrush
**Tree:** Sugar maple           **Song:** "Hail, Vermont!"
**Entered Union:** March 4, 1791 (14th)
**Capital:** Montpelier (population, 7,856)
**Largest Cities** (with population): Burlington, 39,004; Rutland, 17,605
**Important Products:** machine tools, furniture, scales, books, computer parts, foods, dairy products, apples, maple syrup
**Places to Visit:** Green Mountain National Forest; Shelburne Museum
**WEB SITE** *http://www.state.vt.us*

**DID YOU KNOW?** *Vermont is famous for its granite, marble, scenery, and maple syrup. Vermont passed the first constitution (1777) to prohibit slavery and to allow all men to vote. The first ski tow in the United States was established in Vermont in 1934.*

# VIRGINIA (VA)

*Old Dominion*

**Population** (1998): 6,791,345 (12th)
**Area:** 42,326 sq. mi. (35th) (109,391 sq. km.)
**Flower:** Dogwood    **Bird:** Cardinal
**Tree:** Dogwood    **Song:** None
**Entered Union:** June 25, 1788 (10th)
**Capital:** Richmond
**Largest Cities** (with population): Virginia Beach, 430,385; Norfolk, 233,430; Richmond, 198,267; Chesapeake, 192,342; Newport News, 176,122
**Important Products:** transportation equipment, textiles, chemicals, printing, machinery, electronic equipment, food products, coal, livestock, tobacco, wood products, furniture
**Places to Visit:** Colonial Williamsburg; Busch Gardens, Williamsburg; Arlington National Cemetery; Mount Vernon (George Washington's home); Monticello (Thomas Jefferson's home); Shenandoah National Park
**WEB SITE** *http://www.state.va.us*

**DID YOU KNOW?** *Virginia was the birthplace of eight presidents (Presidents W. H. Harrison, Jefferson, Madison, Monroe, Taylor, Tyler, Washington, Wilson), more than any other state. The first permanent English settlement in the New World was in Virginia.*

# WASHINGTON (WA)

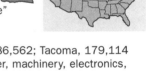

*Evergreen State*

**Population** (1998): 5,689,263 (15th)
**Area:** 70,637 sq. mi. (19th) (182,950 sq. km.)
**Flower:** Western rhododendron    **Bird:** Willow goldfinch
**Tree:** Western hemlock    **Song:** "Washington, My Home"
**Entered Union:** November 11, 1889 (42nd)
**Capital:** Olympia (population, 39,006)
**Largest Cities** (with population): Seattle, 524,704; Spokane, 186,562; Tacoma, 179,114
**Important Products:** aircraft, lumber and plywood, pulp and paper, machinery, electronics, computer software, aluminum, processed fruits and vegetables
**Places to Visit:** Mount Rainier, Olympic, and North Cascades national parks; Mount St. Helens; Seattle Center, with Space Needle and monorail
**WEB SITE** *http://www.state.wa.us*

**DID YOU KNOW?** *Grand Coulee Dam, on the Columbia River, is the world's largest concrete dam. Mount Rainier is the tallest volcano in the contiguous 48 states (those that border each other). Washington is known for its apples, timber, and fishing fleets.*

# WEST VIRGINIA (WV)

*Mountain State*

**Population** (1998): 1,811,156 (35th)
**Area:** 24,231 sq. mi. (41st) (62,759 sq. km.)
**Flower:** Big rhododendron    **Bird:** Cardinal
**Tree:** Sugar maple    **Songs:** "The West Virginia Hills"; "This Is My West Virginia"; "West Virginia, My Home Sweet Home"
**Entered Union:** June 20, 1863 (35th)
**Capital and Largest City:** Charleston (population, 56,098)
**Other Large Cities** (with population): Huntington, 53,941; Wheeling, 33,311
**Important Products:** coal, natural gas, fabricated metal products, chemicals, automobile parts, aluminum, steel, machinery, cattle, hay, apples, peaches, tobacco
**Places to Visit:** Harpers Ferry National Historic Park; Grave Creek Mound, Moundsville; Monongahela National Forest
**WEB SITE** *http://www.state.wv.us*

**DID YOU KNOW?** *West Virginia's mountain scenery and mineral springs attract many tourists. The state is one of the biggest coal states. West Virginia was part of Virginia until West Virginians decided to break away, in 1861.*

# WISCONSIN (WI)

*Badger State*

**Population** (1998): 5,223,500 (18th)
**Area:** 65,499 sq. mi. (22nd) (169,642 sq. km.)
**Flower:** Wood violet     **Bird:** Robin
**Tree:** Sugar maple     **Song:** "On, Wisconsin!"
**Entered Union:** May 29, 1848 (30th)
**Capital:** Madison
**Largest Cities** (with population): Milwaukee, 590,503; Madison, 197,630; Green Bay, 102,076; Racine, 82,572; Kenosha, 86,888
**Important Products:** paper products, printing, milk, butter, cheese, foods, food products, motor vehicles and equipment, medical instruments and supplies, plastics, corn, hay, vegetables
**Places to Visit:** Dells of the Wisconsin; Cave of the Mounds, near Blue Mounds; Milwaukee Public Museum; Circus World Museum, Baraboo; National Railroad Museum, Green Bay
**WEB SITE** http://www.state.wi.us

**DID YOU KNOW?** *Wisconsin is known as America's Dairyland; more recently it has also become a major manufacturing state. The first kindergarten in America was opened in Wisconsin in 1865.*

# WYOMING (WY)

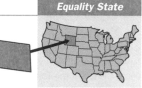

*Equality State*

**Population** (1998): 480,907 (50th)
**Area:** 97,818 sq. mi. (9th) (253,349 sq. km.)
**Flower:** Indian paintbrush     **Bird:** Meadowlark
**Tree:** Plains cottonwood     **Song:** "Wyoming"
**Entered Union:** July 10, 1890 (44th)
**Capital and Largest City:** Cheyenne (population, 53,729)
**Other Large Cities** (with population): Casper, 48,800; Laramie, 26,583
**Important Products:** oil, natural gas, petroleum (oil) products, cattle, wheat, beans
**Places to Visit:** Yellowstone and Grand Teton national parks; Fort Laramie; Buffalo Bill Historical Center, Cody
**WEB SITE** http://www.state.wy.us

**DID YOU KNOW?** *Wyoming is the home of the first U.S. national park (Yellowstone). Established in 1872, Yellowstone has 10,000 geysers, including the world's tallest active geyser (Steamboat Geyser).*

# PUERTO RICO (PR)

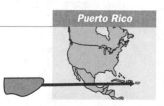

*Puerto Rico*

**History:** Christopher Columbus landed in Puerto Rico in 1493. Puerto Rico was a Spanish colony for centuries, then fell to the United States in 1898 after the Spanish-American War. In 1952, still associated with the United States, Puerto Rico became a commonwealth with its own constitution.
**Population** (1997): 3,828,506
**Area:** 3,508 sq. mi. (9,086 sq. km.)
**Flower:** Maga     **Bird:** Reinita
**National Anthem:** La Borinqueña
**Capital and Largest City:** San Juan (population, 433,705)
**Other Large Cities** (with population): Bayamón, 231,845; Carolina, 188,427; Ponce, 189,988
**Important Products:** chemicals, food products, electronic equipment, clothing and textiles, industrial machinery, coffee, sugarcane, fruit, hogs
**Places to Visit:** San Juan National Historic Site; beaches and resorts

**DID YOU KNOW?** *Puerto Ricans have most of the rights of American citizens, but cannot vote in U.S. presidential elections and do not pay federal income tax. That would change if Puerto Rico becomes a state. In 1998, Puerto Rico voted to remain a commonwealth.*

# How the STATES

Alabama comes from *Alibamu*, which was the name of the town of a Creek Indian tribe.

Alaska comes from *alakshak*, the Aleutian (Eskimo) word meaning "peninsula" or "land that is not an island."

Arizona comes from an American Indian word meaning "little spring" or "little spring place."

Arkansas is a variation of *Quapaw*, the name of a Sioux Indian tribe. *Quapaw* means "downstream people."

California is the name of an imaginary island in a Spanish story. It was named by Spanish explorers of Baja California, a part of Mexico.

Colorado comes from a Spanish word meaning "reddish." It was first given to the Colorado river because of its reddish color.

Connecticut comes from an Algonquin Indian word meaning "beside the long tidal river."

Delaware is named after Lord De La Warr, the English governor of Virginia in colonial times.

Florida, which means "flowery" in Spanish, was named by the explorer Ponce de Leon, who landed there during the Spanish flower festival.

Georgia was named after King George II of England, who granted the right to create a colony there in 1732.

Hawaii probably comes from *Hawaiki,* or *Owhyhee,* the native Polynesians' name for their homeland.

Idaho's name is of uncertain origin, but it may come from a Kiowa Apache name for the Comanche Indians.

Illinois is the French version of *Illini,* an Algonquin Indian word meaning "men" or "warriors."

Indiana means "land of the Indians."

Iowa comes from the name of an American Indian tribe that lived on the land that is now the state.

Kansas comes from a Sioux Indian word that possibly meant "people of the south wind."

Kentucky comes from an Iroquois Indian word, possibly meaning "meadowland."

Louisiana, which was first settled by French explorers, was named after King Louis XIV of France.

Maine means "the mainland." English explorers called it that to distinguish it from islands nearby.

Maryland was named after Queen Henrietta Maria, wife of King Charles I of England, who granted the right to establish an English colony there.

Massachusetts comes from an Algonquin Indian word meaning "at the big hill."

Michigan comes from the Chippewa Indian words *mici gama*, meaning "great water" (referring to Lake Michigan).

Minnesota got its name from a Dakota Sioux Indian word meaning "cloudy water" or "sky-tinted water."

Mississippi is probably derived from two Chippewa Indian words meaning "great river" or "father of the waters," or from an Algonquin word.

Missouri comes from an Algonquin Indian term meaning "river of the big canoes."

Montana comes from a Latin or Spanish word meaning "mountainous."

# Got Their NAMES

**Nebraska** comes from "flat river" or "broad water," an Omaha or Otos Indian name for the Platte River.

**Nevada** means "snowy or "snow-covered" in Spanish. Spanish explorers gave the name to the Sierra Nevada Mountains.

**New Hampshire** was named by an early settler after his home county of Hampshire, in England.

**New Jersey** was named for the English Channel island of Jersey.

**New Mexico** was given its name by a Spanish explorer in Mexico.

**New York**, first called New Netherland, was renamed for the Duke of York and Albany after the English took it from Dutch settlers.

**North Carolina**, the northern part of the English colony of Carolana, was named for King Charles I.

**North Dakota** comes from a Sioux Indian word meaning "friend" or "ally."

**Ohio** is the Iroquois Indian word for "fine or good river."

**Oklahoma** comes from a Choctaw Indian word meaning "red man."

**Oregon** may have come from *Ouaricon-sint,* a name on a French map that was once given to what is now called the Columbia River. That river runs between Oregon and Washington.

**Pennsylvania**, meaning "Penn's woods," was the name given to the colony founded by William Penn.

**Rhode Island** may have come from the Dutch Roode Eylandt (red island) or may have been named after the Greek island of Rhodes.

**South Carolina**, the southern part of the English colony of Carolana, was named for King Charles I.

**South Dakota** comes from a Sioux Indian word meaning "friend" or "ally."

**Tennessee** comes from the name the Cherokee Indians gave to their ancient capital. The name was given to the Tennessee River. The state was named after the river.

**Texas** comes from a word meaning "friends" or "allies," used by the Spanish to describe some of the American Indians living there.

**Utah** comes from a Navajo word meaning "upper" or "higher up."

**Vermont** comes from two French words, *vert* (green) and *mont* (mountain).

**Virginia** was named in honor of Queen Elizabeth I of England, who was known as the Virgin Queen because she never married.

**Washington** was named after George Washington, the first president of the United States.

**West Virginia** got its name from the people of western Virginia, who formed their own government during the Civil War.

**Wisconsin** comes from an Algonquin Indian name for the state's principal river. The word, meaning "the place where the waters come together," was once spelled *Ouisconsin.*

**Wyoming** comes from an Algonquin Indian word meaning "at the big plains," "large prairie place," or "on the great plain."

# WASHINGTON, D.C.
## The Capital of the United States

**Area:** 69 square miles
**Population:** 543,213
**Flower:** American beauty rose
**Bird:** Wood thrush

**HISTORY.** Washington, D.C., became the capital of the United States in 1800, when the U.S. government moved there from Philadelphia. The city of Washington was especially designed and built to be the capital. It was named after George Washington, the first president of the United States. Many of its major sights are located on the Mall, an open grassy area that runs from the Capitol to the Potomac River.

**Capitol**, which houses the United States Congress, is at the east end of the Mall, on Capitol Hill. The dome of the Capitol's rotunda can be seen from many parts of the city.

**Franklin Delano Roosevelt Memorial,** honoring the 32nd president of the United States, was dedicated in 1997. The memorial is wheelchair accessible. The walls are carved with sayings of the president and First Lady Eleanor Roosevelt.

**Jefferson Memorial,** a circular marble building located near the Potomac River. At night, it is floodlit and very impressive.

**Korean War Veterans Memorial,** dedicated in 1995, is at the west end of the Mall. It shows a group of 19 troops ready for combat.

**Lincoln Memorial,** at the west end of the Mall, is built of white marble and styled like a Greek temple. Inside is a large, seated statue of Abraham Lincoln. His Gettysburg Address is carved on a nearby wall.

**National Archives,** on Constitution Avenue, is the place to see the Declaration of Independence, the Constitution, and the Bill of Rights.

**National Gallery of Art,** on the Mall, is one of the world's great art museums. Older paintings and sculptures are housed in the West Building, while 20th-century art is housed in the newer East Building.

**Smithsonian Institution** has 14 museums, including the National Air and Space Museum and the Museum of Natural History. The National Zoo is part of the Smithsonian.

**U.S. Holocaust Memorial Museum** presents the history of the Nazis' murder of over six million Jews and millions of other people from 1933 to 1945. The exhibit *Daniel's Story* tells the story of the Holocaust from a child's point of view. It is for eight-year-olds and older. The other exhibits are for visitors 11 years old or older.

**Vietnam Veterans Memorial** has a black-granite wall shaped like a V. Names of the Americans who lost their lives or are still missing in the Vietnam War are inscribed on the wall.

**Washington Monument,** a white marble pillar, or obelisk, standing on the Mall and rising to over 555 feet. From the top, there are wonderful views of the city.

**White House,** at 1600 Pennsylvania Avenue, has been the home of every U.S. president except George Washington.

**Women in Military Service for America Memorial,** dedicated in 1997, is at the entrance to Arlington National Cemetery. It honors the 1.8 million women who have served in the U.S. armed forces.

# NATIONAL PARKS

**M**ost national parks are large and naturally beautiful and have a wide variety of scenery. They are visited by millions of people each year. The world's first national park was Yellowstone, established in 1872. Since then, the American government has set aside a total of 54 national parks. Fifty-two of the parks in the United States are listed below.

Two outside the United States are in the Virgin Islands and American Samoa.

You can find out more about national parks by writing to the National Park Service, Department of the Interior, 1849 C Street NW, Washington, D.C., 20240.

**WEB SITE** For information on-line, go to: *http://www.nps.gov/parks.html*

## Acadia (Maine)
47,678 acres; established 1929
Rugged coast and granite cliffs; seals, whales, and porpoises; highest land along the East Coast of the U.S.

## Arches (Utah)
73,379 acres; established 1971
Giant natural sandstone arches, including Landscape Arch, over 100 feet high and 291 feet long

## Badlands (South Dakota)
242,756 acres; established 1978
A prairie where, over centuries, the land has been formed into many odd shapes with a variety of colors

## Big Bend (Texas)
801,163 acres; established 1935
Desert land and rugged mountains, on the Rio Grande River; dinosaur fossils

## Biscayne (Florida)
172,924 acres; established 1980
A water-park on a chain of islands in the Atlantic Ocean, south of Miami, with beautiful coral reefs

## Bryce Canyon (Utah)
35,835 acres; established 1928
Odd and very colorful rock formations carved by centuries of erosion

## Canyonlands (Utah)
337,570 acres; established 1964
Sandstone cliffs above the Colorado River; rock carvings from an ancient American Indian civilization

## Capitol Reef (Utah)
241,904 acres; established 1971
Sandstone cliffs cut into by gorges with high walls; old American Indian storage huts

## Carlsbad Caverns (New Mexico)
46,766 acres; established 1930
A huge cave system, not fully explored, with the world's largest underground chamber, called "the Big Room"

## Channel Islands (California)
256,334 acres; established 1980
Islands off the California coast, with sea lions, seals, and sea birds

## Crater Lake (Oregon)
183,224 acres; established 1902
The deepest lake in the United States, carved in the crater of an inactive volcano; lava walls up to 2,000 feet high

## Death Valley (California, Nevada)
3,367,628 acres; established 1994
Largest national park outside Alaska. Vast hot desert, rocky slopes and gorges, huge sand dunes; hundreds of species of plants, some unique to the area; variety of wildlife, including desert foxes, bobcats, coyotes

## Denali (Alaska)
4,741,800 acres; established 1980
Huge park, containing America's tallest mountain, plus caribou, moose, sheep

**Dry Tortugas (Florida)**
64,700 acres; established 1992
Colorful birds and fish; a 19th-century
fort, Fort Jefferson

**Everglades (Florida)**
1,508,490 acres; established 1934
The largest subtropical wilderness within
the U.S.; swamps with mangrove trees,
rare birds, alligators

**Gates of the Arctic (Alaska)**
7,523,898 acres; established 1984
One of the largest national parks; huge
tundra wilderness, with rugged peaks
and steep valleys

**Glacier (Montana)**
1,013,572 acres; established 1910
Rugged mountains, with glaciers, lakes,
sheep, bears, and bald eagles

**Glacier Bay (Alaska)**
3,225,484 acres; established 1986
Glaciers moving down mountainsides to
the sea; seals, whales, bears, eagles

**Grand Canyon (Arizona)**
1,217,403 acres; established 1919
Mile-deep expanse of multicolored
layered rock, a national wonder

**Grand Teton (Wyoming)**
310,027 acres; established 1929
Set in the Teton Mountains; a winter
feeding ground for elks

**Great Basin (Nevada)**
77,180 acres; established 1986
From deserts to meadows to tundra;
caves; ancient pine trees

**Great Smoky Mountains**
(North Carolina, Tennessee)
521,621 acres; established 1934
Forests, with deer, fox, and black bears,
and streams with trout and bass

**Guadalupe Mountains (Texas)**
86,416 acres; established 1966
Remains of a fossil reef formed 225
million years ago

**Haleakala (Hawaii)**
28,091 acres; established 1960
The largest crater of any inactive
volcano in the world

**Hawaii Volcanoes (Hawaii)**
209,695 acres; established 1961
Home of two large active volcanoes,
Mauna Loa and Kilauea, along with a
desert and a tree fern forest

**Hot Springs (Arkansas)**
5,549 acres; established 1921
47 hot springs that provide warm
waters for drinking and bathing

**Isle Royale (Michigan)**
571,790 acres; established 1931
On an island in Lake Superior; woods,
lakes, many kinds of animals—and no
roads

**Joshua Tree (California)**
792,750 acres; established 1994. Large desert with rock formations and unusual desert plants, including many Joshua trees; fossils from prehistoric times; wildlife, including desert bighorn

**Katmai (Alaska)**
3,674,541 acres; established 1980
Contains the Valley of Ten Thousand
Smokes, which was filled with ash
when Katmai Volcano erupted in 1912

**Kenai Fjords (Alaska)**
652,048 acres; established 1980
Fjords, rain forests, the Harding
Icefield; sea otters, seals; a breeding
place for many birds

**Kings Canyon (California)**
461,901 acres; established 1940
Mountains and woods and the highest
canyon wall in the U.S.

**Kobuk Valley (Alaska)**
1,750,737 acres; established 1980
Located north of the Arctic Circle, with
caribou and black bears; archeological
sites indicate that humans have lived
there for over 10,000 years

**Lake Clark (Alaska)**
2,619,859 acres; established 1980
Lakes, waterfalls, glaciers, volcanoes, fish and wildlife

**Lassen Volcanic (California)**
106,372 acres; established 1916
Contains Lassen Peak, a volcano that began erupting in 1914, after being dormant for 400 years

**Mammoth Cave (Kentucky)**
52,830 acres; established 1941
The world's longest known cave network, with 144 miles of mapped passages

**Mesa Verde (Colorado)**
52,122 acres; established 1906
A plateau covered by woods and canyons; the best preserved ancient cliff dwellings in the U.S.

**Mount Rainier (Washington)**
235,613 acres; established 1899
Home of the Mount Rainier volcano; thick forests, glaciers

**North Cascades (Washington)**
504,781 acres; established 1968
Rugged mountains and valleys, with deep canyons, lakes and glaciers

**Olympic (Washington)**
922,651 acres; established 1938
Rain forest, with woods and mountains, glaciers, and rare elk

**Petrified Forest (Arizona)**
93,533 acres; established 1962
A large area of woods turned into stone; American Indian pueblos and rock carvings

**Redwood (California)**
110,232 acres; established 1968
Groves of ancient redwood trees, and the world's tallest trees

**Rocky Mountain (Colorado)**
265,727 acres; established 1915
Located in the Rockies, with gorges, alpine lakes, and mountain peaks

**Saguaro (Arizona)**
91,444 acres; established 1994
Forests of saguaro cacti, some 50 feet tall and 200 years old

**Sequoia (California)**
402,482 acres; established 1890
Groves of giant sequoia trees; Mount Whitney (14,494 feet)

**Shenandoah (Virginia)**
197,406 acres; established 1926
Located in the Blue Ridge Mountains, overlooking the Shenandoah Valley

**Theodore Roosevelt (North Dakota)**
70,447 acres; established 1978
Scenic badlands and a part of the old Elkhorn Ranch that belonged to Theodore Roosevelt

**Voyageurs (Minnesota)**
218,200 acres; established 1971
Forests with wildlife and many scenic lakes for canoeing and boating

**Wind Cave (South Dakota)**
28,295 acres; established 1903
Limestone caverns in the Black Hills; a prairie with colonies of prairie dogs

**Wrangell-Saint Elias (Alaska)**
8,323,618 acres; established 1980
The biggest national park, with mountain peaks over 16,000 feet high

**Yellowstone (Idaho, Montana, Wyoming)**
2,219,791 acres; established 1872
The first national park and world's greatest geysers; bears and moose

**Yosemite (California)**
761,236 acres; established 1890
Yosemite Valley; highest waterfall in North America; mountain scenery

**Zion (Utah)**
146,598 acres; established 1919
Deep, narrow Zion Canyon and other canyons in different colors; Indian cliff dwellings over 1,000 years old

# UNITED STATES CROSSWORD PUZZLE

Try filling in these boxes. If you need to do research for answers, look in the United States chapter.

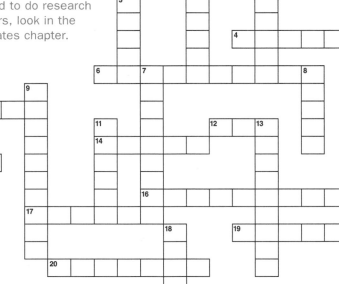

## ACROSS
1. Last name of 15th U.S. president; he never married
4. Building in Washington, D.C., that houses the U.S. Congress
6. George Washington belonged to this political party
10. Name of this Midwestern state means "fine or good river"
12. These initials stand for the Environmental Protection Agency
14. First word in the name of the smallest state
15. Postal abbreviation for Alabama
16. The president heads this branch of government
17. This state out West is known as the sunflower state
19. The state bird of Michigan
20. The U.S. Senate has 100 of these; the House has 435

## DOWN
1. Nickname for Wisconsin (first word only)
2. Honolulu is the capital of this state
3. This state in the Northeast has rocky coasts and high tides
5. Last name of first woman appointed to the U.S. Supreme Court
7. The capital of Iowa
8. Austin is the capital of this state in the Southwest
9. Nickname for Nebraska (first word only)
10. Mistletoe is the flower of this Southwestern state
11. Landscape Arch is in this Utah national park
13. First U.S. astronaut to walk on the moon (last name)
18. President Bill Clinton's vice president (last name)

*Answers are on pages 317–320.*

 **WEATHER**

**❓ Where is the coldest place in the world?**
*You can find the answer on page 299.*

# Naming Hurricanes

For many years, violent storms have been given names. Until early in the 20th century, people named storms after saints. Then, in 1953, the U.S. government began to use women's names for hurricanes. Men's names began to be used in 1978.

| HURRICANE NAMES FOR 2000 | |
|---|---|
| **In the North Atlantic:** | **In the Eastern Pacific:** |
| Alberto, Beryl, Chris, Debby, Ernesto, Florences, Gordon, Helene, Isaac, Joyce, Keith, Leslie, Michael, Nadine, Oscar, Patty, Rafael, Sandy, Tony, Valerie, William | Aletta, Bud, Carlotta, Daniel, Emilia, Fabio, Gilma, Hector, Ileana, John, Kristy, Lane, Miriam, Norman, Olicia, Paul, Rosa, Sergio, Tara, Vicente, Willa, Xavier, Yolanda, Zeke |

## Hurricane Mitch

From October 26 to November 4, 1998, Hurricane Mitch battered parts of Central America with fierce winds and rains that caused mudslides and washed away entire villages. The ferocious storm, which hit Honduras and Nicaragua hardest, left more than 11,000 people dead and thousands missing, and more than $5 billion in damages. This makes Mitch one of the worst hurricanes in history.

## The Speed of Wind

This Beaufort Scale at right is used to measure the speed of wind. The U.S. Weather Service also uses the numbers 13 to 17 for winds of hurricane speed.

0 Calm   4 Moderate Breeze   8 Gale   12 Hurricane

| 0 | Calm | (under 1 mph) |
|---|---|---|
| 1 | Light Air | (1-3 mph) |
| 2 | Light Breeze | (4-7 mph) |
| 3 | Gentle Breeze | (8-12 mph) |
| 4 | Moderate Breeze | (13-18 mph) |
| 5 | Fresh Breeze | (19-24 mph) |
| 6 | Strong Breeze | (25-31 mph) |
| 7 | Near Gale | (32-38 mph) |
| 8 | Gale | (39-46 mph) |
| 9 | Strong Gale | (47-54 mph) |
| 10 | Storm | (55-63 mph) |
| 11 | Violent Storm | (64-72 mph) |
| 12 | Hurricane | (over 72 mph) |

# Weather Words

**air mass** A large amount of air at a certain temperature and humidity.

**atmospheric pressure** Pressure on the Earth's surface from the weight of the atmosphere. Rising pressure usually means calm, clear weather. Falling pressure usually leads to storms. A high is an area of high atmospheric pressure. A low is an area of low pressure.

**climate** Average weather conditions for an area over a long time period.

**front** Boundary between two air masses.

**humidity** Amount of water vapor (water in the form of a gas) in the air.

**meteorologist** A person who studies the atmosphere, weather, and weather forecasting.

## Precipitation

**precipitation** Water that falls from clouds as rain, snow, hail, or sleet.

**rain** Water falling in drops.

**freezing rain** Water that freezes as it hits the ground.

**sleet** Drops of water that freeze in cold air and reach the ground as ice pellets or a mixture of snow and rain.

**hail** Frozen raindrops that are kept in the air by air currents. Water keeps freezing on the hailstone until it is so heavy that it falls to the ground.

**snow** Ice crystals that form in clouds and fall.

**blizzard** A heavy snowstorm with strong winds.

## Storms

**cyclone** A circulating storm that forms over warm tropical oceans. Also the name for a hurricane in the Indian Ocean.

**hurricane** A circulating storm with wind speeds of 73 miles per hour or more. It is called a typhoon in the western Pacific Ocean and a cyclone in the Indian Ocean.

**monsoon** A system of winds that changes direction between seasons.

**tropical storm** A circulating storm with wind speeds from 39 to 73 mph; can turn into a hurricane.

**tornado** Violently circulating winds of more than 200 mph form a dark funnel reaching from the cloud to the ground.

Tornadoes, also called "twisters," are violent winds that spin in the shape of a funnel at speeds of 200-250 miles per hour or more. A tornado can suck up and destroy anything in its path! Tornadoes form when winds change direction, speed up, and spin around before a thunderstorm. When this happens, the National Weather Service issues a **tornado watch**. A **tornado warning** is announced when a tornado has actually been seen in the area.

**WEB SITE** You can read more about tornadoes at: *http://www.nsw.noaa.gov/om/tornado.htm*

# Taking Temperatures

**HOW TO MEASURE TEMPERATURE** Two systems for measuring temperature are used in weather forecasting. One is Fahrenheit (abbreviated F). The other is Celsius (abbreviated C). Another word for Celsius is Centigrade. Zero degrees (0°) Celsius is equal to 32 degrees (32°) Fahrenheit.

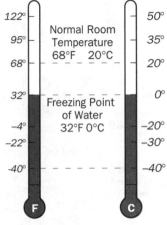

## To Convert Fahrenheit Temperatures to Celsius:

1. Subtract 32 from the Fahrenheit temperature value.
2. Then multiply by 5.
3. Then divide the result by 9.
   **Example:** To convert 68 degrees Fahrenheit to Celsius, 68 − 32 = 36; 36 x 5 = 180; 180 ÷ 9 = 20

## To Convert Celsius Temperatures to Fahrenheit:

1. Multiply the Celsius temperature by 9.
2. Then divide by 5.
3. Then add 32 to the result.
   **Example:** To convert 20 degrees Celsius to Fahrenheit,
   20 x 9 = 180; 180 ÷ 5 = 36; 36 + 32 = 68

## THE HOTTEST AND COLDEST PLACES IN THE WORLD

| CONTINENT | HIGHEST TEMPERATURE | LOWEST TEMPERATURE |
|---|---|---|
| Africa | El Azizia, Libya, 136°F (58°C) | Ifrane, Morocco, −11°F (−24°C) |
| Antarctica | Vanda Station, 59°F (15°C) | Vostok, −129°F (−89°C) |
| Asia | Tirat Tsvi, Israel, 129°F (54°C) | Verkhoyansk, Russia, and Oimekon, Russia, −90°F (−68°C) |
| Australia | Cloncurry, Queensland, 128°F (53°C) | Charlotte Pass, New South Wales, −9°F (−23°C) |
| Europe | Seville, Spain, 122°F (50°C) | Ust'Shchugor, Russia, −67°F (−55°C) |
| North America | Death Valley, California, 134°F (57°C) | Snag, Yukon Territory, −81°F (−63°C) |
| South America | Rivadavia, Argentina, 120°F (49°C) | Sarmiento, Argentina, −27°F (−33°C) |

### HOTTEST PLACES IN THE U.S.

| State | Temperature | Year |
|---|---|---|
| California | 134°F | (1913) |
| Arizona | 128°F | (1994)* |
| Nevada | 125°F | (1994)* |

### COLDEST PLACES IN THE U.S.

| State | Temperature | Year |
|---|---|---|
| Alaska | -80°F | (1971) |
| Montana | -70°F | (1954) |
| Utah | -69°F | (1985) |

*Tied with a record set earlier*

**WEB SITE** To read more about the weather try the Weather Channel at:
http://www.weather.com

❷ **How many feet are in a fathom?**
*You can find the answer on page 301.*

# The Earliest MEASUREMENTS

We use weights and measures all the time—you can measure how tall you are, or how much gasoline a car needs. People who lived in ancient times—more than 1,000 years ago—developed measurements to describe the amounts or sizes of things. The first measurements were based on the human body and on everyday activities.

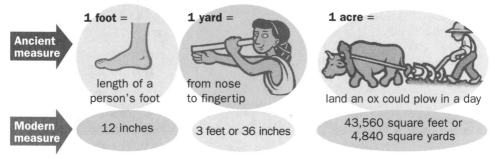

| | 1 foot = | 1 yard = | 1 acre = |
|---|---|---|---|
| **Ancient measure** | length of a person's foot | from nose to fingertip | land an ox could plow in a day |
| **Modern measure** | 12 inches | 3 feet or 36 inches | 43,560 square feet or 4,840 square yards |

# Measurements We Use Today

The system of measurement used in the United States is called the U.S. customary system. Most other countries use the metric system. A few metric measurements are also used in the United States, such as for soda, which comes in 1-liter and 2-liter bottles. In the tables below, abbreviations are given in parentheses the first time they are used.

| LENGTH, HEIGHT, and DISTANCE | AREA |
|---|---|
| The basic unit of **length** in the U.S. system is the **inch**. Length, width, depth, thickness, and the distance between two points all use the inch or larger related units. | Area is used to measure a section of a flat surface like the floor or the ground. Most area measurements are given in square units. Land is measured in acres. |
| 1 foot (ft.) = 12 inches (in.)<br>1 yard (yd.) = 3 feet or 36 inches<br>1 rod (rd.) = 5 ½ yards<br>1 furlong (fur.) = 40 rods or 220 yards or 660 feet<br>1 mile (mi.) (also called statute mile) = 8 furlongs or 1,760 yards or 5,280 feet<br>1 league = 3 miles | 1 square foot (sq. ft.) = 144 square inches (sq. in.)<br>1 square yard (sq. yd.) = 9 square feet or 1,296 square inches<br>1 square rod (sq. rd.) = 30 ¼ square yards<br>1 acre = 160 square rods or 4,840 square yards or 43,560 square feet<br>1 square mile (sq. mi.) = 640 acres |

## CAPACITY

Units of **capacity** are used to measure how much of something will fit into a container. **Liquid measure** is used to measure liquids, such as water or gasoline. **Dry measure** is used with large amounts of solid materials, like grain or fruit.

**Dry Measure.** Although both liquid and dry measures use the terms "pint" and "quart," they mean different amounts and should not be confused. Look at the lists below for examples.

1 quart (qt.) = 2 pints (pt.)
1 peck (pk.) = 8 quarts
1 bushel (bu.) = 4 pecks

**Liquid Measure.** Although the basic unit in liquid measure is the **gill** (4 fluid ounces), you are more likely to find liquids measured in pints or larger units.

1 gill = 4 fluid ounces
1 pint (pt.) = 4 gills or 16 ounces
1 quart (qt.) = 2 pints or 32 ounces
1 gallon (gal.) = 4 quarts = 128 ounces

For measuring most U.S. liquids,
    1 barrel (bbl.) = $31\frac{1}{2}$ gallons
For measuring oil,
    1 barrel (bbl.) = 42 gallons

**Cooking measurements.** Cooking measure is used to measure amounts of solid and liquid foods used in cooking. The measurements used in cooking are based on the **fluid ounce**.

1 teaspoon (tsp.) = $\frac{1}{6}$ fluid ounce (fl. oz.)
1 tablespoon (tbsp.) = 3 teaspoons or $\frac{1}{2}$
                fluid ounce
1 cup = 16 tablespoons or 8 fluid ounces
1 pint = 2 cups
1 quart = 2 pints
1 gallon = 4 quarts

## VOLUME

The amount of space taken up by an object (or the amount of space available within an object) is measured in **volume**. Volume is usually expressed in **cubic units**. If you wanted to buy a room air conditioner and needed to know how much space there was to be cooled, you could measure the room in cubic feet.

1 cubic foot (cu. ft.) =
    1,728 cubic inches (cu. in.)
1 cubic yard (cu. yd.) = 27 cubic feet

## DEPTH

Some measurements of length are used to measure ocean depth and distance.

1 fathom = 6 feet
1 cable = 120 fathoms or 720 feet
1 nautical mile = 6,076.1 feet or
                1.15 statute miles

## WEIGHT

Although 1 cubic foot of popcorn and 1 cubic foot of rock take up the same amount of space, they wouldn't feel the same if you tried to lift them. We measure heaviness as **weight**. Most objects are measured in **avoirdupois weight** (pronounced a-ver-de-POIZ), although precious metals and medicines use different systems.

1 dram (dr.) = 27.344 grains (gr.)
1 ounce (oz.) = 16 drams or
                437.5 grains
1 pound (lb.) = 16 ounces
1 hundredweight (cwt.) = 100 pounds
1 ton = 2,000 pounds
(also called short ton)

# The METRIC System

**D**o you ever wonder how much soda you are getting when you buy a bottle that holds 1 liter? Or do you wonder how long a 50-meter swimming pool is? Or how far away from Montreal, Canada, you would be when a map says "8 kilometers"?

Every system of measurement uses a basic unit for measuring. In the U.S. customary system, the basic unit for length is the inch. In the metric system, the basic unit for length is the **meter**. The metric system also uses **liter** as a basic unit of volume or capacity and the **gram** as a basic unit of mass. The related units are made by adding a prefix to the basic unit. The prefixes and their meanings are:

| milli- = $^1/_{1,000}$ | deci- = $^1/_{10}$ | hecto- = 100 |
|---|---|---|
| centi- = $^1/_{100}$ | deka- = 10 | kilo- = 1,000 |

**For example:**

| | | |
|---|---|---|
| millimeter (mm) = $^1/_{1,000}$ of a meter | milligram (mg) = $^1/_{1,000}$ of a gram |
| centimeter (cm) = $^1/_{100}$ of a meter | centigram (cg) = $^1/_{100}$ of a gram |
| decimeter (dm) = $^1/_{10}$ of a meter | decigram (dg) = $^1/_{10}$ of a gram |
| dekameter (dm) = 10 meters | dekagram (dg) = 10 grams |
| hectometer (hm) = 100 meters | hectogram (hg) = 100 grams |
| kilometer (km) = 1,000 meters | kilogram (kg) = 1,000 grams |

**T**o get a rough idea of what measurements equal in the metric system, it helps to know that a liter is a little more than a quart. A meter is a little over a yard. And a kilometer is less than a mile.

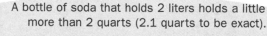

A bottle of soda that holds 2 liters holds a little more than 2 quarts (2.1 quarts to be exact).

A football field is 100 yards long. It is a little more than 90 meters (91.4 meters to be exact).

**DID YOU KNOW?** *Did you know that the metric system is used for measurements in the Olympic Games? Here are a few Olympic Game measurements and what they are equal to in U.S. customary units.*

*A 50-meter swimming pool is 54.7 yards long. A 400-meter freestyle swimming race is 437 yards.*

*A 10-kilometer race covers 6.2 miles. A 50-kilometer walk is 31.1 miles.*

*A 1,000-meter speed-skating race is six-tenths of a mile, or a little over half a mile. A 5,000-meter race is a little over 3 miles. (Remember that 1,000 meters = 1 kilometer. A 1,000-meter race is the same as a 1-kilometer race, and a 5,000-meter race is the same as a 5-kilometer race.)*

You can check the numbers above by using the conversion charts on the following page. A calculator will be a big help with this. For example, if you multiply 50 meters (the length of an Olympic swimming pool) by 1.0936, you get 54.68 yards. When rounded off, that becomes 54.7 yards.

# How to Convert Measurements

Do you want to convert feet to meters or miles to kilometers? You first need to know how many meters are in one foot or how many kilometers are in one mile. The tables below show how to convert units in the U.S. customary system to units in the metric system and how to convert metric units to U.S. customary units.

If you want to convert numbers from one system to the other, a calculator would be helpful for doing the multiplication.

| CONVERTING U.S. CUSTOMARY UNITS TO METRIC UNITS | | | CONVERTING METRIC UNITS TO U.S. CUSTOMARY UNITS | | |
|---|---|---|---|---|---|
| If you know the number of | Multiply by | To get the number of | If you know the number of | Multiply by | To get the number of |
| inches | 2.5400 | centimeters | centimeters | .3937 | inches |
| inches | .0254 | meters | centimeters | .0328 | feet |
| feet | 30.4800 | centimeters | meters | 39.3701 | inches |
| feet | .3048 | meters | meters | 3.2808 | feet |
| yards | .9144 | meters | meters | 1.0936 | yards |
| miles | 1.6093 | kilometers | kilometers | .621 | miles |
| square inches | 6.4516 | square centimeters | square centimeters | .1550 | square inches |
| square feet | .0929 | square meters | square meters | 10.7639 | square feet |
| square yards | .8361 | square meters | square meters | 1.1960 | square yards |
| acres | .4047 | hectares | hectares | 2.4710 | acres |
| cubic inches | 16.3871 | cubic centimeters | cubic centimeters | .0610 | cubic inches |
| cubic feet | .0283 | cubic meters | cubic meters | 35.3147 | cubic feet |
| cubic yards | .7646 | cubic meters | cubic meters | 1.3080 | cubic yards |
| quarts (liquid) | .9464 | liters | liters | 1.0567 | quarts (liquid) |
| ounces | 28.3495 | grams | grams | .0353 | ounces |
| pounds | .4536 | kilograms | kilograms | 2.2046 | pounds |

❷ **What are some Chinese inventions of long ago that affect our lives today?**
*You can find the answer on page 308.*

# Highlights of WORLD HISTORY

The section on World History is divided into five parts. Each part is a major region of the world: the Middle East, Africa, Asia, Europe, and the Americas. Major historical events from ancient times to the present are described under the headings for each region.

## THE ANCIENT MIDDLE EAST 4000 B.C.–1 B.C.

### 4000–3000 B.C.

- The world's first cities are built by the Sumerian peoples in Mesopotamia, southern Iraq.
- Egyptians develop a kind of writing called hieroglyphics.
- Sumerians develop a kind of writing called cuneiform.

*Giza, Great Pyramid of Cheops, Egypt*

**2700 B.C.** Egyptians begin building the great pyramids in the desert. The pharaohs' (kings') bodies are buried in them.

**1792 B.C.** First written laws are created in Babylonia. They are called the Code of Hammurabi.

### Achievements of the Ancient Middle East

Early peoples of the Middle East:
❶ Studied the stars (astronomy).
❷ Invented the wheel.
❸ Created alphabets from picture drawings (hieroglyphics and cuneiform).
❹ Established the 24-hour day.
❺ Studied medicine and mathematics.

**1200 B.C.** Hebrew people settle in Canaan in Palestine after escaping from slavery in Egypt. They are led by the prophet Moses.

### The Ten Commandments

Unlike most early peoples in the Middle East, the Hebrews believed in only one God (monotheism).

*Trail to top of Mount Sinai*

They believed their faith was given to Moses in the Ten Commandments on Mount Sinai when they fled Egypt.

**1000 B.C.** King David unites the Hebrews in one strong kingdom.

### Ancient Palestine

Palestine was invaded by many different peoples after 1000 B.C., including the Babylonians, the Egyptians, the Persians, and the Romans. It came under Arab Muslim control in the 600s and remained mainly under Muslim control until the 1900s.

**336 B.C.** Alexander the Great, King of Macedonia, builds an empire from Egypt to India.

**Around 4 B.C.** Jesus Christ, the founder of the Christian religion, is born in Bethlehem. He is crucified about A.D. 29.

## Islam: A Religion Grows in the Middle East

**570–632** Muhammad is born in Mecca in Arabia. In 610, as a prophet, he proclaims and teaches Islam, a religion which spreads from Arabia to all the neighboring regions in the Middle East and North Africa. His followers are called Muslims.

### The Koran

The holy book of Islam is the Koran. It was related by Muhammad beginning in 611. The Koran gives Muslims a program they must follow. For example, it gives rules about how one should treat one's parents and neighbors.

**632** Muhammad dies. By now, Islam is accepted in Arabia as a religion.

**641** Arab Muslims conquer the Persians.

**660–900** Islam begins to spread to the west into Africa and Spain under the Arab rulers known as the Umayyads.

*Dome of the Rock, Jerusalem*

**1071** Muslim Turks conquer Jerusalem.

**1095–1291** Europeans try to take back Jerusalem and other parts of the Middle East for Christians during the Crusades.

### The Spread of Islam

The Arab armies that went across North Africa brought great change:

❶ The people who lived there were converted to Islam.

❷ The Arabic language replaced many local languages as an official language. North Africa is still an Arabic-speaking region today, and Islam is the major faith.

### Achievements of Muslims

The Umayyad Empire that stretched across Africa and the Middle East is known for many great achievements. Muslims:

❶ Studied math and medicine.

❷ Translated the works of other peoples, including the Greeks and Persians.

❸ Created governments throughout the empire.

❹ Wrote great works on religion and philosophy.

**1300–1900s** The Ottoman Turks, who were Muslims, created a huge empire beginning in 1300, covering the Middle East, North Africa, and part of Eastern Europe. The Ottoman Empire fell apart gradually, and European countries took over portions of it beginning in the 1800s.

**1914–1918** World War I begins in 1914. By its end, the Ottoman Empire has been broken apart. Most of the Middle East falls under British and French control.

**1921** Two new Arab kingdoms are created: Transjordan and Iraq. The French take control of Syria and Lebanon.

**1922** Egypt becomes independent from Britain.

### Jews Migrate to Palestine

Jewish settlers from Europe began migrating to Palestine in the 1880s. They wanted to return to the historic homeland of the Hebrew people.

In 1945, after World War II, many Jews who survived the Holocaust migrated to Palestine. Arabs living in the region opposed the Jewish immigration. In 1948, after the British left, war broke out between the Jews and the Arabs.

## THE MIDDLE EAST 1948–1990s

**1948** The state of Israel is created.

### The Arab-Israeli Wars

Israel's Arab neighbors (Egypt, Jordan, and Syria) attack the new country in 1948 but fail to destroy it. Israel and its neighbors fight wars again in 1956, 1967, and 1973. Israel wins each war. In the 1967 war, Israel captures the Sinai Desert from Egypt and the area known as the West Bank from Jordan.

**1979** Egypt and Israel sign a peace treaty. Israel gradually returns the Sinai to Egypt.

### The Middle East and Oil

Much of the oil we use to drive our cars, heat our homes, and run our machines comes from the Arabian peninsula in the Middle East. For a brief time in 1973-1974, Arab nations would not let their oil be sold to the United States because of its support of Israel. After that, the United States has tried not to rely so much on oil imports.

### The 1990s

❶ In 1991, the United States and its allies go to war with Iraq after Iraq invades neighboring Kuwait. The conflict, known as the Persian Gulf War, results in the defeat of Iraq's army. Iraq signs a peace agreement but is accused by the United States and others of violating the peace terms, especially of making weapons for chemical and germ warfare.

❷ Israel and the Palestine Liberation Organization (PLO) agree to work toward peace (1993). In 1995, Prime Minister Yitzhak Rabin of Israel is assassinated. Benjamin Netanyahu, a critic of Rabin's peace policies, becomes prime minister. Negotiations continue, but go slowly. In 1999, Netanyahu loses office and Ehud Barak becomes prime minister.

## ANCIENT AFRICA 3500 B.C.–A.D. 900

### Ancient Africa

In ancient times, especially from around 3500 B.C. to A.D. 100, northern Africa was dominated by the Egyptians, Greeks, and Romans. However, we know very little about the lives of ancient people in Africa south of the Sahara Desert (sub-Saharan Africa).

The people of Africa south of the Sahara did not have written languages in ancient times. What we learn about them comes from such things as weapons, tools, and other items from their civilization that have been found in the earth.

**500 B.C.** The Nok culture becomes strong in Nigeria, in West Africa. The Nok use iron for tools and weapons. They are also known for their fine terra-cotta sculptures of heads.

**300 B.C.** Bantu-speaking peoples in West Africa begin to move into eastern and southern Africa.

**A.D. 100** The Kingdom of Axum in northern Ethiopia is founded by traders from Arabia and becomes a wealthy trade center for ivory.

**400** Ghana, the first known African state south of the Sahara Desert, rules the upper Senegal and Niger river region. It controls the trade in gold that is being sent from the southern parts of Africa north to the Mediterranean Sea.

**660s–900** The Islamic religion begins to spread across North Africa and into Spain. The Arabic language takes root in North Africa, replacing local languages.

**900** Arab Muslims begin to settle along the coast of East Africa. Their contact with Bantu people produces the Swahili language, which is still spoken today.

**1050** The Almoravid Kingdom in Morocco, North Africa, is powerful from Ghana to as far north as Spain.

**1230** The Mali Kingdom begins in North Africa. Timbuktu, a center for trade and learning, is its main city.

**1464** The Songhai Empire becomes strong in West Africa. By 1530, it has destroyed Mali. The Songhai are remembered for their bronze sculptures.

**1505–1575** Portuguese settlement begins in Africa. Portuguese people settle in Angola and Mozambique.

### The African Slave Trade

Once Europeans began settling in the New World, they needed people to harvest their sugar. The first African slaves were taken to the Caribbean. Later, slaves were taken to South America and the United States. The slaves were crowded onto ships and many died during the long journey. Shipping of African slaves to the United States lasted until the early 1800s.

### 1770–1835

❶ Dutch settlers arrive in southern Africa. The Dutch in South Africa are known as the Boers.

❷ Shaka the Great forms a Zulu Empire in eastern Africa. The Zulus are warriors.

❸ The "Great Trek" (march) of the Boers north takes place. They defeat the Zulus at the Battle of Bloody River.

*Zulu doll*

### 1880s: European Colonies in Africa

European settlers start moving into the interior of Africa and forming colonies in the mid-1800s. The major European countries with colonies in Africa were:

❶ **Great Britain:** East and Central Africa, from Egypt to South Africa.

❷ **France:** Most of West Africa and North Africa.

❸ **Spain:** Parts of Northwest Africa.

❹ **Portugal:** Mozambique (East Africa) and Angola (West Africa).

❺ **Italy:** Libya (North Africa) and Somalia (East Africa).

❻ **Germany:** East Africa, Southwest Africa.

**1899: Boer War** The South African War between Great Britain and the Boers begins. It is also called the Boer War. The Boers accept British rule but are allowed a role in government.

**1948** The white South African government creates the policy of apartheid, the total separation of blacks and whites.

### 1950s: African Independence

African colonies begin to receive their independence in the 1950s from European countries.

**1983** Droughts (water shortages) lead to starvation over much of Africa.

**The 1990s** Apartheid is ended in South Africa. Nelson Mandela, a black freedom fighter, becomes South Africa's first black president in 1995. Warfare between two groups, the Hutus and Tutsis, breaks out in Rwanda and Burundi in the mid-1990s. About 500,000 people, mainly Tutsi, are killed, and approximately two million refugees flee.

## ANCIENT ASIA 4000 B.C.–1 B.C.

**4000 B.C.** Communities of people settle in the Indus River Valley of India and Pakistan and the Yellow River Valley of China.

**2500 B.C.** Cities of Mohenjo-Daro and Harappa in Pakistan become centers of trade and farming.

 **1600 B.C.** Shang peoples in China build walled towns and use a kind of writing based on pictures. This writing develops into the writing Chinese people use today.

**1500 B.C.** The Hindu religion (Hinduism) begins to spread throughout India.

**1027 B.C.** Chou peoples in China overthrow the Shang and control large territories.

**700 B.C** In China, a 500-year period begins in which many warring states fight one another.

**563 B.C.** Prince Siddhartha Gautama is born in India. He becomes known as the Buddha—which means the "Enlightened One"—and is the founder of the Buddhist religion (Buddhism).

**551 B.C.** The Chinese philosopher Confucius is born. His teachings— especially the rules and morals about how people should treat each other and get along—spread throughout China and are still followed today.

### Two Important Asian Religions

Many of the world's religions began in Asia. Two of the most important were:

❶ **Hinduism.** Hinduism began in India and has spread to other parts of southern Asia and to parts of the Pacific region.

❷ **Buddhism.** Buddhism also began in India and spread to China, Japan, and Southeast Asia.

Today, both religions have millions of followers all over the world.

### 320–264 B.C.: India

❶ Northern India is united under the emperor Chandragupta Maurya.

❷ Asoka, emperor of India, begins to send Buddhist missionaries throughout southern Asia to spread the Buddhist religion.

**221 B.C.** The Chinese ruler Shih Huang Ti makes the Chinese language the same throughout the country. Around the same time, the Chinese begin building the Great Wall of China. It is 1,500 miles long and was meant to keep invading peoples from the north out of China. The Great Wall is still visited by people today.

**202 B.C.** The Han people in China overthrow Shih Huang Ti.

### During the Rule of the Han, the Chinese:

❶ Invented paper.
❷ Invented gunpowder.
❸ Studied astronomy.
❹ Studied engineering.
❺ Invented acupuncture to treat illnesses.

*The Great Wall of China*

**320** The Gupta Empire controls northern India. The Guptas are Hindus. They drive the Buddhist religion out of India. The Guptas are well known for their advances in the study of mathematics and medicine.

**618** The Tang dynasty begins in China. The Tang are famous for inventing the compass and for advances in surgery and the arts. They trade silk, spices, and ivory as far away as Africa.

**932** The Chinese begin to make books in large numbers by using wood blocks for printing.

**960** The Northern Sung Dynasty in China is known for advances in banking and paper money.

**1000** The Samurai, a warrior people, become powerful in Japan. They live by a code of honor called Bushido.

**1180** The Angkor Empire is powerful in Cambodia. The empire became widely known for its beautiful temples.

*Detail of Angkor Wat temple, Cambodia*

**1215** The Mongol people of Asia are united under the ruler Genghis Khan. He builds a huge army and creates an empire that stretches all the way from China to India, Russia, and Eastern Europe.

**1264** Kublai Khan, the grandson of Genghis Khan, rules China as emperor from his new capital at Beijing.

**1368** The Ming Dynasty comes to power in China. The Ming drive the Mongols out of China.

### 1467–1603: War and Peace in Japan
❶ Civil war breaks out in Japan. The conflicts last more than 100 years.
❷ Peace comes to Japan under the military leader Hideyoshi.
❸ The Shogun period begins in Japan, and lasts until 1868. Europeans are driven out of the country and Christians are persecuted.

### 1526–1556: The Moguls in India
❶ The Mogul Empire in India begins under Babur. The Moguls are Muslims who invade and conquer India.
❷ Akbar, the grandson of Babur, becomes Mogul emperor of India. He attempts to unite Hindus and Muslims but does not succeed.

**1644** The Ming Dynasty in China is overthrown by the Manchu peoples. They allow more Europeans to trade in China.

**1739** Nadir Shah, a Persian warrior, conquers parts of western India and captures the city of Delhi.

### What Indian Civilizations Did
Many civilizations grew in India over thousands of years of history. Among their achievements were:
❶ Great literature, especially Sanskrit literature and language.
❷ Great architecture, such as the Taj Mahal, a mausoleum (tomb) built in 1629 under the Moguls.
❸ Great world religions, including Hinduism and Buddhism.

## MODERN ASIA 1800s–1900s

**1839** The Opium War takes place in China between the Chinese and the British. The British and other Western powers want to control trade in Asia. The Chinese want the British to stop selling opium to the Chinese. Britain wins the war.

**1858** The French begin to take control of Indochina (Southeast Asia).

**1868** The Shogunate dynasty ends in Japan. The new ruler is Prince Meiji. Western ideas begin to influence the Japanese.

### The Japanese in Asia
Japan became a powerful country during the early 20th century. It was a small country with few raw materials of its own. For example, Japan had to buy oil from other countries. The Japanese army and navy took control of the government during the 1930s. Japan soon began to invade some of its neighbors. In 1941, the United States and Japan went to war after Japan attacked the U.S. Navy at Pearl Harbor, Hawaii.

**1945** Japan is defeated in World War II after the U.S. drops atomic bombs on the Japanese cities of Hiroshima and Nagasaki.

**1947** India and Pakistan become independent from Great Britain, which had ruled them as colonies since the mid-1800s.

**1949** China comes under the rule of the Communists led by Mao Zedong.

### China Under the Communists
The Communists brought great changes to China. Private property was abolished, and the government took over all businesses and farms. China became more isolated from other countries.

### 1950–1953: The Korean War
North Korea, a Communist country, invades South Korea. The U.S. and other nations join to fight the invasion. China joins North Korea. The Korean War ends in 1953. Neither side wins.

### 1954–1975: The Vietnam War
The French are defeated in Indochina in 1954 by the Vietminh. The Vietminh are Vietnamese fighters under the leadership of the Communists headed by Ho Chi Minh. The U.S. sends troops to fight in the Vietnam War in 1965 on the side of South Vietnam against Ho Chi Minh and Communist North Vietnam. The U.S. withdraws from the war in 1973. In 1975, South Vietnam is defeated and taken over by North Vietnam.

**1972** President Richard Nixon visits Communist China. Relations between China and the United States improve.

**1989** Chinese students protest for democracy, but the protests are crushed by the army in Tiananmen Square.

**The 1990s** The economies of Japan, South Korea, Taiwan, and some other Asian countries show great growth in the early 1990s. But, by the late 1990s, several Asian nations are in serious financial trouble. The British, rulers of Hong Kong, return it to China in 1997. China builds its economy, but is accused of violating human rights.

*Hong Kong*

## ANCIENT EUROPE 4000 B.C.–300 B.C.

**4000 B.C.** People in many parts of Europe start building monuments out of large stones called megaliths. Examples can still be seen today, including Stonehenge in England.

*Stonehenge*

### 2500 B.C.–1200 B.C.: The Minoans and the Mycenaeans

❶ People on the island of Crete (Minoans) in the Mediterranean Sea built great palaces and became sailors and traders.

❷ People in the city of Mycenae in Greece built stone walls and a great palace.

❸ Mycenaean people invaded Crete and destroyed the power of the Minoans.

### The Trojan War

The Trojan War was a conflict between invading Greeks and the people of Troas (Troy) in Southwestern Turkey around the year 1200 B.C. Although little is known today about the real war, it has become a part of Greek poetry and mythology. According to a famous legend, a group of Greek soldiers hid inside a huge wooden horse. The horse was pulled into the city of Troy. Then the soldiers jumped out of the horse and conquered Troy.

**1200 B.C.** Celtic peoples in Northern Europe settle on farms and in villages and learn to mine for iron ore.

### Some Achievements of the Greeks

The early Greeks were responsible for:

❶ The first governments that were elected by people. Greeks invented democratic government.

❷ Great writers such as the poet Homer, who made up the *Iliad*, a long poem about the Trojan War.

❸ Great philosophers such as Socrates, Plato, and Aristotle.

❹ Great architecture, like the Parthenon in Athens, which can still be seen (see below).

**700 B.C.** Etruscan peoples rule most of Italy until 400 B.C. They build many cities and become traders.

**431 B.C.** The Peloponnesian Wars begin between the Greek cities of Athens and Sparta. The wars end in 404 B.C. when Sparta wins.

**338 B.C.** King Philip II of Macedonia in northern Greece unites the cities of Greece and defeats Sparta.

**336 B.C.** Philip's son Alexander becomes king. He conquers lands and makes an empire from the Mediterranean Sea to India. He is known as Alexander the Great. For the next 300 years, Greek culture dominates this vast area.

## EUROPE 300 B.C.–A.D. 800s

### 264 B.C.–A.D. 476: Roman Empire

The city of Rome in Italy begins to expand and captures surrounding lands. The Romans gradually build a great empire and control all of the Mediterranean region. At its height, the Roman Empire includes Western Europe, Greece, Egypt, and much of the Middle East. The Roman Empire lasts until A.D. 476.

### Roman Achievements

1 Roman law. Many of our laws are based on Roman law. Romans had the first independent judges and protected the rights of women and children.

2 Great roads to connect their huge empire. The Appian Way, south of Rome, is a Roman road that is still in use today.

3 Aqueducts to bring water to the people in large cities.

4 Great sculpture. Roman statues can still be seen in Europe.

5 Great architecture. The Colosseum, which still stands in Rome today, is an example of great Roman architecture.

**45 B.C.** Julius Caesar becomes the leader of Rome but is murdered one year later by rivals in the Roman army.

*The Colosseum, Rome, Italy*

**29 B.C.** Octavian becomes the first emperor of Rome. He takes the name Caesar Augustus. A peaceful period of almost 200 years begins.

### The Christian Faith

Christians believe that Jesus Christ is the Son of God. The history and beliefs of Christianity are found in the New Testament of the Bible. Christianity spread slowly throughout the Roman Empire. The Romans tried to stop the new religion and persecuted the Christians. They were forced to hold their services in hiding, and some were crucified. Eventually, more and more Romans became Christian.

**337** The Roman Emperor Constantine the Great becomes a Christian. He is the first Roman emperor to be a Christian.

**410** The Visigoths and other barbarian tribes from northern Europe invade the Roman Empire and begin to take over its lands.

**476** The last Roman emperor is overthrown.

**The Byzantine Empire,** centered in modern-day Turkey, was made up of the eastern half of the old Roman Empire. Byzantine rulers extended their power into western Europe. The great Byzantine Emperor Justinian ruled parts of Spain, North Africa, and Italy. The city of Constantinople (now Istanbul, Turkey) became the capital of the Byzantine Empire in 520.

**768** Charlemagne becomes king of the Franks in northern Europe. He rules a kingdom that includes parts of France, Germany and northern Italy.

**800** Feudalism becomes important in Europe. Feudalism means that poor farmers are allowed to farm a lord's land in return for certain services to the lord.

## EUROPE 800s–1500s

**898** Magyar peoples from lands east of Russia found Hungary.

**900** Viking warriors and traders from Scandinavia begin to move into the British Isles, France, and parts of the Mediterranean. They remain for 200 years.

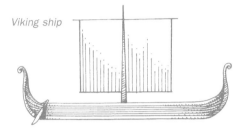

*Viking ship*

**989** The Russian state of Kiev becomes Christian.

**1066** William of Normandy, a Frenchman, successfully invades England and makes himself king. He is known as William the Conqueror.

### 1095–1291: The Crusades
In 1095, Christian European kings and nobles sent armies to the Middle East to try to capture the city of Jerusalem from the Muslims. Between 1095 and 1291 there were about ten Crusades. The Europeans briefly captured Jerusalem. But in the end, the Crusades did not succeed. One of the most important results of the Crusades was that trade increased between the Middle East and Europe.

### 1215: The Magna Carta
The Magna Carta is a document signed by King John of England and the English nobility. The English king agreed that he did not have absolute power and had to obey the laws of the land. The Magna Carta was an important step toward democracy.

**1290** The beginning of the Ottoman Empire. It is controlled by Turkish Muslims who conquer lands in the eastern Mediterranean and the Middle East.

### 1337–1453: War and Plague in Europe
❶ The Hundred Years' War (1337) begins in Europe between France and England. The war lasts until 1453 when France wins.
❷ The bubonic plague begins in Europe (1348). The plague, also called the Black Death, is a deadly disease caused by the bite of infected fleas. Perhaps as many as one third of the people of Europe die from the plague.

**1453** The Ottoman Turks capture the city of Constantinople and rename it Istanbul.

### 1517: The Reformation
The Reformation led to the breakup of the Christian church into Protestant and Roman Catholic branches in Europe. It started when the German priest Martin Luther opposed some teachings of the Church. He broke away from the pope (the leader of the Catholic church) and said that people should read the Bible themselves.

**1534** King Henry VIII of England breaks away from the Roman Catholic church. He names himself head of the English (Anglican) church.

**1558** The reign of King Henry's daughter Elizabeth I begins in England. During her long rule, England's power grows.

**1588** The Spanish Armada (fleet of warships) is defeated by the English navy as Spain tries to invade England.

## MODERN EUROPE 1600s–1990s

**1600** The Ottoman Turks attack central Europe. They take control of territories in the Balkan region of southeastern Europe.

**1618** The Thirty Years' War begins in Europe. The war is fought over religious issues. Much of Europe is destroyed in the conflict, which ends in 1648.

**1642** The English civil war takes place. King Charles I fights against the forces of the Parliament (legislature). The king's forces are defeated and he is executed in 1649. But his son, Charles II, eventually returns as king in 1661.

**1762** Catherine the Great becomes the Empress of Russia. She allows religious freedom and extends the Russian Empire.

### 1789: The French Revolution
The French Revolution ended the rule of kings in France and led to democracy there. At first, however, there were wars, much bloodshed, and times when dictators took control. King Louis XVI and Queen Marie Antoinette were overthrown in the Revolution and executed in 1793.

**1804** Napoleon Bonaparte, an army officer, declares himself Emperor of France. Under his rule, France conquers most of Europe by 1812.

**1815** Napoleon's forces are defeated by the British and German armies at Waterloo (in Belgium). Napoleon is exiled.

**1848** Revolutions break out in countries of Europe. People force their rulers to make more democratic changes.

### 1914–1918: World War I in Europe
At the start of World War I in Europe (1914), Germany and Austria-Hungary opposed England, France, and Russia (the Allies). The United States joined the war in 1917 on the side of the Allies. The Allies won in 1918.

**1917** The Russian Revolution takes place. The czar (emperor) is overthrown. The Bolsheviks (Communists) under Vladimir Lenin take control of the government. The country is renamed the Soviet Union.

**1933** Adolf Hitler becomes the dictator of Germany. He persecutes Jews and tries to take the territory of neighboring countries.

### 1939–1945: World War II in Europe
Germany and Italy fought against England, France, the Soviet Union, and the United States (the Allies) in Europe. Germany surrendered in May 1945. During the war, the Germans killed almost 6 million Jews (the Holocaust).

**1945** The Cold War begins. It is a 45-year period of tension between the United States and the Soviet Union. Both countries build up their armies and make nuclear weapons but do not go to war.

**The 1990s** Communist governments in Eastern Europe are replaced by democratic ones, and Germany becomes one nation. The Soviet Union breaks up. The European Union (EU), made up of 15 countries, takes steps toward greater European unity. Poland, Hungary, and the Czech Republic join the North Atlantic Treaty Organization (NATO). NATO bombs Yugoslavia in an effort to protect Albanians driven out of the Kosovo region.

## THE AMERICAS 4000 B.C.–A.D. 1600s

**4000** B.C. People in North America gather plants for food and hunt animals using stone-pointed spears.

**3000** B.C. People in Central America begin growing corn and beans for food.

**1500** B.C. Mayan people in Central America begin to live in small villages.

**500** B.C. People in North America begin to hunt buffalo for meat and skin for clothing.

**100** B.C. The city of Teotihuacán is founded in Mexico. It becomes the center of a huge empire extending from central Mexico to Guatemala. Teotihuacán contains many large pyramids and temples.

**A.D. 150** Mayan people in Guatemala build many centers for religious ceremonies. They create a calendar and learn mathematics and astronomy.

*Mayan pyramid, Yucatan, Mexico*

**900** Toltec warriors in Mexico begin to invade lands of Mayan people. Mayans leave their old cities and move to the Yucatan Peninsula of Mexico.

**1000** Native Americans in the southwestern United States begin to live in settlements called pueblos. They learn to farm.

**1325** Mexican Indians known as Aztecs create huge city of Tenochtitlán and rule a large empire in Mexico. They are warriors who practice human sacrifice.

**1492** Christopher Columbus sails from Europe across the Atlantic Ocean and lands in the Bahamas, in the Caribbean. This is the first step toward the founding of European settlements in the Americas.

**1500** Portuguese explorers reach Brazil and claim it for Portugal.

**1510** Africans are first brought to the Americas as slaves.

**1519** Spanish conqueror Hernán Cortés travels into the Aztec Empire in search of gold. The Aztecs are defeated in 1521 by Cortés. The Spanish take control of Mexico.

### Why Did the Spanish Win?

How did the Spanish defeat the powerful Aztec Empire in such a short time? One reason is that they had better weapons. Another is that the Aztecs became sick and died from diseases brought by the Spanish. Because the Aztecs never had these illnesses before and did not have immunity to them, they became sick from contact with Europeans.

**1534** Jacques Cartier of France explores Canada.

**1583** The first English colony in North America is set up in Newfoundland, Canada.

**1607** English colonists led by Captain John Smith settle in Jamestown, Virginia. Virginia was the oldest of the Thirteen Colonies that turned into the United States.

**1682** The French explorer Robert Cavalier sieur de La Salle sails down the Mississippi River. The area is named Louisiana after the French King Louis XIV.

## THE AMERICAS 1700s

### European Colonies in the Americas

By 1700, most of the Americas are under the control of Europeans:

Spain: Florida, southwestern United States, Mexico, Central America, western South America.
Portugal: eastern South America.
France: central United States, parts of Canada.
England: eastern U.S., parts of Canada.
Holland: New York.

### 1700

European colonies in North and South America begin to grow in population and wealth.

### 1775-1783: American Revolution

The American Revolution begins in 1775 when the first shot is fired in Lexington, Massachusetts. The 13 British colonies in North America become independent under the Treaty of Paris, signed in 1783.

## THE AMERICAS 1800s–1990s

### Simón Bolívar: Liberator of South America

In 1810, Simón Bolívar began a revolt against Spain. He fought for more than 10 years against the Spanish and became president of the independent country of Greater Colombia in 1824. As a result of his leadership, 10 South American countries had become independent from Spain by 1830.

### South American Independence

| COUNTRY | YEAR OF INDEPENDENCE |
|---|---|
| Argentina | 1816 |
| Bolivia | 1825 |
| Brazil[1] | 1822 |
| Chile | 1818 |
| Colombia | 1819 |
| Ecuador | 1830 |
| Guyana[2] | 1966 |
| Mexico | 1821 |
| Paraguay | 1811 |
| Peru | 1824 |
| Suriname[3] | 1973 |
| Uruguay | 1825 |
| Venezuela | 1821 |

❶ Brazil was governed by Portugal.
❷ Guyana was a British colony.
❸ Suriname was a Dutch colony.

### 1810–1910: Mexico's Revolution

In 1846, Mexico and the United States go to war. Mexico loses parts of the Southwest and California to the United States. A revolution in 1910 overthrows Porfirio Díaz.

**1867** The Canadian provinces are united as the Dominion of Canada.

### 1898: The Spanish-American War

Spain and the United States fight a brief war in 1898. Spain loses its Caribbean colonies Cuba and Puerto Rico, and the Philippines in the Pacific.

### U.S. Power in the 1900s

During the 1900s the United States influenced affairs in Central America and the Caribbean. The United States sent troops to Mexico (1916-1917), Nicaragua (1912-1925), Haiti (1915-1934; 1994-1995), Dominican Republic (1965), Grenada (1983), and Panama (1989). In 1962, the United States went on alert when the Soviet Union put missiles on Cuba, only 90 miles from Florida.

**The 1990s** In 1994, the North American Free Trade Agreement (NAFTA) is signed to increase trade between the United States, Canada, and Mexico. Relations between the United States and Cuba remain hostile, with the U.S. banning all trade with Cuba.

# ANSWERS TO PUZZLES

## ANIMALS

Page 43: **ANIMAL PUZZLE**

**1** vertebrate; **2** reptile; **3** elephant; **4** fish; **5** whale; **6** cat; **7** sow; **8** fossils; **9** troop; **10** horned; **11** deer; **12** ermine; **13** Cape; **14** lion; **15** lamb; **16** ant; **17** pre; **18** ten; **19** giant.

Note: All the letters are used.

| V | E | R | T | E | B | R | A | T | E |
|---|---|---|---|---|---|---|---|---|---|
| D | E | E | R | M | I | N | E | A | R |
| E | E | P | A | C | W | O | S | C | P |
| N | E | T | F | H | B | M | A | L | O |
| R | G | I | A | N | T | N | A | I | O |
| O | S | L | I | S | S | O | F | O | R |
| H | E | E | L | E | P | H | A | N | T |

## COMPUTERS

Page 62: **BINARY PUZZLE**

The words are: binary, moon, millennium.

Page 65: **INTERNET TREASURE HUNT**

The Web answers are: S<u>O</u>CKS, <u>M</u>ACARONI, <u>PE</u>NNSYLVANIA AVEN<u>UE</u>; MOERI<u>T</u>H<u>E</u>RIUM, TCYTHYO<u>S</u>TEGA, BINA<u>R</u>Y CODE, MICR<u>O</u>PROBES, I<u>O</u>, DECIMA<u>L</u>.

The secret message is COMPUTERS ARE COOL!

## ENVIRONMENT

Page 80: **ENVIRONMENT PUZZLE**

**1** trash; **2** water; **3** trees; **4** compost; **5** recycling; **6** bats; **7** fossil; **8** oil; **9** dump; **10** ozone; **11** fuel; **12** global; **13** soil.

| R | E | C | Y | C | L | I | N | G |
|---|---|---|---|---|---|---|---|---|
| L | I | O | X | T | R | E | E | S |
| D | U | M | P | O | Z | O | N | E |
| X | J | P | W | A | T | E | R | E |
| G | L | O | B | A | L | I | O | S |
| F | O | S | S | I | L | E | U | F |
| B | A | T | S | H | S | A | R | T |

## GEOGRAPHY

Page 89: **HELP TOBY GET HOME**

**1** South Street; **2** West Street; **3** east, south; **4** East Street; **5** Pond, north; **6** east; **7** south, west; **8** books.

Page 90: **MOUNTAIN CLIMBING PUZZLE**

|   | S | T | H | E | L | E | N | S |
|---|---|---|---|---|---|---|---|---|
|   | V | E | S | U | V | I | U | S |
|   | K | R | A | K | A | T | O | A |
| P | I | N | A | T | U | B | O |   |
| A | C | O | N | C | A | G | U | A |
|   |   | U | N | Z | E | N |   |   |
| K | O | S | C | I | U | S | K | O |
| M | C | K | I | N | L | E | Y |   |

Page 90: **MATCH THE SIGHT WITH THE SITE.**
❶ Angel Falls . . . . . . . . . . . . . . b. Venezuela
❷ Death Valley . . . . . . . . . . . . . e. California
❸ The Nile RIver . . . . . . . . . . . . a. Egypt and Sudan
❹ Dead Sea . . . . . . . . . . . . . . . d. Israel and Jordan
❺ Mount Everest . . . . . . . . . . . . c. Tibet and Nepal

Page 90: **RIVERS AND MORE RIVERS**
Henry Hudson—Hudson; Lewis and Clark—Missouri and Columbia; Livingstone—
Zambezi; de la Salle—Mississippi; Champlain—St. Lawrence

## HEALTH
Page 97: **DOCTOR PUZZLE**
Here are some words that can be formed from DERMATOLOGIST, not counting plural words.

**3-letter words:** age, ago, aid, aim, ale, arm, art, dam, die, dig, dim, dog, dot, ear, eat, ego, era, got, lad, lag, led, leg, let, log, lot, mad, mat, met, oar, old, rag, ram, rat, red, rim, rod, roe, sag, sat, sit, tad, tag, tar, tea, tot

**4-letter words:** aide, dale, dame, dart, date, dole, dome, doom, door, dorm, dram, emit, gale, game, germ, girl, gist, goal, goat, gold, gram, lame, last, lead, lime, list, load, loom, lose, lost, made, maid, mail, male, malt, meat, mist, moat, mode, mole, mood, moor, moot, more, most, ogle, omit, rail, rest, road, roam, rode, role, rose, room, root, sail, sale, salt, same, silo, sled, slid, slog, soot, stag, star, stir, stem, tail, tale, tame, teal, team, tear, term, test, tide, tied, tile, time, toad, tool, toot

**5-letter words:** alert, dream, drool, goose, grade, grate, great, groom, loose, loser, medal, metal, model, moose, motor, older, omega, remit, roost, slate, slide, stage, staid, stair, stale, stare, steam, start, steal, stole, stood, stool, store, storm, toast, total, totem, trade, trail, trial, tried

**6-letter words:** derail, detail, disarm, malted, master, mister, retail, sailed, sailor, stride, target

**7-letter words:** starlet, toasted, toaster  **8-letter word:** gloomier  **9-letter word:** gloomiest

## LANGUAGE

Page 107: ❶ to be off base; ❷ dog-eat-dog; ❸ flip your wig.

Page 111: **PICTURE WORD PUZZLE**

❶ long underwear; ❷ what goes up must come down; ❸ three little pigs; ❹ little league; ❺ somewhere over the rainbow; ❻ butterfly; ❼ misunderstanding; ❽ read between the lines; ❾ I understand; ❿ man overboard; ⓫ ring around the rosie; ⓬ uphill battle.

## MUSIC AND DANCE

Page 135: **MUSIC PUZZLE**

❶ tuba; ❷ brass drum; ❸ bassoon; ❹ violin

## NATIONS

Page 160: **NATIONS PUZZLE**

No nations start with W or X.

## NUMBERS

Page 177: **ROMAN NUMERALS**

2000 is MM.

Page 180: **NUMBERS PUZZLES**

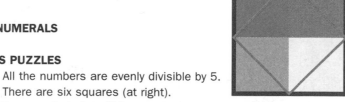

**Square 1:**   All the numbers are evenly divisible by 5.

**Square 2:**   There are six squares (at right).

**Magic Square:**   Top row: 8, 1, 9; middle row: 7, 6, 5; bottom row: 3, 11, 4

**Through the Threes:** One route goes 6, 12, 3, 30, 18, 66, 27, 21, 15, 24, 36, 33, 99, 90.

Page 181: **NUMBERS CROSSWORD PUZZLE**

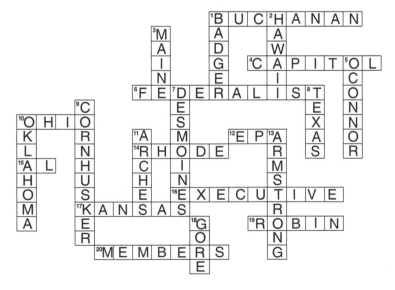

| ¹1 | ²1 | 0 | | ³1 | ⁴1 | | ⁵5 |
|---|---|---|---|---|---|---|---|
| | 0 | | ⁶7 | | 0 | | 0 |
| ⁷1 | 0 | 0 | 0 | 0 | 0 | ⁸0 | 0 |
| | 0 | | | | | 1 | |
| ⁹1 | | | ¹⁰1 | 9 | ¹¹2 | | ¹²1 |
| | ¹³7 | | 7 | | 2 | | 1 |
| ¹⁴9 | | ¹⁵3 | | ¹⁶4 | 5 | | 5 |
| 2 | | ¹⁷2 | 5 | | | ¹⁸1 | 0 |

**SIGNS AND SYMBOLS**

Page 223: **NUMBERS FOR LETTERS**

The message is: Welcome to the new millennium.

**SECRET MESSAGE PUZZLE**

The message is: Hello from The World Almanac for Kids.

**UNITED STATES**

Page 272: **TERI TERRIFIC'S TOUR**

❶ Arizona; ❷ New Mexico, Arizona, Texas, Colorado, Oklahoma; ❸ Washington;
❹ Wyoming; ❺ Utah; ❻ Arizona, Nevada; ❼ Oregon; ❽ Florida.

Page 296: **UNITED STATES CROSSWORD PUZZLE**

# INDEX

# ILLUSTRATION AND PHOTO CREDITS

This product/publication includes images from the Corel Stock Photo Library which are protected by the copyright laws of the U.S., Canada, and elsewhere. Used under license.

## ILLUSTRATION

Dolores Bego **76, 82, 86, 87, 182, 194, 215**, Teresa Anderko **39, 53, 93, 106, 107, 120, 219, 270**, T.D. King **25, 26, 27, 29, 30**, Olivia McElroy **95**

## PHOTOGRAPHY

**9:** Leonardo DiCaprio, © Kalpesh Lathigra/Liaison International; John Glenn, © NASA; Britney Spears, © Mark J. Terrill/AP/Wide World Photos; Brandy, © Kevork Djansezian/AP/Wide World Photos; *Antz,* © Dreamworks/Neal Peters Collection; Shaquille O'Neal, © Harry How/AllSport. **10:** Will Smith, © Reed Saxon/AP/Wide World Photos. **11:** Keri Russell, © Jeff Slocumb/Outline Press; Brandy, © Kevork Djansezian/AP/Wide World Photos. **12:** DiCaprio, © Kalpesh Lathigra/Liaison International. **13:** Adam Sandler, © Jon Farmer, Touchstone Pictures/Courtesy of the Kobal Collection; Sarah Michelle Gellar, © Dale Berman/Outline Press. **14:** Tara Lipinski, © Shaun Botterill/AllSport; Glenn, © NASA. **15:** Michael Jordan, © Mark J. Terrill/AP/ Wide World Photos. **16:** *Episode 1: The Phantom Menace,* © Lucasfilm Ltd. & ™. All Rights Reserved. Used Under Authorization. **17:** *Antz,* © Dreamworks/ Neal Peters Collection; Alicia Silverstone, © Peter Sorel/New Line Cinema. **18:** 'N Sync, © Melanie Edwards/Retna; The Backstreet Boys, © Steve Sands/Outline Press. **19:** Britney Spears, © Mark J. Terrill/AP/Wide World Photos. **20:** Mark McGwire, Sammy Sosa, © Reuters/Ray Stubblebine/Archive Photos. **21:** O'Neal, © Harry How/AllSport; Jeff Gordon, © Jamie Squire/AllSport. **22:** Martina Hingis, © Jack Atley/AllSport; Ricky Hamilton, © Andy Lyons/ AllSport. **23:** John Elway, © Al Bello/AllSport. **24:** Princes William & Harry, © Express Newspapers/Archive Photos; Piccard and Jones, © Alain Morvan/Liaison International. **45:** Boccioni painting, © Scala/Art Resource, NY. **49:** *Snowflake Bentley* by Mary Azarian, Courtesy of Houghton-Mifflin. **50:** *Island of the Blue Dolphins* by Frank O'Dell, Courtesy of Bantam Doubleday. **54:** Petronas Towers, © V. Miladinovic/Sygma. **81:** Globe, © Tom Van Sant/The Stock Market. **113:** Child laborer, © Riccardo Chot Kifox/AP/Wide World Photos. **116:** 1999 quarter, Courtesy of the U.S. Mint. **123:** *Mulan,* © The Everett Collection/Walt Disney Productions; *Dr. Dolittle,* © The Neal Peters Collection/20th Century Fox. **124:** *The Wizard of Oz,* © The Kobal Collection, Courtesy of MGM. **125:** Melissa Joan Hart , © Kobal Collection /Paramount Pictures. **128:** Brandy, © Larry Ford/ Outline Press; Adam Sandler, © Steve Sands/Outline Press; **131:** Williamsburg, Courtesy of the Colonial Williamsburg Foundation. **132:** Celine Dion, © The Everett Collection/Kraig Geiger. **137:** *The Lion King,* © Joan Marcus/Courtesy of Walt Disney Productions. **185:** NASA logo, © NASA. **189:** Astronaut on Moon, © NASA. **190:** Space shuttle, © NASA. **203:** *The Prince of Egypt,* © Everett Collection/Courtesy of Dreamworks. **204:** Lauryn Hill, © Fox/The Neal Peters Collection; Tony Award, © Tony Awards/ Courtesy of Keith Sherman & Assoc. **218:** Exploratorium, Courtesy of the San Francisco Exploratorium. **225:** Roger Clemens, © Andy Lyons /AllSport. **227:** NBA logo, © National Basketball Assoc.; Vince Carter, © Robert Laberge/AllSport. **228:** Ethan Brand, © Jonathan Daniel/AllSport. **229:** AFL/NFL logos, © The NFL Properties. **230:** Terrell Davis, © Al Bello/AllSport. **231:** Ricky Williams, © Stephen Dunn/AllSport. **234:** Se Ri Pak, © Vince Laforet/AllSport. **235:** Wayne Gretzky, © Elsa Hasch/AllSport. **237:** Carl Lewis, © Stu Forster/AllSport. **238:** Michelle Kwan, © Phil Cole/AllSport. **239:** Zach Thornton, © Doug Pensinger/AllSport; **240:** Amy Van Dyken, © All Bello/AllSport. **241:** Pete Sampras, © Clive Brunskill/ AllSport. **242:** UN Building, Courtesy of the United Nations/A. Brizzi. **249:** Supreme Court, Courtesy of the Supreme Court Historical Society. **256-260:** U.S. Presidents 1-36, © 1967 by Dover Publications. **261:** President Nixon, Courtesy of Richard Nixon Library; President Ford, Courtesy of the Gerald R. Ford Museum; President Carter, Courtesy of the Jimmy Carter Library; President Reagan, Courtesy of the Ronald Reagan Library; President Bush, Courtesy of Bush Presidential Material Project; President Clinton, Courtesy of the White House. **262:** Martha Washington, Abigail Adams, Dolley Madison, Eleanor Roosevelt, Jacqueline Kennedy, © 1967 by Dover Publications; Hillary Rodham Clinton, Courtesy of the White House. **269:** Astronaut on Moon, © NASA. **297:** Hurricane Mitch, © Victor R. Caivano/AP/Wide World Photos. **298:** Tornado, © J. Pat Carter/AP/Wide World Photos

## FRONT COVER

Rosie O'Donnell, © Jesse Froman/Outline; Rollerblader, © Kate Photography

# THE WORLD ALMANAC FOR KIDS
# "2000 IN 2000" CONTEST

## Win An All-Expense-Paid Trip For Four To Washington D.C.

To celebrate the arrival of the Year 2000, The World Almanac for Kids is sponsoring the "**2000 In 2000 Contest**." One Grand Prize winner will be chosen from among the entries received, plus 2,000 Runners-up.

▶ **One Grand Prize winner** will receive an all-expense-paid trip for four to Washington D.C.

▶ **2,000 Runners-up** will receive a specially designed World Almanac for Kids T-shirt

The Grand Prize includes transportation to Washington D.C., lodging for four nights, and three meals per day for four days. The winner will receive a special, guided tour of the Library of Congress, the opportunity to meet with a member of Congress, plus the chance to visit such noted national landmarks as the White House, the Capitol, the Washington Monument, the Lincoln Memorial, Ford's Theater, the Smithsonian Air & Space Museum, and much more.

To enter, kids must write and explain who they think are the three most important people in the world today, and why. Entry is limited to kids aged 6-14, and all entries must be received by February 29, 2000. All entries must include the respondent's name, complete address, age, and daytime phone number.

## Send your entry via mail, fax, or e-mail to:

**World Almanac Books**
**World Almanac for Kids**
**"2000 In 2000" Contest**
1 International Blvd., Suite #630
Mahwah, NJ  07495
**Fax:** (201) 529-6901
**E-mail:** wabooks@aol.com

## The World Almanac for Kids "2000 In 2000" Contest Rules